Globalization in Question

Globalization in Question

The International Economy and the Possibilities of Governance

SECOND EDITION

Paul Hirst and Grahame Thompson

Polity Press

This edition published in 1999 by Polity Press in association with Blackwell Publishers Ltd.

Editorial office:
Polity Press
65 Bridge Street
Cambridge CB2 1UR, UK

Marketing and production:
Blackwell Publishers Ltd
108 Cowley Road
Oxford OX4 1JF, UK

Published in the USA by
Blackwell Publishers Inc.
Commerce Place
350 Main Street
Malden, MA 02148, USA

ISBN 0-7456-2163-5
ISBN 0-7456-2164-3 (pbk)

Library of Congress Cataloging-in-Publication Data

Hirst, Paul Q.
  Globalization in question / Paul Hirst and Grahame Thompson. – 2nd ed.
      p.   cm.
  Includes bibliographical references and index.
    ISBN 0-7456-2163-5 (alk. paper). – ISBN 0-7456-2164-3 (pbk. : alk. paper)
    1. International economic relations.   2. International business enterprises.   3. Investments, Foreign.   I. Thompson, Grahame.   II. Title.
  HF 1359.H575   1999
  337 – dc21   99-31062
                                                                              CIP

A catalogue record for this book is also available from the British Library.

Typeset in 10 on 11¹/₂ pt Times
by Best-set Typesetter Ltd., Hong Kong
Printed in Great Britain by MPG Books, Bodmin, Cornwall

This book is printed on acid-free paper.

Contents

Figures

Tables

Preface to the Second Edition

This new edition is a complete rewrite of the original work. Each chapter has been thoroughly revised and the data updated wherever possible. Some 50 per cent is new material which has been added. The first edition was widely discussed and also gave rise to a good deal of controversy. This was inevitable, given that many of its claims were counterintuitive and cut across the new conventional wisdom. Its main thrust was to challenge fashionable ideas about economic globalization by reference to the available evidence. In the new edition we have avoided replying point by point to our various critics. To do so would be tedious and impede the presentation of our own case. Critics are entitled to their opinions, and often have radically different views of the global economy from our own.

Evidence is another matter. What we have done is to try to respond where our critics have claimed that our evidential materials were either methodologically or factually flawed. This is done where appropriate in the body of the text. We have also added discussion of matters that were neglected or omitted in the first edition, or which have become salient in the period since it was published. Thus we have given considerable space to the issue of the impact of the internationalization of economic relations on the welfare state, to various debates about the concept of 'competitiveness', to the Asian crisis and to the relationships between the North and the South in terms of their wage rates and living standards. The major changes we have made are as follows:

- Chapters 3 and 4 of the original edition on foreign direct investment and the degree of national concentration of the sales and assets of multi-national companies have been merged into a single new chapter 3, and the evidence has been completely recast and updated.

- A completely new chapter 4 has been added which considers the impact of North–South trade in manufactured goods on employment in the advanced countries, and also considers the various meanings of the concept of 'competitiveness' and the degree to which they are legitimately applicable to national economies.
- Chapter 5 on the developing economies and globalization has been completely changed to the extent that it is a new chapter and concentrates on the causes of the Asian crisis and its consequences for the widespread view that the liberalization of investment and capital movements will boost growth in the world economy and promote development in the less advanced countries.
- Chapter 6 is a new addition which considers whether the welfare state can survive in its present form in Western Europe in the face of increased international economic competition and intensified capital mobility.
- Chapter 8 on the European Union has been completely revised to take account of new issues, and in particular the advent of monetary union.

Despite these extensive changes, the basic focus of the book remains the same as before. It concentrates on assessing the state of the international economy and the scope and possibilities for extended economic governance at both the international and national levels. We challenge the concept of 'globalization' that has been dominant in public economic discourse for the past decade. This claims that there has been a rapid and recent intensification of international trade and investment such that distinct national economies have dissolved into a global economy determined by world market forces. Economic liberals have been highly successful in using this supposed state of affairs to advocate that public policy should continue to reinforce the deregulation of trade, investment and capital movements. Globalization is seen as a positive trend that will benefit consumers by increasing the scale and allocative efficiency of markets for both goods and capital. National regulation is held to be futile, and welfare and workers' rights above a low international norm will simply damage national competitiveness and result in a loss of international investment. This economic liberal view is pernicious: both because it is founded on a largely erroneous series of factual claims and because it demands policies that result in established entitlements being sacrificed in favour of market-based increases in growth that will prove illusory.

The current crises that began in Asia in 1997 have badly dented the credibility of the economic liberal agenda for the world economy. But such views still remain entrenched among business elites and the international technocracy. In the absence of a demonstration that the international economy is actually very different from these claims and that alternative economic policies are not only possible but more effective, these views will still prevail by default. Our challenge to this version of globalization and the pessimistic left-wing views that parallel it – even as they criticize it – is thus still relevant and politically important. Economic globalization is a concept with real effects. It has helped to blight lives in Asia. It is still advanced to challenge welfare- and growth-orientated policies in Europe, portraying social democracy as a political project rendered obsolete by the demise of the nation-state as an effective economic regulator.

We are not merely sceptical about globalization, but advocate an alternative view of the international economy and its governance. Our account is compatible with growing and deepening international connectedness in trade and investment, an open world economy of interlinked trading nations. Those who see extreme globalizers as one pole of the debate and see people who deny globalization as the other, putting themselves conveniently in the sensible middle ground, are thus doing us and the issue a disservice.

We have chosen to concentrate on the economic arguments about globalization and their political consequences, and largely to ignore other types of discussions which use the concept. To broaden the discussion to include sociology, cultural studies and social geography would be to dilute the issues we believe to be salient and to lessen the political impact of our arguments. There are also theoretical reasons for our reserve in these matters and our focus on the economy. This is partly because economic processes and outcomes drive and constrain most of the cultural and social phenomena that are included in the more extensive and all-encompassing versions of the concept of globalization. Thus these arguments too are frequently dependent on which of the hypotheses about the tendencies of the international economy is closest to being right.

Our reserve is also because globalization has become the new grand narrative of the social sciences. We say this less out of any commitment to the sensibilities of postmodernism – we have none – than because we feel the concept offers more than it can deliver. Globalization has given a role and salience to sociological theory that it has lacked for two decades. The main conception of globalization in sociology and cultural studies treats global processes and the local responses to them as part of a long-run tendency towards the dissolution of local and national 'societies' in which causes within cultural or political borders predominantly determine social outcomes.

The problem with this literature is that it omnivorously gathers together the effects of often very different cultural, economic and social processes under the common concept of globalization, treating them as instances of a wider phenomenon. Yet there may be only instances and no phenomenon. The consistency of these consequences, the causalities driving them, and the means of verifying them and referring them back to the general concept are far from rigorously specified. Globalization is above all a literature of anecdote, inference and reliance on the accumulation of isolated facts removed from context. Clearly some things are changing rapidly in the cultural industries, in information processing and communications, but whether these support the grander sociological conceptions of globalization is a moot point. In the end, if sociologists and cultural theorists can use the concept profitably, then they should do so. We do not wish to imply that all analysis which uses the concept is neither enlightening nor useful. But it is crucial to keep arguments of different kinds and levels separate unless they can be properly linked by a real general theory. It would be a pity if the fuzziness of so much of the conceptualizing about globalization leads sociologists to believe that they are committed to specific propositions about trends in the international economy that chiefly benefit economic liberals. The more meanings the concept takes on, the greater the danger is that they begin to co-refer without really correlating.

To return to our central concerns, the issue of the nature of the international economy and the scope for its governance is important because the answer dictates whether it may be possible to achieve certain goals. Thus, containing volatility in world markets while promoting growth is vital if goals such as reducing unemployment in the developed countries, preserving welfare institutions, and promoting prosperity and a more just distribution of resources in the developing countries can be achieved at all. Confronted with political realities and the sheer scale of the inequalities within and between countries, it is difficult to be optimistic. Yet there is scope for greater governance at supranational and national levels, and for a politics that tries to link prosperity and fairness. If the arguments of the extreme globalists were true, such a politics would be impossible. That is the point of the book.

Acknowledgements

Inevitably a book like this creates many debts: we are especially grateful to Lars Bo Kaspersen and Jonathan Zeitlin for invaluable suggestions and references, to Jason Edwards for help with the bibliography and permissions, to John Hunt for design work on the graphics. In addition, Doreen Pendlebury at the Open University and Jane Tinkler at Birkbeck College aided in preparing the manuscript.

The authors and publishers are grateful to the following for permission to use copyright material.

American Economic Association for tables 2.2 and 2.3, drawing on tables A-21 and A-23 in A. Maddison, 'Growth and slowdown in advanced capitalist economies: techniques of quantitative assessment', *Journal of Economic Literature*, 25, no. 2 (1997), pp. 649–98; and table 4.4 drawing on table 1 in A. Wood, 'How trade hurt unskilled workers', *Journal of Economic Perspectives*, 9, no. 3 (1995), pp. 57–80.

Bank for International Settlements for table 2.7 reproduced from table V.1 in its Annual Report, Geneva, 1996–7, p. 79.

Cambridge University Press for figure 4.7 reproduced from J. Stopford and S. Strange (with J. S. Henley), *Rival States, Rival Firms: Competition for World Market Shares*, Cambridge, 1991.

Cornell University Press for figure 4.6 reproduced from Jeffrey A. Hart, *Rival Capitalists: International Competitiveness in the United States, Japan, and Western Europe*. Copyright © 1992 by Cornell University.

Greenwood Publishing Group, Inc. for figure 2.3 reproduced from figure 19.1 in W. J. Serow et al. (eds), *Handbook on International Migration*, Greenwood Press, 1990.

The Guardian for figure 5.1 reproduced from *The Guardian*, 13 January 1998, p. 17.

Institute of International Finance for table 5.1.

International Monetary Fund for table 2.11 reproduced from *International Financial Statistics Yearbook*, 1986 and 1997.

David Miles and Merrill Lynch for figure 2.5 reproduced from David Miles, 'Globalization: the facts behind the myth', *The Independent*, 22 December 1997.

MIT Press Journals for table 3.13 reproduced from table 4 in Louis W. Pauly and Simon Reich, 'National structures and multinational corporate behavior: enduring differences in the age of globalization', *International Organization*, 51, no. 1 (Winter 1997), pp. 1–30. © 1997 by the IO Foundation and the Massachusetts Institute of Technology.

OECD for table 2.8 reproduced from table 10 in M. Edey and K. Hviding, 'An assessment of financial reform in OECD countries', OECD Economics Department, Working Paper 154, 1995; and table 2.10 from table 1 in *Financial Market Trends*, no. 69 (Feb. 1998).

Office for Official Publications of the European Communities for figure 2.6 reproduced from 'Advancing financial integration', *European Economy*, Supplement A, no. 12 (Dec. 1997), © European Communities.

Oxford University Press for table 4.5 reproduced from J. Fagerberg, 'Technology and competitiveness', *Oxford Review of Economic Policy*, 12, no. 3 (1996), p. 41.

World Economic Forum, Geneva, for figure 4.10 reproduced from The Global Competitiveness Report 1997.

World Trade Organization for figure 3.1 reproduced from chart II.1 in *International Trade: Trends and Statistics*, Geneva, 1995, p. 29.

Every effort has been made to trace copyright holders but if there are any errors or omissions in the list, the publishers will be glad to correct them at the first opportunity.

Acronyms and Abbreviations

APEC	Asia-Pacific Economic Cooperation
ASEAN	Association of South East Asian Nations
BIS	Bank for International Settlements
BWS	Bretton Woods system
CAP	Common Agricultural Policy (of the EU)
DM	Deutschmark
EAT	East Asian trading countries
ECB	European Central Bank
ECU	European Currency Unit
EMS	European Monetary System
EMU	European Monetary Union
ERM	exchange rate mechanism (Europe)
EU	European Union
FDI	foreign direct investment
FTA	free trade area
G3	Europe, Japan, North America (the Triad)
G5	'group of five' countries: France, Germany, Japan, UK, US
G7	G5 plus Canada and Italy
G8	G7 countries plus Russia
G10	G7 countries plus Belgium, The Netherlands, Sweden, Switzerland (actually eleven)
G22	an informal group of the most significant countries in the international financial system
G30	an informal group of the most important developed and developing countries in the international economic system
GATT	General Agreement on Tariffs and Trade

GDFCF	gross domestic fixed capital formation
GDP	gross domestic product
GDR	German Democratic Republic
G-IMS	government-led international monetary system
GNP	gross national product
GS	Gold Standard
H-O/S-S	Heckscher-Ohlin/Stolper-Samuelson model of international trade
IBRD	International Bank for Reconstruction and Development (World Bank)
ILE	interlinked economy
ILO	International Labour Organization
IMF	International Monetary Fund
IOSCO	International Organization of Securities Commissions
IPE	international political economy
ISO	International Standards Organization
LDC	less developed country
M&A	mergers and acquisitions
MEP	Member of the European Parliament
MERCOSUR	Southern Cone Common Market (Latin America)
M-IMS	market-led international monetary system
MITI	Ministry of International Trade and Industry (Japan)
MNC	multinational company
NAFTA	North American Free Trade Agreement
NGO	non-governmental organization
NIC	newly industrializing country
NATO	North Atlantic Treaty Organization
NTT	New Trade Theory
OECD	Organization for Economic Co-operation and Development (members are the leading advanced market economies, including Australia, Canada, Japan, New Zealand, Western Europe, and the US plus Mexico, South Korea and Turkey)
OPEC	Organization of Petroleum Exporting Countries
OTC	over-the-counter (financial trading)
PPP	purchasing power parity
R&D	research and development
RULC	relative unit labour cost
S&A	subsidiaries and affiliates
SAF	Swedish employers' federation
TNC	transnational companies
TVEs	town and village enterprises (China)
UNCTAD	United Nations Conference on Trade and Development
WTO	World Trade Organization
VAT	value-added tax

1

Introduction: Globalization – a Necessary Myth?

Globalization has become a fashionable concept in the social sciences, a core dictum in the prescriptions of management gurus, and a catch-phrase for journalists and politicians of every stripe. It is widely asserted that we live in an era in which the greater part of social life is determined by global processes, in which national cultures, national economies and national borders are dissolving. Central to this perception is the notion of a rapid and recent process of economic globalization. A truly global economy is claimed to have emerged or to be in the process of emerging, in which distinct national economies and, therefore, domestic strategies of national economic management are increasingly irrelevant. The world economy has internationalized in its basic dynamics, it is dominated by uncontrollable market forces, and it has as its principal economic actors and major agents of change truly transnational corporations that owe allegiance to no nation-state and locate wherever on the globe market advantage dictates.

This image is so powerful that it has mesmerized analysts and captured political imaginations. But is it the case? This book is written with a mixture of scepticism about global economic processes and optimism about the possibilities of control of the international economy and about the viability of national political strategies. One key effect of the concept of globalization has been to paralyse radical reforming national strategies, to see them as unfeasible in the face of the judgement and sanction of international markets. If, however, we face economic changes that are more complex and more equivocal than the extreme globalists argue, then the possibility remains of political strategy and action for national and international control of market economies in order to promote social goals.

We began this investigation with an attitude of moderate scepticism. It was clear that much had changed since the 1960s, but we were cautious about the more extreme claims of the most enthusiastic globalization theorists. In particular it was obvious that radical expansionary and redistributive strategies of national economic management were no longer possible in the face of a variety of domestic and international constraints. However, the closer we looked the shallower and more unfounded became the claims of the more radical advocates of economic globalization. In particular we began to be disturbed by three facts. First, the absence of a commonly accepted model of the new global economy and how it differs from previous states of the international economy. Second, in the absence of a clear model against which to measure trends, the tendency to casually cite examples of the internationalization of sectors and processes as if they were evidence of the growth of an economy dominated by autonomous global market forces. Third, the lack of historical depth, the tendency to portray current changes as unique and without precedent and firmly set to persist long into the future.

To anticipate, as we proceeded our scepticism deepened until we became convinced that globalization, as conceived by the more extreme globalizers, is largely a myth. Thus we argue that:

1   The present highly internationalized economy is not unprecedented: it is one of a number of distinct conjunctures or states of the international economy that have existed since an economy based on modern industrial technology began to be generalized from the 1860s. In some respects, the current international economy is *less* open and integrated than the regime that prevailed from 1870 to 1914.

2   Genuinely transnational companies appear to be relatively rare. Most companies are based nationally and trade multinationally on the strength of a major national location of assets, production and sales, and there seems to be no major tendency towards the growth of truly international companies.

3   Capital mobility is not producing a massive shift of investment and employment from the advanced to the developing countries. Rather foreign direct investment (FDI) is highly concentrated among the advanced industrial economies and the Third World remains marginal in both investment and trade, a small minority of newly industrializing countries apart.

4   As some of the extreme advocates of globalization recognize, the world economy is far from being genuinely 'global'. Rather trade, investment and financial flows are concentrated in the Triad of Europe, Japan and North America and this dominance seems set to continue.

5   These major economic powers, the G3, thus have the capacity, especially if they coordinate policy, to exert powerful governance pressures over financial markets and other economic tendencies. Global markets are thus by no means beyond regulation and control, even though the current scope and objectives of economic governance are limited by the

divergent interests of the great powers and the economic doctrines prevalent among their elites.

These and other more detailed points challenging the globalization thesis will be developed in later chapters. We should emphasize that this book challenges the strong version of the thesis of *economic* globalization, because we believe that without the notion of a truly globalized economy many of the other consequences adduced in the domains of culture and politics would either cease to be sustainable or become less threatening. Hence most of the discussion here is centred on the international economy and the evidence for and against the process of globalization. However, the book is written to emphasize the possibilities of national and international governance, and as it proceeds issues of the future of the nation-state and the role of international agencies, regimes and structures of governance are given increasing prominence.

It is one thing to be sceptical about various uses of the concept of globalization, it is another to explain the widespread development and reception of the concept since the 1970s. It will not do to wheel out the concept of 'ideology' here, for this view is so widespread that it covers the most diverse outlooks and social interests. It covers the political spectrum from left to right, it is endorsed in different disciplines – economics, sociology, cultural studies and international politics – and it is advanced both by theoretical innovators and traditionalists. The literature on globalization is vast and varied. We deliberately chose not to write this book by summarizing and criticizing this literature, in part because that would be a never-ending enterprise given the scale and rate of publication on the topic, but mainly because we concluded that the great bulk of the literature that considered the international economy was based on untenable assumptions, for example, that globalization was an accomplished fact. Hence we decided to examine the evidence against concepts that could specify what a distinctive global economy would look like but which did not presuppose its existence.

We are well aware that there is a wide variety of views that use the term 'globalization'. Even among those analysts who confine themselves to strictly economic processes some make far more radical claims about changes in the international economy than others. It might therefore be argued that we are focusing too narrowly in concentrating on delineating and challenging the most extreme version of the thesis of economic globalization. Indeed, in criticizing such positions we might be held to be demolishing a straw man. On the contrary, we see these extreme views as strong, relatively coherent and capable of being developed into a clear ideal-typical conception of a globalized economic system. Such views are also important in that they have become politically highly consequential. The most eloquent proponents of the extreme view are very influential and have tended to set the tone for discussion in business and political circles. Views that shape the perception of key decision-makers are important, and thus are a primary target rather than a marginal one. The advocates of 'globalization' have proposed the further liberalization of the international economy and the deregulation of domestic economies. This advocacy has had serious effects in Asia and in emerging financial markets, leading to economic crisis, unemployment and impoverishment. The view we attack may have been dented by the Asian crisis but it is not dead. It remains strong in the developed countries, where it has sustained the rhetoric of 'competitiveness' and the belief that the extensive welfare states of Northern and Western Europe are a constraint on economic performance that they can no longer afford in an internationalized economy. These myths still need puncturing before they do impossible damage to both social stability and economic performance.

Some less extreme and more nuanced analyses that employ the term globalization are well established in the academic community and concentrate on the relative internationalization of major financial markets, of technology and of certain important sectors of manufacturing and services, particularly since the 1970s. Emphasis is given in many of these analyses to the increasing constraints on national-level governance that prevent ambitious macroeconomic policies that diverge significantly from the norms acceptable to international financial markets. Indeed, we ourselves have over some time drawn attention to such phenomena in our own work.

Obviously, it is no part of our aim here to deny that such trends to increased internationalization have occurred or to ignore the constraints on certain types of national economic strategy. Our point in assessing the significance of the internationalization that has occurred is to argue that it is well short of dissolving distinct national economies in the major advanced industrial countries, or of preventing the development of new forms of economic governance at the national and international levels. There are, however, very real dangers in not distinguishing clearly between certain trends towards internationalization and the strong version of the globalization thesis. It is particularly unfortunate if the two become confused by using the same word, 'globalization', to describe both. Often we feel that evidence from more cautious arguments is then used carelessly to bolster more extreme ones, to build a community of usage when there needs to be strict differentiation of meanings. It also confuses public discussion and policy-making, reinforcing the view that political actors can accomplish less than is actually possible in a global system.

The strong version of the globalization thesis requires a new view of the international economy, as we shall shortly see, one that subsumes and subordinates national-level processes. Whereas tendencies towards internationalization can be accommodated within a modified view of the world economic system, that still gives a major role to national-level policies and economic actors. Undoubtably this implies some greater or lesser degree of change; firms, governments and international agencies are being forced to behave differently, but in the main they can use existing institutions and practices to do so. In this way we feel it makes more sense to consider the international economic system in a longer historical perspective, to recognize that current changes, while significant and distinctive, are not unprecedented and do not necessarily involve a move towards a new type of economic system. The strong economic versions of the globalization thesis have the advantage that they clearly and sharply pose the possibility of such a change. If they are wrong they are still of some value in enabling us to think out what *is* happening and why. In this sense, challenging the strong version of the thesis is not merely negative but helps us to develop our own ideas.

However, the question remains to be considered of how the myth of the globalization of economic activity became established as and when it did. In answering, one must begin with the ending of the post-1945 era in the turbulence of 1972–3. A period of prolonged economic growth and full employment in the advanced countries, sustained by strategies of active national state intervention and a managed multilateral regime for trade and monetary policy under US hegemony, was brought to an end by a number of significant changes. Thus we can point to:

1   The effects of the collapse of the Bretton Woods system and the 1973 and 1979 OPEC oil crises (which massively increased oil prices) in producing turbulence and volatility in all the major economies through the 1970s into the early 1980s. Significant in generating such turbulence and undermining previous policy regimes was the rapid rise in inflation in the advanced countries brought about by domestic policy failures, the international impact of US involvement in the Vietnam War, and the oil price hikes of 1973 and 1979.

2   The efforts of financial institutions and manufacturers, in this period of turbulence and inflationary pressure, to compensate for domestic uncertainty by seeking wider outlets for investments and additional markets; hence the widespread bank lending to the Third World during the inflationary 1970s, the growth of the Eurodollar market, and the increasing ratios of foreign trade to GDP in the advanced countries.

3   The public policy acceleration of the internationalization of financial markets by the widespread abandonment of exchange controls and other market deregulation in the late 1970s and early 1980s, even as the more extreme forms of volatility in currency markets were being brought under control by, for example, the development of the European Monetary System (EMS) in 1979 and the Louvre and Plaza accords in the 1980s.

4   The tendency towards 'deindustrialization' in Britain and the United States and the growth of long-term unemployment in Europe, promoting fears of foreign competition, especially from Japan.

5   The relatively rapid development of a number of newly industrializing
     countries (NICs) in the Third World and their penetration of First World
     markets.
6   The shift from standardized mass production to more flexible produc-
     tion methods, and the change from the perception of the large, nation-
     ally rooted, oligopolistic corporation as the unchallengeably dominant
     economic agent towards a more complex world of multinational enter-
     prises, less rigidly structured firms and the increased salience of
     smaller firms – summed up in the widespread and popular concept of
     'post-Fordism'.

These changes are undoubted and they were highly disturbing to those
conditioned by the unprecedented success and security of the post-1945
period in the advanced industrial states. The perceived loss of national
control, the increased uncertainty and unpredictability of economic relations, and rapid institutional change were a shock to minds conditioned to
believe that poverty, unemployment and economic cycles could all be controlled or eliminated in a market economy based on the profit motive. If
the widespread consensus of the 1950s and 1960s was that the future
belonged to a capitalism without losers, securely managed by national
governments acting in concert, then the later 1980s and 1990s have been
dominated by a consensus based on contrary assumptions, that global
markets are uncontrollable and that the only way to avoid becoming a loser
– whether as nation, firm or individual – is to be as competitive as possible.
The notion of an ungovernable world economy is a response to the collapse
of expectations schooled by Keynesianism and sobered by the failure of
monetarism to provide an alternative route to broad-based prosperity and
stable growth. 'Globalization' is a myth suitable for a world without illusions, but it is also one that robs us of hope. Global markets are dominant,
and they face no threat from any viable contrary political project, for it is
held that Western social democracy and socialism of the Soviet bloc are
both finished.

One can only call the political impact of 'globalization' the pathology of
overdiminished expectations. Many overenthusiastic analysts and politicians have gone beyond the evidence in overstating the extent of the
dominance of world markets and their ungovernability. If this is so, then we
should seek to break the spell of this uncomforting myth. The old rational-
ist explanation for primitive myths was that they were a way of masking
and compensating for humanity's helplessness in the face of the power of
nature. In this case we have a myth that exaggerates the degree of our helplessness in the face of contemporary economic forces. If economic relations
are more governable (at both the national and international levels) than
many contemporary analysts suppose, then we should explore the possible
scale and scope of that governance. It is not currently the case that radical

goals are attainable: full employment in the advanced countries, a fair deal for the poorer developing countries and widespread democratic control over economic affairs for the world's people. But this should not lead us to dismiss or ignore the forms of control and social improvement that could be achieved relatively rapidly with a modest change in attitudes on the part of key elites. It is thus essential to persuade reformers of the left and conservatives who care for the fabric of their societies that we are not helpless before uncontrollable global processes. If this happens, then changing attitudes and expectations might make these more radical goals acceptable.

Models of the international economy

We can only begin to assess the issue of globalization if we have some relatively clear and rigorous model of what a global economy would be like and how it represents both a new phase in the international economy and an entirely changed environment for national economic actors. Globalization in its radical sense should be taken to mean the development of a new economic structure, and not just conjunctural change towards greater international trade and investment within an existing set of economic relations. An extreme and one-sided ideal type of this kind enables us to differentiate *degrees* of internationalization, to eliminate some possibilities and to avoid confusion between claims. Given such a model it becomes possible to assess it against evidence of international trends and thus enables us more or less plausibly to determine whether or not this phenomenon of the development of a new supranational economic system is occurring. In order to do this we have developed two basic contrasting ideal types of international economy, one that is fully globalized, and an open international economy that is still fundamentally characterized by exchange between relatively distinct national economies and in which many outcomes, such as the competitive performance of firms and sectors, are substantially determined by processes occurring at the national level. These ideal types are valuable in so far as they are useful in enabling us to clarify the issues conceptually, that is, in specifying the difference between a new global economy and merely extensive and intensifying international economic relations. Too often evidence compatible with the latter is used as though it substantiated the former. With a few honourable exceptions, the more enthusiastic advocates of globalization have failed to specify that difference, or to specify what evidence would be decisive in pointing to a structural change towards a global economy. Increasing salience of foreign trade and considerable and growing international flows of capital are not *per se* evidence of a new and distinct phenomenon called 'globalization'. As we shall see in chapter 2, they were features of the international economy before 1914.

Type 1: An inter-national economy

We shall first develop a simple and extreme version of this type. An *inter-national economy* is one in which the principal entities are national economies. Trade and investment produce growing interconnection between these still national economies. Such a process involves the increasing integration of more and more nations and economic actors into world market relationships. Trade relations, as a result, tend to take on the form of national specializations and the international division of labour. The importance of trade is, however, progressively replaced by the centrality of investment relations between nations, which increasingly act as the organizing principle of the system. The form of interdependence between nations remains, however, of the 'strategic' kind. That is, it implies the continued relative separation of the domestic and the international frameworks for policy-making and the management of economic affairs, and also a relative separation in terms of economic effects. Interactions are of the 'billiard ball' type; international events do not directly or necessarily penetrate or permeate the domestic economy but are refracted through national policies and processes. The international and the domestic policy fields either remain relatively separate as distinct levels of governance, or they work 'automatically'. In the latter case adjustments are not thought to be the subject of policy by public bodies or authorities, but are a consequence of 'unorganized' or 'spontaneous' market forces.

Perhaps the classic case of such an 'automatic' adjustment mechanism remains the Gold Standard, which operated at the height of the Pax Britannica system from mid-nineteenth century to 1914. Automatic is put in inverted commas here to signal the fact that this is a popular caricature. The actual system of adjustment took place very much in terms of overt domestic policy interventions (see chapter 2). The flexibility in wages and prices that the Gold Standard system demanded (the international value of currencies could not be adjusted since these were fixed in terms of gold) had to be engendered by governments through domestic expenditure-reducing policies to influence the current account and through interest rate policy to influence the capital account.

Great Britain acted as the political and economic hegemon and the guarantor of this system. But it is important to recognize that the Gold Standard and the Pax Britannica system was merely one of several structures of the international economy in this century. Such structures were highly conditional on major sociopolitical conjunctures. Thus the First World War wrecked British hegemony, accelerating a process that would have occurred far more slowly merely as a consequence of British industrial decline. It resulted in a period of protectionism and national autarchic competition in the 1930s, followed by the establishment of American hegemony after the Second World War and by the reopened international economy of the Bretton Woods system. This indicates the danger of assuming that current major changes in the international economy are unprecedented and that they are inevitable or irreversible. The lifetime of a prevailing system of international economic relations in this century has been no more than thirty to forty years. Indeed, given that most European currencies did not become fully convertible until the late 1950s, the full Bretton Woods system after the Second World War only lasted upwards of thirteen to fourteen years. Such systems have been transformed by major changes in the politico-economic balance of power and the conjunctures that have effected these shifts have been large-scale conflicts between the major powers. In that sense, the international economy has been determined as to its structure and the distribution of power within it by the major nation-states.

The period of this worldwide inter-national economic system is also typified by the rise and maturity of the multinational corporation, as a transformation of the large merchant trading companies of a past era. From our point of view, however, the important aspect of these multinational companies is that they retain a clear national home base; they are subject to the national regulation of the home country, and by and large they are effectively policed by that country.

The point of this ideal type drawing on the institutions of the *belle époque* is not, however, a historical analogy: for a simple and automatically governed international economic system *like* that before 1914 is unlikely to reproduce itself now. The current international economy is relatively open, but it has real differences from that prevailing before the First World War: it has more generalized and institutionalized free trade through the WTO, foreign investment is different in its modalities and destinations – although a high degree of capital mobility is once again a possibility – the scale of short-term financial flows is greater, the international monetary system is quite different and freedom of labour migration is drastically curtailed. The pre-1914 system was, nevertheless, genuinely international, tied by efficient long-distance communications and industrialized means of transport.

The communications and information technology revolution of the late twentieth century has further developed a trading system that could make day-to-day world prices: it did not create it. In the second half of the nineteenth century the submarine intercontinental telegraph cables enabled the integration of world markets (Standage 1998). Modern systems dramatically increase the possible volume and complexity of transactions, but we have had information media capable of sustaining a genuine international trading system for over a century. The difference between a trading system in which goods and information moved by sailing ship and one in which they moved by steam ships and electricity is qualitative. If the theorists of globalization mean that we have an economy in which each part of the world is linked by markets sharing close to real-time information, then that began not in the 1970s but in the 1870s.

Type 2: A globalized economy

A *globalized economy* is a distinct ideal type from that of the inter-national economy and can be developed by contrast with it. In such a global system distinct national economies are subsumed and rearticulated into the system by international processes and transactions. The inter-national economy, on the contrary, is one in which processes that are determined at the level of national economies still dominate and international phenomena are out-comes that emerge from the distinct and differential performance of the national economies. The inter-national economy is an aggregate of nation-ally located functions. Thus while there is in such an economy a wide and increasing range of international economic interactions (financial markets and trade in manufactured goods, for example), these tend to function as opportunities or constraints for nationally located economic actors and their public regulators.

The global economy raises these nationally based interactions to a new power. The international economic system becomes autonomized and socially disembedded, as markets and production become truly global. Domestic policies, whether of private corporations or public regulators, now have routinely to take account of the predominantly international deter-minants of their sphere of operations. As systemic interdependence grows, the national level is permeated by and transformed by the international. In such a globalized economy the problem this poses for public authorities of different countries is how to construct policies that coordinate and integrate their regulatory efforts in order to cope with the systematic interdepen-dence between their economic actors.

The first major consequence of a globalized economy would thus be that its governance is fundamentally problematic. Socially decontextualized global markets would be difficult to regulate, even supposing effective co-operation by the regulators and a coincidence of their interests. The prin-cipal difficulty is to construct both effective and integrated patterns of national and international public policy to cope with global market forces. The systematic economic interdependence of countries and markets would by no means necessarily result in a harmonious integration enabling world consumers to benefit from truly independent, allocatively efficient market mechanisms. On the contrary, it is more than plausible that the populations of even successful and advanced states and regions would be at the mercy of autonomized and uncontrollable (because global) market forces. Inter-dependence would then readily promote *dis-integration* – that is, competi-tion and conflict – between regulatory agencies at different levels. Such conflict would further weaken effective public governance at the global level. Enthusiasts for the efficiency of free markets and the superiority of corporate control compared with that of public agencies would see this as a rational world order freed from the shackles of obsolete and ineffective national public interventions. Others, less sanguine but convinced globalization *is* occurring, like Cerny (1998), see it as a world system in which there can be no generalized or sustained public reinsurance against the costs imposed on localities by unfavourable competitive outcomes or market failures.

Even if one does not accept that the full process of globalization is taking place, this ideal type can help to highlight some aspects of the importance of greater economic integration within the major regional trade blocs. Both the European Union (EU) and the North American Free Trade Area (NAFTA) will soon be highly integrated markets of continental scale. Already in the case of the EU it is clear that there are fundamental problems of the integration and coordination of regulatory policies between the different public authorities at Union, national and regional level.

It is also clear that this ideal type highlights the problem of weak public governance for the major corporations. Even if such companies were truly global, they would not be able to operate in all markets equally effectively and, like governments, would lack the capacity to reinsure against unexpected shocks relying on their own resources alone. Governments would no longer be available to assist as they have been for 'national champions'. Firms would therefore seek to share risks and opportunities through intercorporate investments, partnerships, joint ventures, etc. Even in the current internationalized economy we can recognize such processes emerging.

A second major consequence of the notion of a globalizing international economy would be the transformation of multinational companies (MNCs) into transnational companies (TNCs) as the major players in the world economy.[1] The TNC would be genuine footloose capital, without specific national identification and with an internationalized management, and at least potentially willing to locate and relocate anywhere in the globe to obtain either the most secure or the highest returns. In the financial sector this could be achieved at the touch of a button and in a truly globalized economy would be wholly dictated by market forces, without deference to national monetary policies. In the case of primarily manufacturing companies, they would source, produce and market at the global level as strategy and opportunities dictated. The company would no longer be based on one predominant national location (as with the MNC) but would service global markets through global operations. Thus the TNC, unlike the MNC, could no longer be controlled or even constrained by the policies of particular national states. Rather it could escape all but the commonly agreed and enforced international regulatory standards. National governments could not adopt particular and effective regulatory policies that diverged from these standards to the detriment of TNCs operating within their borders. The TNC would be the main manifestation of a truly globalized economy.

Julius (1990) and Ohmae (1990, 1993), for example, both consider this trend towards true TNCs to be well established. Ohmae argues that such 'stateless' corporations are now the prime movers in an interlinked economy (ILE) centred on North America, Europe and Japan. He contends that macroeconomic and industrial policy intervention by national governments can only distort and impede the rational process of resource allocation by corporate decisions and consumer choices on a global scale. Like Akio Morita of Sony, Ohmae argues that such corporations will pursue strategies of 'global localization' in responding on a worldwide scale to specific regionalized markets and locating effectively to meet the varying demands of distinct localized groups of consumers. The assumption here is that TNCs will rely primarily on foreign direct investment and the full domestication of production to meet such specific market demands. This is in contrast to the strategy of flexibly specialized core production in the company's main location and the building of branch assembly plants where needed or where dictated by national public policies. The latter strategy is compatible with nationally based companies. The evidence from Japanese corporations which are the most effective operators in world markets favours the view that the latter strategy is predominant (Williams et al. 1992). Japanese companies appear to have been reluctant to locate core functions like R&D or high value-added parts of the production process abroad. Thus national companies with an international scope of operations currently and for the foreseeable future seem more likely to be the pattern than the true TNCs. Of course, such multinational companies, although they are nationally based, are internationally orientated. Foreign markets influence their domestic strategies and foreign competitors their production processes. Although MNCs continue to trade substantially *within* their national economies, significant percentages of foreign sales influence their actions. The point, however, is that this is not new; companies in the long boom period after 1945 were influenced in this way too, and were successful only if they met the standards of international competition.

A third consequence of globalization would be the further decline in the political influence and economic bargaining power of organized labour. Globalized markets and TNCs would tend to be mirrored by an open world market in labour. Thus while companies requiring highly skilled and productive labour might well continue to locate in the advanced countries, with all their advantages, rather than merely seek areas where wages are low, the trend towards the global mobility of capital and the relative national fixity of labour would favour those advanced countries with the most tractable labour forces and the lowest social overheads relative to the benefits of labour competence and motivation. 'Social democratic' strategies of enhancement of working conditions would thus be viable only if they assured the competitive advantage of the labour force, without constraining management prerogatives, and at no more overall cost in taxation than the average for the advanced world. Such strategies would clearly be a tall order and the tendency of globalization would be to favour management at the expense of even strongly organized labour, and, therefore, public policies sympathetic to the former rather than the latter. This would be the 'disorganized capitalism' of Lash and Urry (1987) with a vengeance, or it could be seen as placing a premium on moderate and defensive strategies where organized labour remains locally strong (Scharpf 1991, 1997).

A final and inevitable consequence of globalization is the growth in fundamental multipolarity in the international political system. In the end, the hitherto hegemonic national power would no longer be able to impose its own distinct regulatory objectives in either its own territories or elsewhere, and lesser agencies (whether public or private) would thus enjoy enhanced powers of denial and evasion vis-à-vis any aspirant 'hegemon'. A variety of bodies from international voluntary agencies to TNCs would thus gain in relative power at the expense of national governments and, using global markets and media, could appeal to and obtain legitimacy from consumers/citizens across national boundaries. Thus the distinct disciplinary powers of national states would decline, even though the bulk of their citizens, especially in the advanced countries, remained nationally bound. In such a world, national military power would become less effective. It would no longer be used to pursue economic objectives because 'national' state control in respect of the economy would have largely disappeared. The use of military force would be increasingly tied to non-economic issues, such as nationality and religion. A variety of more specific powers of sanction and veto in the economic sphere by different kinds of bodies (both public and private) would thus begin to compete with national states and begin to change the nature of international politics. As economics and nationhood pulled apart, the international economy would become even more 'industrial' and less 'militant' than it is today. War would be increasingly localized; wherever it threatened powerful global economic interests the warring parties would be subject to devastating economic sanction.

The argument in outline

We have spent some time elaborating this idea of a globalized international economy and contrasting it to that of an inter-national one. This is to try to clarify exactly what would be involved in making the strong claim that we are either firmly within a globalizing economy, or that the present era is one in which there are strong globalizing tendencies. To diagnose the position conclusively is a difficult task. This task is made harder because of a number of specific and politically driven changes in the international economy after the First World War. Chief among these have been the collapse in hegemonic leadership during the interwar period and then the decline of the Pax Americana – from the early 1970s onwards.

The world trading system has never just been an 'economy', a distinct system governed by its own laws. In this sense the term 'international economy' has always been a shorthand for what is actually the product of the complex interaction of economic relations and politics, shaped and reshaped by the struggles of the great powers. It appears that the international economy has been most open when the trading system has been sustained by a hegemonic power which, for reasons of its own perceived interests, has been willing to accept the costs of underwriting the system. If the globalizers are correct, then all this is about to come to an end. British hegemony was followed by a period of turbulence and competition between the great powers after 1918. Are we currently witnessing a slightly different period of turbulence after the weakening of American hegemony in the early 1970s, or the formation of an entirely new global system in which economic laws finally prevail over political power and thus can eschew a guarantor?

US economic and military power made the Pax Americana possible after 1945: it was a deliberate political attempt to reopen the international economy that was remarkably successful. The liberal multilateral market system created by the US permitted the massive growth in world trade that helped to fuel the long boom. But US hegemony was multidimensional and it is by no means clear that it is entirely over. Militarily the US is still hegemonic in the sense that its strength ensures that no other state can use political power to restructure the international economy. In this sense the Pax continues; the US remains the only possible guarantor of the world free trading system against politically inspired disruption and thus the openness of global markets depends on American policy. The US also remains the largest single national economy and the power-house of world demand. Even though US monetary policy is unable to operate hegemonically and unilaterally, the dollar remains the medium of world trade. Thus the US has more than residual elements of hegemony and no obvious political competitors, neither the EU nor Japan being capable of taking over its world role or wishing to do so.

The immediate conjuncture of the weakening of US hegemony led to conditions in which it might appear that a globalized economy could emerge. The crisis of the early 1970s led to a monetary regime of totally floating exchange rates. These developments, combined with fashionable theories, led to the policies of the abandonment of exchange controls and the liberalization of international financial markets. The floating exchange rate regime quickly began to exhibit perverse 'overshooting'. At the same time the OPEC hikes in oil prices (a coordinated national policy action of the oil exporters) increased the volatility of the international economy by producing inflationary crises in the advanced nations, massive increases in the liquidity of the OPEC countries and a massive growth of borrowing by the Third World (leading subsequently to a debt crisis and recessions, particularly in Latin America). These changes also produced a generalized recession in the advanced world and a widespread increase in government indebtedness. The US changed from being a major creditor nation and became a massive capital importer, principally to fund its trade deficit with Japan.

The point is that these changes were conjunctural, although important in their effects and large in scale, and that they were at least in part driven by policy. The period of extreme volatility and turbulence did not last for long. The monetary regime of the totally floating rate was replaced by partial reregulation through the creation of the European Monetary System in 1979, and the Plaza and Louvre accords between the G7 advanced industrial countries in the 1980s. The old post-1945 multilateral order was not restored, but a drift into uncontrolled market forces, on the one hand, or negative competition between the major emerging trading blocs, on the other, were prevented. The recent Uruguay Round of the GATT Treaty has helped, despite conflicts and divergent interests over agricultural products, financial services and intellectual property rights, to keep the world trading system both open and at least potentially subject to calculable rules. Thus the maximum point of change in the post-1945 international regime does not seem to have produced an acephalous system based on unregulated supranational markets.

The next major move towards such a system, the economic liberal push of the early 1990s, has also failed to produce such an outcome. The financial crisis that began in Asia in 1997 has produced a substantial if belated and sometimes counterproductive intervention by international agencies and the United States, leading to the new phase of the preventative mobilization of large sums to forestall contagion, as in the case of Brazil. Likewise, there have been strong calls for the reregulation of financial markets and a growth in scepticism about the value of short-term financial flows. The stalling of the proposed Multilateral Agreement on Investment, which would have liberalized national regimes of investment regulation, is a clear indication that the project of creating a world economy based solely on market forces is, if not in full retreat, at least in suspension.

The history of the international economy will be considered in the next chapter: we rehearse these issues here to register the purely contingent nature of many of the events that have often been interpreted as a structural transformation in the international economy. Many of these trends have been reversed or interrupted as the international economy has evolved. This goes to make the point, then, that we should be cautious in a wider sense of ascribing structural significance to what may be conjunctural and temporary changes, dramatic though some of them have been.[2]

The strong concept of a globalized economy outlined above acts as an ideal type which we can compare to the actual trends within the international economy. This globalized economy has been contrasted to the notion of an inter-national economy in the above analysis in order to distinguish its particular and novel features. The opposition of these two types for conceptual clarity conceals the possibly messy combination of the two in reality. This makes it difficult to determine major trends on the basis of the available evidence. These two types of economy are not inherently mutually exclusive; rather in certain conditions the globalized economy would *encompass and subsume* the inter-national economy. The globalized economy would rearticulate many of the features of the inter-national economy, transforming them as it reinforced them. If this phenomenon occurred there would thus be a complex combination of features of both types of economy present within the present conjuncture. The problem in determining what is happening is to identify the dominant trends: either the growth of globalization or the continuation of the existing inter-national patterns.

It is our view that such a process of hybridization is not taking place, but it would be cavalier not to consider and raise the possibility. Central in this respect is the evidence we present later (chapter 3) for the weak development of TNCs and the continued salience of MNCs and also the ongoing dominance of the advanced countries in both trade and FDI. Such evidence is consistent with a continuing inter-national economy, but much less so with a rapidly globalizing hybrid system. Moreover, we should remember that an inter-national economy is one in which the major nationally based manufacturers and the major financial trading and service centres are strongly externally oriented, emphasizing international trading performance. The opposite of a globalized economy is not thus a nationally inward-looking one, but an open world market based on trading nations and regulated to a greater or lesser degree by both the public policies of nation-states and supranational agencies (chapter 7). Such an economy has existed in some form or another since the 1870s, and has continued to re-emerge despite major setbacks, the most serious being the crisis of the 1930s. The point is that it should not be confused with a global economy.

The rest of this book is organized as follows. In chapter 2 the history of the international economy and its regimes of regulation is considered in some detail. In particular we contrast the economic integration of the Gold Standard period before 1914 with the international economy developing during the 1980s and early 1990s. The analysis looks at a wide range of measures of integration and finds that there is nothing unprecedented about the levels of integration experienced at present, in either the real or the monetary economy. The governed nature of the international system is stressed, and the relationships between domestic and international activity during different periods are explored.

Chapter 3 combines an analysis of trade and FDI with an assessment of how far modern major companies are truly transnational. FDI is key to the proposition that capital mobility is restructuring the world economy. Here we consider the distribution of FDI and the issue of its regulation, relative to but also as distinct from that of international trade. The continued dominance of the Triad economic blocs – North America, Europe and Japan – in trade, in FDI flows and stocks and in world income distribution is stressed. The rest of the chapter presents the evidence on the economic role of MNCs and explores the best and most recent available data to show that companies are not becoming footloose global capital but in large part remain rooted in one of the three regions of the Triad. The two aspects of this chapter thus consider the nature of the international economy of real goods and services through a thorough examination of the strategies of international companies and real resource flows. The overall conclusion is that the globalization of production has been exaggerated: companies remain closely linked to their home bases, and for good reasons are likely to remain so.

Chapter 4 also considers two distinct but related issues. The first part emphasizes that trade between the three blocs, while accounting for a high percentage of world trade, is modest in comparison to their GDP. Trade with developing countries is also modest in scale and not leading to either a reduction in Triad dominance or to excessive import penetration by newly industrializing economies. This provides a backdrop to an analysis of whether competition and import penetration from low wage NICs are substantially contributing to unemployment and deindustrialization in the developed world. After an extensive review of the literature and evidence, the verdict is 'not proven': the effects have yet to be strongly demonstrated. The second issue is that of 'international competitiveness', a central plank of much modern rhetoric on economic policy. The different meanings of competition are reviewed and assessed, the differences between nations and companies are emphasized and a sceptical eye is cast on the discussion of this issue as inspired by the management literature.

Chapter 5 considers the issue of the developing countries and globalization, and in particular whether a regime of free trade and capital mobility would lead to a market-based take-off by most of the developing world – large countries like China, India, Indonesia and Brazil included. The Asian crisis has cast serious doubt on such predictions, common in the 1990s. The chapter examines the causes of the Asian crisis, attempting to assign appropriate weightings to the effects of short-term capital flows and domestic policy failings respectively. The policy options for the developing countries are then considered and limited strategic controls on capital movements advocated.

Chapter 6 considers the claim that increased international openness has both increased the shocks on domestic economies and reduced the ability to found and sustain the welfare systems necessary to cope with them. It concentrates on Western Europe and adopts a comparative perspective. It shows how small highly internationalized states like Denmark and the Netherlands have been able to sustain and reform their welfare states in a period of apparently intensifying international competition. It then considers how a much larger state, Italy, has managed to achieve major reform in its system through democratic consultation. Finally it discusses whether the further integration of markets in the EU will promote competition for closer regulation of welfare entitlements and worker's rights, and concludes that it need not.

Chapter 7 examines the present structure of governance of the world economy, particularly the financial system, and goes on to consider the possibilities for economic regulation at international, national and regional levels. We conclude that there is real potential for developing regulatory and management systems, that the international economy is by no means out of control, but that there is a lack of political will at present to gain extra leverage over undesirable and unjust aspects of international and domestic economic activity.

Chapter 8 moves on to examine the European Union as the most developed trade bloc and discusses the issue of the future evolution of its institutions. In particular the creation of the euro is considered, along with its impact both on economic policy within Europe and on the EU's place in the world system. The outcomes here, we argue, will be crucial to whether the international economy develops with a minimalist or a more extended regulatory regime.

Chapter 9 examines the political dimensions of governance, exploring the changing role and capacities of the nation-state and the possible roles that such entities may perform in promoting and legitimating extended governance in the international system. Our argument here is that far from the nation-state being undermined by the processes of internationalization, these processes strengthen the importance of the nation-state in many ways.

2

Globalization and the History of the International Economy

The 'globalization' of economic activity and the governance issues it raises are often thought to have appeared only after the Second World War, and particularly during the 1960s. The post-1960 era saw the emergence of MNC activity on the one hand and the rapid growth of international trade on the other. Subsequently, with the collapse of the Bretton Woods semi-fixed exchange rate regime in the 1971–3 period, the expansion of international securities investment and bank lending began in earnest as capital and particularly money markets rapidly internationalized, adding to the complexity of international economic relations and heralding what is often thought to be the genuine globalization of an integrated and interdependent world economy. In this chapter we scrutinize this popular history and trace the main periods of the internationalization of economic activity, which will be shown to have developed in a cyclical and uneven fashion. The key issue at stake in our assessment is the changing autonomy of national economies in the conduct of their economic activity.[1]

MNCs, TNCs and international business

The history of the internationalization of business enterprises is a long one, in no way confined just to the period since 1960. Trading activities, for instance, date from the earliest civilizations, but it was the Middle Ages in Europe that marked the initiation of systematic cross-border trading operations carried out by institutions of a private corporate nature (though often with strong state backing and support). During the fourteenth century, for instance, the Hanseatic League organized German merchants in the conduct of their Western European and Levantine commerce – which

involved them in agricultural production, iron smelting and general manufacturing. Around the same time the Merchant Adventurers organized the
sale of UK-produced wool and cloth to the Low Countries and elsewhere.
In addition, Italian trading and banking houses occupied a key position in
the general internationalization of business activity during the early
Renaissance period. By the end of the fourteenth century it is estimated
that there were as many as 150 Italian banking companies already operating multinationally (Dunning 1993, pp. 97–8).

During the seventeenth and eighteenth centuries state patronage
extended as the great colonial trading companies were established: the
Dutch and British East India companies, the Muscovy Company, the Royal
Africa Company and the Hudsons Bay Company came into existence.
These pioneered wholesale trading operations in what were to become the
leading colonial areas.

However, it is the development of international manufacturing as the
Industrial Revolution took hold that presents the closest precursor to the
modern-day MNC. Here the early pre-eminence of British firms as multinational producers becomes apparent. Initially North and South America
presented the most favourable investment opportunities, but these were
soon followed by Africa and Australasia. There is some dispute as to
whether 'colonial investments' should be considered a true precursor of
foreign direct investment, but production abroad for the local market began
in this way. Technical and organizational developments after the 1870s
allowed a wider variety of similar products to be produced domestically and
abroad within the boundaries of the same firm, while the exploration and
development of minerals and other raw material products also attracted
large amounts of FDI (Dunning 1993, ch. 5).

One of the problems with such a retrospective classification, however,
is that the modern concepts of 'direct' investment on the one hand (involving some notion of managerial control from abroad) and 'portfolio' investment on the other (involving the acquisition of securities issued by foreign
institutions so as to claim returns without any associated control or management participation) were only drawn in the early 1960s, at the same time
as the term MNC was itself introduced. The US Department of Commerce
had reported outward FDI from 1929, but this was the exception.

Despite this lack of consistently classified data it is generally agreed that
manufacturing multinationals appeared in the world economy after the
mid-nineteenth century and that they were well established by the First
World War. International business activity grew vigorously in the 1920s as
the truly diversified and integrated MNC matured, but it slowed down
during the depressed 1930s and war-torn 1940s, and began a fluctuating
expansion again after 1950.

There have been two approaches to quantifying the growth of international business over time. The first involves looking at whatever statistics
on international investment are available, generating additional data, and

Table 2.1   Estimated totals of FDI stocks and trade values at the outbreak of the First World War (current US$m)

	FDI in 1914 (by country of origin)	Manufacturing exports in 1913
UK	8,172	1,928
US	2,652	896
Germany	2,600	1,824
France	1,750	813
Netherlands	925	n.a.
World total	n.a.	7,227

Sources: FDI: UK, Corley 1994; Germany, Schröter 1984; US and France, Dunning 1993; Netherlands, Gales and Sluyterman 1993: all drawn from Jones 1994. Trade: Lewis 1981, app. 4, p. 67

then reclassifying these on the basis of modern distinctions. The second approach focuses on the businesses themselves. It traces the history of firms and the internationalization of their activity, which involves counting multinationals and their business affiliations over time (Jones 1994).

Estimates of FDI held by the leading countries in 1914, and trade values in 1913, are shown in table 2.1. In terms of the estimated value of manufacturing exports shown in the second column, the UK and Germany were the leading exporters of manufactures at the outbreak of the First World War, and were over twice as important as the US and France. Yearly export values were already less than accumulated FDI stocks by this time.

The analysis of companies and their history also shows the developed nature of international production before the First World War. The pioneer country here was the UK, but there was also a surprising extent of multinational production organized by the smaller advanced economies. Company-based analysis reveals that a good deal of this early FDI was modest in scale, though extensive in scope, and often came from quite small foreign companies (Jones 1994).

Trade and international integration

A better statistical base is available for exploring the trends in international trade. Again the history of this part of international economic activity goes back a long way. But good statistical evidence exists from 1830 onwards (Maddison 1962, 1987; Lewis 1981). The important period from our point of view concerns developments this century, and particularly from the First World War. A similar pattern emerges here as in the case of FDI, though perhaps more pronounced in its features. The volume of world foreign trade expanded at about 3.4 per cent per annum between 1870 and 1913. After

Table 2.2   Volume of exports, 1913–1984 (1913 = 100)

	France	Germany	Japan	Netherlands	UK	US
1913	100.0	100.0	100.0	100.0	100.0	100.0
1929	147.0	91.8	257.9	171.2	81.3	158.2
1938	91.0	57.0	588.3	140.0	57.3	125.7
1950	149.2	34.8	210.1	171.2	100.0	224.6
1960	298.4	154.7	924.4	445.1	120.0	387.9
1973	922.4	514.3	5,672.7	1,632.1	241.9	912.0
1984	1,459.5	774.0	14,425.2	2,383.7	349.1	1,161.5

Source: Maddison 1987, table A-21, p. 694

1913 trade was adversely affected by the growth of tariffs, quantitative restrictions, exchange controls and then war, and it expanded by less than 1 per cent per annum on average between 1913 and 1950. After 1950, however, trade really took off to grow at over 9 per cent per annum until 1973. Between 1973 and the mid-1980s the growth rate fell back to nearer the late nineteenth-century levels, with expansion at a rate of only 3.6 per cent (see also figure 3.1 on p. 70).

The experience of six main economies in the development of export volumes between 1913 and 1984 is shown in table 2.2, indicating the different rates of volume growth and their fluctuations. Clearly, there was a definite fall in the volume of world trade during the 1930s. The brunt was borne first by Germany and the UK, then by France, and to a lesser extent by the US and the Netherlands. Japan suffered only as a consequence of the Second World War.

The relationship between growth in output and in trade is a central one for international economics analysis. It is not our intention to explore the theoretical links between these here (see Kitson and Michie 1995). However, trade growth from 1853 to 1872 was already faster than the growth in world production, while from 1872 to 1911 it grew at about the same rate. Between 1913 and 1950 there was a devastating decline in both the rate of growth of trade (0.5 per cent per annum) and of output growth (1.9 per cent per annum). Only since 1950 has there been a consistent expansion of trade relative to production, even during the cyclical downturn after 1973 (see also chapter 3).

Migration and the international labour market

A third broad area of analysis in the context of the history of the international economy concerns migration and its consequences for the integration of the global labour market. It is generally agreed that migration is becoming (or has become) a 'global phenomenon' (see, for instance, Serow et al. 1990, p. 159; Segal 1993, ch. 7; Castles and Miller 1993, ch. 4). However, by global these authors mean that, since the mid-1970s in particular, many more countries have been affected by migration, that there has been a growing diversity of areas of origin for migrants, and that migrants are of a wider range of socioeconomic statuses than ever before. Thus for these authors globalization registers a quantitative change in the extent and scope of migration rather than a feature of a potentially different socioeconomic order.

There are a number of different kinds of migrants. Clearly the early slave trade was a form of 'involuntary' migration (it is estimated that 15 million slaves were moved from Africa to the Americas before 1850: Castles and Miller 1993, p. 48). Refugees and asylum seekers can also be considered as migrants. But for the purposes of our analysis we focus on 'voluntary' migration. The period considered extends from the 'mass migration' after 1815 (mainly from Europe) to the emergence and extension of labour migration of the 'guest worker' variety after the Second World War.

It is difficult to judge exactly how many migrants there have been since 1815, so all the following numbers should be treated with some caution. Castles and Miller (1993) report that there could have been as many as 100 million migrants of all kinds in 1992 (including some 20 million refugees and asylum seekers, and 30 million overseas workers). They point out, however, that this represented only about 1.7 per cent of the world population. Thus the vast majority of the world's population remain in their country of origin.

The greatest era for recorded voluntary mass migration was the century after 1815 (figure 2.1). Around 60 million people left Europe for the Americas, Oceania, and South and East Africa. An estimated 10 million voluntarily migrated from Russia to Central Asia and Siberia. A million went from Southern Europe to North Africa. About 12 million Chinese and 6 million Japanese left their homelands and emigrated to East and South Asia. One and a half million left India for South East Asia and South and West Africa (Segal 1993, p. 16: the statistics for Indian migration are probably severely underestimated here).

Between the two world wars international migration decreased sharply. To a large extent this was in response to the depressed economic conditions during much of the interwar period, but it was also due to restrictive immigration policies instigated in many of the traditional recipient countries, particularly the United States.

An upsurge in international migration began in the post-1945 period, particularly involving Europe and the United States once again (Livi-Bacci 1993). This was the period, however, of the relative growth of migration from the developing countries to the developed ones (figure 2.2), and the

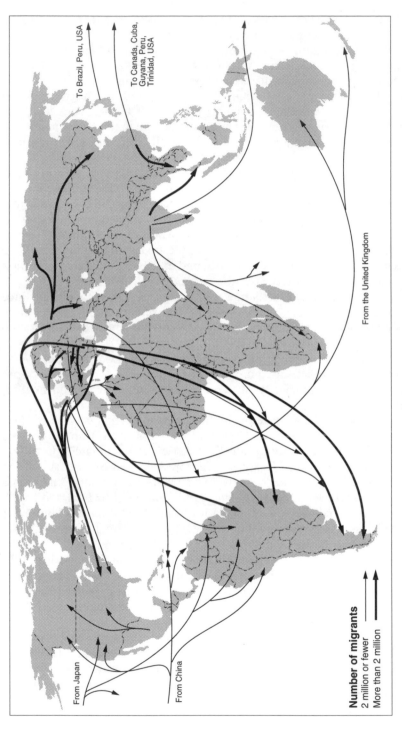

Figure 2.1 Global voluntary migrations, 1815–1914
Source: Based on Segal 1993, p. 17

To Brazil, Peru, USA

To Canada, Cuba, Guyana, Peru, Trinidad, USA

From the United Kingdom

From Japan

From China

Number of migrants
2 million or fewer
More than 2 million

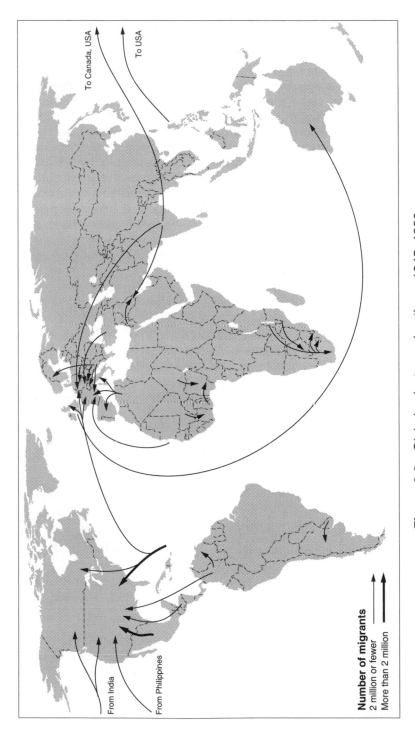

Figure 2.2 Global voluntary migrations, 1945–1980

Source: Based on Segal 1993, p. 21

introduction of the 'guest worker' phenomenon. During the 1970s and 1980s global trends favoured the controlled movements of temporary workers on a 'guest' basis, with entry for immigrants restricted to the highly skilled or those with family already in the country of destination.

It is generally agreed that the United States has been, and remains, the great immigrant country. Figure 2.3 neatly summarizes the history of immigration into the US, which mirrors the trends in the history of migration for the world as a whole sketched above. The steady growth of migration to the US in the period after the Second World War is evident from this graph. The accumulated proportion of migrants in the US in 1995 was 8.7 per cent (Papademetriou 1997–8, p. 17). For the 1980s estimates of global flows of migrants run at approximately 25–30 million a year (Segal 1993, p. 115). Up to 4 million of these were refugees and a good proportion of the others consisted of new temporary migrant workers (workers with the intention of returning home). The pattern of mass family migration has yet to repeat itself in the way that it operated in the period up to the First World War.

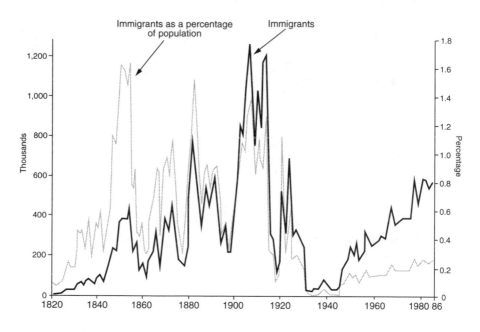

Figure 2.3   Legal immigration to the United States, 1820–1986 (numbers and as a percentage of population)

Source: Serow et al. 1990, fig. 19.1

The relative openness and interdependence of the international system

A key question posed by the preceding analysis is whether the integration of the international system has dramatically changed since the Second World War. Clearly, there has been considerable international economic activity ever since the 1850s, but can we compare different periods in terms of their openness and integration?

One way of doing this is to compare trade to GDP ratios. Table 2.3 provides information on these for a range of countries. Apart from the dramatic differences in the openness to trade of different economies demonstrated by these figures (compare the US and the Netherlands), the startling feature is that trade to GDP ratios were consistently higher in 1913 than they were in 1973 (with the slight exception of Germany where they were near enough equal). Even in 1995, Japan, the Netherlands and the UK were still less open than they were in 1913, with France and Germany only slightly more open. The US was the only country that was considerably more open than it was in 1913. There have been a number of objections to these figures, and this controversy is reviewed in the appendix to this chapter.

As we will see in chapter 4, concentrating on just the period after the Second World War shows a steady growth in trade openness, with a particularly dramatic entry of the East Asian economies into the international trading system.

Getting back to the longer term trends, however, the evidence also suggests greater openness to capital flows in the pre-First World War period compared to more recent years. Grassman (1980), measuring 'financial openness' in terms of current account balance to GNP ratios, finds no increase in openness between 1875 and 1975: indeed there is a decline in capital movements for his leading six countries (Great Britain, Italy,

Table 2.3   Ratio of merchandise trade to GDP at current prices (exports and imports combined), 1913, 1950, 1973 and 1995

	1913	*1950*	*1973*	*1995*
France	35.4	21.2	29.0	36.6
Germany	35.1	20.1	35.2	38.7
Japan	31.4	16.9	18.3	14.1
Netherlands	103.6	70.2	80.1	83.4
UK	44.7	36.0	39.3	42.6[a]
US	11.2	7.0	10.5	19.0

[a] 1994.

Sources: Figures from 1913 to 1973 derived from Maddison 1987, table A-23, p. 695; figures for 1995 derived from *OECD National Accounts, 1997*, country tables

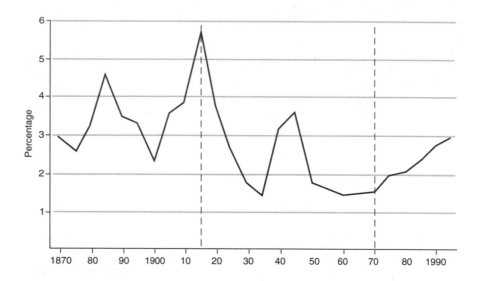

Figure 2.4   International capital flows among the G7 economies, 1870–
1995 (as percentage of GDP)

Source: Adapted from Howell 1998, fig. 7

Sweden, Norway, Denmark and the US). This is even the case for the
post-Second World War period, though from the mid-1970s there is some
sign of an increasing trend in financial openness. Measuring things slightly
differently, the figures shown in figure 2.4 confirm the general finding of a
decrease in openness among the G7 countries from a peak in 1913, but with
a steady increase after 1970.

In addition, Lewis reports that capital exports rose substantially over the
thirty years before the First World War, though they were subject to wide
fluctuations. But when a comparison is made with the years 1953–73, the
order of magnitude of capital exports was much lower in the latter period
(Lewis 1981, p. 21). Finally, in a comprehensive comparison of the pre-1914
Gold Standard period with the 1980s, Turner (1991) also concludes that
current account imbalances and capital flows, measured in relation to GNP,
were larger before 1914 than in the 1980s.

Thus, using gross figures for ratios of trade and capital flows relative to
output confirms that 'openness' was greater during the Gold Standard
period than even in the 1990s. But these gross figures could disguise important differences between the periods. As the appendix to this chapter points
out, the composition of output might be important in judging the real extent

of interdependence. In the case of financial flows we should also recognize the change in their character and the significance of the financial regimes under which they took place. In the high Gold Standard period long-term capital dominated international capital flows. In the recent period there has been a switch to shorter-term capital. In addition, a wider range of countries have now been included under the international capital movement umbrella.

This issue is discussed at greater length below but at this stage it is worth pointing to the nature of the Gold Standard as a quintessential fixed exchange rate system compared to the floating rates of the 1980s and 1990s. In a fixed exchange rate regime, short-term capital flows are highly interest-rate elastic, with only small changes in interest rates causing significant capital movements (though this also means that the sensitivity of capital flow to interest rates can limit the variability of short-term interest rates as well). Some of the capital flows could thus be accounted for by the significant differences in the pattern of interest rate variation as between the two periods, though, again, the postwar Bretton Woods system did not show any greater interest rate variability than the Gold Standard period (Turner 1991, table 2, p. 16).

Moving away from trade and capital flows for the moment, we can now look at the implications of the trends in international migration. First, it must be emphasized that these are contained within the twin considerations of the labour market and governmental policy. A world market for labour just does not exist in the same way that it does for goods and services. Most labour markets continue to be nationally regulated and only marginally accessible to outsiders, whether legal or illegal migrants or professional recruitment. Moving goods and services is infinitely easier than moving labour. Even a rapid and sustained expansion of the world economy is unlikely to significantly reduce the multiple barriers to the movement of labour. Other than in the context of regionally developing free trade agreements of the EU type, freedom of labour movement still remains heavily circumscribed. Even the NAFTA explicitly excludes freedom of movement of persons, though there is *de facto* freedom between Canada and the US, and enormous illegal flows between Mexico and the US. Extraregional migration of all kinds is a small percentage of global labour movements. Most migration is of the country next door variety. During the nineteenth century the mass movement of workers to the sources of capital was accepted and encouraged; now it is rejected except as a temporary expedient.

In as much as there is global international migration for employment, it is concentrated on the Gulf states, North America and Western Europe. A crude estimate of this category gives a figure of about 20 million in 1990 (prior to the Gulf War, which saw a massive return home, particularly of Third World migrant workers, from the Gulf states). This form of international labour force reached its peak in the early 1970s. The worldwide recession and subsequent developments like the Gulf War interrupted the growth of temporary migrant employment. A large proportion of these workers are illegally residing and working abroad. Legal expatriate workers tend to be in the managerial, skilled and technical employment categories.

One consequence of these levels of international migration and employment is that remittances of money home now constitute an important component of international financial flows and of the national incomes of some small states. It is estimated that remittances rose from $3,133 billion in 1970 to $30,401 billion in 1988 (Segal 1993, p. 150). But this still represents less than 5 per cent of the total value of world trade, though it has been increasing at a faster pace than has the value of that trade. This suggests either that the incentives to move this kind of labour have grown relative to the movements of goods and services, or that the rewards to this kind of labour have risen independently. The latter explanation could in turn be because more of the migrants are now to be found in the higher income categories of employment. The days of the unskilled, low income migrant seem to be numbered, though considerable scope may remain for continued temporary female migration to undertake domestic tasks in the richer countries.

Indeed, this is where government policy enters the picture explicitly. Policy is tightening on the growth in numbers of migrant workers, and even more so on the rights to permanent family immigration. There are differences here, particularly between Europe and the US, with the latter still maintaining a more open and liberal regime (Livi-Bacci 1993, p. 41). But as Castles and Miller suggest: 'Prospects are slim for significant increased legal migration flows to Western democracies over the short to medium term . . . Political constraints will not permit this . . . [There is] some room for highly skilled labour, family reunification and refugees, but not for the resumption of massive recruitment of foreign labour for low level jobs' (1993, pp. 265–6). The adverse labour market conditions in the advanced countries and difficulty of providing work for existing citizens and resident alien workers will mean the curtailment of unwanted and illegal immigration.

Two sets of more general points are worth making in the light of these remarks. The first is that there have been phases of massive international migration over many centuries and there seems nothing unprecedented about movements in the post-Second World War period, or those in more recent decades. The second related point is that in many ways the situation between 1815 and 1914 was much more open than it is today. The supposed era of 'globalization' has not seen the rise of a new unregulated and internationalized market in labour migration. In many ways, the world's underprivileged and poor have fewer international migratory possibilities nowadays than they had in the past. At least in the period of mass migration there was the option to uproot the whole family and move in the quest for better conditions, a possibility that seems to be rapidly shrinking for equivalent sections of the world's population today. They have little choice but to remain in poverty and stick it out. The 'empty lands' available to

European and other settlers in the US and Canada, South America, southern Africa and Australia and New Zealand just do not exist today, with a concomitant loss of 'freedom' for the world's poor.

Things look different for the well off and privileged however. Those with professional qualifications and technical skills still have greater room for manoeuvre and retain the option to move if they wish. The 'club class' with managerial expertise, though relatively few in number in terms of the global population, are the most obvious manifestation of this inequity in long-term migratory opportunities.

Another strong contemporary feature of the international system that is often invoked as an indicator of 'globalization' is the emergence of large discriminatory regional trading blocs like the EU, NAFTA and APEC (Asia-Pacific Economic Cooperation). We will have much to say about these institutions in later chapters but here it is worth pointing to the historical precedents for these kinds of bodies. A marked discrimination in trade and investment patterns was produced during the colonial empire period in the nineteenth century. For the French and British empires the biases to trade between the colonial power and its colonies were between two and four times greater than would have been expected given the 'natural' economic fundamentals that determine trade, such as the size of the countries involved, GDP per capita, proximity and common borders. The biases were even higher for Belgium, Italy and Portugal and their overseas dependencies. In fact, the concentration of trade with the countries that made up British and French empires did not peak until 1938; it declined steadily following the independence movements after the post-Second World War, but did not reach unity until as late as 1984 (Frankel 1997, p. 126). Trade within the Austro-Hungarian Empire, before it broke up at the end of the First World War, was also four or five times what it would have been if determined simply by the natural fundamentals (Frankel 1997, p. 119). The case of Japan and its 'co-prosperity sphere' is shown in table 2.4. Note that in 1990 the simple average share of trade confined to the East Asian countries was about the same as it was in 1913, and lower than in 1938 (Pertri 1994). Intra-East Asian investment integration was higher in 1938 than it was in the early 1990s.

Thus it was in the 1930s that regionalism was probably at its height. There was a definite discriminatory sterling bloc, overlapping imperfectly with the British Empire/Commonwealth. Then there was a group of countries that remained on the Gold Standard, and a subsection of central and south-eastern European countries that gravitated towards Germany. The US erected trade barriers, and formed a partial dollar bloc with the Spanish-speaking countries adjacent to North America. According to Frankel, all these were heavily discriminatory – though some more than others – except for the partial dollar bloc (Frankel 1997, pp. 127–8). The differences between the blocs have, however, been emphasized by Eichengreen and Irwin (1995, 1997). Sterling bloc countries traded disproportionately among

Table 2.4 East Asian trade as a share of total trade for different countries (exports plus imports as percentage of total trade)

	1913	1925	1938	1955	1990
China	65	46	70	43	59
Indonesia	32	38	26	32	60
Taiwan	–	–	99	50	42
Japan	41	47	70	22	29
Korea	–	–	100	35	40
Malaysia	44	39	35	30	37
Philippines	18	15	11	17	43
Thailand	62	71	65	52	51
Simple average	42	43	59	35	45
Excluding Korea, Taiwan	42	43	46	33	47
Excluding Korea, Taiwan and Japan	42	42	41	35	50

Higher percentages indicate greater trade intensity.
Source: Adapted from Pertri 1994, table 10.1, p. 111

themselves, and discrimination increased during the 1930s, while those remaining on the Gold Standard were more disparate. In as much as they erected barriers between themselves, this reduced trade discrimination.

There have thus been several earlier periods of regionalization, some of which were more intense than the present period. What is distinctive about the present situation, however, is the formation of larger formal *de jure* free trade area (FTA) blocs, and the extension of their *de facto* influence over a wider range of countries and areas. For the first time there are three almost continent-wide blocs (that is the EU, NAFTA, and Japan plus some of East Asia) either firmly established or in proto-existence.

As a preliminary conclusion, then, we can say that the international economy was in many ways more open in the pre-1914 period than at any time since, including from the late 1970s onwards. International trade and capital flows, both between the rapidly industrializing economies themselves and between these and their various colonial territories, were more important relative to GDP levels before the First World War than they probably are today. Add to this the issue of international migration just explored and we have an extraordinarily developed, open and integrated international economy at the beginning of this century. Thus the present position is by no means unprecedented.

International monetary and exchange rate regimes

An issue thrown up by the previous analysis is the existence of general monetary and exchange rate regimes under which economic activity takes place and by which the international economy is ordered and governed. In broad

Table 2.5   History of monetary and exchange rate regimes

Regime	Period
1 International Gold Standard	1879–1914
2 Interwar instability	1918–1939
(a) Floating	1918–1925
(b) Return to Gold	1925–1931
(c) Return to floating	1931–1939
3 Semi-fixed rate dollar standard	1945–1971
(a) Establishing convertibility	1945–1958
(b) Bretton Woods system proper	1958–1971
4 Floating rate dollar standard	1971–1984
(a) Failure to agree	1971–1974
(b) Return to floating	1974–1984
5 EMS and greater Deutschmark zone	1979–1993
6 Plaza-Louvre intervention accords	1985–1993
7 Drift towards renewed global floating	1993–
(a) Broad multilateral surveillance	1993–1997
(b) Final end of the dollar peg	1997–

Sources: Compiled from Eichengreen 1990, 1994; McKinnon 1993; and authors' own assessments

terms we can divide the twentieth century into a number of fairly discrete periods as far as these regimes are concerned, as indicated by table 2.5.

There are two important preliminary points to note about this table. The first is the diversity of regimes it displays. It is often thought that there have been just two regimes in the twentieth century, the Gold Standard and the Bretton Woods system – the former breaking down in the interwar period and the latter in the post-1973 period. These are indeed two of the main systems characterizing the twentieth century, but they are not the exclusive ones. In addition, there are important subperiods within some of the regimes depicted. All in all a rather more complex picture of international economic orders and systems needs to be painted if we are to have an adequate analysis.

Secondly, other than the number of regimes, what is striking about the table is the short period of time over which they have operated. Only the Gold Standard existed for more than thirty years, while most of the others operated for considerably less. Clearly, what is designated here as 'interwar instability' does not conform to any obvious regime since the 'rules of the game' during this period defy a consistent characterization. Thus we have split this period into three subperiods, none of which can be said to display exclusive (or inclusive) system-like features since arrangements were very fluid and overlapping, being either in decay or in embryonic reconstruction (sometimes both at the same time).

The regime emerging immediately after the Second World War is characterized as a 'semi-fixed rate dollar standard', which has two subperiods. This is really a period of significant stability in exchange rates since few and only slight adjustments were made, but they were possible and sanctioned within this regime.[2] The period in its entirety is often classified as the Bretton Woods system (BWS), after the agreement signed in 1944, but we prefer to divide it into two subperiods, since full current account convertibility of the major currencies was not established until the end of 1958 (though this was a condition of the 1944 treaty). Thus the Bretton Woods system proper only operated for some thirteen years between 1958 and 1971,[3] perhaps a surprisingly short period of time.

The following period is designated the 'floating rate dollar standard'. The tumultuous events of 1971–4 are termed here the 'failure to agree' subperiod. This was a time during which the international community gave up any attempt to collectively manage its exchange rates after the Nixon administration unilaterally suspended convertibility of the US dollar against gold in August 1971 and subsequently devalued. Despite various plans and schemes designed to shore up the previous system during this period, the writing for it was already on the wall. But the advent of 'flexible' rates did little to dislodge the dollar as the *de facto* standard for the conduct of official and most private international monetary transactions. Also, this subperiod, despite its designation as a 'return to floating', displayed a definite set of 'rules of the game' in the conduct of international monetary transactions, and these were closely adhered to by the industrialized countries involved (McKinnon 1993, pp. 26–9; also see below).

Although the period of floating rates lasted for ten years, an important subperiod interrupts this after the EMS was established in 1979. This is termed a 'greater Deutschmark zone' to indicate the central importance of the German currency in acting as the standard for the other European currencies in the European Monetary System. The EMS began to unscramble after the autumn of 1992 with first the departure of a number of its key currencies and then the widening of the bands in which the remaining currencies were allowed to fluctuate. Further devaluations of the Spanish peseta and Portuguese escudo followed in early 1995. The remains of the EMS, in this modified form, functioned until 1999, however, when it was transformed with the inauguration of European Monetary Union (EMU).

The sixth regime characterized in table 2.5 follows the Plaza and Louvre accords struck in 1985 and 1987, which had as their objective the stabilization (and, indeed, initially the reduction) of the value of the US dollar against the two other main currency blocs: the EMS-DM zone and that of the Japanese yen. Formally these accords introduced broad 'target zones' for exchange rates between the three currency blocs (the G3), allowing 'interventions' for stabilization around these rates (with concomitant sterilization of monetary impacts), and sanctioned the adjustment of the central rates according to 'economic fundamentals' when necessary. Monitoring by the G3 continued with a successful agreement in 1995 to reverse the slide of the dollar against the yen. After that the yen began to depreciate against the US dollar. However, it is arguable whether there was ever a real commitment to managing the rates actively against market sentiment, and thereby also to managing the G3 economies more generally (see also chapter 8). This is why, when this is considered alongside the partial demise of the EMS after 1992, we suggest a final possible regime, emerging in 1993–4, that hints at a drift towards floating rates like the more obvious floating rate regime of 1974–84. Initially the period was marked by broad multilateral surveillance. After the financial turmoil in 1997 and 1998, however, the last vestiges of an international dollar peg were swept away as most of the remaining East Asian countries were forced to break with the dollar. Of course, this may all change as quickly again if the euro is gradually consolidated after 2000.

The main point of this brief history of international monetary arrangements is, first, to demonstrate the governed nature of the system throughout much of this century (with the possible exception of the twenty interwar years). Secondly, it is to suggest that there is nothing radically unusual about the present period. In these terms, there remains at least a quasi-system of order and governance. Thirdly, given the volatile nature of the international regimes and their short lived character, there is no reason to believe that things cannot change significantly in the future, even the near future. The length of regimes may be getting shorter. But even if they are not, thirty years looks like an absolute maximum before strains begin to pull things apart (or perhaps push things together again). With this in mind we should remember that what is often thought to have been the key regime 'watershed' year of 1973 was already twenty-five years behind us by 1998.

Openness and integration: what is at stake?

Returning to the broad issue of integration preliminarily discussed above, the actual measurement of the degree of integration in financial markets is difficult both theoretically and empirically. Economic analysis in this area tends to be driven by the idea of 'efficient (international) financial market' theory; that is, that capital markets operate competitively to allocate (international) savings and investment so as to equalize returns on capital. Thus key indicators of the degree of integration would be measures such as interest rates as between countries or the value of the same shares on domestic and international stock markets: the nearer these are to equality as between different national financial markets, the more integrated the international economy has become. With a fully integrated capital market there would be single international rates of interest on short-term and long-term loans, and a single share or bond price, other things remaining equal.

Of course, the key constraint here is the 'other things remaining equal' one. In reality they just do not, so the task of empirical analysis from within this dominant perspective is to account for, and then adjust for, these 'imperfections' so as to arrive at a proxy measure of the degree of 'true' integration.[4] As might be expected, all this requires some formidable assumptions to be made, ones that few other than the truly converted *cognoscenti* might either appreciate or accept. However, despite some scepticism about this underlying approach, it is worth considering its main results.[5]

The degree of international financial integration could be analysed in a number of forms and at a number of levels (Frankel 1992; Herring and Litan 1995; Harris 1995). These can be grouped under three overlapping headings: those associated with interest rate differentials; those associated with differential prices of securities; and those associated with real resource flows and capital mobility. We deal with each of these in turn, beginning with a discussion of the relationships between interest rates and exchange rates.

One of the most straightforward indicators of financial integration concerns offshore markets like that for Eurocurrencies. Formally, measures of offshore financial market integration can be established in terms of covered interest rate parities. This implies that depositors can receive the same return on whatever Eurocurrency they hold, taking into account the cost involved in protecting against possible exchange rate changes. Such interest rate parity seems to hold in the Eurocurrency markets. A more developed form of integration would be when offshore and onshore markets are closely linked, but it is here that difficulties begin to arise. Banking regulations and capital controls establish a separation between these two spheres, and these have often been introduced and maintained for public policy reasons. But with the progressive harmonization of banking regulations and the abandonment of capital controls this form of integration was effectively established between the advanced countries by 1993: thus covered interest rate parity between national rates has now also been more or less achieved.

Deeper forms of integration would be signalled by first uncovered interest rate parity and then real interest rate parity between deposits in different currencies. If the first condition holds, expected returns on investments in different currencies are the same when measured in terms of a single currency, so that capital flows equalize expected rates of return regardless of exposure to exchange rate risk. This introduces an unobservable variable into the calculation, the 'speculative premium' associated with changes in expectations. In the case of real interest rate parity, differential inflation rates are already anticipated in the nominal rates, so that real exchange rates are maintained and capital flows serve to equalize real interest rates across countries. While tests to measure the presence of these latter two forms of integration are complex and controversial, real interest rate parity seemed far from established by the mid-1990s, so that the level of international financial integration fell short of what would prevail in a truly integrated system. By contrast, the Gold Standard period was one where short-term interest rates were closely correlated, and there was a strong tendency for real rates of return to be equalized internationally (Turner 1991, pp. 16–17).

The second broad approach is to focus on asset prices in different national financial systems. Here one problem is to distinguish domestic influences on prices from international ones, but there is a *prima facie* case that stock markets are closely linked, with disruption in one being quickly transmitted to others (so-called 'contagion'). In this context it is changes in the 'volatility' of price movements that would represent an indicator of increased globalization, not the existence of links as such, and the evidence on this score remains at best ambiguous (Harris 1995, pp. 204–6). In fact, historically based studies have reinforced the impression of greater financial integration, measured in these terms, in the pre-First World War period. From within the broad perspective of the efficient capital market approach, Neal (1985) focused on asset price movements during the main financial crises occurring between 1745 and 1907. He measured the rapidity with which financial panics spread between one financial centre and another. This analysis found that there was already a surprisingly high degree of capital market integration between European financial centres as early as the mid-eighteenth century, but suggested that the degree of financial integration did not develop much further between then and 1900. Zevin, in his survey of a wide range of the financial integration literature, reports on a number of measures supporting the highly integrated nature of the pre-First World War international economy. He sums up thus:

> All these measures of transnational-securities trading and ownership are substantially greater in the years before the First World War than they are at present. More generally, every available descriptor of financial markets in the late nineteenth and early twentieth centuries suggests that they were more fully integrated than they were before or have been since. (Zevin 1992, pp. 51–2)

The Gold Standard period was thus also the one displaying the most interdependent and integrated international economy in terms of security markets, the extent of which seems yet to have been repeated.

How did the international financial system adjust so rapidly when technological developments were so primitive? In fact, the idea that the contemporary era of communications technology is unprecedented again needs to be challenged. The coming of the electronic telegraph system after 1870 in effect established more or less instantaneous information communications between all the major international financial and business centres (Standage 1998). By the turn of the century a system of international communications had been established that linked parties together much in the way that the contemporary Internet does. Although the networks were not so developed in terms of individual subscribers, corporate and institutional linkages were dense and extensive. Compared to a reliance on the sailing ship (and even steam propulsion), the telegraph marked a real qualitative leap in communications technology, in many ways more important than the shift into computer technology and telematics after 1970.

A third important related approach in trying to identify the extent of financial integration involves measuring real resource flows: can increased financial integration be implied from increased capital mobility? In this case it is the relationship between national savings and investment that becomes the object of analysis. This approach has generated the most extensive literature, but its results remain controversial.

The more integrated the capital markets, the more mobile capital will become internationally and the more likely it is that domestic savings and investment will diverge. If there were a completely integrated global financial system, domestic investment would not be fundamentally constrained by domestic savings, and the correlation between savings and investment would be broken. Thus national economies will lose their ability to 'regulate' or 'determine' domestic investment. In fact, this is just another way of pointing to the key role of interest rate differentials as a measure of integration and as the determinant of investment. As openness increases, domestic savings become irrelevant to domestic investment since interest rates converge and savings and investment adjust accordingly.

But national savings–investment correlations have not unambiguously declined in the 1980s and 1990s, during the period of capital market liberalization and floating exchange rates. Careful analysis by Bosworth (1993, pp. 98–102) and by Obstfeld (1993, e.g. p. 50) shows this not to be the case (despite the less than careful commentary by some others, for instance Goldstein and Mussa 1993, p. 25). The persistence of the correlation between national savings and investment, first established in 1980 (Feldstein and Horioka 1980), well into a period of financial liberalization, deregulation and supposed global integration, testifies to the continued robust relative autonomy of financial systems, and this despite the (sometimes desperate) attempts by conventional economic analysts to prove otherwise (e.g. Bayoumi 1990). Table 2.6 brings together previous OLS (ordinary least squares) estimates of a simple gross savings–investment equation and adds our own estimates for the period 1991–5.

The β coefficient can be interpreted as the 'savings retention coefficient': the proportion of incremental savings that is invested domestically (Feldstein and Bacchetta 1991, p. 206). Thus, over the period 1991–5, for every dollar saved in the main OECD countries, 67 cents would have been

Table 2.6 Savings and investment correlations, 1900–1995

			$(I/Y)_i = a + \beta(S/Y)_i + u_i$			
	1900–1913	*1926–1938*	*1960–1974*	*1974–1980*	*1981–1990*	*1991–1995*
β	0.774	0.959	0.887	0.867	0.636	0.67
	(0.436)	(0.082)	(0.074)	(0.170)	(0.108)	(0.086)
R²	0.26	0.94	0.91	0.56	0.64	0.75

Data from 1960 are for 22 main OECD-member developed economies.
I = investment; Y = national income; S = savings; u = error term.
Figures in brackets beneath β coefficients are standard errors.
Sources: 1960–74, Feldstein and Horioka 1980, table 2, p. 231; 1991–5, authors' own estimates; all other years, Obstfeld 1993

invested domestically. Clearly the interwar period and that directly after the Second World War represented the high points of a 'closed' international financial system on this measure. Between 96 per cent and 89 per cent of incremental domestic savings was invested domestically. There was a decline in this ratio during the 1980s and 1990s, but the value of the β coefficient eased up in the first half of the 1990s. (Most of this decline can probably be attributed to the lagged effects of the collapse in the savings ratio of a single country, the US, after 1979: Frankel 1992 and chapter 7 below). These coefficients were also lower than that for the high Gold Standard period of 1900–13, which is often thought to have been the pinnacle of an 'open' international financial system as well. However, note that the R² correlation coefficient has become stronger since 1974–80. All in all, this analysis does not as yet indicate any dramatic change in the relationship between domestic saving and investment during the period of 'globalization'.[6]

So long as governments continue to target their current accounts, retain some sovereignty within their borders (so that at least the threat of government intervention in cross-border capital movements remains) and differentially regulate their financial systems, investors cannot think about domestic and foreign assets in the same way. Different national financial systems are made up of different institutions and arrangements, with different conceptions of the future and assessments of past experience, and thus operate with different modalities of calculation. All these features factor into a continued diversity of expectations and outlooks which cannot all be reduced to a single global marketplace or logic. What is more, even the most committed of the integrationists who have looked at national saving–investment correlations tend to conclude that the less developed countries (LDCs) and most NICs remain largely out of the frame as far as this form of financial integration is concerned. Thus, even for the integration enthusiasts, there are limits to the extent of the 'globalization' of financial markets.[7]

However, the basic Feldstein–Horioka findings, while proving very robust and reproducible, have attracted heavy criticism, mainly because they seem so counterintuitive. Against the conclusion that the high correlation between national savings and investment is the result of a lack of financial integration are arguments that (a) it might reflect net flows, which disguise much larger gross flows; (b) if the data are disaggregated into private and public sector flows, lower correlations appear for solely private sector behaviour, so that it is government policy that accounts for the strong overall relationship (Bayoumi 1990); (c) floating exchange rates and associated uncertainties have lowered capital mobility (Bayoumi and Rose 1993); (d) the close correlations may be because of exogenously determined productivity shocks and the way they are handled domestically (Ghosh 1995); and finally (e) although the original findings are robust, they have been fatally undermined by the emergence of the large US balance of payments deficits since the mid-1980s, and this has yet to be properly picked up by econometric analyses (Frankel 1992).

Clearly, there are a number of possible reasons for the high correlation between aggregate savings and investment. Most of the points just made do not so much undermine this relationship as serve to explain it in the context of a range of contemporary conditions. One problem is to distinguish those points that pertain to the determinants of real capital investment flows as opposed to overall financial ones. With the exception of the final point, they do not undermine the result of a continued separation of capital markets: they provide reasons for the finding which are compatible with a continued relatively unintegrated international financial system – one that continues to allow for more national autonomy than might be generally appreciated. In a longer-term perspective, Zevin compares the post-1960 findings with a similar type of analysis for the 1890s onwards. This only confirms his other results showing that the Gold Standard period was an era of more effective capital mobility and financial openness than that from the 1960s onwards. Investment-savings autarky was much less between 1870 and 1910 (Zevin 1992, table 3.2, p. 57). Below and in chapter 7 we return to point (e) above – concerning the significant change in the post-1985 period vis-à-vis the USA – but this pertains to general financial flows between the US and Japan and not just real resource flows.

One further possible explanation for these results, particularly over the recent period, has to do with the rate of return on financial investments in different economies. If there is no significant difference in the return on financial investment then we would not expect a large redistribution of capital relative to savings compared to a situation where there was extreme variation in returns. Thus the current situation of low financial asset mobility could be accounted for by a general convergence of returns as between different economies. In fact there was considerable convergence of underlying productivity between the main industrial economies over the period from 1962 to 1993, though with a striking general decline in productivity levels (which has yet to be reversed). Of course, this does not preclude intense short-term movements of funds between financial centres in search of small arbitrage gains on currency transactions, which is something that has characterized contemporary currency markets (indeed, underlying convergence may encourage this very activity). We discuss this further below and in chapters 5 and 7.

However, with respect to convergence – which itself could constitute a measure of the integration between economies – indications of this emerged for the major economies as their real economic business cycles synchronized in the mid-1970s and early 1980s. But this was reversed during the upturn of the late 1980s to early 1990s when a general desynchronization set in (OECD 1994a, pp. 37–43). Thus it is inappropriate to read too much into any measure of 'convergence' as an indicator of integration which does not have a long-term empirical provenance or carry robust explanatory significance.[8]

Of particular importance in this context was the growing asymmetric relationship between the G3 countries over the 1970s and 1980s in terms of financial flows, even though the close relationships between their domestic savings and investment levels did not alter much (Bosworth 1993, ch. 3). While there was a decline in the savings ratios in most advanced countries, so that investment ratios also fell, there was a stronger fall of both of these in the US than in other countries. The US in effect imported capital to make up for a decline in its domestic saving, and not to sustain higher levels of investment. This happened along with the emergence there of a persistent current account deficit. This led to financing problems in the context of the so called 'twin deficits'. However, how far these international financing problems were the result of the twin deficits rather than the abandonment of fixed exchange rates and of capital controls and financial market deregulation remains a point of dispute. In chapter 7 we discuss this issue further.

The importance of this assessment of openness and integration is obvious. It has to do with the ability of distinct national economies to devise and regulate their own economic policies. The fact that the degree of constraint on national economies in the Gold Standard period seems to have been consistently greater than at any time since should not blind us to the problems and issues facing economies because of the level of integration at the present time. It is certainly the case that, on the basis of some of the measures discussed above, the level of economic integration has increased since 1960 – though this is not obvious on just the savings–investment measure, except perhaps for the most recent period. In addition, it would be difficult to accept that the qualitative dimension has been constant over the entire period since 1870. The number and range of financial instruments has changed dramatically since 1960, for instance, and with them new problems of management and regulation have arisen (Turner 1991; Cosh, Hughes and Singh 1992). Before we look at the internationalization of money and short-term capital markets, however, we need to look to the more mundane areas of financial integration to see whether the underlying framework for the operation of capital markets has radically changed in the recent period. Money markets are probably more highly integrated than are capital markets. But it is capital markets that most immediately affect the economic prospects for the long-term growth of national economies.

Recent developments in international financial market activity

These issues can be first approached by investigating the cross-border transactions and holdings of bonds and equities between countries and in various domestic financial institutions. As a percentage of GDP the cross-border *transactions* in bonds and equities have escalated since the mid-1970s, as shown in table 2.7. But if this is looked at from a slightly different angle, changes may not appear quite so dramatic.

For instance, tables 2.8 and 2.9 give two different sources for the actual *holdings* of foreign bonds and equities in the accounts of institutional investors (not just transactions between countries), expressed as a percentage of their total holdings. The case of table 2.8 demonstrates a general trend of growth in the importance of foreign securities since 1980 (with the exception of Austria).

The figures for 1993 in table 2.8 can be compared with those shown for the same year in table 2.9. In the case of the US there is a significant discrepancy between the data in the two tables for pension funds, though for the other countries common to both tables the figures are reasonably close. For most countries the foreign securities holdings by their institutional

Table 2.7   Cross-border transactions in bonds and equities (as a percentage of GDP)

	1975	1980	1985	1989	1990	1991	1992	1993	1994	1995	1996
United States	4	9	35	101	89	96	107	129	131	135	164
Japan	2	8	62	156	119	92	72	78	60	65	84[a]
Germany	5	7	33	66	57	55	85	171	159	172	200
France	–	5	21	52	54	79	122	187	201	180	227[b]
Italy	1	1	4	18	27	60	92	192	207	253	468
Canada	3	10	27	55	64	81	113	153	212	194	258

Transactions are gross purchases and sales of securities between residents and non-residents.
[a] Based on settlement data.
[b] Jan.–Sep. at an annual rate.
Source: BIS 1996–7, table V.1, p. 79

investors were in the 10–30 per cent range, with only the Netherlands, Ireland and New Zealand having a stake over 30 per cent. (The dramatically contrasting cases of Hong Kong and Singapore shown in table 2.9 are discussed in a moment.)

What the figures for 1993 in both tables demonstrate, however, is the enormous variation between countries in terms of the importance of foreign holdings. Some financial systems are clearly much more 'open' than others on this measure. Of the G5 countries, the UK and Japan are much more 'open' than are the US, Germany and France.

Table 2.8   Institutional investors' holdings of foreign securities, 1980–1993 (percentage of total securities holdings)

	1980	1985	1990	1993
United States[a]				
Private pension funds[b]	1.0	3.0	4.1	7.1
Mutual funds	–	–	4.0[c]	8.0
Japan				
Postal life insurance	0.0	6.7	11.6	12.3
Private insurance companies	8.1	23.2	29.9	22.3
Canada				
Life insurance companies	2.2	2.3	2.4	3.1
Pension funds	6.1	6.6	7.0	10.6
Italy				
Insurance companies	–	–	13.6	12.2
United Kingdom				
Insurance companies[d]	6.3	14.1	14.6	–
Pension funds[e]	10.8	17.3	23.2	–
Australia				
Life insurance companies	–	–	14.0	18.8
Austria				
Insurance companies	14.1	11.6	10.1	9.9
Investment funds	27.0	13.2	18.7	25.1
Belgium				
Insurance companies	5.5	8.6	5.2	–
Netherlands				
Insurance companies	6.9	22.9	20.2	26.0
Private pension funds	26.6	28.1	36.6	36.9
Public pension funds	14.7	9.9	16.6	20.2
Sweden				
Insurance companies	–	1.5[f]	10.5	12.3

[a] Per cent of total assets held by these funds.
[b] Tax exempt funded schemes (excluding individual retirement accounts).
[c] 1991.
[d] Long-term funds.
[e] Pension funds exclude central government sector but include other public sector funds.
[f] 1987.
Source: Edey and Hviding 1995, table 10, p. 33

Table 2.9 The internationalization of pension fund
investments (percentage held in international bonds and
equities), 1993

US	4
Japan	14
Germany	3
UK	27
France[a]	5
Canada[b]	9
Australia	16
Belgium	29
Ireland	35
Switzerland	6
New Zealand	34
Hong Kong	60
Singapore	0

[a] At end of 1991.
[b] At end of 1992.
Source: HM Treasury 1996, compiled from tables A2.1 (p. 24)
and A2.3 (p. 26)

Indeed, if we look at this in a slightly different way we continue to see
the structural differences between financial systems. Table 2.10 shows the
distribution of corporate equity as between different types of shareholder
in a range of OECD countries. Apart from indicating the basic differences
between the ownership structure of so-called 'insider' and 'outsider' (or
'market-based') financial systems ('insider' systems being those where
shares are owned by parties that are institutionally linked to the company,
'outsider' systems those where shares are owned by a dispersed set of shareholders), the table also demonstrates the variation in foreign holdings of
shares. Two of the 'outsider' systems (the UK and the US) have among the
lowest proportions, along with two of the 'insider' group (Germany and
Japan). On this classification it is Australia, Sweden and France that have
the highest measure of 'internationalization'. The 'big four' economies of
the US, Japan, Germany and the UK – with 11 per cent or less of their equity
stake held abroad in 1996 – can surely hardly constitute a clear case of
globalization?

From all these figures what is clear is that there is no obvious convergence of all the advanced countries to a common openness position. By and
large the differences between them seem to have been maintained, indicating continued variation in the characteristics and structures of their
domestic financial systems. Thus, up to the mid-1990s at least, the operation
of 'globalization' did not seem to have forced the domestic financial institutions of the advanced countries to have fundamentally broken with the

Table 2.10   Distribution of outstanding listed corporate equity among different categories of shareholders in selected OECD countries (percentage at year-end 1996)

	United States	Japan	Germany	France	United Kingdom[a]	Sweden	Australia
Financial sector	46	42	30	30	68	30	37
Banks	6	15	10	7	1	1	3
Insurance companies and pension funds	28	12	12	9	50	14	25
Investment funds	12		8	11	8	15	–
Other financial institutions	1	15[b]	–	3	9	–	9[c]
Non-financial enterprises	–	27	42	19	1	11	11
Public authorities	–	1	4	2	1	8	–
Households	49	20	15	23	21	19	20
Rest of the world	**5**	**11**	**9**	**25**	**9**	**32**	**32**
Total	100	100	100	100	100	100	100

[a] United Kingdom figures are for end 1994.
[b] For Japan, pension and investment funds are included in 'other financial institutions'.
[c] Australian figures are for end Sep. 1996; investment funds are included in 'other financial institutions'.
Source. OECD 1998a, table 1

historical variation in their character, though there had been some increase in their overall internationalization.

Particular attention is drawn to the figures for Singapore and Hong Kong in table 2.9. Neither of these countries could be argued to have escaped the full rigours of internationalization over the recent period. Both have remarkably open economies and have been the centres for similar kinds of 'global integration' forces (in terms of trade openness, for instance, in 1993 the sum of imports and exports relative to GDP for Hong Kong and Singapore was 252 per cent and 279 per cent respectively). But in one these institutional investors had zero foreign participation and in the other 60 per cent. This difference must be accounted for by different policy choices. Those in charge of the Singapore Central Provident Fund were required to invest only in domestic financial assets, whereas those running the Hong Kong funds went for a completely different option (though there was probably some external indirect leakage from the Singapore Fund) (see Ramesh 1993 for a discussion of the politics of Singapore's Central Provident Fund).

Table 2.11 Foreign assets and liabilities as a percentage of assets of commercial banks for selected countries, 1960–1996

	1960	1970	1980	1990	1996
France					
Assets	–	16.0	30.0	24.9	30.9
Liabilities	–	17.0	22.0	28.6	30.2
Germany					
Assets	2.4	8.7	9.7	16.3	16.0
Liabilities	4.7	9.0	12.2	13.1	12.9
Japan					
Assets	2.6	3.7	4.2	13.9	13.8
Liabilities	3.6	3.1	7.3	19.4	10.6
Netherlands					
Assets	18.4	23.1	33.0	33.5	33.2
Liabilities	7.1	22.2	33.9	31.2	34.1
United Kingdom					
Assets	6.2	46.1	64.7	45.0	47.0
Liabilities	13.9	49.7	67.5	49.3	48.8
United States					
Assets	1.4	2.2	11.0	5.6	2.6
Liabilities	3.7	5.4	9.0	6.9	8.2

Source: IMF, *International Financial Statistics Yearbook*, 1986 and 1997

Similar comments could be made about the operation of commercial banks. An increase in the importance of foreign assets and liabilities in their balance sheets is evident from table 2.11, mainly attributable to a growth between 1960 and 1980, since when the positions have tended to stabilize. (There are some exceptions to this, notably in the case of Sweden, which experienced a rapid growth over almost the entire period 1960–96, to reach one of the highest levels in 1996.) But there remains a great variation between the economies shown, largely based on entrenched historical differences.

The final point to make here is to look at the 'bottom line', as it were, of the internationalization of financial systems by assessing the importance of foreign assets ultimately owned by households as a proportion of their total financial assets. Thus we are still concentrating on the holdings only of financial assets, but looking at their importance in household wealth. The problem with the figures presented so far is that they do not cover the entire financial system. As table 2.10 indicated, there are many non-bank and non-financial institutional holdings of financial assets.

Figures for households are plotted in figure 2.5 for the end of 1995. A variation between countries similar to the patterns outlined above emerges, and with great diversity among them. But only two countries show a foreign

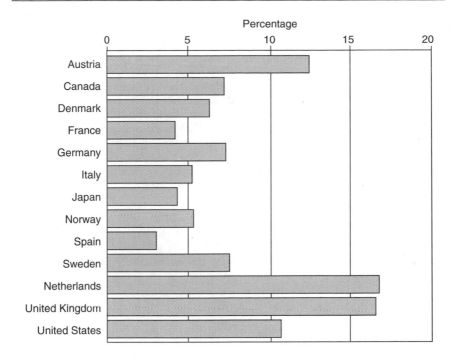

Figure 2.5 Percentage of financial assets ultimately owned by households held in overseas bonds and equities, end of 1995

Source: Merrill Lynch Research/*The Independent*, 22 Dec. 1997, p. 19

proportion of over 15 per cent. Around 10 per cent and below is the norm. Broadly speaking, then, people's financial wealth still remains a domestic affair: it stays at home.

What the data in these tables, and in figure 2.5, indicate is the continued pertinence of domestic policy choices, something rather ignored by the globalization analysis. We must presume that 'globalization' has had little impact on these choices in the case of Hong Kong and Singapore, for instance, since both of them have been subject to more or less the same external pressures. The causes are purely 'domestic'. Similarly in the case of the advanced industrial economies: it has been policy choices (and mistakes) that have driven the move towards greater interdependence and internationalization, as displayed for instance in table 2.9, not some mysterious process of 'globalization'. For instance, take the remarks of two commentators who more or less unambiguously welcome the moves towards greater openness and integration:

> In some sense, authorities have suffered the fate of getting what they asked for. They wanted greater participation by foreign investors in their government debt markets, in part to make it easier to finance larger fiscal and external balances. They wanted a more efficient financial system that would erode the power of local monopolies and offer savers a higher rate of return and firms a lower cost of capital. They welcomed innovations that provided a wider range of hedging possibilities against volatile asset prices, and that made it more convenient to unbundle risks. They wanted to regain business that had migrated to the off-shore centres in search of a less restrictive regulatory environment, and to level the playing field against foreign competitors. Much of that has taken place. But along with it has also come the creation of an enormous pool of mobile, liquid capital whose support, or lack of it, can often be the measure of difference in the success of stabilization, reform, exchange rate, and tax policy. (Goldstein and Mussa 1993, p. 42)

Despite their complacency, these authors have a point. Though, along with them, we are not suggesting here that *everything* was just the result of either deliberate policy choices or mistakes by the authorities.

Similar remarks could be made about the other ways of measuring and assessing the degree of international financial integration discussed above: real interest rate convergence, equity price movements, offshore and onshore yields, covered or uncovered interest rate parity, international portfolio diversity, etc. To quote Goldstein and Mussa again:

> Even though there is by now a burgeoning literature that addresses directly the measurement of international capital market integration, it has proven difficult to reach firm and clear conclusions about the degree – if not the trend – of integration. This ambiguity reflects the fact that no single method of measuring the degree of integration is completely free of conceptual and technical difficulties that cloud its interpretation. (Goldstein and Mussa 1993, p. 14)

Caution remains the order of the day. It is still reasonable to argue, for instance, that short-term interest rates are set nationally, and that even long-term interest rates are fundamentally driven by the decisions of important state authorities, as in the US, Japan and Germany, rather than totally by the anonymous forces of global markets.

Even those alternative approaches that do not concentrate directly or indirectly on financial integration, like those that stress comparisons of consumption paths between countries, cannot reach an unambiguous conclusion that financial integration has taken place (Bayoumi and MacDonald 1995).

Short-term lending

Broadly speaking, the period since the liberalization moves of the 1970s has seen an upsurge in international financial activity associated with three

Table 2.12 Borrowing on international capital markets, 1976–1997 (US$bn, annual averages)

	1976–80	1981–5	1986–90	1991	1992	1997
Securities[a]	36.2	96.4	234.7	332.1	357.2	916.7
Loans	59.4	72.0	103.1	116.0	117.9	390.4
Committed back-up facilities		35.2	18.7	7.7	6.7	2.7
Uncommitted facilities[b]			70.9	80.2	127.7	459.5
Total	95.6	203.6	427.4	536.0	609.5	1,769.3
% change on previous year				+23.2	+13.7	+50.6

[a] International and foreign bonds and, as from 1986, issues of international equities.
[b] Mainly euro-commercial paper and medium-term note programmes.
Sources: Financial Market Trends (OECD), no. 55 (June 1993); no. 58 (June 1994); no. 69 (Feb. 1988), p. 49

developments: increased extent of international lending, financial innovation and financial agglomeration. In this section we concentrate on the latter two.

The prodigious growth of international lending is indicated in table 2.12. In 1998 it was anticipated that total loans would be over US$2,000 billion – a 2,000-fold increase on the late 1970s position. A key development is the growth of 'securitization': the displacement of conventional loan business (traditionally conducted by banks) by the issue of marketable bonds and other securities. The other significant feature is the growth of 'uncommitted facilities', particularly in the eurobond market.

As part of these processes, financial innovation has become rife, which itself involves several features. The range of new instruments is shown in table 2.13. Since most of these are derivative of the move towards security lending – they provide borrowers and lenders with the possibility of hedging against the risk of interest rate and exchange rate movements – they are collectively termed 'derivatives'. A lot of these are very esoteric instruments, which are quite difficult to understand, monitor or control. In part this is because new ways of trading have emerged, in particular over-the-counter (OTC) markets in which intermediaries deal among themselves in large monetary volumes, bypassing the established exchanges which use traditional trading floors.

The importance of these OTC instruments can be seen in table 2.13. By 1991 their worth was larger than that of exchange-traded instruments and was more than 50 per cent that of the total of foreign currency claims of all banks reporting to the Bank for International Settlements (BIS). They have shown spectacular growth during the 1990s. Such instruments are often

Table 2.13 Growth in markets for selected derivative instruments: notional principal amounts outstanding at end year, in US$bn equivalent, 1986–1997

	1986	1990	1997
Exchange-traded instruments[a]	**588**	**2,291**	**12,207**
Interest rate futures	370	1,454	7,489
Interest rate options[b]	146	600	3,640
Currency futures	10	16	52
Currency options[b]	39	56	33
Stock market index features	15	70	217
Options on stock market indices[b]	8	95	777
Over-the-counter instruments[c]	**500e**	**3,451**	**25,453**[d]
Interest rate swaps[e]	400e	2,312	19,171[d]
Currency and cross-currency interest rate swaps[e,f]	100e	578	1,560[d]
Other derivative instruments[e,g]	–	561	4,723[d]
Memorandum item: Cross-border plus local foreign			
currency claims of BIS reporting banks	4,031	7,578	–

e = estimate
[a] Excludes options on individual shares and derivatives involving commodity contracts.
[b] Calls plus puts.
[c] Only data collected by International Securities Data Association (ISDA). Excludes information on contracts such as forward rate agreements, over-the-counter currency options, forward foreign exchange positions, equity swaps and warrants on equity.
[d] 1996.
[e] Contracts between ISDA members reported only once.
[f] Adjusted for reporting of both currencies.
[g] Caps, collars, floors and swap options.
Sources: *Financial Market Trends* (OECD), no. 55 (June 1993), table 3, p. 26; BIS 1998, table VIII.5, p. 155

traded 'off-balance sheet' – they earn a fee income rather than constituting part of a financial institution's asset or liability structure. These developments provide opportunities for intermediaries to engage in risk arbitrage in a lower-cost and less regulated environment, but they thereby raise important new problems of systemic exposure to risk. The overall growth in financial derivatives between 1986 and 1997 is shown in figure 2.6. Note that the trading of these instruments is more or less totally confined to the big three financial centres associated with the Triad. We discuss these problems again in chapter 5.

Financial innovation continues apace. The latest developments represent a resurgence of bond instruments with so-called 'dragon bonds' and 'global bonds'. 'Dragon bonds' are issued and traded simultaneously just on East Asian markets, while their 'global' counterparts are issued and traded in all major international financial centres on a round-the-clock basis.

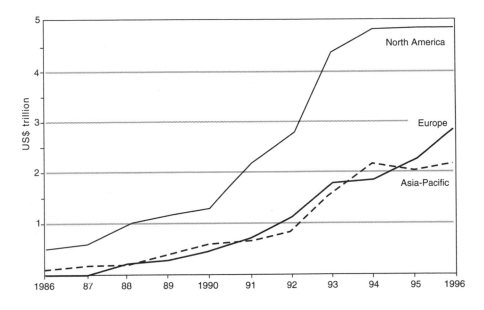

Figure 2.6 Financial derivatives: notional amount outstanding on
organized exchanges (year end)

Source: European Union 1997a, chart 18, p. 15

After the first global bond was marketed by the World Bank in 1989,
this market expanded to over US$100 billion by mid-1994, capturing 8
per cent of total external bond issue in that year (OECD 1994b, table 1,
p. 57).

This latest development in bond markets testifies to the strength of
the trend towards internationalization in the world's financial systems.
But, as mentioned above, the penetration of foreign assets into domestic
institutional investment markets is still relatively light. The United States,
in particular, remains highly undiversified and autonomous on this score. In
as much as global trading of securities and derivatives exists, it still tends
to remain within a single region (North America, Europe or Asia-Pacific).

But again there is a trend in the government bond market towards
further openness. The average foreign penetration of national government
bond markets in advanced countries increased from 10 per cent in 1983 to
15 per cent in 1989 (Turner 1991); for the EU countries, it increased only
from 19 per cent in 1987 to 26 per cent in 1993 (European Union 1997a,
table 13, p. 14).

The final issue to discuss in this subsection is the development of financial conglomerates. The international financial services industry is increasingly characterized by a small number of highly capitalized securities and banking houses which are global players with diversified activities. In part this is the result of the continuing trend towards predominantly institutional investment. 'Collective saving' is a strengthening feature of all OECD countries, so the institutions managing these funds could become key international players.

Broadly speaking, there is worldwide excess capacity in this industry, leading to intense competitive pressures to which cost-cutting and diversification are the strategic commercial responses. As a result, the financial conglomerates operate through very complex and often opaque corporate structures. Attempts at risk transfer between a shrinking number of players are legion, and even between the different components of the companies themselves. Thus contagion risk, market risk and systemic risk have all increased, presenting new and important regulatory problems for governments and international bodies (see chapter 5).

An important point to note about the present era as compared with the Gold Standard period is that the recent growth of international lending has not just dramatically increased the range of financial instruments: it has changed the whole character of capital flows. As mentioned above, late nineteenth-century lending was mainly long term in nature, going to finance investment in real assets. Even that part of total flows consisting of investment in financial assets was mainly used to finance real investment. This is no longer so. The explosion of aggregate lending had until very recently been made up almost exclusively of financial assets. Only since the mid-1980s has substantial real investment reappeared with the growth of FDI (see chapters 3 and 4).

The overall picture: history, the current situation and immediate future

In the final part of this chapter we review the changing nature of national economic management and its interaction with international mechanisms of integration so as to chart the broad contours of the present situation facing the international economy. This has as its objective an analysis of the implications of the main regimes identified in table 2.5 for economic autonomy.

To a large extent the Gold Standard must act as a benchmark in this discussion because of its pivotal position as the first integrated economic mechanism and the key features it displayed. The system carries great ideological and theoretical significance since it was not only 'voluntarily' entered into by the parties involved (there was no 'founding treaty'), but it is also supposed to have embodied the principle of 'automaticity' in its operation and adjustments. In most orthodox accounts, other subsequent systems are measured against the Gold Standard – and, it must be added, often found wanting.

The basics of the system involve the fixing of an official gold price for each currency, combined with the free export and import of gold with no current or capital account restrictions. The persistent movement of gold into or out of a country is then permitted to influence the domestic money supply in each country. Thus the issue of bank notes and coinage is directly linked to the level of gold reserves. Any short-run liquidity crisis (that is, a gold drain) is first met by lending by the central bank at premium rates ('lender of last resort' facility). If the gold price ('mint parity') has to be suspended, this should only be temporary, and convertibility is restored as soon as possible – if necessary with the aid of domestic deflationary policies. Here arises the crucial link between domestic and international conditions: there must be domestic wage and price/cost flexibility to allow the nominal price level to be determined endogenously by the worldwide demand and supply of gold. Thus the Gold Standard (GS), in so far as it actually functioned along these lines, represented the quintessential integrated economy, where 'national autonomy' was minimal.

As might be expected, the GS never worked quite in this automatic manner. Great difficulty was experienced at times in generating the deflationary domestic measures that the system implied as a condition of its operation. This led to various 'gold devices' that cushioned the domestic economy from the full rigours of gold movements, most important among these being disguised changes in the exchange rates of the domestic currency against gold to protect reserves or to maintain the level of domestic economic activity (so called 'massaging of the gold points'). Despite this, however, the exchange rates stayed within remarkably narrow bands between 1870 and 1914.[9] The system also required a remarkable degree of cooperation between central bankers because all manner of discretionary judgements and actions were necessary if the system was to function – there were a good many asymmetrical adjustments that needed to be made which in effect circumvented the formal rules.

Within the terms of the GS there was no single currency that provided the nominal anchor for the money supply or price level, since that was done by the system as a whole and by the supply and demand for gold. No single country took responsibility for monitoring 'the money supply' which was the supposed key to the success of the system, not even the British authorities. It was the UK's commitment to free trade (along with its ability to police this) and the depth of its financial markets in London that supported the system, however, and provided the key political anchor for its effective functioning. The economic weakness of the Gold Standard arose from the way supply and demand shocks were designed to be outside any national jurisdiction, so that volatile economic activity was magnified, a constant feature of the system. In addition, any excessive accumulation of gold stocks by a single country could also trigger off a generalized deflation of the system, whether it was involuntary or not.

It is the instability of the interwar years that still haunts the international economic system, and provides the main reason for the concern and uncertainty associated with current trends in the international economy. The constant worry of the international community is to avoid a repeat of this period, when, as we have seen, international (and domestic) economic activity fell dramatically (foreign trade fell by two-thirds between 1929 and 1933, comprehensive capital controls were introduced and devaluations and deflations took place). Even in 1938, trade volume was barely 90 per cent of its 1929 level, despite a full recovery in world production. In the wake of all this, belligerent protectionist power blocs emerged which eventually fought to challenge one another's existence.

The Bretton Woods system was designed so as to avoid the external constraint imposed on national economies by the GS, which had operated so disastrously in the interwar period. What was needed was flexibility to support nationally decided policies, on the one hand, but enough stability to avoid competitive devaluations, on the other. The solution negotiated at Bretton Woods was for a fixed but adjustable system, linked to the dollar standard as numeraire (the base value for the system). Currencies were fixed in terms of the US dollar, which itself was to be convertible into gold; 'fundamental disequilibriums' were adjustable with International Monetary Fund (IMF) consent; national economies were given autonomy to pursue their own price level and employment objectives unconstrained by a common nominal price anchor. National capital markets were kept relatively separate by sanctioning capital controls on transactions other than current ones, and the domestic impacts of exchange rate interventions were 'sterilized' by drawing on official exchange reserves and IMF credits, which thereby acted as the buffers between domestic and international monetary conditions, adding to domestic autonomy.

The well-known and tortuous story of how the BWS fared and its shortcomings in the postwar period will not be repeated here. Its key feature was a reliance on American 'passivity', and when this was no longer viable (because of fears of the loss of American international competitiveness) neither was the system itself. The remarks above are designed to demonstrate (a) that this was a definite regime, and (b) how the issue of (relative) national economic autonomy was built into that regime. What the BWS demonstrated, however, was that there was no economic autonomy, in the terms laid out so far, for the US economy if the system was to function as described. This may sound odd given the leading role that the US played in the international economy over the period and the way it is perceived as dictating the 'rules of the game' to its own advantage. But one of the paradoxes here is that, strictly speaking, once those rules were in place the behaviour of the US economy was just as circumscribed by them as was the conduct of the other economies in the system, if in different ways.

The US could not 'choose' its own price and employment level independently of others. It had to remain passive in terms of its exchange rate, hold minimal reserves of foreign exchange, provide liquidity to the system by acting as its creditor, and anchor the world price of internationally tradable goods in terms of dollars by its own domestic monetary policy. If there was to be no international inflation, then that domestic monetary policy was constrained by the dictates of a system in which partner choices were paramount – *formal* American monetary independence was just that.[10] Clearly, up to a point this also benefited the US since so long as it remained the strongest export economy in such a system, it required a stable exchange rate and an inflation-proof regime. However, as this position changed, and as the US manoeuvred for some domestic economic advantage, the system collapsed.

The floating rate regime that followed the unsuccessful attempts to shore up the BWS in the period of the 'failure to agree' was one designed again to increase national economic autonomy. But the rules of this game changed surprisingly little from the period before. As mentioned above, the US dollar remained the 'currency of choice' for the conduct of international monetary transactions – largely because of its path-dependent embeddedness. The US also continued to remain relatively 'passive' in the face of changes in the dollar's value, though other countries conducted systematic interventions to try to stabilize their own currency dollar-equivalent rates. In the short run, other countries' national money supply policies were set so as to adjust to the relative weaknesses of their exchange rates vis-à-vis the dollar (reducing domestic money supply when currency value against the dollar weakened, increasing it as that value strengthened, that is, the non-sterilization of exchange rate movements); while in the long run, secular adjustments in the par values were sanctioned so as to set national price level and money supply targets independently of the policy of the US (this being the major change on the previous system). The US, on the other hand, no longer tried to anchor a common world price level, but conducted its own monetary and exchange rate policy independently of what other countries were doing.

One (unintended) consequence of this relative autonomy in the conduct of monetary policies was an increase in the 'world's' money supply. As the dollar weakened between 1971 and 1980 (implying a strengthening of other currencies against the dollar), the money supplies of other countries increased. The passivity of the US, by contrast, meant that it did not offset this with a reduction of its own money supply. Inflation resulted. Then when the dollar unexpectedly strengthened after 1980, the adjustment took the form of severe deflations and world output contracted sharply. Thus, perhaps somewhat bizarrely, this period saw the closer and deeper integration of the international economy as the business cycles of all the main participants synchronized and became more pronounced. A regime designed to increase autonomy (by allowing exchange rates to float and enabling independent monetary policies) had actually led in the opposite direction. There is an important lesson to be learned here, about the need to design particular rules for whatever governance mechanism is adopted.

Of course that lesson was partly learned in the case of the attempt to stabilize exchange rates associated with the period of the Plaza-Louvre accords. The US abandoned its 'hands off' policy and initiated an attempt at more concerted action to manage exchange rates with 'discrete but clustered' interventions. The rules of this game were mentioned above. There were seventeen such concerted interventions between 1985 and 1992, most of which worked successfully in moving the exchange rates at least in the direction anticipated – and often against the prevailing trend. Thus at the level of exchange rates this cooperation between the G3 countries implied a heavier interdependence between them. But they were exercising their 'autonomy' independently of those outside the G3 framework, these other countries having to support – or not oppose – any G3 intervention (by buying or selling dollars with their national currency when the dollar was either weak or strong).

Quite whether the G3 regime remains robust is a moot point, however. The key issues are the existence or otherwise of 'target zones' and how seriously they are taken; whether the implied sterilization works (itself leading to differences in short-term interest rates between financial centres); and the macroeconomic effects of both of these. Without direct and more continuous coordination of policies (as opposed to indirect and discrete cooperation), exchange rate volatility is likely to remain high and international inflationary effects and output fluctuations serious. We take up some of these issues again in chapter 7.

A good many of the points made above in connection with the various international regimes could be repeated for the case of the European Monetary System (EMS). This system in many ways paralleled the rules of the fixed rate dollar standard of the Bretton Woods system, though it has had different objectives. The EMS, for instance, had as one of its objectives the successive convergence of national macroeconomic policies at an unchanging par value of the exchange rates, which can be interpreted as an eventual commitment to complete (economic and political) integration of the European Union economies. This strong convergence/union theme was something missing from the BWS. The EMS also fixed the par value of exchange rates of the participants in terms of a basket of EMS currencies, weighted according to the relative country size, though the Deutschmark became the *de facto* anchor of the system much like the dollar under the BWS. Its formal rules included a commitment to keeping currency values stable within bilateral bands, though adjustments in par values were allowed to reposition price levels with the agreement of the EMS (all this before eventual convergence or full monetary union). Central bank intervention was also sanctioned if breaching of the bilateral rate bands was threatened.

The *de facto* operation of the system was to stabilize national exchange rates vis-à-vis the DM (partly because of the DM's importance in the currency basket), increasingly using the DM as the intervention currency; adjusting short-term monetary targets and interest rates so as to support exchange rate interventions; organizing long-term money growth so that domestic inflation in tradable goods converged to, or remained the same as, price inflation in Germany; and to progressively liberalize capital controls. Germany, much like the US in the case of the BWS and the floating rate regime, was thus to remain 'passive' in respect of foreign exchange rates of other members, but to anchor the DM (and therefore the EMS) price level for tradables by adopting an independently chosen German monetary policy.

The history of this system is well known. What it provided – indeed was explicitly designed to provide – was a reduction of autonomy, in relation to monetary policy at least, for the participants (see Thompson 1993, ch. 4, and chapters 7 and 8 below for a discussion of its implications for other aspects of macroeconomic management, particularly that of fiscal policy). The country gaining the most formal autonomy was Germany, but rather like in the case of the US discussed above, if the system was to operate properly German policy would also have to be heavily constrained by the 'burden' of managing the system overall, and would have had to circumscribe its own objectives at times in the interest of the other members. However, this has proved the crunch point in terms of the success or otherwise of the EMS. Partly as a consequence of constitutional issues – summed up in the so-called 'Emminger letter' (see Kenen 1995, pp. 183–4) – and partly because of domestic political reasons, the Bundesbank has not been required to fully support partner currencies in times of EMS crisis. The result has been to undermine its credibility as a regime of financial governance. The fuller implications of the emergence of EMU after 1999 will be discussed in chapter 8.

The basic point to be drawn from the analysis above is that for the foreseeable future the real character of the international system will be that of one dominated by the Triad countries and their regional clusters or allies. We have entered a period when three large economic formations look to have emerged, the relative size and importance of which are indicated in tables 2.14 and 2.15.

In terms of GDP the EU and the US are about equal, with Japan about half as big (though in terms of GDP per capita Japan leads the EU and the US). As far as shares of world exports of goods only are concerned, while there has been some convergence, the three blocs seem to have stabilized, with the EU at 25 per cent, the US at 20 per cent and Japan at 19 per cent (and falling slightly) (see figure 7.2, p. 198).

Most of the other data in tables 2.14 and 2.15 relate to the currency role of the three big countries/blocs. This is important in terms of the future of the international economic and financial system as the euro is introduced

Table 2.14 United States, Japan and the European Union: relative economic size and relative use of currencies (percentages)

	United States	Japan	EU15
Relative economic size			
Shares of world GDP, 1996	20.7	8.0	20.4
Shares of world exports, 1996[a]	15.2	6.1	14.7
Relative use of currencies[b]			
World trade, 1992	48.0	5.0	31.0
World debt securities, Sept. 1996	37.2	17.0	34.5
Developing country debt, end 1996	50.2	18.1	15.8
Global foreign exchange reserves, end 1995	56.4	7.1	25.8
Foreign exchange transactions, Apr. 1995[c]	41.5	12.0	35.0

[a] Goods plus services, excluding intra-EU.
[b] Shares denominated in currency (or currencies) of country (or EU).
[c] Shares adjusted for double counting that arises from the fact that each transaction involves two currencies.
Source: World Bank 1997, table 12, p. 71

Table 2.15 The international role of the main Triad currencies

(a) Official role

Share of total official currency holdings (%)

	End 1973	End 1983	End 1995
US dollar	76.1	71.1	61.5
European currencies[a]	14.3	15.8	20.1
of which, German mark	7.1	11.7	14.2
Yen	0.1	4.9	7.4

Number of currencies linked to:

	1983	1994	1994 (% of world GNP)
US dollar	34	25	1.53
European currencies (incl. the ECU)	18	19	0.25

(b) Currency use in international trade

Share of the main currencies as regards use in international trade

	1980		1992	
	% of world exports	Internationalization ratio[b]	% of world exports	Internationalization ratio[b]
US dollar	56.4	4.5	47.6	3.6
German mark	13.6	1.4	15.5	1.4
Yen	2.1	0.3	4.8	0.6

continued:

Table 2.15 *continued*

(c) Transactions on foreign exchange markets

Breakdown of transactions by currency[c]

	April 1989	April 1992	April 1995
US dollar	90	82	83
German mark	27	40	37
Yen	27	23	24
Other	56	55	56
Total as %[d]	200	200	200

(d) Currency in which financial assets and liabilities are denominated

Share of outstanding international bonds

	End 1981	End 1992	End 1995
US dollar	52.6	40.3	34.2
European currencies	20.2	33.0	37.1
of which, German mark	n.a.	10.0	12.3
Yen	6.9	12.4	15.7

Share of world private portfolio

	End 1981	End 1992	End 1995
US dollar	67.3	46.0	39.8
European currencies	13.2	35.2	36.9
of which, German mark	n.a.	14.7	15.6
Yen	2.2	6.9	11.5

[a] Pound sterling, German mark, French franc, Dutch guilder.
[b] Ratio of world exports denominated in currency relative to that country's exports.
[c] Gross turnover. Daily averages.
[d] Since any transaction on the foreign exchange market involves two currencies, the total of the proportions of transactions involving a given currency is 200%.
Sources: European Union 1997b, Annex 2, p. 18, drawing on, for (a), IMF annual reports; for (b), European commission; for (c), BIS, surveys of activities on foreign exchange market; for (d), BIS, international banking and financial activity, and authors' own calculations

at the turn of the century. These data indicate broadly (1) that the US dollar still remained the *lingua franca* of the international financial system in the mid-1990s; (2) that the European currencies have made some inroads into this role, particularly in terms of transactions on foreign exchange and portfolio investments; and finally (3) that the yen is a relatively unimportant currency for international transactions, but has gained some advantage as a denominator of assets (largely as a consequence of the appreciation of the yen against the US dollar and the Deutschmark up to 1996).

The implications of these trends are that the relationship between the US and Europe looks to be becoming the key one for international governance, and this will be accelerated if the euro is eventually successfully introduced and becomes a rival to the dollar. This will tend to reinforce the dominance of the two main blocs in the Triad. This is especially so as the Japanese economy has faltered in the 1990s, and as the crisis in the Far East and Latin America matured during 1998. Without a sustained recovery in Japan, the centre of gravity of the international system will shift to the North Atlantic. Thus the future for extended international governance essentially hangs not on global market forces but on the old-fashioned differences of interest between the US, the EU and (to a lesser extent) Japan. This is far from comforting, but it is as well to know from whence one's problems come, and that they are still driven by the classic problem of the divergent interest of states, or of the political entities that are successors to them like the EU. Far from a fully integrating 'globalized world economy', we still inhabit an essentially 'internationalized' one, if one now conditioned heavily by a regionalized triadic bloc structure.

Conclusion

We have striven to argue a number of points in this chapter. First, that the level of integration, interdependence, openness, or however one wishes to describe it, of national economies in the present era is not unprecedented. Indeed, the level of autonomy under the Gold Standard in the period up to the First World War was much lower for the advanced economies than it is today. This is not to minimize the level of integration now, or to ignore the problems of regulation and management it throws up, but merely to register a certain scepticism over whether we have entered a radically new phase in the internationalization of economic activity.

The second point has been to argue that governance mechanisms for the international economy have been in place over almost the entire twentieth century, in one form or another. This is just as much the case today as it was at the start of the century. We may not like the particular mechanisms that are established now and how they work, but they are there all the same. The issue then becomes how to devise better or more appropriate ones.

Thirdly, we have argued that there are some new and different issues of economic interdependence in the present era which are particular to it. Our argument is not that things have remained unchanged: quite fundamental reorganizations are going on in the international economy to which an imaginative response is desperately needed. This is an issue we take up later in the book.

Finally, we have traced the trajectory of 'national economic autonomy' through the various regimes of governance operating over the twentieth century. This has shown that such autonomy has oscillated between periods of strong and then weak forces, and that it has operated with various degrees of effectiveness. Perhaps the overall trajectory of this assessment is to point to the impossibility of complete national economic autonomy as the twentieth century has progressed. The debacle of the floating rates regime of 1974–85 seems, if nothing else, to have confirmed the demise of this form of governance as a viable long-term objective in the present era.

Appendix: The Trade to GDP Ratio Controversy

The fact that the data included in table 2.3 above find that the degree of trade openness for the advanced economies was not much different in the mid-1990s than it was at the end of the *belle époque* has attracted some critical comment, particularly from those who remain wedded to a strong globalization thesis. Two main issues are involved.

The first derives from Maddison's OECD survey of the historical trends in the world economy, which shows the degree of trade openness as the ratio of exports to GDP, *measured at constant 1990 prices* (Maddison 1995). The data in table 2.3, by contrast, are measured in terms of current market prices (and combine exports and imports).

The consequences of Maddison's readjustment can be seen from table A2.1, where his data are reproduced, along with the contrasting current price data. For the latter measure the degree of openness indicator is recalculated to be comparable to the Maddison estimates: (exports + imports) × 1/2.

Both sets of figures agree that there was a reduction in the degree of openness between 1913 and 1950. But the main effect of calculating the figures at constant prices is that the degree of openness is much greater in 1992 than it was in 1913. In fact, the changes here are dramatic. For Western Europe as a whole the ratio increased from 16.3 per cent in 1913 to 29.7 per cent in 1992. Thus integration and 'globalization' appear much greater in the mid-1990s than at the end of the *belle époque*.

However, 'constant price' comparisons are very misleading (Glyn 1998, p. 6). Export prices rise more slowly than do prices for output as a whole. This is because productivity in the export sector is systematically greater than it is in the economy as a whole. Where this is the case, constant price calculations exaggerate the openness ratio. In effect, current prices correct

Table A2.1   Merchandise exports as a percentage of GDP, advanced countries

	1913		1950		1973		1992	
	M	H&T	M	H&T	M	H&T	M	H&T
France	8.2	17.7	7.7	10.6	15.4	14.5	22.9	17.8
Germany	15.6	17.6	6.2	10.0	23.8	17.6	32.6	28.5
Japan	2.4	15.7	2.3	8.5	7.9	9.1	12.4	9.1
Netherlands	17.8	51.8	12.5	35.1	41.7	40.0	55.3	42.6
UK	17.8	22.3	11.4	18.0	14.0	19.7	21.4	18.0
US	3.7	5.6	3.0	3.5	5.0	5.2	8.2	7.6

Sources: M = Maddison 1995, derived from table 2.4, p. 38; H&T = Hirst and Thompson, table 2.3 above, and *OECD National Accounts*, 1995

for the differential between the growth of export prices and the general price level, so current prices are the best ones to focus on.

But the degree of openness is further exaggerated by both these sets of figures in that they include the import content of exports (and, by analogy, any export content of imports in the case of our calculations). True trade dependence should be calculated net of these.

In fact, the ratio of trade to GDP is likely to exaggerate the extent of openness of economies even further because exports and imports are measured in terms of sales while GDP is a value-added concept. Since sales are roughly twice as big as GDP, these ratios should be halved. However, in terms of tracking *changes* in openness, the usual trade to GDP ratio can suffice, since the ratio of sales to GDP has not changed much over time in the advanced economies (Borjas, Freeman and Katz 1997, p. 10). This caveat about trade measured as sales and GDP as value-added should be borne in mind as the analysis proceeds in the main text. For greater accuracy as to the extent of globalization, all the ratios might be cut by a half.

Before we move on it is worth reintroducing the Maddison analysis in terms of what it says about the degree of integration of the developing economies into the international system. Table A2.2 provides data for a selection of Asian and Latin American countries. Note that the Asian economies show a general increase in trade dependency, except for India, while it decreases for the three Latin American countries. Given the exaggerations generated by these figures, as just discussed, more accurate estimates would no doubt indicate an even greater decrease in Latin American openness relative to the position in 1913, and probably reverse the position for some of the Asian economies as well.

The second objection is a more serious one. This concerns the denominator in the calculations. GDP is made up of a number of components which

Table A2.2   Merchandise exports of developing countries as a percentage of GDP, all at 1990 prices

	1913	1950	1973	1992
Developing Asia				
China	1.4	1.9	1.1	2.3
India	4.7	2.6	2.0	1.7
Indonesia	2.2	3.3	5.0	7.4
Korea	1.0	1.0	8.2	17.8
Taiwan	2.5	2.5	10.2	34.4
Developing Latin America				
Argentina	6.8	2.4	2.1	4.3
Brazil	9.5	4.0	2.6	4.7
Mexico	10.8	3.5	2.2	6.2
Total world	8.7	7.0	11.2	13.5

Source: Maddison 1995, derived from table 2.4, p. 38

Table A2.3   Ratio of merchandise trade (half the sum of exports and imports) as a percentage of total merchandise value-added (method A) and as a percentage of GDP by method of calculation in table 2.3 above (method B)

	1913		1960		1970		1990	
	Method A	Method B	Method A	Method B	Method A	Method B	Method A	Method B
France	23.3	15.5	16.8	9.9	25.7	11.9	53.5	17.1
Germany	29.2	19.9	24.6	14.5	31.3	16.5	57.8	24.0
Japan	23.9	12.5	15.3	8.8	15.7	8.3	18.9	8.4
UK	76.3	29.8	33.8	15.3	40.7	16.5	62.8	20.6
US	23.2	6.1	9.6	3.4	13.7	4.1	35.8	8.0

Method B gives the equivalent to table 2.3 calculations for all years (though note how these differ slightly for 1913).
Source: All figures derived from Feenstra 1998, table 1, p. 33 and table 2, p. 35

are changing at different rates. In particular the sectoral composition of nominal GDP has shifted away from the production of merchandise goods towards the production of services, particularly publicly provided services. Given that services tend not to be so intensively internationally traded as are merchandise products, it might be more appropriate to express such merchandise trade in terms of tradable goods production only. A way of measuring this is as the value-added of the merchandised sector of the economy. Such calculations are shown in table A2.3 for some of the countries considered in this chapter, but for slightly different years. However, it is still possible to compare these with similar calculations for merchandise trade to overall GDP figures as given in table 2.3 above.

Comparing merchandise trade to value-added output data between 1913 and 1990, France, Germany and the US are the three countries showing an unambiguous increase in openness, whereas even on these figures Japan and the UK remain less open (see also Irwin 1996, table 1, p. 42 for US figures).

Of course, once one begins to adjust estimates along these lines all sorts of alternatives present themselves. For instance, merchandise trade is itself composed of manufactures, raw materials and agricultural goods, each of which could be treated separately. Similar comments could be made about merchandise value-added, which (in Feenstra's analysis used above) is made up of agriculture, mining and manufacturing – for the US – plus construction and public utilities in the other countries (which are usually classified in the service sector of the economy, so even here the data is not entirely consistent between countries). Also, services are increasingly being introduced into international trade. And here again we could differentiate between the different kinds of service activity which are more or less open to international trade, for instance, as between construction, transportation, public utilities, wholesale and retail trade, finance, insurance, real estate and 'other' services.

The difficulty, then, is to know quite where to stop in terms of these possible disaggregations and further adjustments. Given all the alternatives, we prefer to work with a single simple measure. The trade to GDP ratio at current prices has the advantage of continuity, and it expresses the way the *total* economy is or is not being integrated into the international system.

3

Multinational Companies and the Internationalization of Business Activity

The Consequences of 'Globalization' for National Systems

This chapter moves away from the history of the international trading and financial system. It concentrates on the major changes in the structure of the international economy since the early 1980s, particularly in terms of the internationalization of production. One of the key changes identified and explored here is the increased salience of, and rapid growth in, foreign direct investment (FDI). In the period 1945–73 the dominant factor driving the world economy was growth in international trade; from the early 1980s onwards, it is argued, it has been growth in FDI. It should be noted, however, that in this chapter we develop a critique of this particular measure of the internationalization of production.

In this chapter we are more concerned with those international mechanisms that have an impact on the structure of and growth in the real economy: trade and FDI. International short-term financial flows, which expanded rapidly after the abandonment of semi-fixed exchange rates and capital controls in the 1970s, are analysed elsewhere (chapters 2, 5 and 7). Clearly, these short-term capital flows have some indirect impact on economic growth since they affect national exchange rates and interest rates, but we contend that they mainly redistribute success – and more often failure – around the international system, and add little to the structural capacity of economies to generate long-term aggregate growth.

It is multinational companies (MNCs) that are the agents responsible for FDI. The strategies of these organizations as they shape the role and distribution of FDI are central to the analysis that follows. As we shall see, that distribution is socially and geographically uneven on a world scale. FDI is heavily concentrated in the advanced industrial states and a small number of rapidly developing industrial economies. This analysis is complemented later in the chapter by a detailed empirical investigation into the geographical distribution of advanced country business activity, contrasting its home and foreign concentrations.

As we shall see, there still remain massive and important national differences in the attractiveness of locations for investment and other business activity. Countries vary considerably in the effectiveness of their economies in delivering FDI advantages to multinational firms that cannot be ignored. Successful MNCs are those that can tap into those specific advantages. These advantages are not just ones associated with the cost of labour. Companies also need national legal and commercial policy provisions to protect their investments, constraints that prevent them being entirely extraterritorial, as we emphasize in chapters 7 and 9.

The literature on 'national systems of innovation' (Lundvall 1992; Nelson 1993; McKelvey 1991; Porter 1990), 'production regimes' (Wilkinson 1983; Rubery 1994), and on 'national business systems' (Whitley 1992a, 1992b) is instructive here. These authors point to real differences in the way countries have traditionally gone about their innovative activity and established their typical business environment, and how business is conducted therein. But the role of MNCs in the development of the global economy has become of central importance in the analysis of the degree to which these national systems are thought to be in a process of fundamental transformation. Without the extensive development of MNCs, the way companies operate could be regarded as closely tied to domestic institutional structures. These domestic institutional structures were recognized as being differentially configurated as between the advanced industrial countries, with, it has been argued, a profound impact on the economic performances of both the companies inhabiting those systems and the economies to which they were closely articulated (see Hollingsworth and Boyer 1996; Lazonick and O'Sullivan 1996; Soskice 1991; Whitley 1992b; Whitley and Kristensen 1996, 1997).

With the advent of 'globalization', however, and the dramatic advance of the multinational firm, this conception of the central importance of various 'national systems' (of business, innovation, labour relations, finance, production, etc.) is now often thought to be under siege as business practices rapidly internationalize. Firms are now supposed to roam the globe in search of cheap but efficient production locations that offer them the largest and most secure and profitable return on competitive success. The precise impact of these internationalizing processes on the nature of the socially and economically embedded national (or regional) business systems has become the subject of much analysis and speculation (see Chesnais 1992; Dicken, Forsgren and Malmberg 1994; Mueller 1994; Tiberi-Vipraio 1996).

This chapter is concerned to do a number of things. The first is to explore the overall significance of MNC activity and the geographical concentration of traditional measures such as FDI and trade. We also supplement this with the analysis of other measures of international inequality.

Secondly, in this context, we analyse whether the advance of MNC activity has been quite so rapid and widespread as is often assumed by the strong globalization thesis, and particularly so fast as to seriously undermine the continuation of a national or local business system. This will involve the examination of a range of measures of the internationalization of economic activity, not just the expansion of FDI, which is the measure most often used to bolster the strong globalization thesis. This part of the chapter is quantitative in character. For too long, loose generalizations about the extent and nature of the internationalization of business activity have served to obscure the issue. The likelihood of a collapse of national systems of business and innovation needs to be evaluated by a serious evidential test. Until we know the true extent of such internationalization, and whether it is indeed increasing as rapidly and dramatically as is often argued, there is little point in speculating about its precise impact on the embeddedness of national systems.

One problem here is that there is no unambiguous evidence available or single statistical indicator that can point to the true position. Thus a good deal of the chapter is designed to present a range of indicators and to assess the strengths and weaknesses of each.

The chapter then moves on to look at the possible forms of the internationalization of business activity identified in the context of the review of these different measures. This is done in relation to the debate about the continued relevance of national systems of business and innovation. Finally, the implication of these trends for economic performance and the nature of the international economy are briefly examined.

MNCs in the mid-1990s

There were an estimated 45,000 parent MNCs in the mid-1990s controlling about 280,000 affiliated organizations (United Nations 1997, from which much of the following information is drawn). Of these, 37,000 (about 82 per cent) were 'home based' in the fourteen major developed OECD countries. Ninety per cent of MNC headquarters are in the developed world.

In 1996 the stock of FDI was US$3.2 trillion. The MNCs controlling this stock were responsible for (domestic and international) sales of US$7 trillion. This was much more than the total of world trade at US$5.2 trillion in 1996. Only 8 per cent of the stock of FDI had its origins with a developing country's MNCs, though these accounted for about 15 per cent of flows (see WTO 1997, chart IV.1, p. 44).

Some 80 per cent of US trade was conducted by MNCs, which is a not untypical proportion for the developed countries as a whole. For total US trade as much as 40 per cent was estimated to be *intra*-MNC trade. Intra-MNC trade – that conducted within the boundaries of the company, involving transfers across borders between different parts of the organization – is both difficult to ascertain and to assess. Clearly, MNCs' FDI and trade are very closely linked, but important changes are occurring here and differences in the patterns between the two are emerging: we will have more to say about these in a moment.

There is great concentration in FDI. The hundred largest MNCs controlled about one-fifth of total global foreign assets, had US$2 trillion of foreign sales and employed 6 million workers in 1995. In as much as these distinctions can still be made, 60 per cent of MNC stock was associated with manufacturing, 37 per cent with services and only 3 per cent with the primary sector. It is the growth in service sector FDI that has been a particular feature of the latest surge in overall investment levels.

Character of FDI and trade

The 'long boom' after the Second World War was typified by a massive increase in world trade and domestic (and, until recently, to a lesser extent foreign) investment. The prosperity of the international economy was in large part based on these trends – it was 'export driven'. The main characteristics of this period can be seen in figure 3.1, which shows the 'export gap' between the growth of world output and that of exports: that is, exports increasing at a much faster rate than production between 1950 and 1994.

Since the early 1980s, however, a different trend has emerged, to be seen in figure 3.2. Here what is striking is the sudden increase in FDI flows in the mid-1980s, particularly to the industrial countries. Export growth was eclipsed by this expansion of FDI. For instance, between 1985 and 1995 FDI flows expanded at an average rate of 18.4 per cent compared with an annual rate of 11 per cent for global merchandise trade, and 8.5 per cent for world GDP.

As indicated in figure 3.2, the flows to the advanced countries fell away significantly in the recession years of the early 1990s, but with a continued strong growth to the developing countries. The importance of the developing countries can be seen from the data in table 3.1.

While it was the flows to the developing countries that were still exceptional in 1995–6 (accounting for 34 per cent of total flows), the pattern established for the advanced countries in the early 1980s began to reassert itself again after 1992. With the emerging markets crisis of 1997–8, we would expect this boom in flows to the developing countries to have dramatically changed, but in which direction is not clear. If uncertainty and recession prevail, the flows should abate. If these economies are liberalized and 'opened up' to Western merger and acquisition (M&A) activity, the flows might expand.

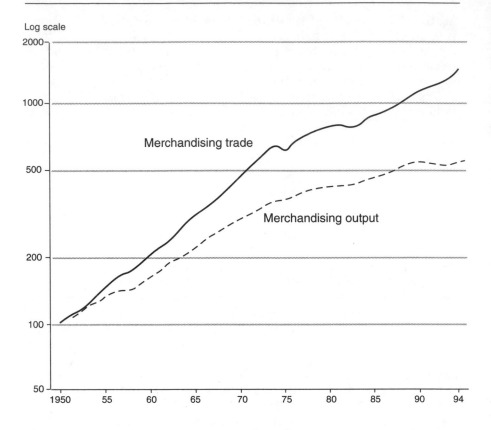

Figure 3.1   Long-term trends in world merchandise trade and output,
1950–1994 (volume indices, 1950 = 100)

Source: WTO 1995, chart II.1, p. 29

The reasons for the upsurge after 1992 are many. In the more recent period it probably represented a response to the significant liberalization of foreign investment as the barriers to FDI continued to fall in both the advanced and developing countries.

Triad power and influence

Any discussion of the diverse strategies and tactics of firms and govern-ments in the context of FDI should not blind us to an overarching feature of these relationships, illustrated in table 3.2. Sixty per cent of the flows of

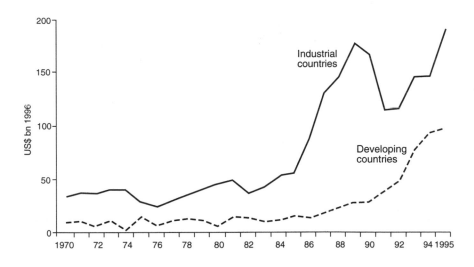

Figure 3.2   The trends in real foreign direct investment flows, 1970–1995
(1996 US$ billions)

Source: IFC 1997, fig. 2.4, p. 16

Table 3.1   Net FDI flows to developing countries, 1973–1993 (US$bn, annual averages)

	1973–6	1977–82	1983–9	1990–3
Africa	1.1	0.8	1.1	1.4
Asia	1.3	2.7	5.2	19.8
Middle East and developing Europe	−1.0	2.5	2.6	1.6
Latin and South America	2.2	5.3	4.4	11.0
Total	3.7	11.2	13.3	34.2

Rounding may mean totals differ from additions of specific areas.
Source: Derived from IMF 1994, table 7

FDI over the period 1991–6 were between just the members of the Triad
bloc, which also accounted for 75 per cent of the total accumulated stock
of FDI in 1995. North America, Europe and Japan have dominated as both
the originators and destinations for international investment. In the case of
investment the flows have been particularly intense between North
America and Western Europe. Japan remained a net exporter of FDI in
1996 to both the other areas (see figure 3.3 on p. 78 below).

Table 3.2   Populations and inward FDI flows, 1991–1996

	Population 1996		Investment flows 1991–6[a]	
	(m)	%	(US$m)	%
World total	5,753.726	100	1,455,280	100
A				
USA and Canada	295.248		317,618	
Western Europe				
(EU12 + EFTA)	413.534		526,299	
Japan	125.761		29,106	
Total	834.543	14.5	873,023	60
B				
Ten most important developing countries in terms of FDI flows[b]	1,834.555	31.9	349,267	24 (73% of FDI flows to developing economies)
A + B		46.4		84

[a] 1996 estimates.
[b] Argentina, Brazil, China, Hungary, Indonesia, Malaysia, Mexico, Poland, Singapore, Thailand.
Sources: For investment flows, United Nations 1997, calculated from Annex, table B1; for population levels, *World Bank Atlas 1998*

One proviso here is that, as mentioned above, there has been a growing importance of some developing countries as the *source* of FDI on the basis of their indigenous MNC activity. In particular this trend has affected the rapidly growing East Asian countries, and a few in Latin America. While important trends, these developments do not as yet threaten to undo the pattern outlined above of the continued dominance of the Triad in FDI (see also chapter 4).

FDI, trade and income inequalities

What are the issues and consequences associated with the pattern of concentration of FDI described above? The rest of the data presented in table 3.2, along with the information in tables 3.3, 3.4 and 3.5 below, identify some of the issues. Here there is a division into two areas, A and B, showing population sizes and distributions of global FDI, trade and GNP for different groups of countries.

The first level, A, concerns only the Triad countries, which made up 14.5 per cent of world population in 1996, but attracted 60 per cent of FDI flows over the first half of the 1990s.[1] The second level, B, adds the populations of the ten most important developing countries in terms of FDI flows over

Table 3.3   Distribution of trade, 1996 (exports only)

	Including intra-EU trade		Excluding intra-EU trade	
	US$bn	%	US$bn	%
Total	5,270	100	3,960	100
A				
USA and Canada	826	15.7	836	21.0
Western Europe (EU12 and EFTA)	2,240	42.5	928	23.4
Japan	411	7.8	411	10.4
Total		66.0		54.8
B				
Ten most important developing countries in terms of 1991–6 FDI flows (see table 3.2)	641	12.2	641	16.2
A + B		81.5		71.0

Source: WTO 1997, vol. 2, calculated from table 1.5, p. 3, and table 1.6, p. 4

Table 3.4   GNP, 1996 (US$m, at market prices)

	US$m	% of world total
A		
USA and Canada	8,003,414	
Western Europe	8,941,093	
Japan	5,149,185	
Total	22,093,692	74.9
B		
Ten most important developing countries in terms of FDI flows 1991–6 (see table 3.2)	2,995,122	10.1
A + B		84.1

Source: *World Bank Atlas 1998*, calculated from table on 'Economy', pp. 42–3

the period (together receiving 73 per cent of all non-Triad flows and accounting for another 32 per cent of world population). Adding these together (A + B, shown near the bottom of table 3.2) gives a total of 46 per cent of the world's population in receipt of 84 per cent of FDI flows (down from 92 per cent over the 1980s). But the group of countries included under level B is dominated by China with a population of over 1.2 billion in 1996. It is unlikely that all China's population is benefiting equally from inward FDI. It is known that FDI is highly concentrated in the coastal provinces,

Table 3.5 Global distribution of GNP in 1996

Economies		GNP		Population	
Per capita income (US$)	No. of economies	(US$m)	%	(m)	%
Low ($785) or less	63	1,596,837	5.4	3,236	56.2
Lower middle ($786–3,115)	63	1,962,719	6.7	1,125	19.6
Upper middle ($3,116–9,635)	31	2,178,234	7.4	473	8.2
High ($9,636) or more	53	23,771,825	80.6	916	15.6
World total	210	29,509,614	100	5,754	100

Source: *World Bank Atlas 1998*, based on table on p. 38

particularly in the south. Thus if we were to include only the populations of the eight Chinese coastal provinces, along with Beijing province, to give a rough estimate of where the FDI is actually going within China, this recalculation would suggest that it is only 30 per cent of the world's population that received 84 per cent of the FDI flows.

On the basis of these admittedly rough and ready calculations, between 54 per cent and 70 per cent of the world's population was in receipt of only 16 per cent of global FDI flows in the first half of the 1990s. In other words, between a half and two-thirds of the world was still virtually written off the map as far as any benefit from this form of investment was concerned. The question is, for how long can this kind of severe inequality continue?

What is more, this inequality is paralleled by the case of trade. Table 3.3 shows the distribution of world trade (exports) in 1996. The table is divided into two main parts: the first part includes intra-European trade, while the second part excludes it. On the basis of this evidence, the equivalent of A + B from table 3.2 accounted for between 82 per cent and 71 per cent of trade in 1996, again demonstrating significant inequality compared to the populations involved.

If we now look at the 'bottom line' of these developments, table 3.4 indicates the persistence of inequality in the international distribution of income for the dominant FDI investment groups of countries (measured in terms of GNP). Furthermore, table 3.5 shows the general distribution of global income in 1996, matching GNP and populations for a wider number of country groupings.

In fact, this distribution changed little over the 1970s and 1980s (Hirst and Thompson 1996, fig. 3.7, p. 71), and indeed became more unequal rather than less after the 1970s. What all these measures show goes against the sentiment that benefits will 'trickle down' to the less well-off nations and regions as investment and trade are allowed to follow strictly market signals. Inequalities are dramatic, remain stubborn to change and, in terms of GNP, grew slightly during the 1970s and 1980s. The only salutory lesson here is that the inequalities in terms of FDI flows and trade eased a little from the position over the 1980s.

There are good ethical arguments against this situation. Its consequences for the living conditions, life expectancy and security of the world's poor are obvious. It should not be *allowed* to go on and we should do something about it urgently as a matter of *conscience*. Ethics, however, have rarely moved economists, Western policy-makers and company executives: they need other rationales in terms of economic and business opportunities. These non-ethical arguments are therefore emphasized here, that is, the practical economic and political objections to the continuation of these trends. These objections concern the self-interest of the successful in not neglecting the world's poor.

One of these implicates problems for world order. With an increasingly interconnected international system and the majority of the world's population excluded from prosperity, even greater political, social, environmental and, therefore, *economic* disruption of the world economy can be anticipated. This is not a new argument but it is one worth re-emphasizing in the contemporary conditions of the absence of superpower rivalry and an increasing plurality of antagonistically poised voices and social forces. Greater disruption in and by the 'periphery' now tends to have more immediate consequences within the 'core', and the 'core' itself is not immune from many of these trends: it 'imports' the consequences of poverty. The pressure on Europe and the US of refugees and migrants fleeing conflict and poverty is obvious (chapter 2). Any new migration and its containment constitute a major new security risk, and this is likely to be exacerbated by the continuing reproduction of extreme inequality in the distribution of wealth on a global scale.

Secondly, there are good economic arguments in terms of direct benefits to the First World against the continuation of this unequal situation. Even while the high levels of concentration between members of the Triad were developing in the 1980s, this did not prevent them from falling into recession. Indeed the post-1973 period more generally has been one of continued economic difficulties for many of the advanced countries of the Triad. One of the reasons for this could be the relative growth of cross-border merger and acquisition expenditure at the expense of 'new establishment' investment in the 1980s. M&A activity has expanded dramatically in the Triad countries (see below). The significance of this is that it may mean simply the transfer of ownership and speculative activity, rather than involving any net new productive investment. Be that as it may, stagnant aggregate demand, the underutilization of resources and excess capacity, and an inability to launch a sustained world recovery and upturn have all typified this period. What this hints at is the need for a more balanced redistribution of world resources, a generation of new effective demand on a world scale, so as to generate a robust long-term recovery in the Triad as well as some hope for a sustainable upturn among the so far excluded countries of the 'South'. Spare capacity in the Triad is matched by excess but frustrated demand in the South. What is required is some mechanism (and the political will) to redistribute between them. It is to the credit of UNCTAD that it has been one of the few international voices to have consistently argued this case (for a recent effort see UNCTAD 1993). Both rich and poor countries would benefit by such a move, and it would be in their joint long-term interests to engineer it.

As it stands, however, any of this looks unlikely. But there must be a question mark hanging over whether the existing situation as analysed above is sustainable even in its own terms over the long run. How can a 'global system', however partial in its truly internationalized features, manage when two-thirds of its population is systematically excluded from the benefits of that system while the limited prosperity it does generate is increasingly concentrated among the already employed and successful in the wealthy 14 per cent of the world and a few client states?

The advance of the MNC: traditional measures

Returning to the issues of the internationalization of production, FDI has been a feature of the international economy for more than a hundred years. There is thus an accumulated stock inherited from the past. This is shown for the years 1980 to 1995 in table 3.6, expressed as a percentage of GDP. As might be expected there has been a growth in its importance relative to GDP since 1980: at the world level it has more than doubled from 4.6 per

Table 3.6 Inward FDI stock as a percentage of GDP, 1980–1995

	1980	1985	1990	1995
World	**4.6**	**6.5**	**8.3**	**10.1**
Developed economies	**4.8**	**6.0**	**8.3**	**9.1**
of which, EU	5.5	8.2	10.9	13.4
(UK)	11.7	14.0	22.3	28.5
(Germany)	4.5	6.0	7.4	6.9
US	3.1	4.6	7.2	7.7
Japan	0.3	0.4	0.3	0.3
Developing economies	**4.3**	**8.1**	**8.7**	**15.4**
of which, Latin America and Caribbean	6.4	10.8	11.6	18.4
(Brazil)	6.9	11.3	8.1	17.8
Asia	3.5	7.3	7.3	14.2
South, East and South East Asia	3.8	6.5	8.7	15.1
Central and Eastern Europe	–	**0.1**	**1.3**	**4.9**

Source: Compiled from United Nations 1997, Annex, table B6

cent to 10.1 per cent. But the absolute levels in 1995 still remained modest for most countries and groupings. The UK was a conspicuous exception among the larger advanced countries. At the other end of the spectrum, Japan remained largely untouched by inward FDI (and even its outward stock, at 6 per cent of GDP in 1995, was modest). It is surely debatable whether a stock of foreign-owned productive activity of around 10 per cent or less of GDP for most of the advanced countries is as yet sufficient to dislodge any indigenously embedded national business system. It could be argued to have been more important for a small number of rapidly developing countries that have relied on FDI as the main stimulant to their development strategies, but even this can be challenged (see the discussion around table 3.11 below, and the analysis in chapter 5).

Many quite reasonable adjustments to these FDI flow and stock figures could be undertaken to make them more representative of the 'true' position that they are designed to measure. For instance, the stock figures are calculated in terms of historic costs whereas they should perhaps be readjusted to current values, which would no doubt increase their significance somewhat (Graham 1996, pp. 10–13).

But there is a range of other problems in taking FDI flows or stocks as the single most useful measure of the internationalization of productive activity. FDI has become the premier indicator because it is the most standardized international measure available. But even among the advanced industrial economies there are surprising differences in the calculations of FDI flows, as figure 3.3 reveals

This presents estimates of the FDI flows between the Triad countries in 1994 calculated by the three main collection agencies in Europe, the US and Japan. Note that there is only a single case of agreement in these figures: that between Europe and Japan calculated by Eurostat and the Bank of Japan. All the other calculations show different estimates, some very different, as in the case of EU flows to the US (ECU 6.4 billion by Eurostat, 16.2 billion by the US Department of Commerce). Thus it is impossible to be confident of the actual flows of FDI even between the Triad countries. Perhaps we need to look at different and more appropriate indicators, which present a somewhat different picture of the extent of internationalized business activity.

Contrary to common claims, FDI is not a measure of the assets held in affiliated firms. Rather it measures what is happening on the liabilities side of companies' balance sheets. FDI flows are made up of changes in the shares, loans and retained earnings of affiliated companies that are operating abroad, though in a number of countries the reporting of FDI does not include retained earnings (hence, in part, the discrepancies shown in figure 3.3). These have become an important element in the amount of activity conducted abroad (so in this sense, FDI might *underestimate* the extent of this activity in some countries). But in general the FDI measure is likely to *overestimate* this activity. It is not only that companies massage their

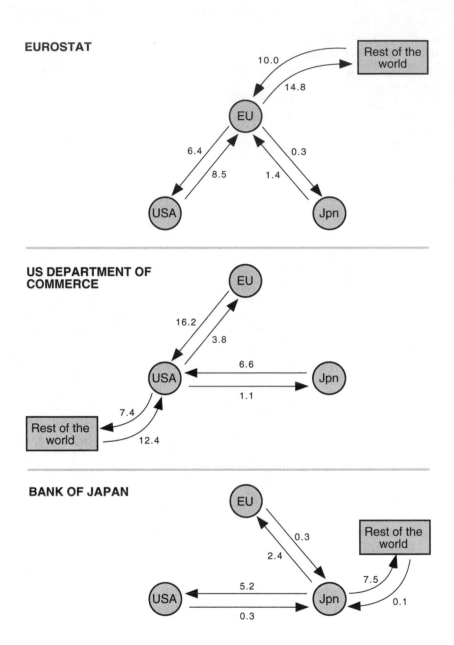

Figure 3.3 FDI flows between the Triad countries, 1994 (ECU bn), according to three sets of calculations

Source: Derived from European Union 1997c, p. 22

liabilities for tax purposes – and this has nothing necessarily to do with their ability to produce from their assets – but a major form of FDI liability management, namely the purchase of existing company shares and bonds, also need have no direct relationship to changing the productive capacity of the assets so acquired. If a foreign company acquires an already existing domestic company's liabilities through a merger or acquisition, but does not alter the asset structure of the acquired company, there is no necessary increase in the productive potential in the country where it has invested. However, this would appear as an inward flow of FDI. There has been a dramatic growth in the extent of M&A activity internationally, stimulated particularly by the privatization programme embarked on by both the advanced and latterly the developing countries. In 1996 nearly 50 per cent of global FDI flows were made up of cross-border mergers and acquisitions (United Nations 1997, p. 9) and this is expected to increase as a proportion in the future (p. 36).

Thus what is needed are new measures of internationalization that capture more of what is going on on the asset side of companies' balance sheets, or which look directly at productive activity accounted for by foreign affiliates as registered in a country's national accounts. But here there are major problems of access to relevant and appropriate information.

Alternative company-based measures

In any scrutiny of company accounts, for instance, it is important to recognize what companies are doing on their 'home' territory at the same time as they are investing and operating abroad. FDI flows only capture what companies are 'lending' to their affiliates abroad, not what they are at the same time investing in their home country or territory. Even where there is some assessment of MNCs according to the extent of their foreign-owned *assets*, the companies included are usually those already classified by the extent of their *foreign*-owned assets, thereby prematurely skewing the analysis in favour of the overseas orientation of company activity (e.g. United Nations 1997, table 1.7, pp. 29–31).

In work reported in detail elsewhere, we have developed three large-scale cross-sectional data sets designed to circumvent some of these problems (see Hirst and Thompson 1996; Allen and Thompson 1997). The first of these contains information for 1987 on the sales, assets, profits, and subsidiaries and affiliates of over 500 manufacturing and service MNCs from five countries: Canada, Germany, Japan, the UK and the US. The second set contains information for 1990 on these aspects for just manufacturing multinationals. The third set gives data for sales and assets for 1993 of over 5,000 MNCs from six countries: France, Germany, Japan, the Netherlands, the UK and the US.[2] The fact that these data are classified for home territory activity as well as for that conducted overseas by companies from these countries allows us to judge more accurately the extent of the internationalization of their activity. Note that these data do not indicate flows across borders but the results of such flows as expressed in terms of the ex-post economic activity they have engendered.

A way of integrating the analysis of the data sets for different years can be seen in table 3.7, which reports the geographical distribution of manufacturing subsidiaries and affiliates (S&As) of MNCs headquartered in five countries for 1987 and 1990. Some interesting differences between the countries emerge. First, just 41 per cent of Japanese S&As were home country based in 1990 (58 per cent for S&As based in Japan and South East Asia), while 78 per cent of German S&As were located in Europe. Other than this difference, home-country based S&As were also evident elsewhere, though for US and Canadian firms Europe was a particularly important site for S&As. Clearly, the US and Canada operate much like a single integrated North American economy for US and Canadian international firms. Perhaps surprisingly the UK was not as well represented in the US as might have been expected. But Latin America figured as a relatively important destination for all the countries in the case of S&As.

These data are summarized in table 3.8 in terms of the proportions allocated to the home country or region. Canada is the least 'home centred' economy, followed by the US and Japan. Germany remains highly concentrated in Europe. Indeed, its concentration on this area seems to have increased a little between 1987 and 1990.

Tables 3.9 and 3.10 provide added comparable results for sales and assets, integrating the 1993 analysis into the picture and also looking at the service sector position. Table 3.9 provides the relevant figures for sales activity. It compares the percentage distribution of MNC sales to the home region for the country company sets for which there was data in 1987, 1990 and 1993 (the 'home region' is common for these data, and includes the home country).[3] Clearly, although these data should be treated with some caution, they provide a reasonable guide to the magnitudes involved. The importance of the home base for manufacturing sales remained about the same for Germany, the UK and the US between 1987 and 1993, whereas it increased for Japan. For services there was a decrease for Japan and the US, and a slight increase for the UK.

As far as asset data is concerned, the results of a similar exercise are presented in table 3.10.[4] Overall these display slightly less bias to the home country/region than do the sales figures (which is perhaps surprising – we might have expected MNCs sales to be more internationalized than their assets). In as much as one can draw any generalizations from these figures, it seems that manufacturing asset distributions became more biased to the home country/region between the late 1980s and early 1990s, while for services US companies became less concentrated. (We are less happy about drawing any strong conclusions from Japanese data, however, particularly as far as services are concerned.)

Table 3.7 Distribution of subsidiaries and affiliates of manufacturing MNCs headquartered in five countries, 1987 and 1990 (percentages)

	Europe		US		Canada		Africa		SE Asia		Japan		Middle East		Caribbean		Latin America		Pacific Rim		Other	
	1987	1990	1987	1990	1987	1990	1987	1990	1987	1990	1987	1990	1987	1990	1987	1990	1987	1990	1987	1990	1987	1990
Canada	27	31	22	23	34	24	1	2	3	4	2	1	0	0	2	3	5	6	4	4	1	1
Germany	76	78	7	8	3	2	2	2	3	3	2	1	0	0	0	0	5	4	2	1	0	0
Japan	15	17	13	14	2	2	1	1	13	17	49	41	1	1	0	0	5	4	2	3	0	0
UK	64	60	13	11	2	3	7	7	5	7	1	1	1	1	0	1	3	3	4	5	0	0
US	27	29	44	38	5	5	2	2	5	7	2	3	1	1	2	2	9	10	3	3	1	0

Source: Authors' data files

Table 3.8 Percentage of manufacturing subsidiaries and affiliates located in home country/region, 1987 and 1990

	1987	1990
Canada	56	47
Germany	76	78
Japan	62	58
UK	64	60
US	58	53

Home country/region here defined as: Canada = Canada and US; Germany = Germany and rest of Europe; Japan = Japan and South East Asia; UK = UK and rest of Europe; US = US, Canada and Latin America.
Source: Authors' data files

Table 3.9 MNCs' sales to home country/region as a percentage of total sales, 1987, 1990 and 1993

	Manufacturing			Services	
	1987	1990	1993	1987	1993
Canada	n.a.	77	n.a.	n.a.	n.a.
Germany	72	75	75	n.a.	n.a.
Japan	64	65	75	89	77
UK	66	59	65	74	77
US	70	63	67	93	79

n.a. = not available.
Source: Authors' data files

Table 3.10 MNCs' assets in home country/region as a percentage of total, 1987, 1990 and 1993

	Manufacturing			Services	
	1987	1990	1993	1987	1993
Canada	n.a.	74	n.a.	n.a.	n.a.
Japan	n.a.	n.a.	97	77	92
UK	52	48	62	n.a.	69
US	67	66	73	81	77

n.a. = not available.
Source: Authors' data files

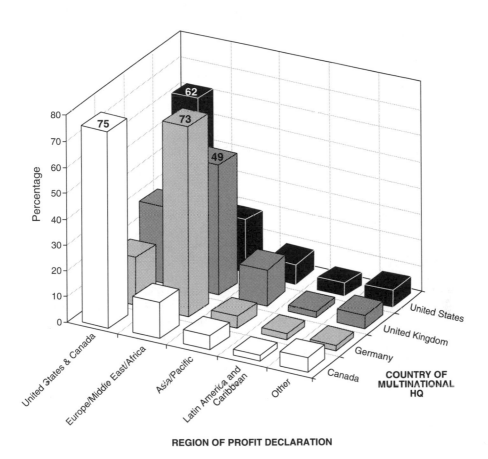

Figure 3.4 Percentage distribution between regions of gross profits of multinationals headquartered in the US, UK, Germany and Canada, 1990

Source: Authors' data files

Finally we can turn to profit data. This area is the least satisfactory from the point of view of data availability, and only the results shown in figure 3.4 could be generated. It provides gross profit distributions for four sets of country manufacturing companies for 1990. Profit distribution follows the pattern established by other indicators: the centrality of 'home country/region' as the site of profit declaration (if not generation – these data do not allow us to distinguish between where profits were generated and where they were declared). Clearly manufacturing companies in the

UK, and to a lesser extent the US, are the ones most open to profit declaration in other than the home region/country.

These data are clearly not ideal since for the most part the way the data
are recorded in company accounts only allows for the allocation of their
activities as within or outside their 'home region' by a single definition (see
p. 80, note 3). However, for some of the data and countries, and for some
years, it was possible to disaggregate this into a home *country* allocation
(as shown to a large extent in table 3.8, and for 1993 data on the other
measures), which confirmed the basic home-centredness of the data as
presented in these tables and the figure (see Allen and Thompson 1997, in
particular).

The main conclusion to be drawn from this analysis is an obvious one.
The 'home oriented' nature of MNC activity along all the dimensions
looked at remains significant, even if this could be a regionally centred
one. Thus MNCs still rely on their 'home base' as the centre for their
economic activities, despite all the speculation about globalization. From
these results we should be reasonably confident that, in the aggregate,
international companies are still predominantly MNCs (with a clear
home base to their operations) and not TNCs (which represent footloose
stateless companies, see chapter 1). As indicated above, there are two
aspects to this home-centredness. One is the role of the 'home country',
and the other that of the 'home region'. As far as the data can be
disaggregated, in 1993 home country biases were as significant as the
home region biases found in 1987. Given that for 1987 and 1990 it is only
possible to specify an aggregated regional breakdown, then strictly speaking the three cross-sectional analyses can only be compared on this basis.
But these confirm that as much as between two-thirds and three-quarters
of MNC aggregate business activity remains centred on the home region in
this sense.

However, it is worth raising a possible caveat to this conclusion, which
will be additionally explored below. A strong feature of the globalization
thesis is that joint ventures, partnerships, strategic alliances and liaisons
are drawing firms into increasingly interdependent international networks
of business activity. The relatively 'open' dispersion of S&As as demonstrated by tables 3.7 and 3.8 could indicate to this. A potential problem,
then, with the *quantitative* data presented here is that they do not capture
this *qualitative* change in company business strategies. The fact that only 25
to 30 per cent of company activity is conducted abroad does not of itself
tell us anything about the strategic importance of that 25 to 30 per cent to
the overall business activity of firms. It might represent the key to their per-
formative success both internationally *and* domestically. The fact that we
have seen a wider international dispersion of S&As could be taken as an
indicator of this 'networking' trend in operation. We address this further
below.

Measures of internationalization from national accounts data

The adjustments to measures of internationalization made up to now do not exhaust those needed to properly assess the popular belief that MNCs are now so footloose that they are undermining the continued viability of national economies or national systems of business. They need supplementing by examining the extent of internationalization in relation to overall national output, and then with that derived directly from national account statistics. This gives some added insights into the true extent of internationalization.

The data in table 3.11 show the estimated gross product that MNC foreign affiliates were responsible for producing compared to the GDP of various country groupings and the world total. Note that for the developed countries this only increased from 5.1 per cent in 1982 to 5.4 per cent in 1994 (despite the massive increase in FDI flows over this period); for the developing countries it increased from 6 per cent to 9.1 per cent (admittedly a 50 per cent increase); and the world total overall grew from 5.2 per cent to 6.0 per cent. But these hardly seem dramatic levels or major growth rates for the crucial developed countries where fears of the end of national business systems are most pronounced.

In addition, the data in table 3.12 show the relative importance of FDI inflows as a contribution to the gross domestic fixed capital formation (GDFCF) in a range of country groupings. Again, what is significant here is the relative *un*importance of FDI flows in their contribution to domestic investment (even accepting the criticisms of this measure as outlined above). In a number of cases the contribution of FDI to GDFCF actually fell in the mid-1990s from that averaged over the late 1980s. It is clear from these figures that economies cannot borrow their way to prosperity via a

Table 3.11   Gross product of MNCs' foreign affiliates as a percentage of GDP, 1982, 1990 and 1994

	1982	1990	1994
World	**5.2**	**6.7**	**6.0**
Developed countries	**5.1**	**6.7**	**5.4**
European Union	5.7	8.6	7.7
North America	5.1	6.7	5.2
Developing countries	**6.0**	**7.0**	**9.1**
Latin America and the Caribbean	7.6	9.3	10.3
Asia	5.6	5.9	8.6
South East Asia	5.0	7.0	9.0
Central and Eastern Europe	**0.1**	**1.1**	**2.3**

Source: United Nations 1997, adapted from table A4, p. 267

Table 3.12 Share of inward FDI flows in gross domestic fixed capital formation, 1985–1995 (percentages)

	Average 1985–1990	1991	1992	1993	1994	1995
World	5.1	3.1	3.3	4.4	4.5	5.2
Developed economies	5.5	3.2	3.2	3.7	3.5	4.4
of which, EU	9.1	5.4	5.5	5.9	5.0	6.8
(UK)	13.7	9.4	9.8	11.0	6.8	13.2
(Germany)	1.6	1.0	0.6	0.4	0.2	1.7
US	5.3	3.1	2.4	4.9	4.8	5.9
Japan	0.2	0.2	0.2	–	0.1	–
Developing economies	8.0	4.4	5.1	6.6	8.0	8.2
of which Latin America and Caribbean	11.3	7.8	8.1	7.2	10.3	11.0
(Brazil)	3.1	1.4	3.0	1.3	3.0	4.7
Asia	7.6	3.4	4.2	6.5	7.2	7.5
South, East and South East Asia	9.7	3.8	4.7	7.5	8.3	9.0
Central and Eastern Europe	1.0	0.4	0.8	7.9	5.0	5.2

Source: Compiled from United Nations 1997, Annex, table B.5

reliance on FDI. What remains crucial to domestic development strategies are domestic savings, which still remain the main source of financial resources for domestic investment in all advanced and developing economies. It is still the nature of domestic financial systems that is crucial to the long-run developmental success of different economies.

Finally, it is worth considering other detailed attempts to assess the extent of internationalized production as derived directly from national accounts and measures of national output. For 1990, for instance, Lipsey, Blomström and Ramstetter (1995) calculated that foreign-based output amounted to only about 7 per cent of overall world output (see also table 3.11 above), up from 4.5 per cent in 1970 (Lipsey 1997, p. 2). Although the share was higher in 'industry' (including manufacturing, trade, construction and public utilities) at about 15 per cent in 1990 (up from 11 per cent in 1977), it was negligible in 'services', which amounted to 60 per cent of total world output in 1990. By 1995 foreign-based output was estimated to have increased to 7.5 per cent of total world output, hardly a dramatic and earth-shattering change.

The story of US international firms is interesting in its own right. Their overseas output peaked in 1977 at about 8 per cent of US GDP, and has been declining ever since to about 5.5 per cent in 1995. In manufacturing the production by majority-owned US foreign affiliates was 15.5 per cent of US manufacturing output in 1977, reaching over 17 per cent in 1990, but settling back to 16 per cent in 1995, that is, it has remained almost stable over the past twenty years. In terms of employment the trends have been similar. There was a rapid increase in US firms' employment overseas relative to that at home from 1957 to 1977, but since then the trend has been a decreasing one. In 1994 the employment figure for foreign manufacturing affiliates of US firms remained well below its 1977 level. Most of these decreases in the overseas proportion of US firms' production and employment can be accounted for by the relative decline in the importance of the manufacturing sector in the US economy as a whole. In fact, the story of the internationalization of the US manufacturing sector has really been one confined to the inward side. Foreign MNC production in the US as a proportion of GDP rose from almost zero in 1970 to just over 8 per cent in 1995, and in the manufacturing sector from 4 per cent in 1977 to 13 per cent in 1994 (Ramstetter 1998, fig. 8.2, p. 195).

The story of the Japanese economy is almost the reverse of the one for the US. There has been virtually no growth in the importance of overseas production relative to GDP in Japan: indeed, in terms of directly measured output indicators the trend has been a declining one (Ramstetter 1998, fig. 8.2, p. 194). On the other hand, Japanese multinationals have been expanding their activities abroad relative to their production at home. For all Japanese manufacturing companies, the overseas production ratio doubled from 5 per cent in 1985 to nearly 10 per cent in 1996 (for only those companies with overseas affiliates this ratio also doubled, from about 13.5 per cent to 27.5 per cent over the same period: MITI 1997). Given Japanese overall output growth rates, however, absolute levels of these ratios relative to GDP are low and changes have been modest.

Similar calculations as these for the other advanced countries are not readily available. The broad picture is indicated by the data contained in table 3.11. But for the Asia-Pacific region as a whole, Ramstetter (1998) has produced a comprehensive survey along these lines, in particular comparing FDI-based indicators with those derived directly from national accounting data, the results of which are worth quoting:

> FDI-based indicators and foreign MNC shares of production often display very different trends [which] strongly suggests that FDI-related indicators are rather poor indicators of foreign MNC presence. More specifically, since foreign MNC shares of production are clearly more accurate measures of foreign MNC presence, focussing on FDI-related measures apparently leads to significant overestimation of the extent to which MNC presence has grown in the Asia Pacific region since the 1970s. (p. 208)

This remains a salutary warning for all those approaches that stress the simple growth of FDI flows and stocks as indicating the necessary growth of a global business environment. It is these business-based approaches towards globalization and its supposed consequences that form the context for the next part of this chapter.

Business strategy and the future of national systems

Those who claim a dramatic change in the international production environment see this as heralding a new stage of TNC evolution. This involves an uncoupling of companies and networks from distinct national bases, and a move towards a genuine global economy centred on truly global companies. The best example of this argument is the work of Kenichi Ohmae (1990 and 1993). The virtue of Ohmae's case is that he does at least say what he thinks the structure of a truly global, borderless economy would look like: it is summed up in the idea of an 'interlinked economy'. Ohmae argues that 'stateless' corporations are now the prime movers in an interlinked economy (ILE) centred on North America, Europe and Japan. He contends that macroeconomic and industrial policy intervention by national governments can only distort and impede the rational process of resource allocation by corporate decisions and consumer choices on a global scale. The emergence of 'electronic highways' enables anyone, in principle, to 'plug into' the global marketplace. All corporate players need to do is to shake off the burden of a nationally oriented bureaucracy, and the government intervention that goes along with it, and enter the new world of open global marketing and production. The vision is of one large interlinked network of producers and consumers plugged into an efficiently operating 'level playing field' of the open international and globalized economy. International markets provide coordinative and governance mechanisms in and of themselves: national strategies and policy interventions are likely merely to distort them. Like Robert Reich (1992), Ohmae believes that the era of effective national economies, and state policies corresponding to them, is over.

Pace Ohmae, the international economy looks nothing like the ILE and does not seem to be converging towards it. Current practice of international corporations is more complex, and much more akin to an MNC pattern. Strategic alliances are creating an extremely uneven international marketplace, which is being duplicated in both manufacturing and service sectors. To the extent that a globalized economy exists at all, it is *oligopolistically* organized, not organized according to the dictates of the perfectly competitive model as Ohmae and others wish to believe (cf. Gray 1998). The major corporate players are involved in a deadly competitive game, deploying all manner of business strategies to exclude some competing players from their networks while locking others firmly into them. For oligopolists there are massive 'first mover' advantages. If a firm can secure the originating industry standard, for instance, it has the potential to gain enormous benefits by moving down the cost curve to reap economies of scale and scope. The providers of the 'super electronic highways', for instance, compete with one another over standards and conditions of connection, precluding any open plugging in at will (Mansell 1994). They seek to attract the right kinds of customers and 'trap' them by locking them into their own particular standards and connections at the start so that sales can be guaranteed from then on. These companies seek to use market resources and public policy to strongly protect any advantages gained in this way.

It is the typology by Bartlett and Goshal (1989) of different forms of international company that has struck a chord with those researchers concentrating on company form and the analysis of company strategy. Building on their suggestions it is possible to draw a conceptual distinction between four organizational types of global business, using their labels of 'multinational', 'international', 'global' and 'transnational' respectively. The outline characteristics of these types of companies are:

1   those that build on a strong local presence through sensitivity and responsiveness to national differences ('multinational companies');
2   those that exploit parent company knowledge and capabilities through worldwide diffusion and adaptation ('international companies);
3   those that build cost advantages through centralized operations on a global scale ('global companies');
4   those that disperse their activities to relatively independent and specialized units seeking to be globally competitive through multinational flexibility and worldwide knowledge development and learning capabilities ('transnational companies').

Thus broadly speaking these forms proceed from a more national focus to a wider transnational one. An attempt to empirically test for these organizational types found that the most common remained the multinational type, while the least common was the transnational type (Leong and Tan 1993). This finding set the trend for further empirical work that cast doubt on the full development of the global economy and the transnational type of corporate form: the majority of 'international' firms still remain tethered to a definite national country base, confirming the analysis above.

Technology

The issue of innovation and the role of technology is another dimension along which the process of company internationalization is often thought to be rapidly proceeding, and it is used to bolster the argument about the globalization of company activity. Again, there is little systematic company-based evidence about how much of this remains focused on the parent country rather than overseas, but what evidence is available broadly supports the conclusion that this type of activity remains far from fully globalized. For instance, in their analysis of the international distribution of R&D laboratories of 500 major firms, Casson, Pearce and Singh (1992) found some degree of interdependency, but it varied greatly according to the parent countries of firms. Firms from the Netherlands, Switzerland, West

Germany and the UK showed significant foreign orientation (the international to home ratios of laboratories for companies from these countries were all over 60 per cent), while the other nine countries or groupings studied showed considerably lower ratios (the average ratio was 39 per cent). The dominant country in terms of numbers of companies and laboratories, the US, had a ratio of only 31 per cent, confirming it as a relatively 'closed' country on this measure. Countries such as Japan and Sweden remain very closed. In addition, papers by Cantwell (1992), Patel and Pavitt (1992) and Patel (1995) take other measures of technological activity: in patent registration, for example, no more than 10 per cent of patents granted to international firms by the US patent office originated from foreign subsidiaries, and the share of patents coming from foreign subsidiaries did not substantially increase between 1969 and 1986, or between 1986 and 1990 (based on the analysis of 686 of the world's largest manufacturing companies). The home territory remained the dominant site for the location of this form of R&D activity, reinforcing the local innovation system.

But patent registration represents an intermediate 'output' end of innovative activity. When it is supplemented by direct 'input' data associated with R&D expenditures, there is also little evidence of any systematic change in the location or composition of this type of investment as far as the advanced countries are concerned over the period from 1970 to 1990 (Archibugi and Michie 1997). Thus these national and company-based studies conclude that at most only between 10 per cent and 30 per cent of the technological activity of multinationals is likely to be located in foreign subsidiaries. As Patel comments: 'The main conclusion of this paper is that there is no systematic evidence to suggest that widespread globalization of the production of technology has occurred in the 1980s' (1995, p. 151).

However, there is a different way in which technology can interact with the international economy, namely through the technological spillovers arising from trade and R&D expenditure. As discussed in chapter 4, R&D expenditure has traditionally been closely associated with international competitiveness. Although almost the entire world's R&D investment is concentrated in the advanced OECD countries, trade and FDI extend the benefits of this to other countries. The extent of these spillovers can look impressive (Coe and Helpman 1995; Coe, Helpman and Hoffmaister 1997), but they need to be set in the context of the relatively low levels of R&D expenditure conducted abroad by advanced country firms, and the relatively low levels of trade interaction between the OECD and non-OECD countries, as measured in terms of trade to GDP ratios (see chapter 4). In addition, as analysed below, a good deal of contemporary company strategy is to tap into those production locations that provide organizational advantages to their international activities but which do not necessarily involve conventional R&D expenditures.

Behavioural characteristics

These findings about technology are reinforced by the detailed empirical analysis of Pauly and Reich (1997) into the characteristic features of US, German and Japanese MNCs. They argue that there are systematic differences between the strategies adopted by MNCs originating from each of these three countries in the areas of research and development, corporate governance and finance, and investment and intrafirm trade, arising from deeply entrenched socioeconomic institutional characteristics and cultures in the three countries. The broad but complex natures of the US, German and Japanese business systems are still intact, they argue, and they have heavily marked the MNCs originating from these countries as their activities have internationalized. In terms of technological development, Japanese firms conduct remarkably little R&D abroad, while German firms have made significant R&D commitments in the US but little elsewhere. For multinational companies from these two countries, the bulk of their overseas R&D effort is directed either to the customization of products for local markets or to the gathering of knowledge for transfer back home. The companies from these two countries thus organize their overseas R&D either to bolster their domestic innovation systems, or to enhance their capacity to export from their domestic economies: 'trade creating' activity (this conclusion for Japan is strongly confirmed by the analysis of Fransman 1997 and Yoshitomi 1996).

US companies, by contrast, conform closely to their 'national type' in conducting much more of their R&D abroad, and using this to provide substitute overseas production sites for 'trade displacing' activity. These different investment, R&D and trade strategies are reinforced, it is argued, by the domestic corporate governance systems in which the parent companies are located. The well-known nature of the links between banks and commercial enterprises, the complex cross-holding of shares in some of the countries, the differential role of the stock exchanges in each country, and the type of behaviour this engenders, are not being undermined but are being reinforced, according to this analysis. Recognizably different behavioural patterns persist in the leading MNCs' strategic orientation towards the internationalization of their activities. Table 3.13 sums up the conclusions of Pauly and Reich's analysis.

The reorganization of production?

The analysis of Pauly and Reich (1997) provides a bridge between formal quantitative analyses of MNC activity and more qualitative approaches to the organization of the business of innovative product development and competitive success. Often the latter are based on case studies, something relatively ignored by this chapter up to now. In addition, Pauly and Reich essentially stress the effects of particular national business systems on the

Table 3.13   Multinational corporate structures and strategies of three countries

	United States	Germany	Japan
Direct investment	Extensive inward and outward	Selective/outward orientation	Extensive outward; limited competition from inward
Intrafirm trade	Moderate	High	Very high
Research and development	Fluctuating; diversified; innovation oriented	Narrow base/process, diffusion orientation	High, steady growth; high-technology and process orientation
Corporate governance	Short-term shareholding; managers highly constrained by capital markets; risk-seeking, finance-centred strategies	Managerial autonomy except during crises; no takeover risk; conservative, long-term strategies	Stable shareholders; network-constrained managers; takeover risk only within network/aggressive market share-centred strategies
Corporate financing	Diversified, global funding; highly price sensitive	Concentrated, regional funding; limited price sensitivity	Concentrated, national funding; low price sensitivity

Source: Pauly and Reich 1997, table 4, p. 23

companies operating internationally from them. Another way of approaching this issue is to look at what effects the introduction of an MNC from abroad might have on an already established business system. It is time to bring these elements into the picture.

A number of key features of contemporary business reorganization and the role of location for competitive advantage need to be recognized here. The classic way economics tackles the analysis of technology and innovation is via the production function. Production is conceived in a 'linear' form where a series of inputs are marshalled and combined together to produce an output. Innovation is introduced into these models through the addition of another input usually measured by some variable associated with technological advance: number of patents registered, number of scientists and engineers, number and location of R&D laboratories, R&D expenditures, etc. The linear model also describes the innovation process as a sequence of stages: from research to development, then to production, and finally to marketing, with little communication or connection between these stages.

In contrast to this linear model, however, it has become increasingly clear that there is a lot more to innovation than just the application of another 'resource input' or the organization of a sequence of separated stages. Non-linear, looped and feedback models recognize the existence of many 'intangible' assets in the innovation process: those associated with incremental learning and tacit knowledge, with the locational 'milieu' in which companies operate, with the habits, conventions and routines that serve to 'socially organize' the production process, etc. One significant way of expressing these aspects is as 'untraded interdependences' (Storper 1995). They represent an 'asset' that cannot be easily identified as a measurable input into the production process. Rather they exist as locationally specific 'externalities' which firms can only access by actually setting up operations within the location in question. This can account for the significant development of 'innovation without R&D' that is usually associated with local and regional economic districts. In part, this 'innovation without R&D' has to do with process innovation, but it also has to do with incremental product innovations based on how the innovation process is spatially organized. These issues, then, bring back into the picture the spatially and locationally specific business systems as a central element for firms' innovative activity and competitive performance.

Including these considerations enables us to make sense of the way international firms look for particular comparative and competitive strengths in locational advantages associated with national or regional production, innovation and business systems. MNCs thus seek to tap into the advantages offered by particular locations so as to strengthen their overall competitive performance and success. They often look for quite small advantages associated with a specific part of their overall production process, creating complex international divisions of labour based on locational specialization. Take the Jæren district of Norway as an example (Asheim and Isaksen 1997, pp. 317–18). This has specialized in the production of advanced industrial robots. A leading local firm (Trallfa Robot) was taken over by the Swiss-Swedish MNC ABB in the late 1980s (creating ABB Flexible Automation). ABB produced most of its robots for the European car makers in Västerås in Sweden, but instead of restructuring by closing down the Jæren plant and moving production to Sweden, ABB increased capacity and employment in its Norwegian subsidiary in order to capture the specialist externalities available in the local area. In this way the presence of ABB has *strengthened* the local innovative and business system, rather than undermined it.

Another example of a similar process can be seen by the way that German bank multinationals have tapped into the comparative advantages of the City of London's financial system, without necessarily undermining either that system's operation or their own domestic activities (Soskice 1997, pp. 76–7). Deutsche Bank, Dresdner Bank, the Norddeutsche Landesbank and Commerzbank have all moved – or are in the process of moving – their international operations away from Frankfurt to London. But they have maintained their domestic operations – those that support the high skill competence and long-term relationships associated with local manufacturing – within Germany. Similarly, German chemical firms like

BASF, Bayer and Hoechst have run down their biotechnology operations in Germany and concentrated them in the US where there is a technical and organizational advantage. Meanwhile their mainstream high value-added chemical research and production is still concentrated in Germany.

One way of characterizing these changes in how international business is being conducted is in terms of the introduction of sophisticated networks of specialization and value-added. In some sectors these may not even involve any direct investment overseas. The development of cross-border production networks that assemble diverse points of innovation occurs by drawing in independent indigenous suppliers who link into the commodity chain, or chains, of system assembly and standard setting (Borrus and Zysman 1997), without this requiring an explicit physical investment strategy on the part of the lead MNC firm. The MNC acts only as the 'organizer' of the independent part-contractors and subsystem assemblers that occupy the strategic positions in the network. Here we have the internationalization of production without any overseas investment being necessary. Borrus and Zysman probably exaggerate the extent of this as a new paradigm for global competition to be followed by all sectors (they call it 'Wintelism', from the combination of Windows and Intel type production technologies), but it captures elements of a number of well-recognized developments in international business.

An example of this is the way Singapore has developed a comparative advantage in hard disk drive (HDD) production and assembly, based on the technological and organizational innovativeness of its local firms (but also supplemented initially by MNC investment: Wong 1997).[5] Subsequent spin-off developments and new local investment have served to strengthen the production and innovation system. Nor is this based on any labour cost advantage, since direct and indirect labour costs only amount to 6 per cent of the total cost of an HDD (Wong 1997, table 7, p. 199). The Singapore element in several complex transnational production networks for computer equipment is now well established. The key point to recognize from these examples is summed up by Borrus and Zysman:

> This era is [...] one in which an increasingly global market coexists with enduring national foundations of distinctive economic growth trajectories and corporate strategies. Globalization has not led to the elimination of national systems of production. National systems endure; but they are evolving together in a world economy that increasingly has a regional structure. (1997, p. 143)

Conclusion

The argument of this chapter has involved a number of points. The first is that the internationalization of production and trading activity remains extremely unequally distributed, with a domination of the Triad countries and a few favoured rapidly expanding less developed economies. The vast bulk of the world's population is heavily disadvantaged, and almost ignored by these developments. Income distribution is also severely unequal, with little sign that this is changing.

Secondly, the extent of the internationalization of business activity is often exaggerated in both popular and academic accounts; and it is not increasing at a particularly dramatic rate. From the quantitative analysis reported in the first part of the chapter it is reasonable to suggest that between 65 and 70 per cent of MNC value-added continues to be produced on the home territory. This conclusion coincides with the arguments of Tyson (1991), Kapstein (1991) and Lazonick (1993) in their debate with Reich (1990, 1992) about the nature of international business (see also Hu 1992, 1995). The former authors challenged Reich on his assumption that American business had gone 'transnational', and that this did not matter. Tyson pointed out that 'within manufacturing, US parent operations account for 78 percent of total assets, 70 percent of total sales, and 70 percent of total employment of US multinationals in 1988' (p. 38). The analysis reported here confirms this finding for a wider range of countries.

But there has obviously been some internationalization of business activity. Thus a second issue was to assess the strategies of companies originating from different business systems. Despite the home-centredness of the main findings, the remaining activity of the country groupings is quite diverse. That is, the different country MNCs operate in different areas to different extents. The MNCs are not all the same in terms of the geographical spread of their activity outside their home territories, nor in the way they have gone about internationalizing their activities. In this respect it was argued that the production and business systems of the originating countries still marked the MNCs with a particular approach and attitude.

Connected to this is the question of what effects the limited internationalization of business activity is having on national systems of business, production and innovation. Here the argument is that this has yet to develop to such an extent that national systems are being radically undermined, transformed or rendered redundant. Indeed, in many ways these systems are being reinforced and strengthened by the internationalization of business. Firms are locking themselves into the advantages offered by particular locational production configurations, which are enhancing their ability to compete. In addition, the continuation of a clear home-centredness for most MNCs also needs to be recognized as providing them with advantages that they will not easily give up.

Finally, it is worth raising the issue of the 'governance' consequences of this analysis. These are twofold. In the first place, if national systems of production, business and technology still remain relatively firmly embedded, then there is still scope for the management of these in the interests of the stability and productivity of the national economy. Secondly, given that MNCs remain tethered to their home economies, whether these are specified nationally or regionally, the opportunity arises for national or sub-national regional bodies to more effectively monitor, regulate and govern them than if they were genuinely 'footloose capital'.

Thus the overall conclusion of the chapter is that the extent of internationalization and its potential detrimental consequences for the regulation of MNC activity and for national economies is severely exaggerated. International businesses are still largely confined to their home territory in terms of their overall activity: they remain heavily 'nationally embedded'.

4

North–South Trade and International Competitiveness

The relationship between the world's North and South has become a key issue in the debate about the trends towards contemporary 'globalization'. This relationship is now perceived as one of greater integration and of growing flows of trade in manufactured goods from the South to the North. The debate became salient in the late 1970s and early 1980s. It was strongly associated with the apparent sudden integration of the hitherto highly autonomous US economy into the global economic system. Europe, although less of an isolated 'continental' economy than the US, also experienced a similar debate with regard to import penetration from the South. In this chapter we examine the terms of this debate and provide an assessment of these relationships, exploring their character and significance for the globalization thesis.

In the later part of the chapter this discussion of North–South trade is linked to the rise of the discourse of 'international competitiveness'. Here we question why there is now a preoccupation with being 'internationally competitive'. The emphasis on 'competitiveness' threatens to pervade all aspects of economic and social life. This is true for companies and nations, whether their activity is in the internationally traded goods sector or not, whether goods are privately produced or collectively provided: all are now equally subject to the criteria of the discourse of competitiveness. Company strategy and public policy are alike concerned to match supposed international challenges. This is also increasingly so for individuals, who are also required to become 'competitive' in the way they conduct their lives, these demands going under the headings of being 'flexible', 'innovative', 'imaginative', 'entrepreneurial', and so on. This discourse of competitiveness is closely tied to globalization: global markets enforce competition and there is no option but to meet them on their own terms.

The chapter is organized as follows. The first part sets out the issues involved and looks at the historical antecedents to the present North–South debate. There is a review of the theoretical and empirical arguments advanced around that debate, and then the evidence is assessed. Finally, an alternative approach to the dominant ones found in the literature is proposed. The second part of the chapter examines the associated trends in international competitiveness. First we assess the reasons for the growth of interest in the concept. Second we consider the conceptual frameworks that can be brought to bear in assessing it. Third the geo-economic relationship between the major Triad blocs and the secondary players in the international competitiveness game is examined. Fourth we focus on economic competitiveness in particular, and the differences between the competitiveness of firms and nations in terms of the implications for trade theory. The concluding section sums up the implications for the globalization thesis and the lessons to be learned from it.

For the most part this analysis takes us up to the early to mid 1990s, since this represented the high point of the 'trade and globalization' debate focused on here.

What are the issues and problems?

The economic integration between the North and the South was perceived to have rapidly increased from the 1970s onwards and to have reached dramatic levels by the early 1990s. For instance, between 1970 and 1992 in the case of trade in manufactured goods, OECD imports from the newly industrializing countries (NICs)[1] increased from a 4.6 per cent share of OECD manufactured imports to 15.8 per cent. For OECD Europe the proportions went from 2.7 per cent to 8.6 per cent, and for the UK alone from 5.4 per cent to 10.6 per cent (McGiven 1996, chart 1, p. 70). Over the same period, manufactured exports to the NICs as a percentage of total manufactured exports increased from 9.6 per cent to 15.2 per cent for the OECD and from 6.3 per cent to 8.0 per cent for OECD Europe, and decreased for the UK from 8.8 per cent to 8.1 per cent (McGiven 1996, chart 2, p. 70). For the US in 1978, the developing countries as a whole accounted for 29 per cent of US manufactured goods imports and this ratio grew to 36.4 per cent by 1990 (Sachs and Shatz 1994, p. 1). As we shall see, however, concentrating in this way on just the origin of imports from the NICs as a proportion of total imports of the advanced countries can give a misleading impression of the overall level of integration between the North and the South.

But it was this change in the sources of the advanced countries' imports that worried policy-makers, politicians and to a lesser extent economists, and which was the origin of the main concern about the potential effects of globalization on the advanced economies. This is connected to a wider post-Second World War transformation in the openness of economies generally, as measured by their trade to GDP ratios (see below). Since it is with respect to the US economy that these concerns have most prominently emerged, figure 4.1 shows the pattern of the growth in trade penetration for the US economy between 1970 and 1996. The data in the figure should alert us to an important feature of this trade growth. Although the average US trade to GDP ratio expanded from about 8 per cent in 1970 to 18 per cent in 1996, that of imports from the group of less developed countries grew from less than 1 per cent to 4 per cent: by any account this was still a fairly low absolute figure in 1996 (note also that these are total imports not just manufactured imports).[2]

Here it is worth considering the extent of international trade interactions more generally, first of all among the members of the Triad, and then between the 'North' and the 'South' (expressed in terms of national income). The position with respect to the Triad is shown in figure 4.2. The US imported 4.6 per cent relative to GDP from Europe and Japan in 1992 (compared to about 3 per cent from the LDCs: see fig. 4.1b). In terms of manufactured goods, the early 1990s US–NIC trade to GDP ratio was only about 2 per cent of US GDP (but up from approximately 0.3 per cent in 1970). As will be argued below, these are not exactly large ratios, though the rates of growth are more significant (see Krugman 1995, table 4, p. 337; also Krugman and Lawrence 1994).

When comparing 1962 with 1992 what is clear from figure 4.2 is that the growth and extent of trade integration between the countries in the Triad were still very modest in 1992. For instance, only the trade flow between Japan and the US (plus Canada) was greater than 2 per cent of GDP. Comparing the 1962 figures to those for 1992 indicates some shift in emphasis within the Triad, with the greatest change affecting the US, particularly the fall in export proportion to Japan.

The way the US has opened up to the greatest extent in terms of manufactured imports is registered again in figure 4.3 (this is also the case, though to a lesser extent, for manufactured exports). Overall imports of manufactures expanded five times, from 1.54 per cent of US GDP in 1963 to 7.66 per cent in 1992. Neither Europe nor Japan have increased their participation in international trade in manufactures to such an extent.[3]

To bring this analysis further up to date – and also to present it in a slightly different format – the data in table 4.1 indicate the degree of importance of merchandise trade flows in 1996 between the Triad countries and between these and the main East Asian trading nations. What is clear is that adding the East Asian trading nations into the picture does not much change the overall significance of the trade flows between the Triad countries. The extent of intra-Triad trade proper rarely exceeded 2 per cent of GDP in 1996, and did not exceed 4 per cent when the East Asian traders were added.

We now turn to the main focus for this section, North–South trade relationships measured with respect to GDP. These are sketched out in

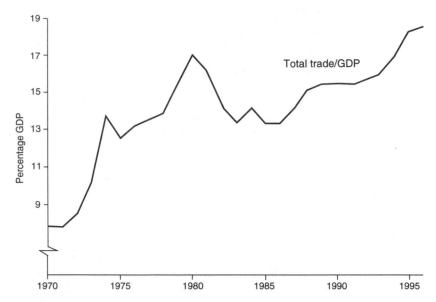

(a) Total US trade (exports plus imports as percentage of GDP)

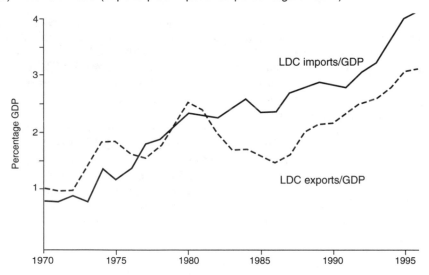

(b) US–LDC trade (trade flows include those with trading partners other than Canada, Japan, Australia, New Zealand, South Africa, members of OPEC and the countries of Western Europe)

Figure 4.1   Trade openness of the US economy, 1970–1996

Source: Adapted from Borjas, Freeman and Katz 1997, fig. 2, p. 11

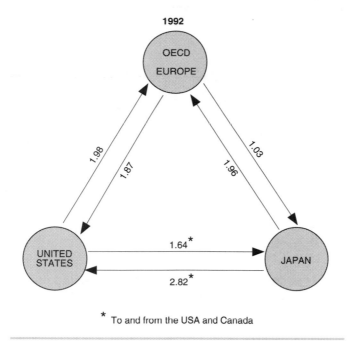

1992

OECD
EUROPE

1.98   1.87   1.03   1.96

UNITED
STATES   JAPAN

1.64*

2.82*

* To and from the USA and Canada

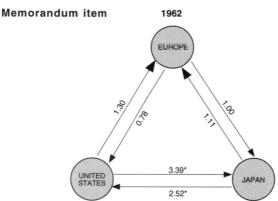

Memorandum item   1962

EUROPE

1.30   0.78   1.00   1.11

UNITED
STATES   JAPAN

3.39*

2.52*

Figure 4.2   Intra-Triad imports and exports as a percentage of GDP,
1992 compared with 1962

Source: Compiled from *OECD Jobs Study: Part 1, Evidence and Explanations*, tables 3.1 and 3.2,
pp. 79 and 80, OECD, 1994

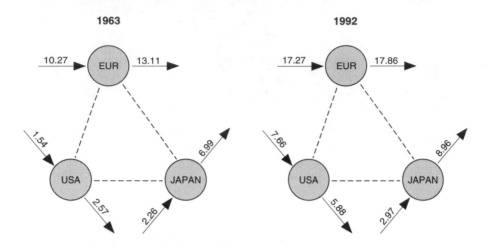

Figure 4.3   Triad trade in manufactures as a percentage of GDP, 1992 compared with 1963 (current prices)

Source: As fig. 4.2

Table 4.1   Merchandise trade flows as a percentage of GDP of originating Triad bloc country, 1996

	To North America	To Western Europe	To Japan (J)	To East Asian traders (EAT)	To J + EAT
From:					
North America	3.5	1.9	0.9	1.4	2.3
Western Europe	1.9	16.9	0.6	1.2	1.8
Japan (J)	2.4	0.6		3.0	3.0
East Asian traders (EAT)	1.4	1.3	2.0	n.a.	
J + EAT	3.8	1.9	2.0		

East Asian traders (EAT): China, Hong Kong, Taiwan, Korea, Malaysia, Thailand, Singapore. *Sources*: *WTO Annual Report 1997*, vol. 2, derived from tables 11.4 (p. 13), 11.6 (p. 15) and 11.8 (p. 17)

figures 4.4 and 4.5. Here the 'North' is taken as the OECD countries, while the 'South' is all non-OECD countries. In figure 4.4 the Triad countries are first shown separately and then aggregated together. Similar proportions for all the Triad countries in their trade relationship with the 'South' are reported for 1992. In addition, these figures point to the much greater

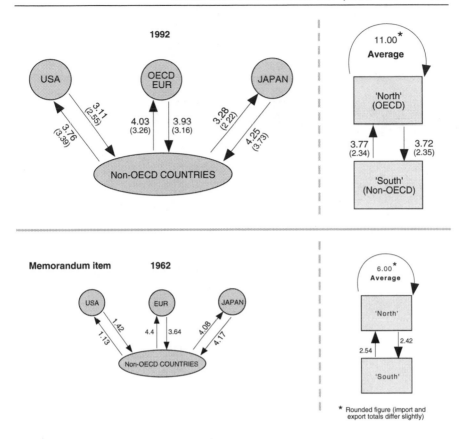

Figure 4.4   North–South trade relationships: trade between the Triad and non-OECD countries (imports and exports of goods as percentage GDP, figures in brackets exclude OPEC trade), 1992 compared with 1962

Source: As fig. 4.2

importance of North–North trade than that between the North and the South as a whole (11 per cent in 1992). Comparing 1962 with 1992 shows that it is the US that was most significantly affected by the growth of North–South trade in terms of ratios of GDP.

Figure 4.5 reveals the extent of overall North–South integration measured in terms of trade in manufactures. While there was some significant growth over thirty years, in terms of OECD GDP, the proportions were still fairly small in 1992, OECD imports from the South being no more than 2.3 per cent of OECD GDP (1.8 per cent for high value-added imports only).[4]

At this stage it is worth summing up what these figures tell us. First of all it is best to compare proportions of trade in terms of national income

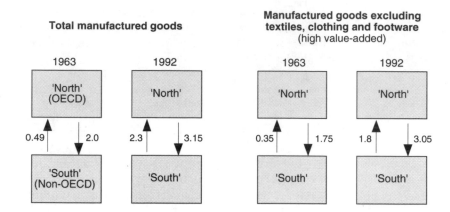

Figure 4.5   North–South trade in manufactures as a percentage of OECD GDP, 1992 compared with 1963

Source: As fig. 4.2

(GDP) to discern the main trends, and particularly the levels of global trade integration. These remained modest in the early and mid 1990s. Secondly, the main changes have been with respect to the position of the US economy within the 'North'. The US economy has shown the biggest propensity to greater openness, largely because its integration began from a very low base in the 1960s.

But what is the problem of North–South relations that these trends and levels are thought to have given rise to? It is the continued 'international competitiveness' of the Northern economies in the production of manufactured goods. Has the growth and greater integration of world trade undermined the manufacturing capacity of the Northern economies as this activity has been relocated to Southern NICs? What has been the impact of this development on employment prospects in the North? Are unemployment and a fall in the real incomes of the less skilled in the North the direct result of the drift of manufacturing jobs to the South? If this were so, then the protectionist sentiment that arose in the US, and to a lesser extent in Europe, in the 1980s would be justified.[5] It is this debate about the causes and consequences of the perceived shift of manufacturing capacity to the South that we take up now.

Broadly speaking, two arguments have been put forward by conventional economics to account for these trends, and more recently they have been joined by a third. The two main arguments concern the effects of trade as opposed to technological developments on employment and wage levels in the North. The third concerns the effects of migration, into the US in particular, on these labour market outcomes. The intention here is not to conduct a blow by blow account of this debate, which is available elsewhere (see Lawrence 1996; Cline 1997, ch. 2; World Bank 1997). Rather we concentrate on key points in the debate and look into the analytical issues raised with respect to the globalization thesis.

Analytical approaches

In conventional economics trade is analysed in the context of the Heckscher-Ohlin/Stolper-Samuelson model of international trade, where trade between countries is driven by comparative advantage and factor endowments. This model, with modifications and variations, is essentially the one deployed by those engaged in the debate about the determinants of US trade with the South. Of course, the Heckscher-Ohlin/Stolper-Samuelson (hereafter H-O/S-S) model is less satisfactory in the context of intra-Triad trade, where it is intra-industry trade that dominates. In this case New Trade Theory (NTT) models are displacing the H-O/S-S factor endowments approach. NTT assumes an oligopolistic market structure, economies of scale (both internal and external), barriers to entry, first mover advantages, technological lock-ins, and the like. These features are what give rise to trade between countries in products with similar factor endowments.

But in the case of the North and the South, where intra-industry trade is much less developed, trade exchange has traditionally been viewed in terms of inter-industry trade. Here trade is between the North, with a highly paid, skilled labour force and a large endowment of advanced capital, and the South, which has a large endowment of unskilled labour and lower wages and levels of capital endowment.[6] The 'natural' pattern of production under these circumstances would be for the North to specialize in high value-added, high skill intensive, technologically advanced products, while the South would specialize in low value-added, low skill intensive and technologically modest products. These would then be traded between the two regions. Thus the migration of manufacturing from the North to the South simply expresses the normal working of the international market system. Its growth is to be expected as a rapidly integrating 'globalization' process based on expanding world markets takes place.

To some extent this pattern of output can be seen from table 4.2. There has been a move away from the production of basic manufactures in the North and a growth of it in the South. But at the same time as complex manufacturing (and traded services) production has been expanding in the North, it has also been growing more rapidly in the South. This has complicated things a little for the simple H-O/S-S framework. In 1990 the non-traded sector was a very similar proportion in both the North and the South, having expanded in both regions since 1970.

Table 4.2   North–South composition of output, 1970 and 1990 (percentage shares of GDP)

	North		South	
	1970	1990	1970	1990
Primary	5.6	4.1	30.6	19.5
Basic manufactures	17.0	12.6	15.0	17.1
Complex manufactures and traded services	26.7	30.0	5.0	7.9
Non-traded sector	52.7	53.4	48.4	55.5

Source: Adapted from Minford, Riley and Nowell 1997, table 2, p. 9

It is in the context of the operation of the general H-O/S-S model that a number of key issues arise. The first concerns the effects of this process of a shift from North to South (if it is operating in this manner) on the labour market conditions in the North.[7] In particular there has been a dramatic undermining of the wages and employment prospects of unskilled labour in the North. This is to be set in the context of a decline in the market power of labour more generally, as real wages fell in the US (and to a lesser and more variable extent elsewhere) during the 1980s and early 1990s (Freeman and Katz 1994). In fact, in the US, inflation-adjusted wages of the less skilled fell in *absolute* terms over the 1980s. Added to this was a generalized growth in wage rate and income inequality in the North and a loss of overall employment security.

Table 4.3 summarizes the position in selected Northern countries with respect to income inequality. With the exception of France and Germany (and possibly Denmark in terms of disposable income), the OECD concludes that there was a general growth in inequality within the countries shown (1997b, p. 51). This was particularly marked in the case of the US, the UK and Italy, which also displayed the highest inequality *levels* in the mid-1990s. What these figures also demonstrate is the considerable variation in the European experience with respect to inequality and labour market outcomes, something returned to later (see also World Bank 1997, chart 25, p. 56).

The question that arises from these data is how this situation came about? Is it mainly due to the growth of trade from the South or are there other reasons? Here the complexity of operationalizing the H-O/S-S approach, and the importance of a range of other considerations that might have accounted for these trends in income distribution, come to the fore. There have been two main lines of analysis, and a subsequent subsidiary one: the trends are attributed to the relocation of manufacturing to the South and the subsequent growth of global trade (an 'international' explanation); to changes in technological developments in the North that have

Table 4.3 Changes in inequality in the North (percentages) and Gini coefficients (figures in brackets)

	Market income	Disposable income
Denmark 1983–94[a]	11.2	−4.9
(1994 level)	(42.0)	(21.7)
Finland 1986–95	11.4	9.7
(1995 level)	(39.2)	(23.0)
France 1979–90	–	−1.7
(1990 level)	–	(29.1)
Germany 1984–94[b]	1.2	6.4
(1994 level)	(43.6)	(28.2)
Italy 1983–93	20.8	12.7
(1993 level)	(51.0)	(34.5)
Netherlands 1977–94	14.2	11.8
(1994 level)	(42.1)	(25.3)
Sweden 1975–94	17.3	0.9
(1994 level)	(48.8)	(23.4)
United States 1974–95	13.1	10.0
(1995 level)	(45.5)	(34.4)
United Kingdom 1977–95/6	20.9	27.6
(1995/6 level)	(52.0)	(37.0)

The higher the Gini coefficient number the higher the inequality; positive changes indicate a growth in inequality.
[a] On other measures Denmark shows a *growth* in inequality.
[b] On other measures Germany shows a *reduction* in inequality.
Sources: UK data derived from *Economic Trends*, no. 520 (Mar. 1997), App. 2, tables 1 and 2, p. 53; all other countries derived from OECD 1997b, table 19, p. 51

worked to the clear disadvantage of the unskilled and manufacturing workers in the North (a 'domestic' explanation); or to the growth of labour migration to the US in particular, especially that of unskilled labour (another 'international' explanation).

The H-O/S-S framework predicts the long-term convergence of factor returns between countries as competitive and relocational processes work themselves out. An interesting parallel investigation arises, then, in the context of the previous era of international integration during the *belle époque* (chapter 2). This was a period that saw unprecedented labour migration, the rapid internationalization of trade and financial flows, and technological advance and its international dissemination. Jeffrey Williamson has analysed the 'convergence thesis' during four distinct periods of internationalization and disengagement experienced by the world economy since the 1830s (Williamson 1995, 1996). The period between 1855 and 1913 saw the most dramatic convergence of real wages (which did not mean their equalization) the world experienced until the late 1980s. For the most part, this convergence was a North–North affair: between real wages in the 'New

World' of Canada, the United States, Australia and Argentina and the 'Old World' of Western Europe. This analysis adds some credence to the trade-as-cause-of-convergence hypothesis, but with a crucial role played by migration (trade accounting for about 30 per cent and migration about 70 per cent of convergence: Williamson 1996, p. 295).

Clearly, such labour migration flows no longer exist – migration from South to North is distinctly modest. Since the skill intensity of technology was much less in the 1890s than in the 1990s, differences here (as proxied by educational levels) did not greatly affect the convergence process, and nor were there particularly strong feedback effects into domestic skilled/unskilled wage rates and labour markets. What this analysis again emphasizes, however, is the fact that contemporary processes of international interconnection, loosely called 'globalization', are by no means unprecedented: although the precise way in which technological development now affects the form of international integration remains potentially of more central concern.

Mechanisms and measures of North–South linkages: results

There are a number of ways of looking at what various factors might contribute to the labour market and income distributional trends mentioned above. First, we could look at the *skill intensity* of the North's imports and exports: the North should export high skill intensive products (and services) and import low skill intensive products (and services). Second, we could concentrate on the *relative price changes* of the low skill intensive and high skill intensive products: the relative price of the low skill intensive products in the North should decline, and vice versa. Third, the *wages* of low skilled labour *relative* to those of high skilled labour should decline in the North. Fourth, *employment* in the North should shift to the high skill intensive output, so that *unemployment* among the low skilled will (temporarily) increase. But, fifth, Northern firms should react to the reduction in the relative wages of unskilled labour by raising the proportions of such labour in the production of *both* high skill intensive and low skill intensive sectors, thereby offsetting the effects in the previous point to some extent. Sixth, we could focus directly on the trends in *technological innovation*, particularly IT, which might lead to a skill-biased technical change (which is in addition to, and independent of, the trend-neutral growth of total factor productivity experienced in advanced economies for over a hundred years). Finally, we could look at the educational and skill trends of *migrants* into (and out of) the North.

This sketches a large canvas. Determining which of these features provides the most significant measure or contribution is not straightforward. Many of these potential effects and candidate influences are highly interdependent and sequentially linked. There is the added problem of constructing relevant counterfactuals. In addition, how should skill be measured – in terms of education, experience, or job classification? As a consequence, estimates of the relative importance of influences vary considerably and are not easily summarized.

Gathered along one dimension are those who think that trade (and hence 'globalization') is the most important contributory factor in the decline of real wages in the US and the plight of unskilled workers in the North as a whole. A key analysis employing the skill factor endowment approach (Wood 1994) found that a substantial proportion of the loss of market power by Northern unskilled workers was the result of the relocation of manufacturing industry and the growth of global trade. Wood argued that taking into account the low skill intensive activities that had already been competitively driven out of the advanced countries (thus looking beyond the *existing* factor proportions in the remaining import-competing industries, the usual approach), and additionally taking into account the fact that a portion of the labour-saving technological change in the North arises from the need for manufacturers to compete with trade from the South, then over 20 per cent of the reduction in the demand for labour in the North was a consequence of trade alone. This claim by Wood was challenged in another influential study by Sachs and Shatz (1994), who estimated a much smaller proportion of trade-related demand influences for the US economy only, much nearer to 6 per cent. Table 4.4 summarizes these estimates, which more or less set the extreme bounds for the generally accepted range of trade-induced influences: between 10 per cent and 20 per cent.

These approaches look at factor (skill) endowments. Thus there is evidence that labour demand has shifted towards skilled workers in advanced countries both *across industries* – in that the share of output produced by low skill intensive industries has fallen relative to that produced by more skill intensive ones – and in terms of demands *within industries* – as firms have shifted away from unskilled towards skilled workers – so that the

Table 4.4 The debate on factor content estimates of the impact of trade with developing countries on demand for labour in 'Northern' manufacturing, 1990 (percentage difference from counterfactual position without trade)

	Wood (All developed economies)	Sachs and Shatz (United States only)
All workers	−10.8	−5.7
Skilled workers	0.3	−4.3
Unskilled workers	−21.5	−6.2
Unskilled minus skilled	−21.8	−1.9

Source: Wood 1995, table 1; see also Sachs and Shatz 1994

prospects of the more skilled workers would seem to have improved even though their relative supply has increased. But, on other evidence, the skill intensity of US manufacturing has risen in both the top end *and* the lower end of the manufacturing sectors: this runs counter to the predictions of the H-O/S-S framework and points to a less than strong impact of trade effects (Krugman and Lawrence 1994, p. 27).

However, these approaches are framed in terms of factor endowments and they can be criticized for not focusing on price changes. This is where the effects of any changes in factor endowments should normally work themselves out. Formally, the H-O/S-S framework operates in terms of price adjustments. There is little evidence that product prices in industrial countries have followed the expected pattern of prices of import-competing, low skill and labour intensive goods falling relative to the prices of high skill embodied and capital intensive goods. The World Bank concludes:

> For manufacturing industries in the industrial countries in the 1980s and 1990s, the prices of goods produced using relatively more skilled labour have for the most part fallen in relation to the prices of goods produced using relatively more unskilled labour. And even after taking into account the effects of technological progress on relative prices, the change in relative prices attributable to international trade has favoured goods produced by low skilled, not high skilled labour. (World Bank 1997, p. 75)

Finally these are partial equilibrium approaches when what is really required is a general equilibrium analysis. Those attempts at providing this (such as Krugman 1995; Cline 1997; Minford, Riley and Nowell 1997) have produced estimates nearer the top end of the spectrum referred to above, with trade contributing about 20 per cent to the rising real wage inequality in the US in the 1980s. In the case of Minford, Riley and Nowell (1997), estimates of these trade effects are even higher, accounting for about 40 per cent of the collapse of Northern unskilled labour employment and wages.[8]

An alternative focus to the trade-as-cause-of-wages-decline approach is to concentrate on the movements of capital in the first instance. The outflow of FDI, with domestic jobs 'exported' to offshore sites, is often thought to be leading to the deindustrialization of the advanced economies and employment loss there. The recent growth of international outsourcing production and the development of value chains, substituting for home production, are an expression of this trend. Thus the activities of MNCs can substitute home exports to other countries by the direct output and supply from offshore production platforms. As we have seen in chapter 3, there is some evidence of this trend developing, but analysis of its importance for the US economy suggests that American firms do not seem to have substituted foreign workers for domestic workers on a large scale (e.g. Feenstra and Hanson 1996). Indeed, the number of foreign workers in US-owned firms peaked in the late 1970s. This trend may be more important for some smaller European economies and Japan, but the problem is how to demonstrate that it is this specific activity that has led to wage inequality rather than other influences.

Other than these moderate 'international' effects, the rest of the collapse in the demand for unskilled labour and wages can be attributable to 'domestic causes'. Here is the second main dimension around which an explanation lies: that of skill-enhancing technical change. From this perspective 'deindustrialization' is in part at least a consequence of the impact of unequal rates of productivity growth in manufacturing and services, which has affected the advanced economies in particular. Those economists who adopt low estimates of the trade influence think the importance of 'international competitiveness' is exaggerated. 'Domestic' influences are more important, and given the generally accepted proportions of between 10 and 20 per cent attributable to trade, 80 to 90 per cent must still be domestic and technological in origin (Krugman and Lawrence 1994; Lawrence and Slaughter 1993). But this is not estimated directly. Technological change cannot be observed and measured with any precision. It is either proxied in equations or emerges as a 'residual' from a production function. Thus skill-biased technical change is invoked as a cause rather than being directly empirically attributable. Usually, it is the low ratios of trade to GDP between the North and the South that act as the background counterfactual here.

Clearly, this type of analysis is not entirely satisfactory. But it serves to indicate that, even with a range of sophisticated econometric and economic modelling techniques, the relative importance of global compared to domestic influences is likely to be low. One problem here is that analyses like those of Wood (1995) cited above, which claim a larger importance for trade effects, already 'account' for some technological change in the estimates because they adjust the counterfactual to include past skill-displacing technical change indirectly induced by international trade with the South. Thus trade and technological change are interdependent and intertwined, so these estimates can be no more than educated guesses. This also leaves room for alternative explanations. Accepting for the moment that the trade influences do lie between 10 and 20 per cent, estimates of the effects of migration (another 'international' explanation) do not add much to this (Borjas, Freeman and Katz 1997). But conventional economic analysis ignores possible explanations other than the indirectly estimated and residual technological change variable.

What is missing from this highly aggregated level of analysis is any focus on the actual strategies of Northern firms, for instance in their dealings with labour. The period from the 1970s has seen an unprecedented attack on labour from the business interest, particularly in the US and the UK. Considering this also raises other structural issues, including the role of bargaining power and collective action. Not all the adjustments can be accounted for simply within the labour market (Howell and Wolff 1991). The period from the New Deal to the mid-1960s in the US was one of a strategic accommodation between business and labour, marked by an acceptance of the legitimate interests of each in the conduct of business activity and in terms of a broad social compromise in economic policy more generally (Roe 1994, part 3; Korten 1995, pp. 1–14). But this compromise was deliberately broken in the mid-1970s in the US and in the UK in particular, just at the time when the increases in inequality referred to above also began to emerge.

What is the possible connection between the loss of market power of manufacturing unskilled workers and the decline in real wages in general? The break in the historical compromise mentioned above saw a renewed attack on the working conditions of American labour, and a release of the constraints on managerial prerogatives and managerial salaries. David Gordon (1996) has documented the consequences of this in detail. His argument is that despite a rhetoric of 'downsizing' in American management speak, the facts go against it. There has been an increase in the numbers and levels of supervisory and management personnel. And this analysis is supported by similar evidence from the UK (Gallie et al. 1998). In addition, the wage bill for this managerial group has expanded at the expense of those very workers who are supervised and managed. In this context a corporate strategy of deliberately undermining the wages of production workers and of cutbacks in shopfloor employment has emerged. This has simultaneously released the restraint on corporate management from rapidly increasing its own remuneration. The coincidental securitization of American savings and the stock market boom have additionally fed the incomes of stockholders. The outcome is the growth in inequality in the US, and to a lesser extent in the UK and elsewhere in Europe.

Here we have the seeds of an alternative explanation for much of the turn against the unskilled worker and the reduction of real wages in the North. This is also an explanation that is resolutely 'domestic' in origin. It provides an account for the missing 80 to 90 per cent that is complementary to that of technical advance.

But this explanation itself is not without its problems. It probably underestimates the extent of downsizing that has occurred in the US. Other accounts testify to a genuine cut in layers of management. It also ignores the increase in high-grade jobs being driven by the growth in technical grade workers in more sophisticated manufacturing processes, who tend to be classified in the supervisory and managerial grades. What is more, the European experience is variable, and it will be useful to deal with this in a little more detail now.

The European experience

The situation in Europe (other than the UK) is often contrasted to the US in terms of the 'inflexibility' of European labour markets. In the US a steep fall in the share of manufacturing employment (though not in absolute numbers, which have remained about the same since 1970), along with a large increase in total civilian employment and relatively low levels of unemployment, mean that the country has absorbed its strong labour supply growth. But this has been at the expense of stagnant earnings, widening income disparities and a substantial amount of poverty among working people. The EU, by contrast, has experienced a fall in manufacturing employment that is both relative and absolute, a very small increase in total employment and high rates of unemployment. But wages levels and income inequalities have not moved so sharply against labour. These differences are put down to a 'flexible' US system that can absorb a growth in the labour supply as wages adjust downwards, and an 'inflexible' European system where, while wage levels for those in employment are maintained, the system cannot create or maintain enough employment opportunities (Siebert 1997).

This rather neat picture is complicated by the facts noted above of the variable growth in inequality among the EU economies. Any shift in the demand away from the less skilled towards the more skilled has had a variable effect on European wage differentials dependent on the particular character of a country's labour market (World Bank 1997, pp. 54–7). As Nickell and Bell (1996) point out, despite the apparent flexibility of wages in the UK, its record on unskilled unemployment was much worse than that of 'rigid' systems like the Netherlands and Germany (p. 303). In particular, while unskilled unemployment was at much the same level in Germany as in the US during the 1980s (and lower than in the UK), German real wages for the bottom decile of male earnings were increasing. This poses the question of how it is that the level of wages for the unskilled was sustainable in Germany – in the early 1990s it was double its US PPP (purchasing power parity) equivalent?

Nickell and Bell argue that this has much to do with the nature of the German education and vocational training system, which produces a more compressed distribution of human capital than the US and UK systems do. In turn this means that there is no large segment of the workforce that simply cannot cope with the employment demands of rapid technical change. The German, Dutch and Swiss educational and training systems put a great deal of emphasis on maintaining high standards for the bottom half of the ability range so as to bring all pupils up to an acceptable level of achievement, and they are prepared to devote resources to this task. Thus we have a picture of a different skill profile in these countries, and in some ways a different practical definition of what 'skill' amounts to. The high skill level of middle-ranking operatives and supervisory staff also helps raise the productivity of the less qualified labour force, which lifts overall productivity above their counterparts in technologically comparable firms in the US and UK. This helps to sustain the high wages of the less skilled in Germany compared to the US, and the lower unemployment rates than in the UK, even though all these countries are suffering from a common move away from unskilled demand.

By looking more generally at the differential institutional natures of labour market operations within Europe, Nickell and Bell (1996; Nickell 1997) are able to clarify the nature of European unemployment. Many labour market characteristics that conventionally appear under the heading of rigidities – like strict employment protection measures and general legislation on labour market standards, or generous levels of unemployment benefits (so long as these are accompanied by pressures on the unemployed to take jobs), or high levels of unionization (so long as these are offset by high levels of coordination in wage bargaining, particularly among employers) – have no observable impact on unemployment, particularly of the unskilled. These patterns are somewhat different from the US, indicating a potentially different problem and explanation.[9]

International competitiveness and globalization

At the root of a concern about the effects of the growth of North–South trade is the question of the continued 'international competitiveness' of the Northern economies. As mentioned above, the issue of international competitiveness has grown alongside the concern about the effects of globalization – they are parallel developments. But there are probably five relatively separate trends that can account specifically for this growth in the discourse of competitiveness.

The first, and most obvious, has to do with the collapse of the Cold War. While the Cold War prevailed, competitiveness remained couched in fundamentally geopolitical terms: the struggle between the two main politico-ideological blocs locked all remaining world issues into a single geomilitary confrontation. Once this was over, the *differences* between countries came newly to the fore, and particularly the differences between them in terms of their economic performance as measured by their 'competitiveness'.

A second important development was the perceived unsuccessful nature of large-scale and grandiose 'industrial policy' initiatives. Twenty-five years ago critical economic analysis was much more concerned about different industrial policies and restructuring initiatives by states. These are now perceived to have been a failure (though we do not endorse the view that all industrial policy initiatives were in fact failures). In the wake of this, it is the emphasis on 'competitiveness' that has taken hold of both the private and public consciousness in terms of economic matters: intervention is to be confined to making markets work better.

A third trend is the move towards policies of liberalization and privatization in terms of domestic institutional changes. Although these are often argued to be the results of internationalization and even the globalization of economic activity, we would suggest that fundamentally they have been driven by domestic decisions and policy changes (e.g. Thompson 1997). Whatever the reason, however, the result has been a reinvigorated emphasis on competition and market-driven solutions to economic problems.

A fourth issue involves the relative 'success' of those mainly intergovernmental organizations of international economic regulation and management that have governed the world economy in the post-Second World War period, such as the OECD, the GATT/WTO, the IMF and the World Bank. The activity of these organizations has resulted in a general opening up of the world economies as protectionist barriers to economic activity were eliminated or drastically reduced. In the absence of tariff barriers or capital controls, the underlying economic competitiveness of different countries has been exposed, hence the growth in concern with this aspect of their economies.

Finally, the growth of interdependences and integrations among the world's major economies since the end of the Second World War, limited though this process is, has served to announce afresh the importance of the relative competitiveness of different countries.

Thus there is a clear relationship between the growth of a concern with international competitiveness and that of 'globalization', something we return to in a moment. First we outline in more detail the main ways in which 'international competitiveness' is discussed in the international political economy literature, since this can act as a frameworking device for the rest of the analysis. We then move on to look specifically at the economics literature, where different conceptions of and emphases on international competitiveness are considered. The discussion is undertaken with the UK position to the forefront, since it is an interesting example, but placed in a comparative international context.

Explanatory frameworks for international competitiveness

The first explanatory framework can be termed the 'domestic interests approach'. Essentially, this looks for the *sources* of international competitiveness, and seeks them in the configuration of *domestic* relations between the 'interest groups' or 'social partners'. It is illustrated in figure 4.6 by Jeffrey Hart's diagram of the positions of postwar advanced industrial economies, where the interest groups in this case are business, labour and the state (Hart 1992).

This is part of a much larger body of literature in the international political economy (IPE) tradition that stresses similar patterns and processes for understanding outcomes for national economic performance. In this analysis, those countries whose economic organization is dominated by an exclusive attachment to a single nodal interest group have suffered relative to those where organization is more broadly balanced. The strategic choice

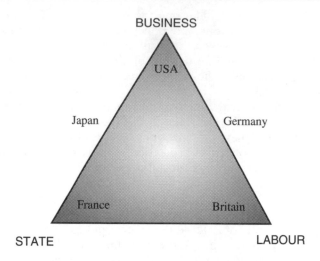

Figure 4.6   The domestic interests approach
Source: Hart 1992, p. 281

offered to the US and Britain, for instance, to improve their competitive performance is to move towards a position similar to the one already occupied by Japan and Germany respectively.

A number of critical comments can be made about this approach. While its continued usefulness should not be totally denied, the overall result looks dated. Britain, for instance, can scarcely still be placed in the position as illustrated – as completely beholden to labour – yet its performance has not greatly improved, continuing to suffer from relative decline. Germany and Japan are also in flux in respect to the 'balanced' position, with a faltering in the latter's economy in particular. In addition there is a question as to the accuracy of the original positioning anyway. Was the state quite so unimportant to the economic success of postwar Germany as suggested by this diagram? Similar comments could be made about the US. And perhaps the key role played by the state in Japan has been exaggerated. Broadly speaking, this analysis relies on a particular configuration of postwar social settlements in each country, one that is now being eroded by neoliberal policy changes and international integrative developments. While the full consequences of these for comparative international competitiveness remain unclear, they reduce confidence in the model as outlined. However, it is important to recognize that the central point of this analysis – the significance of the balance between the social interest groups – remains a pertinent one even if its basis is being eroded.

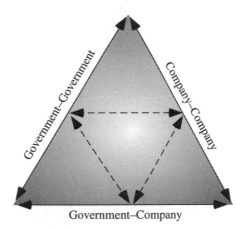

Figure 4.7   The actor interactions approach
Source: Stopford and Strange 1991, p. 22

The second approach stresses the interactions between key actors in the conduct of *international* economic relations rather than domestic ones. Here the actors are more narrowly drawn than in figure 4.6. In figure 4.7 just two key agents are identified – governments and companies – and the issue is the relationships between them. Stopford and Strange (1991), on which figure 4.7 draws, suggest that the key to international competitiveness now lies within the lower righthand corner of the figure. It is government–company relationships (and to a lesser extent company–company relationships) that provide the arenas in which decisions for international competitiveness will be decided or fought over. They see international competitiveness as being conditioned by both comparative and competitive advantages (although the differences between these, and the relative importance attributed to each of them, are not sufficiently distinguished in their analysis, see below). In addition, they pay particularly close attention to the business tactics and strategies of multinational corporations, though without neglecting the role of purely domestic companies. An added feature of the Stopford and Strange approach is to downplay government–government interactions as the strategic site for international competitiveness struggles.

The actor interactions approach highlighted in figure 4.7 has some obvious virtues. But the analysis also suffers from a number of weaknesses. First, its analysis of government–company interactions is directed at the

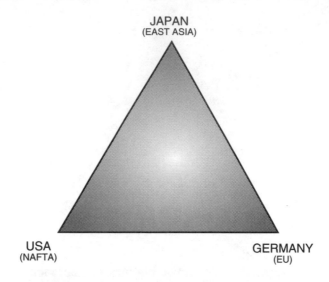

Figure 4.8   The geo-economic approach
Source: Derived from Sandholtz et al. 1992

relationships between the less developed economies and multinational corporations in the main, so the role of the governments of the more developed countries as continued strategic players in their own right is somewhat
neglected. Secondly, the complexity of the strategies, tactics, locational decisions, governmental reactions and the like explored in the analysis does not
lend itself easily to any generalization. The analysis concentrates on agents
at the expense of structures and thus can shed little light on the general
nature of the internationalized economy in which the actors operate. The
sources of competitiveness are thus multiple and unlikely to be system-
atized. It is all 'complex process' with no simple model as to where that
process might lead, either intellectually or practically.

The final approach discussed in this section is illustrated by figure
4.8. The geo-economic approach stresses the strategic interrelationship
between the three main player countries/blocs in the international
system: the Triad. The 1992 analysis by Sandholtz et al. (collectively known
as the Berkeley Roundtable on the International Economy (BRIE))
is overwhelmingly concerned with redefining the nature of international
security, where it sees the issue of international competitiveness as being
critical.

Two main issues drive this analysis: the collapse of the Cold War and
the decline of US hegemony. The first is seen as heralding the potential
end of geopolitics as a new geo-economics based on international

competitiveness replaces it. The emphasis shifts from a predominantly militarily driven system of interstate/interbloc rivalry, based on deep ideological and systemic socioeconomic organizational differences, to a system based around 'peaceful' economic competition between states/blocs with military matters subsidiary to this (at least in the first instance). The second implicates the US's ability to 'manage' the newly evolving system and determine its own security. The decline of hegemony is put down to a decline in economic power and the loss of international competitiveness, so the remedy is obvious – to restimulate the American economy. But how? This question, of course, has preoccupied American analysts since the 1970s.

The geo-economics approach has the advantage of setting the problem of competitiveness squarely within an international system, and one where state/bloc rivalry between the advanced industrial states continues to figure prominently. The thrust of the approach is to look for the possible *consequences* of a differential or similar competitiveness record among the Triad (in terms of its security implications), rather than to concentrate on the *causes* of any differential competitiveness (though this element is by no means neglected). Although the nodal points in figure 4.8 are represented by single countries (Japan, USA and Germany), a feature of the analysis is to link these to the formation of definite economic blocs (indicated by East Asia, NAFTA and the EU). An obvious potential problem here is whether such an East Asian bloc, formed around Japan, is actually emerging: recent events in East Asia might seem to have further undermined this. The EU looks the most coherent bloc (see chapter 8), with NAFTA some way behind in terms of institution building. In so far as there is an East Asian bloc forming around Japan, it is driven by commercial activity rather than by any institution building. Explicit and complex institution building is eschewed by the 'Asian way' and rejected within the APEC process, for instance (Yamazawa 1998).

Exploring the geo-economic approach

The geo-economic approach represents the most fruitful way of thinking about the question of international competitiveness and its implications. As pointed out in chapter 3 the Triad alone was responsible for 60 per cent of FDI flows during the first half of the 1990s, some 66 per cent of trade in 1996, and 75 per cent of world GNP. Since the mid-1980s the growth of FDI has eclipsed that of trade growth and now figures as the central driving force in the international economy. Although the growth of FDI flows declined somewhat in the early 1990s, and their direction of flow moved more in favour of the non-Triad countries, the older pattern began to re-establish itself again after 1992 (see figure 3.2 above, p. 71).

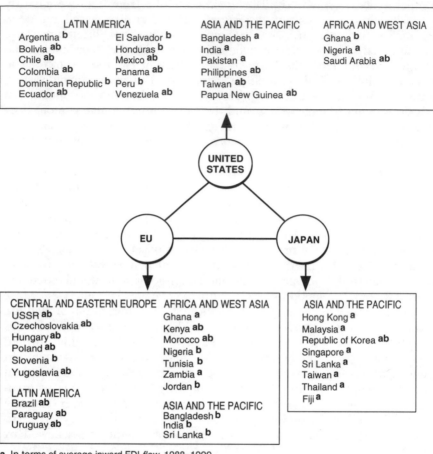

a In terms of average inward FDI *flow*, 1988–1990.
b In terms of inward FDI *stock* for 1990.

Figure 4.9   Foreign direct investment clusters of Triad members, 1990
(economies in which a Triad country dominates inward FDI stocks/flows)
Source: UNCTAD database

In addition, the intra-Triad dominance is reinforced by important subsidiary flows of investment between the three blocs and a geographically discrete group of smaller 'associated' countries. Thus by the mid-1990s relatively isolated clusters of main actor and client states were beginning to emerge, geographically discrete and stabilizing. The essential character of this process is illustrated in figure 4.9, which shows which member of the Triad dominates the inward FDI in particular countries (which was paralleled by trade flows in an even more intensive form).

Thus while *intra*-Triad investment (and trade) relationships were particularly dense, a pattern of further discrete but robust *inter*linkages between each of the Triad members and more marginalized country clusters was also evident. These country groupings tended to be regionally specific and adjacent to one or other of the Triad members. Further, this testifies to the relative *lack of global integration* in FDI flows and stocks since the clusters indicate a geographical and regional discreteness in the relationships between countries. The directions of FDI relationships were first among the Triad countries themselves and then secondly between one or other of the Triad powers and its cluster of client states, rather between these clustered states themselves. Thus the EU countries had their strongest and most intense trade and investment relationships first with other EU countries themselves, and then with the countries of Eastern Europe and with some in North Africa. The US had its strongest and most intense relationships with the other NAFTA countries and the rest of Latin America (and with some in Asia). Finally, Japan had the strongest ties with the other East Asian countries, particularly in terms of investments.

In fact, since this analysis was completed there has been some growth of intra-cluster trade and investment relationships, for instance, between the clusters of countries shown in the square boxes in figure 4.9. Attentive readers will have noticed that mainland China is not included among the countries shown in figure 4.9. But during the 1990s mainland China went on to become the largest single developing country recipient of inward FDI. Most of this is organized by overseas Chinese business interests, so an alternative supply network to those depicted in the figure has emerged. In addition, there has been a rapid growth of inter-cluster trade and investment relationships among some of the countries shown in the square boxes, such as the MERCOSUR countries in the southern cone of South America (if from a very low base). These trends are tending to obscure the picture that emerges from figure 4.9, but as yet they are not strong ones and even if they continue it will take a very long time before the established pattern depicted by the figure is undermined. If we were to take just ten of the countries outside of the Triad which were most favoured in terms of FDI flows in the first half of the 1990s, then together with the Triad these would have accounted for 84 per cent of FDI flows. This highly concentrated pattern has become well established and will take a long time to undo: the Triad will continue to dominate for the foreseeable future.

Measures and trends in international economic competitiveness

This section moves away from the analysis of the overall framework for international competitiveness to look more closely at the idea of international *economic* competitiveness. There are two main ways international competitiveness is discussed in the literature: in terms of 'ability to sell' and 'locational attractiveness'. Accepting for a moment the usefulness of the notion of 'national competitiveness', a country's ability to sell internationally will depend on its relative cost structure, productivity and exchange rate, so the policy areas are clear (Thompson 1987; Auerbach 1996). The ability to sell approach is the traditional one. It focuses on the current account of the balance of payments, particularly the trade account. A premier measure of competitiveness is the relative unit labour cost (RULC), usually in manufacturing.

The locational attractiveness approach arises in the context of the internationalization and efficiency of financial markets, increased capital mobility and the way that intertemporal investment decisions are thought to follow a logic of utility maximization in an interdependent world. This approach stresses how balance of payments adjustments are secured via capital flows, and puts more emphasis on the decisions of private agents in terms of their investment choices and less emphasis on public policy, thus focusing on the capital account of the balance of payments. The premier measures of competitiveness in this approach are FDI and other investment flows. The policy areas here have to do with making a country attractive for investors, so they embrace a wider set of options than just the traditional ones associated with the ability to sell.

Although these two approaches are often presented as though it is a matter of choice between them, they are in fact complementary and interdependent. It is useful to examine how the UK and other main economies have fared in relationship both to ability to sell and ability to attract investment over the post-Second World War period.

In the case of the RULC and 'ability to sell', the long-term trend until the late 1970s was for the UK economy to show an *improving* competitiveness position. There was a dramatic loss of international competitiveness between 1979 and 1981, and then after 1984 a restoration of the longer term trend of improving competitiveness, measured by RULC. The story for the US economy is much the same, though its loss of competitiveness lasted longer in the 1980s (to 1985), before the re-emergence of the older trend. The sources of improvements in the UK were mainly through exchange rate adjustments (devaluations), while for the US they were mainly through domestic labour cost adjustments. Comparing these experiences with those of Japan and Germany is instructive, since the trends in those countries were more or less exactly the opposite. Japan and Germany had been *losing* competitiveness in RULC terms over almost the entire period since the 1960s (Thompson 1987, 1998c).

Thus the counterintuitive paradox here, first noted by Kaldor in the 1970s (Kaldor 1978), was that as the US and the UK were improving their international competitiveness, they were losing on their trade accounts, and while Japan and Germany were losing their international competitiveness, they were improving or maintaining their trade account surpluses. In fact,

Table 4.5   The 'Kaldor paradox' re-examined, twelve industrialized countries, 1978–1994

	Growth in market share for exports[a]	Growth in relative unit labour cost[a]	Growth in GDP per capita at constant prices[a]	Change in R&D as a share of GDP[b]
US	0.08	–1.17	1.36	0.24
Japan	0.95	0.82	2.94	1.10
Germany	–1.03	1.62	1.65	0.23
France	–0.98	–0.18	1.36	0.54
Italy	–0.16	–1.13	2.00	0.59
UK	–0.89	0.81	1.57	–0.01
Canada	–0.10	–0.38	0.97	0.36
Belgium-Luxembourg	–0.89[c]	–2.85[c]	1.70	0.31
Netherlands	–1.53	–1.60	1.23	0.13
Korea	4.85	1.89	6.33[c]	1.16
Taiwan	4.68	3.77	5.94[d]	1.13
Hong Kong	8.36	2.58	5.35[c]	n.a
Regression on growth in market share[e]				
slope		1.17 (0.36)	1.43 (0.21)	4.48 (0.94)
R^2		0.52	0.82	0.71

[a] Annual rate of growth.
[b] Difference between 1992 and 1979 levels of R&D as a share of GDP.
[c] 1978–92.
[d] 1978–91.
[e] Estimated by ordinary least squares with constant term (not reported), standard deviation in brackets, 12 observations except for R&D (11 observations).
Source: Fagerberg 1996, p. 41

this seeming paradox is one shared for a larger range of advanced economies, as shown by the figures in table 4.5.[10] The relationship between the growth in market share of exports and the growth in relative unit labour cost (cols 1 and 2) is *positive* and *greater than 1* (slope 1.17) for the twelve countries examined. Thus as relative unit labour costs increase so does the market share, exactly the opposite to that predicted by conventional theory. Note also the positive relationship between the growth in market share for exports and the change in R&D as a share of GDP (cols 1 and 4). The very strong correlation and high value of the slope indicates the way market share is driven by technological innovation rather than by relative labour costs.

This result is an important one in circumstances where governments insist on driving down their relative labour costs in the name of some expected beneficial effects to their current account: if historical experience is anything to go by there may be no such benefits. To a large extent it is this kind of a result that led to a disillusionment with the RULC measure of international competitiveness, and the rise in popularity of the locational advantage approach. We now examine this in the UK context.

A great deal is made of the record of the UK as a destination for FDI, demonstrating the success of liberalization, deregulation and policies for flexibility adopted in the UK over the past fifteen years or so. However, this success should not be exaggerated. The UK has been a consistent *net exporter* of FDI in every year since the growth of FDI took off in the early 1980s, except for small surpluses in 1982 and 1990. In addition, the UK has been a net exporter of portfolio investment (HM Treasury 1996). During the 1980s it became the largest single outward investor in the world. The result was that in 1995, while the stock of inward FDI was £160 billion, the stock of outward investment was much larger at £219 billion. This would seem to point to the 'locational non-attractiveness' of the UK economy in this regard. The only large industrial economy that displays a long-term locational advantage on this measure is the US, which after 1983 became a consistent net importer of capital (this position changed in the early 1990s, however). The other major European economies and Japan, for instance, have also been net exporters, mainly to the US, the southern EU members and East Asia. This might seem to be expected and unex-ceptional – the rich countries with 'excess' capital exporting it to the poorer ones with high demands – *except* for the highly anomalous position shown by the US. The US proves the rule by undermining the commonly accepted approach.

The argument about the UK's unique attractiveness as a destination for foreign investment in Europe is also undermined by the fact that France had larger FDI inflows than the UK did between 1991 and 1995, despite all the talk about the supposed detrimental effects of the Social Chapter (Barrell and Pain 1997, table 2, p. 65). UK companies were the largest single investor in France over this period. The benefits of inward investment to the UK also tend to be exaggerated given that a growing percentage is accounted for by service industry investments, which have not shown significant increases in productivity, and are mainly the results of takeover and acquisition activity.

An important (policy) issue arises here concerning the quality of official analysis in this area. It is claimed that inward investment has served to pre-serve 770,000 British jobs (HMSO 1996, p. 139), but given the net FDI exporting position, would we not expect there to be an overall *net loss* of jobs as well? British industry is being 'hollowed out' by this process. As far as can be judged there are no official UK calculations of this potential impact. By contrast, other advanced countries do make these kinds of calculations. MITI, for instance, estimates that Japanese multinationals operating abroad employed just under 2 million workers in 1993, while multinationals from overseas operating in Japan employed only 169,000 workers (MITI 1996a, p. 25; 1996b, p. 24).

Secondly, it is claimed that outward FDI added positive flows to the UK balance of payments in terms of interest, profit and dividend receipts: £24 billion in 1995. But the net position was much less, at only £6 billion. In addition, there is a possible loss of *export receipts* to the UK economy as a result of the net export of its investment capital. The MITI studies mentioned above follow up the basic statement of the net employment loss position with a discussion of the possible 'second round' impacts of the net export of FDI. Their argument is that Japanese overseas FDI has had an overall positive impact on the Japanese economy and on Japanese employment (MITI 1996a, pp. 38–42). This is because that investment has stimulated the purchase of Japanese capital goods. Such an 'export inducement effect' has outweighed the 'export substitution effect'. But this is not quantified in the report. It is only asserted, with the proviso that this net positive impact could soon wear off as the overseas investment 'matures'. An important implication of this for the advanced countries, therefore, is that they should establish a serious and ongoing 'social audit' of the full consequences of FDI flows into and out of their economies, so as to provide proper information on which to base public discussion and official decision-making.

Clearly, both the approaches indicated above suffer analytical and policy problems, so perhaps we should not expect too much from either of them. The RULC approach continues to emphasize international cost and price competition. A possible resolution of the 'Kaldor paradox' mentioned above, then, is to highlight 'quality' rather than 'quantity' as the growing determinant of international success (which is itself linked to the technological inventiveness aspect, as indicated above in relation to table 4.5). In principle, this would seem extremely important and potentially fruitful. While it would be impossible to ignore prices and costs altogether, the emphasis is shifting to quality indicators. The disastrous consequences of ignoring quality can be judged by the recent beef crisis in the UK. The Anglo-American tradition tends to leave these important matters either to self-regulation, or to the concerns of the consumption end of economic activity (retail chains and consumer choice), or to universalized information dissemination and packaging. In the EU, and elsewhere, it is managed much more at the production level, or in relation to *local* producer and municipal organizations (who do the monitoring themselves), and has a stronger institutional base. The advantage of establishing, monitoring and regulating quality is that it is not so affected by 'globalization' as are other more overt policy initiatives. It need not implicate treaty commitments already entered into with international organizations governing trade and commerce.

One way this has taken hold internationally (but perhaps only half-heartedly in the UK) is via 'benchmarking' and quality standards like the ISO 9000 process. The problem with this, however, is that it cannot do more than encourage a simple 'copying' of already existing products, techniques and processes, mirroring current best practice. Competitive advantage is gained by an innovative capacity to jump to a new performance plateau. Benchmarking generalizes existing best practice, it locks in the past rather than promoting radical innovation. By and large, British companies in particular are unused to institutionalized innovation and are often openly hostile to the levels of cooperation with labour and other firms that it requires. If companies refuse to cooperate, however, there is little that can be done. In general terms the UK has a smaller stock of 'world class companies' than the size of its economy would warrant. A programme of international benchmarking might serve to even up performance, but in the absence of an appropriate system of innovation it is unlikely to leap ahead of competitors on quality.

An important recent development in the international competitiveness debate is the entry of new private bodies into the field of information gathering and provision. A classic example of this is the World Economic Forum that operates from Geneva. This produces an index of 'international competitiveness' compiled from a range of eighty separate measures. Its 1997 overall ranking is shown in figure 4.10.

Clearly, some of these placings are highly suspect, but journalists and politicians tend to ignore the methodological limitations and only read the headline figures. This kind of an exercise serves to bolster the centrality of the notion of international competitiveness to contemporary economic discussion. The problem with these kinds of rankings is that they depend critically on surveying business opinion – hence they tend to magnify dissatisfaction by managers and reflect plain ignorance of real economic conditions.

The competitiveness of countries and the competitiveness of companies

The introduction of the nature of companies and their attitudes serves to raise a number of other issues associated with international competitiveness. The RULC and FDI measures pertain to economies rather than to companies, and it may be worthwhile trying to keep these two apart at a number of levels. To start with there is the difference between comparative advantage and competitive advantage: the one pertaining to the national economy, the other to the companies that make it up. In terms of conventional trade theory an economy always has a *comparative advantage* in some line of production, so there are always mutual gains from trade. This rather attractive outcome specified by the theory may, however, not be the case if we take seriously the notion of *competitive advantage*. It is not clear that an economy will always have a competitive advantage in some line of production if such an advantage is dependent on the success of its companies. Companies have to *organize* production and this capacity cannot be derived from aggregate economic functions like relative costs. Some countries' companies may be unsuccessful in internationally traded lines of production while other countries' companies are widely successful. This is especially so if we take

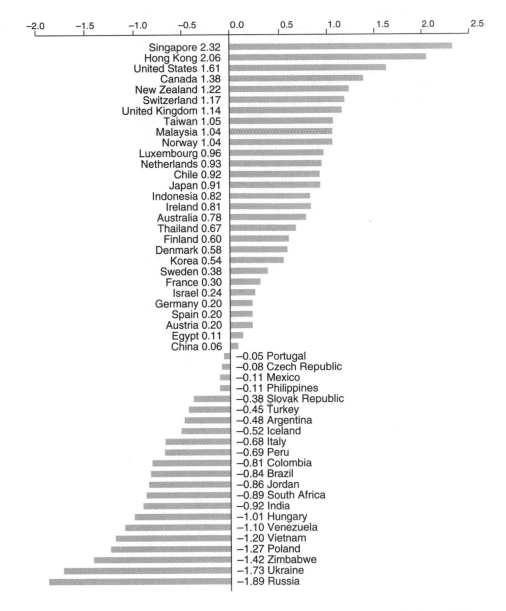

Figure 4.10 World Economic Forum global competitiveness index, 1997

Source: The Global Competitiveness Report 1997, World Economic Forum, Geneva

seriously the literature on dynamic increasing returns modelling (Arthur 1996). Bandwagon effects, positive feedbacks, learning by doing, etc., can all lead to successful cumulative growth trajectories for companies or products, so that they completely outcompete others (and yet these may not necessarily lead to the most efficient or optimal outcomes overall, see also Kaldor 1981). On the other hand, those companies that are outperformed will suffer from a cumulative decline and eventually go out of business.

If one country has a critical mass of internationally competitively successful companies located on its territory, that country will demonstrate a *revealed absolute competitive advantage*, characterized by an increasing share of world trade and/or sustained appreciation of its currency. If a country is unlucky enough to have a set of companies located on its territory who lose out in the competitive struggle, then a cumulative downward spiral might result. Thus, conceptions of revealed *absolute* competitive advantage may be more important than comparative (*relative*) advantage ones. Here we must register a crucial distinction, however. Conceptions of absolute competitive advantage would apply to those sectors, usually manufacturing and services, where competitive advantage can be deliberately created and fostered (either by public policy or the policies pursued by firms). This includes the developments associated with intra-industry trade in particular. Comparative advantage would still seem to apply to those sectors whose success remains dependent on natural comparative factor endowments, like primary production (agriculture and mineral extraction). These formulations, then, add to the critique of the H-O/S-S approach to the skill factor endowment analysis associated with the discussion of the effects of North–South trade made earlier in this chapter.

Even perceptive commentators on these matters often fail to fully register these key conceptual distinctions about trade theory (e.g. Porter 1990; Kay 1994). Kay has argued, for instance, that the UK maintains a national *comparative* advantage in areas where the English language is important (publishing and audio-visual media; tertiary education) and in areas like chemicals and pharmaceuticals, aviation electronics and engines, insurance and some other financial services, and retailing. These have been British success stories, based on the competitiveness of British firms. Clearly, in our terminology, the key to a revealed *competitive* advantage for the UK economy is the competitive advantage of the companies in these fields. It is important, therefore, for both companies and governments to recognize and foster those factors that account for the present conditions of successful company performance, and to nurture those conditions that may constitute new competitive advantages in the future.

From the Kay perspective, however, there is little point in trying to enhance the existing domestic competitive configuration of sectors or branches where other countries and their firms already demonstrate current comparative advantage. Trying to emulate the current comparative success of elsewhere is unlikely to enhance the long-run strengths of the home economy, he argues. However, this can be successful at times, as is shown by the decision to foster the European civilian aircraft industry against the predominant strength of that of the US. Again, Italy should have withdrawn from sectors like clothing and footwear, where low wage countries have a strong comparative advantage: yet these two sectors are major Italian export success stories. Thus, contrary to Kay's argument, a country should not totally write off the potential of a coordinated attempt to emulate or outperform already highly successful international competitor companies.

A further important consequence of stressing the differences between companies and countries is that we can draw a sharper distinction between what might be good for a company and what might be good for an economy. These two do not always coincide. For instance, what firms do to improve their international efficiency and competitiveness may have detrimental effects on the economy as a whole, as in the case of the way the labour market operates to displace problems of employment and training away from firms and on to the economy as a whole. The decisions of companies over FDI mentioned above is another potential example of this mismatch. Thus there may well be very efficient and internationally competitive firms operating in an economy while that economy overall is becoming less internationally competitive or declining relatively. Indeed, this could be the emerging pattern of the UK economy: small 'pockets' of economic efficiency, wealth and competitiveness, coalescing around successful firms or branches of industry, coexisting with a generalized poor performance of the aggregate economy characterized by stagnation, growing poverty, inequality and inefficiency. The future for the UK, therefore, could be a form of 'leopard spot' economy – patches of success against a background of increasing social degradation and poverty.

An important corollary of this is the question as to whether it is sensible to think of countries competing economically at all. While companies clearly compete – they can either grow and expand or go out of business – countries cannot go bankrupt and disappear in the same way if they are not economically successful. They merely get relatively poorer. The only way a country can disappear is if it is conquered by another after a war, or if it agrees to merge with another. Thus the type of competition that countries are involved in *qua* countries is arrayed along quite a different dimension from that given by conventional economics. Clearly, there is some truth in this argument, and in an ultimate sense countries do not compete among themselves in quite the same way as companies do, or with the same consequences. But at another level countries clearly do compete in economic terms, even if just to attract FDI. But their competition is also wider than this, expressed in terms of such diverse characteristics as comparative living standards and military power.

Finally there is one further big difference between firms and nations in regard to their economic activity. Firms tend to 'export' the vast bulk of their produce: well up to 99 per cent, one suspects. They sell it on the market 'outside' of their own institutional boundaries and they do not consume much of it themselves or allow their own workers to do so. Indeed, they do not sell much on the open market to their own workers either. However, this is not the case with nations. The bulk of their product (measured by GDP) is consumed 'internally', and by their own citizens, so that only a small percentage is exported. This varies between countries, of course. While the US exported just over 14 per cent of its GDP in 1996, the UK exported much more at nearly 30 per cent and Germany a slightly lower proportion at 25 per cent. But, as has been pointed out by Krugman (1994a), the three Triad economic blocs as a whole (the US, Japan and the EU) exported about the same amount – 10 to 11 per cent in 1993 (see table 4.6 below: the reason for the differences between individual EU countries and the EU as a whole is accounted for by intra-EU country trade).

The point made by Krugman is that perhaps the emphasis given to trade and international competitiveness in popular economic and political discussion is misplaced if it involves only about 11 per cent of GDP. For the purposes of economic growth and living standards, the real issue then becomes one of changes in national productivity *per se* without worrying too much about the international dimension or international comparisons. Here we revisit the issues raised in the first part of this chapter. It means that considerations of international competitiveness should only pertain to a much smaller section of the economy – the internationally traded sector – and we should resist the 'expansion' of the concern about being 'internationally competitive' to all other aspects of economic life. There remains a large 'sheltered sector', particularly involving welfare expenditures and a large section of the privately traded service economy, that is not – and need not be – subject to all the vagaries and pressures associated with being 'internationally competitive'. Hence the absurdity of using 'international competitiveness' as a justification for driving down wages and conditions in areas such as office cleaning and similar non-tradable service activities. The world's janitors and cleaners do not 'compete'.

Clearly, this argument is all very well and has its place. But it could be accused of complacency. Engaging in international trade has important 'demonstration effects' for domestic economic activity overall and potential 'learning effects' for new exporters. Without it the general level of domestic productivity for those sectors not engaged in international trade could easily fall behind best practice and their activity levels could stagnate. The issue for policy is to strike a balance between competitive performance in the internationally traded sector and conditions in the rest of the economy. The rhetoric of 'competitiveness' should not be used to justify exploitation and 'sweating'. Equally the non-traded sectors must not set the cost floor so high that it damages exporters.

Table 4.6 Developments in the openness of economies, 1972–1996 (sum of exports and imports as a percentage of GDP, market prices)

	1972	1982	1992	1996	1996 (PPP)[a]
US	12	19	22	25	19.4
Japan	19	28	17	19	26.1
EU15	14.2	20.7	14.8	17.2[b]	–
Asian NICs[c]					
Hong Kong	122	146	252	269	248
Singapore	192	321	279	325	316
Taiwan	70	87	74	80	–
Korea	39	62	51	69	47
Thailand	31	42	66	92	31
Indonesia	29	41	48	52	14
Malaysia	63	91	139	202	70
Philippines	30	36	48	85	21
India	7	13	16	24	5
China	–	15	36	37	7
Eastern Europe					
Hungary	67	77	61	59	41
Poland	–	33	35	62	27
Czechoslovakia	–	66	82	125[d]	46[d]

[a] PPP defined as the number of units of a country's currency required to buy the same amount of goods and services in the domestic market as $1 could buy in the US.
[b] 1995.
[c] Sum of merchandise trade (1996) and service trade (1995) expressed as proportion of 1996 GDP.
[d] Czech Republic only.
Sources: Compiled from: *Bank of England Quarterly Bulletin* (Feb. 1996), table B, p. 72; *European Economy* (EU), 42 (1989); 58 (1994); 63 (1997); *Statistical Yearbook of the Republic of China*, 1983, 1993, 1997; *WTO Annual Report 1997*, vol 2, tables 1.5 (p. 4) and 1.7 (p. 5); PPP figures from *World Bank Atlas 1998*

We can also take these arguments one step further by considering the comparative data given in table 4.6. There may be dangers when *too great* a proportion of economic activity is devoted to the international market. Table 4.6 gives data on the general openness of economies (exports plus imports as a percentage of GDP) over the period between 1972 and 1996.

Clearly countries like Thailand, Malaysia, Hong Kong, Singapore, Taiwan, Korea and the Philippines were the vulnerable ones in the international economy. Their whole prosperity was built on exporting, without a large 'sheltered' domestic sector to fall back on. The less vulnerable economies are those like the Triad with 75–80 per cent of their GDP as purely domestic economic activity, able to act as a cushion in times of recession. These economies can more easily ride out any downturn in global economic activity that might be caused by trade policy or other economic changes. Most of the East Asian NICs, for instance, are in effect trade policy captives of either the US, Japan or the EU. In the run-up to the recent crisis they were heavily dependent on these advanced countries, having had large trade surpluses with one or other of them. Changes in domestic policy sentiment in the Triad economies could have serious impacts on the East Asian NICs in the future. The East Asian NICs are clearly highly dependent on the continuation of a liberal and open international trading system, something that still rests largely in the hands of the Triad. Of course, if these NICs mature, they may well follow the characteristics of the older advanced economies and become less dependent on trade for their prosperity. These points should warn us against losing sight of the continued structural vulnerability of the East Asian NICs. Recent events have proved that they were not as competitive as they seemed, or as we were led to fear, as we shall see in chapter 5 when the East Asian crisis is discussed in more detail.

Some final considerations

A great deal is made in policy circles of the need to improve the overall supply side of the older advanced economies, by promoting specific education and training programmes, improving R&D expenditures, creating the 'climate for enterprise', etc. (e.g. HMSO 1994). But we should be modest in our expectations about policies designed to promote international competitiveness organized around the concerns expressed earlier in this chapter. Historical reflection demonstrates that there is no systematic or robust evidence to causally link economic innovativeness, educational levels, R&D expenditures, training competencies, or any of the other worthy but specific supply-side initiatives that are often spoken about, with long-term international economic performance and success (Edgerton 1996). Much more important than these specific measures are the general institutionalized operation of the labour market (for instance, centralized versus decentralized bargaining), the forms of the 'social settlement' between the social partners or organized interest groups, the form of the financial system, the constitutional nature of company governance systems, and so on. The question is, how far are these institutionalized structural features of economies open to reform or policy initiatives? In chapter 6 on the welfare state we shall see some examples of policies that effectively deviate from the previous path of development, most notably in Italy and the Netherlands. However, one must be cautious as to how effectively basic institutions and social patterns can be changed by deliberate public policy.

As a final footnote it should be emphasized that all these approaches concentrate exclusively on *economic* measures of international competitiveness. But it is worth making the point that the narrowly defined way in which the international competitiveness debate has been set up leads to a neglect of other important elements that go to make a nation 'competitive', many of which are non-economic. For instance, the idea that a country can be successful in the modern world without having a lively, innovative, pluralistic and open political and aesthetic culture is hardly credible. Yet these are precisely the issues neglected and dismissed by the headlong rush to redefine everything in terms of economic competence and managerial prerogatives. A country that refuses to actively foster a critical 'culture of ideas' could quickly become marginalized and isolated. This will eventually impact on its 'international competitiveness' in an adverse way.

Conclusions

The are a number of concluding points that arise from the analysis of this chapter.

First, the extent of 'globalization' is once again exaggerated. The figures for intra-Triad and North–South trade point to the continued relative non-integration of the 'global economy'.

Secondly, there are other explanations for the undermining of the living conditions of the unskilled workers in the advanced countries than just the economists' emphasis on trade and/or technical change.

Thirdly, 'domestic' explanations remain more important to the outcomes in these matters than 'international' ones, though these could be complementary.

Fourth, there is a need to disaggregate: Europe is not like the US and there are lots of differences within Europe.

Finally, just as in the case of the discussion of 'globalization', the discussion of 'international competitiveness' must be treated with great caution. The strong globalization thesis serves to disarm policy-makers and undermine strategic thinking about national economic management: similar comments could quite easily be made about the connected discussion of 'international competitiveness'. This chapter has served to introduce the way this term has entered our everyday discourse about economic matters, and to raise issues about the limited usefulness of the concept and some of the ambiguities in the trends it is supposed to embody. There is no need for all economic activity to be subject to the dictates of being 'internationally competitive', and we should be careful to distinguish the operation of companies and of economies in the discussion of the concept.

5

The Developing Economies and Globalization

In the first edition of this book we were confronted with the widespread belief that a substantial proportion of the developing economies were about to achieve a sustained industrial take-off that would transform the world economy. In a typical example of such boosterism, *The Economist* (10 Oct. 1994) predicted that if existing trends were to continue, China would be the world's largest economy in 2020, having overtaken the United States, and that the developing countries would represent over 60 per cent of world output and the developed countries less than 40 per cent (OECD 1997b, fig. 10, p. 43). The experience of sustained economic growth in the first wave of Asian newly industrializing countries – Hong Kong, South Korea, Singapore and Taiwan – had been followed by rapid growth in South East Asia. If other developing countries were able to follow the lessons of the 'Asian miracle', then major countries like India, the laggard states of Latin America, and even Africa could hope to leave economic backwardness behind. The lessons of Asian growth were widely perceived to be stable government, market-friendly policies, and external and internal financial market liberalization to attract foreign investment. The World Bank's 1993 report *The East Asian Miracle* offered a model of growth that, appropriately applied, could be achieved by any country that consistently followed the strategy.

Economic growth in the developing world would thus create a truly global economy. It would restructure the world economy without the need for interventionist policies, such as the regulation of capital markets or attempts to change the terms of trade, or for large transfers of wealth between the developed and developing worlds in the form of aid. It would also benefit the developing world, since economic growth and industrialization in hitherto underdeveloped countries would provide enhanced demand for the sophisticated goods and services in which the developed countries were supposed to specialize.

This optimistic prediction did arouse opposition, but in a form that neither denied the prospects for growth of manufacturing production in developing countries nor the creation of a truly global economy. Rather, the pessimists contended that the effects would be disastrous for the advanced world. Globalization would lead to a 'race to the bottom'. The combination of capital mobility and free trade would lead to a massive transfer of manufacturing output from the high wage industrial countries to low wage developing countries. This would devastate output and employment in the West. The accelerating deindustrialization would impoverish the West, but industrial growth would not benefit the mass of workers in the developing countries. Authoritarian governments would hold down wages in newly industrializing countries. The only true beneficiaries would be Western corporations and capital markets, and the elites of the developing world. The pessimistic case continues to be strongly argued, for example by Greider (1997), Martin and Schumann (1997) and Gray (1998).

Contesting the 'Asian miracle'

Confronted with this climate it was difficult to challenge the central proposition of further sustained growth in Asia and the possibility of its widespread diffusion elsewhere. We were sceptical about such prospects but forced to be cautious in the face of such a solid consensus. In essence we argued two distinct cases.

On the one hand, we claimed that for large countries like India and China the prospects for growth depended on political stability and that stability depended on the capacity to contain uneven development. The ability to incorporate and transform large peasant-based rural sectors is central to successful industrialization. Failure to do so, or to politically contain the losers, leads to political crisis. Alexander Gershenkron (1966) and J. M. Barrington Moore (1967) argued powerfully that it was the failure of societies like Japan and Russia to overcome the legacies of agrarian backwardness and to transform autocratic agrarian-based power structures that led to rebellion against the consequences of modernization. We cited the examples of Russia in 1905 and 1917 and Iran in 1978 to make the point.

On the other hand, we cited the evidence of econometric studies by Krugman (1994b) and Young (1994a, 1994b) that showed that rapid economic growth in the Asian Tigers was based on extraordinarily high levels of factor inputs. There was no 'miracle', just very high rates of investment and once and for all increases in the quality and quantity of the industrial labour force, as traditional non-commercial sectors were run down and mass secondary education was provided for the first time. According to the total factor productivity analysis adopted by Krugman and Young, there was little evidence of more efficient and productive use of resources. Hence, having mobilized hitherto underutilized human resources and combined them with very high levels of capital investment to GDP, there will be once and for all gains that will taper off and growth rates will fall in consequence. Investment will be subject to the law of diminishing returns. Not only was there no Asian miracle, Asian growth was not exceptional. In fact, total factor productivity growth in the Tigers was no better than in some Western countries during their own period of rapid growth after 1945. Thus Hong Kong's total factor productivity grew at a rate of 2.3 per cent per annum between 1966 and 1991, Singapore, South Korea and Taiwan grew at –0.3 per cent, 1.6 per cent and 1.9 per cent per annum respectively during 1966–90, whereas Germany grew at a rate of 3.7 per cent per annum between 1950 and 1973, Canada at 1.8 per cent per annum between 1947 and 1973, France at 3 per cent per annum between 1950 and 1973, and Italy at 3.4 per cent per annum, between 1952 and 1973 (Young 1994b).

The demystification by Krugman and Young was valuable, chiefly because they undermined the economically illiterate hype emanating from Asia and the West alike about the new logic of economic growth based on distinctive Asian institutions and values. They punctured the myth that Asia was exceptional in its industrial efficiency and the sources of its growth. Unintentionally, they also punctured the idea that such rates were easy to achieve, given the right free market policies. Such levels of domestic saving and capital investment as those in Singapore or South Korea are difficult to replicate. Thus a rather different kind of specificity is reconferred on Asian institutions – a point that the normally acute Krugman seems to miss.

This analysis was bound to be controversial. Specific objections have been raised about Young's econometric calculations (*Economist*, 1 Mar. 1997), and also more general objections against the appropriateness of the total factor productivity approach (Singh 1998). Thus it is argued that high rates of investment can continue to enhance productivity: as new machines are bought to replace older ones, the new machines will tend to increase output independently of any improvements in the efficiency of use of the factors of production otherwise. Moreover, it is perfectly possible that highly developed economies like Singapore have not exhausted the ability to dramatically upgrade the quality of their labour inputs by further investments in training and the promotion of widespread higher education. Singapore has expanded R&D expenditure as a proportion of GDP close to German levels, thus offering the possibility of a continuous upgrading of quality in both products and production processes. While Singapore has been heavily dependent on FDI by multinational companies, which accounted for around 70 per cent of manufacturing GDP in 1995 (Ramstetter 1998, table 8.6, p. 199), it does have indigenous high-tech firms. For example, it has developed a regional hub supplying hard disk drives, in

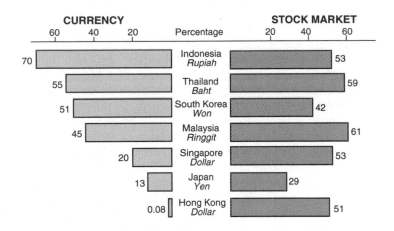

Figure 5.1   Percentage falls in East Asian currencies (against the US dollar) and stock markets (on previous levels) between January 1997 and January 1998

Source: *The Guardian*, 13 Jan. 1998, p. 17

effect an industrial district characterized by flexibly specialized production that can serve as a focus for other developments (Wong 1997; see also chapter 3).

However, these arguments about high self-sustaining growth now appear severely dated in the context of the Asian crisis that began in mid-1997. Scepticism about growth prospects is no longer exceptional or controversial, nor is it confined to Asia, with financial meltdown in Russia in August 1998 and severe turbulence in Latin American markets, particularly in Venezuela and Brazil. Most of the leading rapidly growing economies in South East Asia and also South Korea have suffered major crises in their currency and equity markets and face major contractions in employment and output, see figure 5.1.

The issue now is that the crisis has produced arguments that are no less mythological and problematic than were those of the optimists and pessimists in the period of apparently limitless high growth. The first mythologizing explanation for the crisis is a new twist on the notion of Asian exceptionalism. For growth based on 'Asian values' we now need to substitute a crisis created by 'crony capitalism' (a type of informal capitalism in which networks of personal acquaintances, friends and family play the overwhelming part in determining economic relationships). Those who advance such arguments believe in the theory of efficient capital markets, and see the crisis in Asia as not primarily the product of the behaviour of foreign investors but the result of fundamental flaws in the policies and institutions of the recipient countries. Asia experienced a crisis because its various countries did not liberalize their financial sectors enough. They failed to turn domestic banks into Western-style institutions, with high transparency and allocation based on rational market-oriented criteria. They failed to develop appropriate institutions of national financial supervision and to follow prudent policies to control excessive borrowing. Asia thus failed to the degree that it was different from Western capitalism, and specifically from the United States. This analysis is both complacent about Western institutions, as anyone who remembers the early 1990s Savings and Loan scandal can see, and also superficial. It blames not liberalization of financial markets, but the failure to go far enough. Yet Western institutions committed to the liberalization agenda, such as the IMF and the World Bank, had praised efforts at financial market liberalization in Indonesia, for example.

The second mythologizing explanation is a reverse image of the first. Asia's crisis shows both the existence of the new globalized economy and its inherent destructiveness. The crisis is due to the sudden withdrawal of short-term funds by Western investors and large-scale short selling on foreign exchange and equity markets by speculators. This has severely disrupted the various Asian economies affected without real domestic necessity: it is a crisis made in volatile global markets. Here the sources of the crisis are essentially external. The problems experienced are the side-effects of largely irrational and excessive capital flight and contagion effects that generalized the crisis. The problem with such an analysis, whether advanced by Western radicals or by Asian conservatives (like Malaysia's Prime Minister, Dr Mahathir), is not so much that the markets have not had a major role to play, but that it ignores the domestic dimensions and sources of the crisis. Thus different countries have experienced different degrees of disruption, from what amounts to meltdown in Indonesia, to what seems likely to be a major but essentially salutary setback to a rapidly overheating economy in the case of Malaysia. Moreover, if contagion effects are so powerful and the markets beyond control, why were certain countries, such as Taiwan, virtually unaffected and others, such as Singapore, able to contain the speculative pressure of the markets?

Explaining the Asian crisis

The crisis has also produced a good deal of sensible analysis, which we shall review. It must be emphasized, however, that it took everyone by surprise. Even sceptics like Paul Krugman or ourselves, who sought to deflate expectations about continuing high rates of growth, did not envisage major falls

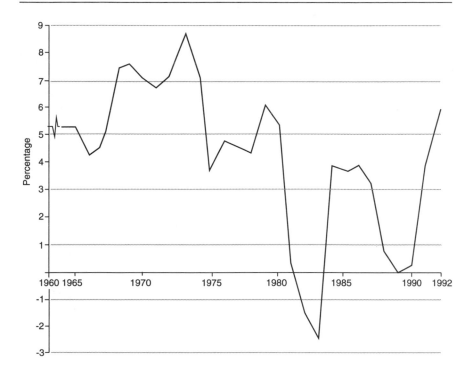

Figure 5.2   Latin American GDP growth rates, 1960–1993 (per cent per annum)

Source: UN National Accounts Yearbooks

in GDP. In the first edition we contrasted Asian and Latin American growth since the 1960s, drawing on the work of Ajit Singh (1993). The successful Asian NICs developed primarily because of domestic capital formation and public investment, with foreign direct investment in a subsidiary role. Latin American countries, by contrast, were open to a massive influx of capital in the 1970s and then suffered violent external shocks that they were unable to master except at the price of savagely deflationary policies imposed on them by the international financial system in the 1980s. The result was that Latin American growth fell from a peak of over 8 per cent per annum in 1973 to below –2 per cent in 1983, and has fluctuated violently thereafter (figure 5.2). The difference in the growth in GDP per capita between East Asia and Latin America was pronounced in the period 1970–90 (see figure 5.3).

As a case for domestically sourced growth and control over access to foreign capital the Asian countries seemed highly impressive. However, this

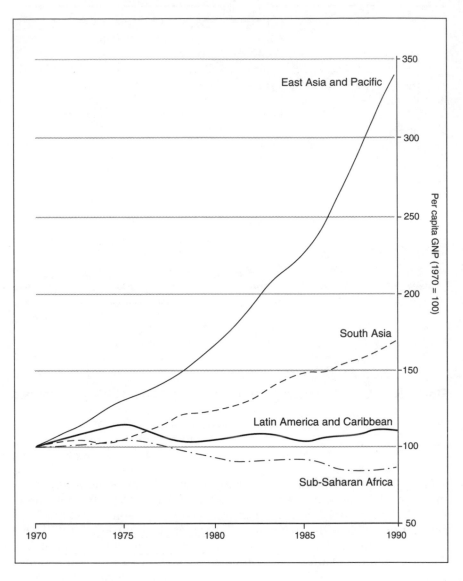

Figure 5.3 GNP growth per capita in East Asia, Latin America, South Asia and sub-Saharan Africa, 1970–1990 (1970 = 100)

Source: Derived from *World Development Indicators*, World Bank, 1997

course requires very high rates of saving relative to GDP. On average, Asian NICs save around 30 per cent of GDP as against around 20 per cent in Latin America. Successful Asian countries expanded their savings–GDP ratios very substantially during the process of growth: thus the ratio in South Korea rose from a very low level of 3.3 per cent during 1955–65 to 21.5 per cent during 1965–73 and 31.2 per cent during 1990–4; in Thailand it rose from 16.7 per cent in 1955–65 to 34.1 per cent in 1990–4 (Williams 1997). The point was soundly made, but out of date. As we were writing the first edition in 1995, relying on data from 1994 and before, the picture was changing rapidly. In early 1997 the first signs of problems in Asia began to be apparent. Rates of growth in exports slowed markedly in 1995–6 – exports in the six Tiger economies rose by 3.5 per cent in 1996 compared with 14.5 per cent in the previous year and an average rate of growth between 1990 and 1996 of 10 per cent (*Economist*, 1 Mar. 1997). GDP growth also slowed in a number of the Tigers – unsurprisingly given the strong export orientation of these economies. Average GDP growth in the region slowed from 9 per cent in 1995 to 7 per cent in 1996 (Grabel 1998). In the mid-1990s several of the Tigers began to accumulate significant levels of foreign debt, in the form of short-term loans to private banks and to a lesser extent portfolio investment. Thus in 1996 Indonesia received the third largest share of private capital inflows ($17.9 billion), Malaysia the fourth largest ($16 billion) and Thailand the sixth largest ($13.3 billion) (Montes 1998a, p. 20). In table 5.1, Wolf (1998a) summarizes the position for the five Asian economies most affected by the crisis: South Korea, Indonesia, Malaysia, Thailand and the Philippines.

From 1994 to 1996 the inflow of funds produced a deepening current account deficit and was marked by heavy lending by foreign commercial banks: the flow of bank lending into the region increased from $24 billion in 1994 to $56 billion in 1996. In 1997 this turned into a net outflow of $21.3 billion. Thus up until 1997 the Tigers were borrowing on a deteriorating economic performance. Has Asia gone the same way as Latin America, and will the early years of the twenty-first century be Asia's equivalent of Latin America's 'lost decade' in the 1980s?

In fact, the two crises are very different, as Paul Krugman (1998) points out. The Latin American crisis was driven primarily by high rates of public borrowing. Latin American governments had built up large budget deficits, leading to accelerating inflation. Inevitably they were faced with pressure on their exchange rates and inadequate reserves to defend them. Once their exchange rates had fallen they were faced with a growing burden of public and private debt to foreign creditors. Latin American countries were forced simultaneously to adopt austerity measures to contain budget deficits and inflation, and to divert a higher proportion of resources to debt repayment, thus substantially reducing domestic output and consumption. By contrast, the Tigers had followed prudent fiscal policies and government budgets were in balance or surplus. Rates of inflation were relatively low. The Asian

Table 5.1   Asian economies: external financing (South Korea, Indonesia, Malaysia, Thailand, Philippines)

	1994	1995	1996	1997 (estimate)	1997 (forecast)
Current account balance	−24.6	−41.3	−54.9	−26.0	17.6
External financing, net	47.4	80.9	92.8	15.2	15.2
Private flows, net	40.5	77.4	93.0	−12.1	−9.4
Equity investment	12.2	15.5	19.1	−4.5	7.9
Direct equity	4.7	4.9	7.0	−7.3	9.8
Portfolio equity	10.6	10.6	12.1	−11.6	−1.9
Private creditors	28.2	61.8	74.0	−7.8	−17.3
Commercial banks	24.0	49.5	55.5	−21.3	−14.1
Non-bank private sectors	4.2	12.4	18.4	13.7	−3.2
Official flows, net	7.0	3.6	−0.2	27.2	24.6
International financial institutions	−0.4	−0.6	−1.0	23.0	18.5
Bilateral creditors	7.4	4.2	0.7	4.3	6.1
Resident lending/other, net[a]	−17.5	−25.9	−19.6	−11.9	−6.7
Reserve excluding gold	−5.4	−13.7	−18.3	22.7	−27.1

[a] Including resident net lending, monetary gold, and errors and emissions.
Source: Institute of International Finance, provisional figures

crisis was brought on not by imprudent public borrowing, but by large-scale private debt and unsustainable booms in asset prices, particularly property, in several countries.

The Asian crisis could not be compared with other currency crises like the turbulence in the European exchange rate mechanism (ERM) in 1992. In that case governments like the UK and Italy were forced to choose between defending a target exchange rate and the unacceptable macroeconomic consequences of doing so. High interest rates were necessary to contain higher than average inflation, and led to deflationary pressures and rapidly rising unemployment. Once that became clear the markets forced the issue, believing devaluation to be inevitable. In the Asian case, as Krugman points out, despite slowing growth in 1996, there was no substantial increase in unemployment, and the currency crisis did not precede the boom and bust cycle in the asset markets but followed on from it.

Krugman sees the crisis as being caused by the inherent temptations to exuberant investment by underregulated financial intermediaries. In a context where investors believe that they are protected from risk by the government (even if that belief is false) they will lend to financial intermediaries with an interest in speculative investments that have high risk but the potential for high reward. These 'Pangloss values', as Krugman calls them, are chosen because the intermediaries believe they can make windfall gains but that investors will be guaranteed against losses. Hence the bubble economy in property and equity asset values is threatened by the inflow of foreign investors forcing it up to unsustainable levels where bad outcomes and losses begin to accumulate. As Lester Thurow points out, 'Bangkok, a city whose per capita productivity is about one-twelfth that of San Francisco, should not have land values that are much higher than those in San Francisco' (1998, p. 22). There is no doubt that Krugman's analysis helps to explain an aspect of the crisis and that there was a significant component of this reckless lending in South East Asian countries like Thailand and Indonesia that precipitated the crisis, but it does not explain the full conjuncture of the crisis.

The key question to ask is why did this burden of short-term foreign debt arise in countries with very high levels of domestic savings? Interest rate differentials are part of the explanation in Thailand and South Korea. But why, given this strong source of domestic capital, did governments open their economies to foreign investors and permit reckless lending by banks and other financial intermediaries? The answer is that they were following Western advice, and receiving praise for it from such institutions as the IMF, which complimented Thailand on its macroeconomic policies in 1996. Policy was driven by conformity with Western doctrine.

The crisis in South East Asia

Manuel Montes (1998a, 1998b) offers the most balanced and penetrating account of the course and causes of the crisis in South East Asia. In what follows, we will concentrate on Thailand, the precipitating country in the crisis. Montes points out that the growth of foreign borrowing and the failure of effective control followed rapidly on the 'twin liberalizations' of the domestic financial system and the external controls on capital and the current account. In Thailand these liberalizations began in 1990: chiefly the removal of exchange controls, the promotion of non-banking capital markets, the removal of caps on interest rates and the abandonment of capital allocation rules. Financial intermediaries took full advantage of these relaxations in policy, borrowing in foreign currencies at lower foreign rates of interest. Thus capital inflows peaked at 12.3 per cent of GDP in 1995 – of this 11.6 per cent was composed of portfolio investment and equity flows rather than long-term FDI (Montes 1998a, p. 20). Foreign investment flows were thus not boosting real domestic output or upgrading manufacturing industry, but contributing to the asset price bubble. In addition, in as much as substantial portions of FDI flows are made up of acquisitions and mergers investment, this is no more of an addition to the stock capital than short-term flows.

The problem is that such major private liabilities will undermine the exchange rate if lenders withdraw substantial short-term funds: Thai reserves were too small to cope with the potential demand. Thailand's ratio of short-term debt to foreign exchange reserves was 121 per cent, with $45.6 billion of short-term debt outstanding and reserves of $37.7 billion in June 1997. Thus private debt can threaten a currency crisis as much as public debt – private markets are not inherently self-restraining. The only way to have avoided this situation, given that liberalization had taken place, would have been to move to a flexible exchange rate. This would have allowed the currency to appreciate as foreign funds flowed in and would have tended to deter excessive foreign borrowing by domestic financial institutions. The problem is that this was not an option: it would increase the burden on manufacturing industry, already suffering from rapidly rising costs and the falling value of the Chinese yuan after 1994 and the Japanese yen after 1995. As the yen fell in value against the dollar, Japanese banks (the major short-term lenders in South East Asia) began to call in loans as they fell due and restrict further lending. The Japanese institutions were faced with a falling stock market, and therefore falling asset values to set against their own liabilities. From 1975, and particularly after the Plaza Accord of 1985, the yen appreciated against the dollar steadily until 1995 (Thompson 1998a, fig. 4.5, p. 104). After 1995 the dollar appreciated substantially against the yen and continued to do so substantially in 1998.

The result was to place the Thai authorities in a difficult dilemma. Manufacturers and exporters needed a cut in the value of the baht, but despite a deteriorating export performance, the effect of devaluing the currency would be to dramatically increase the debt burden. The result was that they had no option but to try to hold on to the existing pegged rate against the dollar. The baht came under pressure in May 1997, but was defended by a substantial expenditure of reserves and with extensive support from other ASEAN central banks. In July 1997, once the scale of the foreign exchange losses became clear, the Thai government abandoned the attempt to maintain the dollar peg and the value of the currency promptly fell: between 1 July 1997 and 24 January 1998 the baht fell 54.6 per cent against the dollar (Montes 1998a, table U.1, p. xv).

Immediately after the Thai devaluation the major currencies in South East Asia thought to be similarly affected – the Malaysian ringgit, the Indonesian rupiah and the Philippine peso – all fell in value as investors sought to protect their assets or to minimize their liabilities: the ringgit fell 44.9 per cent against the dollar by 24 January 1998, the rupiah by 83.6 per cent and the peso by 39.4 per cent (Montes 1998a, table U.1, p. xv). Consequent falls in the respective equity markets further undermined domestic financial systems: stock market falls as of January 1998 relative to January 1997 were for Thailand 59 per cent, Malaysia 61 per cent, Indonesia 53 per cent, Singapore 53 per cent and Korea 42 per cent (figure 5.1, p. 137 above). Falling asset values undermined banks and other companies at the same time as their dollar debts substantially increased the domestic costs of servicing them. In the case of Indonesia the position was further worsened by the effect on domestic demand of the austerity measures required by the IMF – so much so that establishment economists like Jeffrey Sachs (1997, 1998) and Joseph Stiglitz (1997) roundly condemned the IMF for imposing self-defeating conditions that would make external debt more difficult to service. The result of the initial foreign exchange shocks has been a self-reinforcing crisis, where each move downward on one variable triggers slides in others and creates the conditions for fresh decline. Even the assumption that the financial crisis would be compensated for to some extent by an increase in the competitiveness of exporters is not wholly borne out by the facts: into 1998 Indonesian firms found it hard to get trade credit and the same applied to internationally famous but heavily indebted South Korean conglomerates, the chaebols.

The extent of the external shock imposed by speculative lending becomes clear when one takes account of the relative weakness of the financial sectors in these countries. As Montes (1998b) points out, the financial flows to the developing countries since the late 1980s have been far larger as a percentage of GDP than are those to the developed countries: typically around 2 per cent of GDP as against 1 per cent. The difference may not seem so great. However, because the developed countries have complex financial sectors that are larger than their GDP, these flows are relatively small in comparison to the whole financial system, whereas the financial sectors of developing countries are much smaller on average, about 40 per cent of output. Hence the impact of a flow of 2 per cent of GDP is several times the order of magnitude of a 1 per cent flow into a developed country.

South East Asia's crisis was generalized in scale and scope by contagion effects. But should these be seen as crude herd behaviour by panicky foreign investors or as speculative attacks by fast-moving and footloose international financial markets? Neither will quite do. The principal lenders to the five most affected countries were Japanese and EU banks, with just under US$100 billion each outstanding in June 1997. The Japanese were selling precipitously, but not speculatively, to meet their own obligations. The loans outstanding represented 39.2 per cent of the banks' capital (Wolf 1998c). Domestic asset holders started the movement out of local currencies into foreign assets, aware of how precarious the position was. Often they sold to latecoming and ignorant foreign investors, eager to cash in on booming 'emerging markets'. As Lester Thurow remarks: 'What is clear is that crashes are not set off by outside speculators who see the internal weaknesses and attack. The first investors to leave the local market are always the local investors who have the best information' (1998 p. 23). By the time speculators had got to work, the rout had begun. Attempts to blame speculators and threats to ban short-selling in order to curb speculation on the part of Dr Mahathir of Malaysia were not merely ineffective, they led to panic in local markets and spooked the Kuala Lumpur stock exchange, as Ranjit Gill (1998) shows. The international financier George

Soros, Mahathir's chief villain, not only explicitly denied leading speculative attacks, but also challenged the appropriateness and effectiveness of IMF recovery measures.

Indeed, Soros proposed a remedy to counter the threat of excessive flows of short-term funds into developing countries. He advocated setting up an International Credit Insurance Corporation (Soros 1997). That institution would insure international loans to developing countries up to a prudent level. Beyond that, investors would be on their own, the rule of *caveat emptor* would apply and thus they could have no expectation of even an implicit public guarantee. Inevitably such arrangements would make lending beyond the limit risky and to compensate interest rates would be high, thus tending to constrain excessive and imprudent lending. Soros clearly sees this as a form of guarantee that limits moral hazard, and helps to make lending self-limiting.

As many commentators have pointed out, such financial crises brought on by excessive foreign borrowing are neither new nor confined to Asia. Moreover, they are not a unique effect of the global financial markets that are perceived to have emerged since the late 1980s. The principal lenders to Asia are commercial banks, who were also primarily responsible for excessive lending to Latin America during the 1970s. Chile experienced a similar crisis to Thailand's in 1981 and it followed directly from the liberalization of the financial markets. Chile's crisis, in large part the result of following dogmatic economic liberal policies, resulted in a cost of 41.2 per cent of GDP to meet the liabilities of the banking system (Wolf 1998c). Similar costly crises occurred in the early 1980s in other Latin American countries, such as Argentina and Uruguay.

Even if the crisis could have been averted or contained by prompt action by the Thai authorities, it is questionable how far the inflow of short-term funds would have benefited domestic development. Montes (1998a) presents a calculation, drawing on Reisen (1997), that shows that capital inflows raised GDP growth by just 1 per cent in Indonesia and 1.5 per cent in Malaysia, but that GDP fell in the case of Thailand by 0.6 per cent. The efficiency of investment (that is, the ratio of investment to the real GDP growth rate) fell in the case of Malaysia from 30.2 to 23.5 per cent and in Thailand from 34.7 to 23.6 per cent (Montes 1998a, table U.1, p. xv). Thus, for a very modest boost to growth, these countries incurred dangerous and, as it turns out, damaging liabilities. As Montes argues: 'Thailand would have grown by 1.5 percentage points less in the period 1991 to 1996 if Thailand had not relied on foreign savings; this would have meant a compound forgone growth rate of about 12.9 per cent of GDP from 1990 to 1996. This growth sacrifice is smaller in comparison to the 20 per cent of GDP estimated as resources required for rehabilitating the Thai financial system' (1998b, p. 3).

Short-term loans are particularly problematic, since unlike FDI they do not bring foreign expertise or technology. Providing property rights are secure and the trading position sound, direct investors have little to fear from foreign exchange and capital movement controls. Their prime aim is to utilize low wages in countries like Indonesia or locational advantages in the case of Singapore. Those countries with low levels of short-term flows relative to FDI seem to have been less severely affected. Malaysia has had a higher ratio of FDI to short-term loans than Thailand, and, despite a severe devaluation and major turbulence in the equity markets, has not had to seek recourse to the IMF. Singapore has been primarily a recipient of foreign flows in the form of FDI – being one of the largest recipients: next to China, Singapore was the largest recipient in 1988–92. Because of its very low level of short-term foreign indebtedness, Singapore could meet speculative pressures in 1997 by allowing the Singapore dollar to fall against the US dollar. Singapore's large foreign exchange reserves meant that it could sit out the markets, accepting some weakening of economic activity brought on by interest rate rises.

Thus countries that were careful to control short-term lending were not without national strategies for coping with speculative attacks. Taiwan was virtually unaffected by the crisis, because it had been careful to avoid a large debt burden and because its very diverse industrial system, based on small and medium-sized enterprises, was largely funded from domestic sources. Markets are not all-powerful and do not close off all options for national policy, as we shall see later.

Korea's crisis

Reckless policies and an inappropriate importation of the economic liberal agenda can undermine the strongest of the NICs. So far we have concentrated on the crisis in South East Asia. The other major victim of the Asian crisis was South Korea. Korea was no longer a developing country like Thailand. It had joined the ranks of the industrialized countries, becoming a member of the OECD in 1996. As Wade and Veneroso (1998) argue, Korean industrialization had been driven by very high levels of domestic saving and very high levels of lending by national banks to their partner industrial companies in the Korean conglomerates, the chaebols. The very high gearing of the Korean companies enabled them to develop rapidly by pouring large amounts of capital into key projects and to concentrate on building up market share in export markets, rather than needing to be concerned with short-term profitability. They would, therefore, be highly vulnerable to a credit crisis, unless companies enjoyed a long-term and cooperative relationship with the banks and unless these arrangements were underwritten by state macroeconomic policy. South Korea followed a model of 'forced draught' industrialization controlled by a highly authoritarian state focused on development. Large volumes of domestic capital drove investment, but the state directed it into key strategic industries and tried to coordinate the chaebol conglomerates to avoid duplication and overcapacity.

This model could only work well if it concentrated on export-led manufacturing and maintained strong internal controls over bank lending and external capital controls. As Ha-Joon Chang (1998) points out, from the early 1990s the Korean government began to liberalize the domestic financial system. Under the Kim Young Sam government after 1993, external controls were loosened and a large number of new merchant banks licensed. The new economic liberal policies abandoned controls over the chaebols and gave up direction of industrial investment through administrative guidance. The chaebols took advantage of lower interest rates abroad to borrow extensively in foreign currencies. They began to invest in dubious ventures, leading to overcapacity, and with poor prospects for profitability. As Ha-Joon Chang argues, the banks and industrial managements were now free of the constraints of the previous *dirigiste* but relatively honest and even-handed industrial policies. It was then that corruption on a large scale entered the system. Against Western denunciations of the close connections between business and the state as inherent to the Korean model, he observes tartly that 'contrary to common perception, it was under the Kim Young Sam government that a full blown "crony capitalism" was born in Korea' (Chang 1998). Corruption was the product of ill-conceived liberalization, a deviation from the model of a developmental state and not a direct consequence of it.

South Korea was a victim of contagion in that its crisis followed on from that in South East Asia. But attention was focused on Korea by major warning signs. In January 1997 the Hanbo steel company collapsed amid a welter of allegations of corruption and politically inspired unviable investment. In June 1997 the leading chaebol Kia was in crisis. Korea has been hit hard by the falling value of the Chinese yuan and Japanese yen. In 1996 it had a massive current account deficit of $23.7 billion. This followed deficits of $4.5 billion in 1994 and $8.9 billion in 1995 (Chang 1998). Korea also suffered from the growing financial crisis in Japan, as hard-pressed Japanese banks called in short-term loans to meet their own liabilities.

Korea suffered a 49.1 per cent fall in the won relative to the dollar between the onset of the Thai crisis on 2 July 1997 and 24 January 1998 (Montes 1998a, table U-1, p. xv). Korea was forced humiliatingly to seek IMF aid in December 1997. This could be seen as a massive overreaction. Surely the markets were overcompensating? Korea had been heavily indebted before. It had a balanced budget. It had major household name firms like LG, Samsung, and Hyundai. However, once caught out in the game of musical chairs by a financial crisis, the very high levels of indebtedness of the chaebols in comparison with Western companies told against them. As Wade and Veneroso (1998) show, Korean companies are threatened with unsustainable levels of debt to earnings once the flow of capital is stopped and when devaluation drives up the costs of their foreign loans.

Moreover, the prospects of Korean companies trading themselves out of the debt crisis are not good. Korea has specialized in industries that currently have a great deal of overcapacity: semiconductors, bulk chemicals, motor vehicles and shipbuilding. Korea is neither a low cost nor a particularly technologically advanced producer. Its wage costs far exceeded those of less developed NICs and before the crisis its total labour costs per employee were predicted to be comparable to those of France by the year 2000 (Thompson 1995a, table 2, p. 103). Korea is not a technological leader in the way Germany and the US are, although it had been attempting to enhance its R&D capability (Kim and Yi 1997). The prices of one of its major exports, basic memory chips, have collapsed more than twentyfold in a glutted market.

Korea's problem is neither just reckless and virtually unsupervised merchant banks nor incautious investments by the chaebols: it is a matter of economic and industrial structure. By 1996 Korea had come close to being a developed industrial economy, yet its economic performance was dependent on levels of export-led growth that are quite uncharacteristic of developed economies and that were unsustainable in the state of world markets before the Asian crisis, let alone after it. As Jeffrey Henderson (1998) perceptively points out, to join the developed economies newly industrializing countries need to develop companies whose competitiveness is driven by technological advances and institutionalized innovation, not just by lowish labour costs and access to plentiful capital, and they need to upgrade their whole economies, so that widespread prosperity enables an increasing proportion of output to be absorbed by the domestic market. Japan achieved both of these objectives. In 1996 Korea had a trade to GDP ratio of 69 per cent; comparable figures for the EU were 17 per cent, the US 25 per cent and Japan 19 per cent (table 4.6 above, p. 131). Korea, with a relatively small population (45 million in 1996), has built up a manufacturing sector that will be perpetually dependent on a very high level of export of output in order to survive. This makes it exceedingly vulnerable to external shocks, to a downturn in the world economy or to pressure from cost-competitive manufacturers in countries like China as they too upgrade their industries.

This raises broader issues. Two models of development have been in contest in the last decade: the market-oriented model that sees growth deriving from inward investment and recommends internal and external liberalization; and the developmental state model, based on high levels of domestic saving, close cooperation of the state and business, and appropriate external controls in order to boost manufacturing exports (Weiss and Hobson 1995). In the Asian crisis both models have suffered a setback. The IMF still urges financial liberalization and demands inappropriate remedies like public sector austerity, low inflation targets and the raising of interest rates as conditions of its loans. But increasingly these prescriptions are mistrusted by intelligent mainstream opinion. The IMF's policies in Indonesia, for example, are clearly inappropriate if the aim is to restore domestic economic activity so that foreign debts can be serviced and repaid (see the appendix to this chapter, pp. 161–2). Informed opinion is drifting away from promoting the openness of developing countries to external financial flows if it conflicts with the objective of development: a sign of this is the willingness of a leading liberal development economist like Jagdish Bhagwati (1998) to contemplate controls if an effective international lender of last resort cannot be created. In the *Financial Times*, Martin Wolf sums up the options from a liberal perspective very neatly:

> In short, countries have a choice. They must introduce tough and effective western-style regulation, along with credible exchange-rate regimes and tight restrictions on foreign currency liabilities and assets in their financial sectors. Or they must postpone capital account liberalisation. What they must never do is combine ill-regulated and heavily guaranteed financial systems with significant liberalisation of access to international lending. That way lies economic ruin. (1998c)

The problem with the prescription of the option of transparency and careful market supervision is that it demands a level of state capacity that few developing countries can meet. Indeed, few developed countries can maintain the standards advocated: the UK and Sweden, for example, both experienced severe crises as a result of liberalizing domestic financial markets and removing external controls. In effect the model of such a financial system is Singapore. It is a tightly regulated and conformist society with a competent authoritarian regime. But authoritarianism and competence seldom go together and stable democratic regimes are difficult to sustain in developing countries, especially if threatened by economic turbulence. How can Indonesia create open and effective democratic government, for example, when it now has a third of the population in poverty and 25 million people unemployed (a figure comparable to the EU)?

Intelligent liberal economists are concerned to maintain a free trade regime. The danger of substantial financial flows moving rapidly into shallow and weakly regulated markets is that a quite modest volume of lending relative to the total stock of capital in the international financial system may precipitate a widespread financial panic and then damage the real flows of goods and services. The danger of a world deflationary environment is a switch in national policies towards protectionism, as in the 1930s.

The problem is that if the naive version of the liberal model is losing credibility, not only with economists but also with policy-makers in fiercely nationalistic regimes like Malaysia and South Korea, then the developmental state model is in little better shape. The developmental state presupposed an asymmetrical trade regime, in which the developing countries in question benefited from free trade with the developed world and yet maintained tight control on imports themselves. For example, in 1979 imports of manufactures amounted to just 2.4 per cent of Japanese GDP, and even in 1997 just 3 per cent. The South Korean market was similarly protected. This is no longer a viable option in the current WTO free trade regime. Moreover, the advanced countries are less willing to tolerate such asymmetries, fearing competition. The assumption of the developmental state regime, with its strong emphasis on manufactured exports, is that world demand is growing rapidly and that the number of such newly industrialized countries is relatively few. In a context of stagnating demand in the advanced countries induced by restrictive macroeconomic policies that give primacy to low inflation targets, and of widespread attempts to industrialize in the developing world, these strategies are less effective as a general prescription. In this context, only a minority of countries can succeed and achieve full industrialization. In particular, the savings levels of the key Asian countries are wholly exceptional, and will be difficult for other developing nations to copy.

This is not to say that development is impossible, just very difficult. Both ready routes to prosperity seem to be foreclosed. States with high levels of domestic savings will probably be best advised to adopt controls on the capital account. States with low levels of domestic saving should attempt to promote FDI but to discourage excessive short-term financial inflows. How these objectives may be pursued is the subject of the next section. The point to make here is that even if there are no ready-made developmental models, there are options for national policy. States may be constrained by international markets, but, if they avoid policy errors that amplify the destructive effects of market forces, they do have the capacity to contain markets in the interests of national goals.

Policy options for developing countries

It should now be obvious that the combination of thoroughgoing internal and external financial liberalization combined with a rigidly pegged exchange rate is a disaster for developing countries. Given the relative shallowness of their financial markets and the difficulty of constructing appropriate regimes of supervision by domestic authorities and practices of transparency by local firms, the tendencies towards exuberant overborrowing and the excessive growth of credit are difficult to prevent. When capital flight begins, attempts to contain it by defending the exchange rate by the use of foreign currency reserves are generally futile. By the time the panic is underway, the high ratio of short-term debt to reserves has already become clear to investors. Utilizing reserves simply allows investors to exit without altering the eventual necessity of devaluation. The reserves are of more use in a post-crisis situation. Similarly, IMF bail-outs protect foreign creditors, who have often invested incautiously and brought little benefit to the domestic economy, at the expense of domestic employment and output. It is now clear that the IMF cannot mobilize sufficient resources from

OECD countries (and ultimately their taxpayers) to meet a series of closely linked crises: the total of support to Mexico (in 1994–5), to Thailand, Indonesia and to Russia exceeds US$100 billion.

Some other international regime needs to be devised than that of the promotion of financial liberalization, punctuated by frequent crashes and bailouts. That this damages development is now so obvious that establishment opinion has weakened its dogmatic opposition to controls on the capital account in developing countries (for example, the editorial in the *Financial Times* of 2 Sept. 1998). It is also clear that the contagion effects cannot be confined to the developing world, and have the capacity to cause turbulence in the developed world as well. At present an alternative international regime of regulation of financial flows is unlikely to be adopted, unless the developed economies find themselves engulfed in a serious recession too. A combination of weak leaderships and the continued residual grip of economic liberal ideology will mean that the G7 governments will respond to a deepening world recession little better than did the elites of the great powers after 1929. Developing countries will therefore have to take prudential action themselves. They need to slough off the economic fatalism preached by the advocates of globalization and to recognize that national governments do have options, if they are not already in the supervisory grip of the IMF and provided they accept the need to act decisively and consistently.

As we have seen, Malaysia avoided the necessity of calling in the IMF because it had a relatively low ratio of short-term debt to FDI. Dr Mahathir worsened the crisis by talking of controls but not decisively implementing them. As of September 1998 the ringgit has fallen 48 per cent against its position at the onset of the crisis and the stock market 70 per cent against its peak. On 1 September 1998 Mahathir acted decisively and introduced a draconian package of short-term currency controls: trading in ringgit investments by foreign banks has been banned, Malaysian institutions are forbidden to offer credit facilities to foreign banks and stockbrokers, ringgit in circulation outside the country are to be repatriated within one month or they will lose their value, all trade must be conducted in foreign currency, foreigners selling shares must wait for one year before they can exit, and strict controls are imposed on foreigners and residents taking local or foreign currency out of the country (*Financial Times*, 2 Sept. 1998, p. 3). Whether these controls are effective remains to be seen. The aim is to decouple domestic monetary policy from exchange rate policy. Malaysia should be able to reduce interest rates, restoring economic activity and making it easier to repay domestic loans. In a country with a very high domestic savings rate and an authoritarian government, but also strong nationalist sentiment in favour of building the domestic economy, these measures may well work. Malaysia may be able to reflate internally and trade its way out of the crisis. In the longer term this will only work if domestic credit growth is controlled, the domestic loan overhang tackled and irrational prestige projects curtailed.

Malaysia is not alone in adopting interventionist measures. The Hong Kong government has been using its extensive foreign exchange reserves to buy equity and support the local stock market, thereby containing a slide into insolvency by banks and finance companies. China and India, relatively untouched by the crisis, still have extensive foreign exchange and capital account controls. But what options are available more generally to developing countries – less draconian than the Malaysian measures – to contain short-term foreign flows and to prevent excessive growth in domestic credit?

First, there is the option to copy the Chilean policies introduced after the crisis of the early 1980s. Foreign investors are free to engage in portfolio investment, but they have to keep their funds tied up in the country for one year as a minimum. Domestic borrowers are discouraged from taking short-term foreign loans by a requirement that 30 per cent of loan capital on loans of less than one year be deposited in a non-interest account for a substantial period.

Second, exchange rate policy should force foreign investors to recognize the risks they run in short-term loans – tightly pegged exchange rates should be avoided in favour of variable rates or very wide bands.

Third, as Montes (1998b) argues, if financial liberalization is a long-term objective it should be accepted that instant liberalization is counterproductive for many economies and that international institutions might be persuaded to accept the legitimacy of several grades of open capital accounts, from highly regulated to very open. Those with extensive controls would not be stigmatized, but having the lowest rating for openness they would not be required or permitted to accept the most volatile capital inflows. In this way the all-or-nothing advocacy of liberalization would be ended and countries with controls would obtain funds of a certain type and level. Countries could move up the ratings ladder with international approval as their economies increased in ability to absorb external financial flows. Publicly sanctioned ratings could be used to replace the often volatile and capricious valuations of the private ratings agencies. In combination with Soros's suggested International Credit Insurance Corporation, such a regime of degrees of openness could offer considerable security to investors.

Fourth, it may be argued that even allowing for stepped capital account controls, other factors will lead to certain countries being off the investment map altogether, whether for short-term loans or FDI. Indeed, as we have seen in chapter 3, FDI is highly concentrated in a small number of developing countries, as are short-term loans. Many parts of the developing world, and most of Africa, are simply not on the map in corporate boardrooms. The Tobin tax has, as an offshoot of its main objective, which is to curb short-term speculative dealing (see also chapter 7), the aim of creating a fund from receipts that can be invested in developing countries. Whether or not such a tax is possible on all short-term international financial transactions, a simpler tax, that did not attempt to put grit between the gears of short-term financial flows but simply aimed to build up an investment fund, might be more feasible. A tax at a modest rate (say 0.5 per cent) on FDI flows between OECD countries and on flows from OECD countries to the ten largest recipients of FDI in the developing world would be easier to administer and would not deter long-term investors in already favourable locations (Hirst 1998a). The funds thus accumulated would be available at favourable rates for private companies to borrow in order to invest in a schedule of the poorest countries, provided they were backed by an equivalent amount of capital raised commercially. The 50/50 split would discourage unviable investments, but would make it easier for companies to take risks with their investments. Such publicly boosted private investment would be additional to development aid and less subject to the conventional objections to large aid projects. The balance of investment is so distorted on an international scale that some form of intervention is necessary. Believers in efficient markets may take umbrage (Coyle 1998), but they can have little credibility as market outcomes have pushed a large part of the developing world into a recession.

Fifth, banks in developing countries should perhaps be subject to different capital adequacy requirements (Montes 1998a). Currently the requirement under the Basel Accord (which establishes international regulatory standards for banking) is 8 per cent, but governments in many developing countries find it hard to regulate foreign transactions and derivatives trading. Higher ratios (up to 20 per cent) may be necessary. This would help to contain reckless lending, without making unrealistic demands on supervision. Inevitably it would reduce the supply of credit and this may not be a bad thing, given the tendency in rapidly developing countries towards excessive lending and exuberant investment.

Lastly, governments should take action to prevent asset price bubbles getting out of hand. They need to judge the point at which to act decisively to deflate overheating markets. Chasing high nominal growth rates at the ultimate expense of long-term development is counterproductive. The present crisis shows that very little real growth would be foregone by more cautious policies. Montes (1998b) points out that both Taiwan and Singapore acted to check asset bubbles, Singapore in particular introducing controls and fees on property resales in 1996.

Active macroeconomic management and prudential domestic financial regulation can help to prevent crises created by asset price inflation and excessive short-term foreign borrowing. This may be possible while also leaving markets open to foreign investors, especially long-term ones. What this implies is that there are national policy options, given competence and caution by governments. It implies a willingness to concentrate on sustainable growth rather than breakneck development at any price. It implies a rejection of dogmatic free market liberalism, while remaining open to FDI and free trade. Governments like those of Thailand and South Korea did not lack the state capacity to pursue more cautious policies; rather adherence to economic liberal ideology and short-term political interests led to major policy errors. There may be no readily exportable 'Asian miracle', but the countries of Asia are capable of recovering from the crisis, with the possible exception of Indonesia, and returning to a path of slower development. The crisis may have cost the most affected countries a decade and dictated more cautious policies, but it does not show that national states in developing countries are powerless before global market forces. They will be, however, if they continue to accept fully the prescriptions of economic liberalism.

What about China?

With the exception of Indonesia, the Asian countries affected by the crisis have relatively small populations. Countries like Singapore and Taiwan which have weathered the crisis and have succeeded in developmental terms, with GDP per capita about that of some developed economies (Singapore had a per capita income of $26,730 in 1995, as against the UK figure of $18,799), are relatively small, and have been able to include the great bulk of the population in the benefits of modernization. The problem comes with larger countries with large rural sectors (60 per cent of the population and above). Here rapid industrialization may lead to growing disparities between regions and sectors, leading to highly uneven development. The question is whether the political systems of such countries can weather the strains and whether policies of income redistribution and internal development assistance can be put in place without slowing growth substantially. If development remains excessively uneven, then political instability may well choke off the growth process.

The prospects for a rapid narrowing of the vast differences between the developed and developing world turn on the sustained and successful industrial modernization of such large and poor countries as China and India, both with large and backward agrarian sectors. Can such countries begin to include the bulk of the population in prosperity, thus boosting domestic demand and providing the basis for further industrialization?

Consider the case of China first. China has been growing rapidly since 1978. In the 1980s Chinese growth averaged 9.3 per cent per annum and during 1990–6 10.1 per cent (Singh 1998, table 3.2, p. 59). This is the highest in the Asia-Pacific region. China had domestic savings rates of 39.3 per cent of GDP per annum in 1990–4 – again the highest in a region of high savers. China was the largest single recipient of FDI in the 1990s, being second only to the US on a world scale. By 1995 FDI flows represented 5 per cent of GDP and FDI stocks 10 per cent of GDP (Ramstetter 1998, fig. 8.11, p. 206). China received $42.3 billion of foreign investment in 1996.

Thus the record is impressive and if one projects current trends forward, by 2020 China will be the greatest economic power on earth. One should bear in mind the fate of such extrapolations in the past: from the growth rates then current, analysts in the 1960s predicted that the USSR would overtake the United States before the end of the century; in the 1970s it was predicted that Japan would overtake the US in both total output and GDP per capita well before the end of the century. Both predictions now appear ludicrous, but the analogy with past economic history does not make the Chinese case impossible.

One should bear in mind that China is still a relatively closed state-capitalist economy. It still has extensive restrictions on imports and foreign exchange controls. Its domestic markets are highly localized and regional governments still have a high degree of autonomy in economic policy. As Ajit Singh remarks, 'in China 90 per cent of industrial capital is in state hands, and most land is still collectively owned' (Singh 1998, p. 75). Most foreign investment in China comes from Chinese people overseas, especially from territories that are part of the People's Republic or claimed by it, such as Hong Kong and Taiwan: Hong Kong alone is reckoned to be responsible for 60 per cent of the FDI in China (Henderson 1998, p. 379). China still has a wide variety of types of enterprise, but state-owned enterprises, both national and local, and collectively owned town and village enterprises (TVEs) make up the vast bulk of enterprises. China still has a dual economy, part rapidly modernizing NIC, part semi-stagnant and internationally uncompetitive state socialist system, and it has a wide variety of types of rural economy, from successful TVE farms to grinding poverty on independent peasant plots. The point is that China's economy could point several ways.

Far from narrowing, regional disparities in China are widening, with the coastal provinces and Beijing pulling away from the rest. These disparities have increased quite markedly in the 1990s, as a glance at tables 5.2 and 5.3 will show.

Ignoring the difficulties of Chinese official statistics, what matters is the high degree of consistency in the provinces in the two tables and their relative rankings. The official statisticians would have no incentive to overstate regional inequalities. What the two tables show is that per capita income inequality has increased from a factor of 7.5 between the highest and the lowest to 10.9. This is a staggering degree of inequality, and given the continuing regionalization of the economy shows the potential for serious interregional conflicts. The interregional inequality is more serious for political stability than that between classes. China still has an efficient system of political repression and an authoritarian system of labour regulation (Dutton 1992). But China has always suffered from swings between periods of effective centralization and the dispersion and regionalization of authority. China may have a dual economy, but it cannot have a dual state. Regions like Shanghai compare favourably with the most successful of the rapidly modernizing Asian NICs, but elsewhere inefficient state socialist enterprises and grinding rural poverty are still common.

The problem is how a single regime can contain these inequalities? Can the state achieve a broadening and evening up of development? Can private capital and public investment be diverted from the overheating centres of

Table 5.2 Regional inequalities in China, 1990–1991

(a) Five provinces with the highest and lowest per capita incomes, 1991

	1991 GDP per capita (yuan)	Multiple of lowest province per capita GDP	Growth in GDP 1990–1 (%)
Highest			
Shanghai	6,675	7.5	7.0
Beijing	5,781	6.5	7.5
Tianjin	3,944	4.4	6.0
Guangdong	2,823	3.2	17.3
Liaoning	2,707	3.0	5.5
Lowest			
Henan	1,141	1.3	7.0
Gansu	1,133	1.3	6.5
Guangxi	1,058	1.2	12.7
Anhui	1,052	1.2	−3.7
Guizhou	890	1.0	9.9

(b) Five provinces with the highest and lowest growth rates, 1990–1991

	Growth in GDP (%)		Growth in GDP (%)
Highest		*Lowest*	
Guangdong	17.3	Anhui	−3.7
Zhejang	15.4	Tibet	1.6
Fujian	14.7	Shanxi	3.3
Shangdong	13.9	Heilongjiang	3.9
Xinjiang	13.9	Hubei	4.5

Source: *China Statistical Yearbook*, 1993, derived from tables T2.16 (p. 33) and T2.17 (p. 34)

growth towards China's poorer regions? The state must do this if it is to contain the localization of power. China is unlikely to become a democracy, given the vast disparities between regions and classes.[1] But can it retain a stable and competent authoritarian regime? The question cannot be answered at present. The political will to suppress nationalist dissent in Tibet and among the Uighurs is evident: this shows that the state is aware of its fragility and unwilling to yield lest wider centrifugal pressures are given encouragement. If central authority does weaken, and political stability is threatened, then the prospects for wider development radiating out from the current centres of growth will be threatened too.

No sensible person would wish continued economic backwardness on China, which would be to condemn hundreds of millions of people to poverty and wretchedness. A prosperous and outward-looking China would be both a major growing market for the West and a source of peace and stability.

Table 5.3   Regional inequalities in China, 1996

(a) Five provinces with the highest and lowest per capita incomes, 1996

	1996 per capita GDP (yuan)	Multiple of lowest province per capita GDP	Growth in GDP 1995–6 (%)
Highest			
Shanghai	22,275	10.9	13.0
Beijing	15,044	7.2	9.2
Tianjin	12,270	5.9	14.3
Guangdong	9,513	4.5	10.7
Zhejiang	9,455	4.5	12.7
Lowest			
Yunnan/Jiangxi	3,715	1.8	10.4/13.4
Shaanxi	3,313	1.6	10.2
Gansu	2,901	1.4	11.5
Tibet	2,732	1.3	13.2
Guizhou	2,093	1.0	8.9
For comparison			
Hong Kong	193,000	92.1	4.7
Taiwan	107,000	51.1	5.6

(b) Five provinces with highest and lowest average growth rates, 1993–1996

	Growth in GDP (%)		Growth in GDP (%)
Highest		*Lowest*	
Jiangsu	16.2	Quinghai	8.6
Guangdong	16.8	Guizhou	8.7
Anhui	17.6	Heilongjiang	9.1
Zhejiang	17.9	Xinjang	9.1
Fujian	19.4	Nigxia	9.5

Source: *China Statistical Yearbook*, 1997, derived from tables 2.10 (p. 43) and 2.11 (p. 45); Hong Kong data from table 20.3 (p. 785); Taiwan data from table 1.3 (p. 805). Transliterations may vary from the 1993 edition used in table 5.2 above

The statistics offer some comfort for the optimists. Although regional inequalities have widened, the picture for growth rates is more encouraging. For example, Anhui at the lower end of the per capita income table and with a growth rate of −3.7 per cent in 1990–1 now has one of the highest provincial growth rates in the average for 1993–6. In 1990–1 the differential between the lowest and highest positive growth rates was 19.7; in 1993–6 it was 10.8. The *lowest* growth rate in 1993–6 was Quinghai at 8.6 per cent. Hence the possibility that development in poorer and peripheral regions is accelerating.

Even if growth does even out some of the disparities, and people may be less discontented at the wealth of the Shanghai bourgeoisie if their own incomes are rising rapidly by reference to their own past experience, China will still face formidable structural economic problems. China has a relatively low rate of population growth at 1.5 per cent, but it is estimated that its population will still grow from 1,166 billion in 1992 – and 1,215 billion in 1996 to about 1.5 billion in 2025 (*World Bank Atlas*, 1994, pp. 8–9). This assumes that China's draconian population control policies remain in effect. Yet even if they do, and as a paradoxical consequence of the restriction of the birthrate, the population bulge of the 1960s will pass through the generations to give China a very high ratio of older people to the economically active by about 2025. China may have 300 million people over sixty at that date and about the same proportion of older and economically inactive people as Europe is expected to have in 2010 (Kennedy 1993, p. 168). China's economy will have to grow substantially to keep up with its population growth and to provide social welfare. In addition to the burden of the aged, China may have as many as 200 million unemployed or underemployed in the early twenty-first century. If China were able to lift the whole of its population out of poverty it would be a tremendous achievement. To achieve developed country status without destroying the environment and, therefore, the conditions for future economic and social progress would be a miracle.

Of the other large developing countries much less needs to be said, since none offers a credible model of rapid economic growth. India has had relatively low growth rates: during 1965–80 its average annual growth was 3.6 per cent, during 1980–9 5.8 per cent and during 1990–4 3.8 per cent (Singh 1998, table 3.1, p. 58). This performance is hardly dramatic by East Asian and South East Asian standards and was less than a third of China's average rate during 1990–4. India's population has been projected to double from 883 million in 1992 (945 million in 1996) to 1.5 billion in 2025 (Kennedy 1993, p. 183). Hence India will have to grow quite rapidly to stand still. Of other developing and transitional economies with large populations, the prospects of rapid modernization are even more moot. The Russian economy has been contracting in industrial output since 1985. Russia is facing a fiscal and financial crisis of terrifying proportions and also a demographic crisis as birthrates fall and death rates rise. Russia's economy had not effected a transition to a market-based system. The real economy is much smaller than official statistics claim, a consequence of many enterprises being quite literally value-destroying but valuing their output at inflated notional prices (Gaddy and Ickes 1998). The effect of the market 'reforms' since the early 1990s has been to shift Russian enterprises towards a system of non-market exchange in which barter and debts play a more important role than hard cash (W. Tompson 1998). Indonesia's crisis needs no further comment – its economy is expected to shrink by 20 per cent during 1998. Brazil is faced with a financial crisis, probable devaluation, major public expenditure cuts, large-scale urban unemployment, widespread rural poverty and a rapidly growing population.

The excessive optimism of the early 1990s about the prospects for economic growth in the developing world has rapidly turned sour. It is quite clear that the economic liberal vision of a world transformed by the power of free markets has failed. The combination of financial liberalization in the developing world and 'sound money' anti-inflationary policies in the West have produced the worst possible outcome, crisis induced by financial instability, spreading from Asia to other regions of the developing world, and economic stagnation in large parts of the developed world. To achieve economic development and greater fairness in the distribution of income on a world scale, quite different economic policies and large transfers of resources on the basis of need rather than market forces will be required. The politics for such policies and transfers quite simply does not exist.

Enthusiasts for the concept of globalization see the crisis in Asia as the first truly global economic crisis – the contagion spreading from Asia to Russia and Latin America, and maybe on to the West itself. A City economist expressing this view said naively, 'where was Asia in the 1930s?' The answer is quite simple. The Great Crash helped to reinforce tendencies towards fascism and imperialism in Japan, leading to the attempt to construct in the Greater East Asia co-prosperity sphere a trading bloc in which Japan cornered raw materials and secured markets for its industries. Malaysia was plunged into recession as the world price of tin collapsed, cutting its healthy positive contribution to the sterling area's current account. Australia suffered large-scale unemployment and rural poverty. The crisis now is not the same as that brought on by the 1929 crash, the markets are different, but the world economy of the 1920s was highly interdependent and exposed to financial market crises just as the world economy is today. Europe and the US were intimately linked by financial flows: Germany and Austria were heavily dependent on American loans in particular. Colonies and quasi-colonies were very reliant on export markets for their primary products in the industrial metropoles. The economic doctrines that precipitated and prolonged the crisis were very similar to those of today: 'sound money' and *laissez faire*. The world may with luck escape a crisis on the scale of the 1930s, which massively reduced the level of global trade and led to widespread protectionism, but economic liberals have helped to create a world with considerable similarities to the late 1920s. After 1918 the leading powers tried to recreate the institutions of the Gold Standard and the free markets of the *belle époque* and failed to achieve their aim. Perhaps the surge in economic liberal ideology after the 1970s is another attempt, doomed to failure, to create a world driven by free markets. To the extent that the world is not as the economic liberals claim, a truly globalized economy dominated by unregulated market forces, then there is hope that it can be put back together on a less volatile and more sustainable basis.

Appendix: The Asian Crisis

A simple way of representing the Asian crisis can be demonstrated by way of the figure A5.1. This follows the idea that this was essentially a 'crisis of liquidity' and a crisis of the financial system, rather than one driven by 'real fundamentals', which for the most part were sound (Radelet and Sachs 1998). The figure shows two different scenarios: (a) and (b). Part (a) illustrates what the *actual situation* in (some of) the East Asian economies is like, while (b) shows what the *IMF thinks* it is like. Note that for both (a) and (b) the level of liquidity (measured along the horizontal axis as M) is the same at the outset, at OM_0, and the situation is typified by a common level of *excess supply* (X_s) at that liquidity level: aggregate supply (AS) is greater than aggregate demand (AD). This is a reasonable assumption about the facts, since the crisis has left these economies with an excess supply potential.

Returning to the actual situation in (a), the correct policy response under these circumstances is to *expand liquidity* towards M_e, so as to bring supply and demand into equilibrium (which, incidentally, will produce an expansion of the economy to $AS_e \& AD_e$).

The reasons for the necessity of an expansion of liquidity have to do with the nature of company financing conditions as outlined by Wade and Veneroso (1998) and Chang (1998). Unlike Anglo-American corporate financial arrangements, which rely mainly on share capital, East Asian companies are heavily geared and rely much more on fixed interest bank loans. Thus during a financial recession, East Asian companies are harder hit in liquidity terms, and require more generous and sustained liquidity support if they are to ride out the recession successfully. The analysis here represents this argument in a slightly different way and for the economy as a whole.

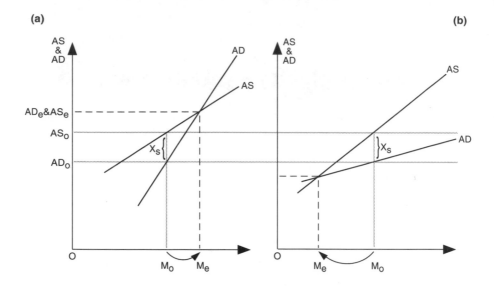

Figure A5.1 The East Asian crisis in a framework of aggregate demand/aggregate supply analysis: actual situation and IMF perspective compared

However, the IMF thinks the situation is actually like that shown in (b), which is its classic response situation for an advanced industrial country of the Anglo-American type. The policy requirement, as it sees it here, is to *reduce liquidity* to OM_e, *deflating the economy* to bring about the alignment of AS and AD. However, note that the application of this policy in the actual case of (a) leads to a worse situation as far as the alignment of AS and AD is concerned, not a better one. It destabilizes the economy rather than stabilizes it.

Clearly, this whole analysis turns on the position and shape of the AS and AD curves in each case. In (a), the actual case in East Asia, the AD curve is more elastic with respect to liquidity than the AS curve. In other words these countries are typified by 'export-led growth', where AD is very sensitive to firms' liquidity conditions. On the other hand, in economies of the Anglo-American type (b), the IMF *assumes* that AS is more sensitive to liquidity changes than is AD (there is therefore a reluctance in the Anglo-American countries to countenance AD policy activism).

6

Can the Welfare State Survive Globalization?

In no area is increased openness to international capital movements and trade seen in more apocalyptic terms than in the case of social welfare. For example, the political theorist John Gray regards the demise of the welfare state as a direct effect of globalization:

> To imagine that the social market economies of the past can renew themselves intact under the forces of downwards harmonisation is the most dangerous of the many illusions associated with the global market. Instead social market systems are being compelled progressively to dismantle themselves, so that they can compete on more equal terms with economies in which environmental, social and labour costs are lowest. (Gray 1998, p. 92)

Many other authors make the same assertion of a race to the bottom, as we have seen in our discussion of labour costs in chapter 4, most notably Martin and Schumann (1997) or Greider (1997).[1]

There is no doubt that welfare states in the advanced countries are now under a variety of sources of strain that push up both costs and the demand for services: high levels of persistent unemployment in many European countries, ageing populations – increasing the costs of pensions and health care – increasing complexity of medical technology, high rates of family break-up and a decline in informal family-centred welfare, and a growing demand for enhanced welfare and social services generally. In the EU the convergence criteria for monetary union have put a general break on public spending and public borrowing in a number of countries, with an impact on welfare entitlements and provision. The question, however, is whether there is an added pressure on welfare entitlements and provision that is due to increasing international openness *per se*. If a race to the bottom is taking place, it should show in a failing economic performance by countries with extensive welfare states. France and Germany are cutting back in order to qualify for EMU, and Germany has the burden of assimilating the former GDR. But both have healthy balance of trade surpluses and their exports continue to grow. France attracted more inward investment than the UK in the period 1991–5 ($19 billion per annum as against $17.2 billion), demonstrating that there are assets other than deregulation and flexible labour markets that attract investors (IMF data cited *Observer*, 27 Apr. 1997). Both have intrinsic structural problems with their welfare states, high unemployment and relatively low growth, but neither is failing to pay its way in world markets.

This may seem an old-fashioned concern, but it is a crude index of competitive performance in international terms. A country, like the UK, that must finance a structural balance of payments deficit is dependent on short-term capital flows as much as a country with a substantial ratio of public debt to GDP is dependent on the bond markets. In a way it might be argued that the real effect of increased international openness to trade and capital movements is to make medium-sized states like France or Germany more like smaller highly internationalized ones like Austria and Switzerland.

In a sense the issue of international exposure is not new; historically a high degree of internationalization has been typical of the smaller advanced countries, and it has induced higher rather than lower levels of public and welfare spending. Very open economies are more exposed to external shocks and must develop means to cushion their firms and workers against them. As Katzenstein (1985) has shown, small, highly internationalized countries like Austria, the Netherlands and Sweden have combined corporatist economic policy-making and traditions of solidarism and consensus-seeking among the organized social interests with high levels of welfare and public provision to protect individuals against the effects of externally generated risks. Corporatism enabled states to adapt macroeconomically, by restraining wages, coordinating economic action by firms and underwriting public policies of industrial support and labour market adjustment. Welfare enabled workers to bear the costs of external shocks while these adaptive measures were taking effect. By offering security to workers, welfare states built political support for consensus policies. Thus a high level of international exposure does not automatically require the responses of cut-throat competition between firms and the slashing of welfare provision. Rodrik (1996) has confirmed these findings of political science by an econometric analysis. This covers government expenditures as a percentage of GDP (excluding interest payments) for twenty-three OECD countries during 1990–2 (Rodrik 1996, fig. 4.2, p. 52). It shows a clear connection between the degree of international openness and the level of government expenditure.

In a later work Rodrik argues: 'Societies that expose themselves to greater amounts of external risk demand (and receive) a larger governmental role as shelter for the vicissitudes of global markets. Hence the conclusion that the social welfare state is the flip side of the open economy!' (1997, p. 53). The issue now is whether such national responses are still possible. Katzenstein's study relates to a period in which controls on capital movements were still in force. John Gray, with characteristic emphasis, claims that the social democratic regime presupposed a closed economy in which capital movements were controlled within a system of semi-fixed exchange rates (1998, p. 88; see also Gray 1996). One should be careful here to decouple welfare systems and Keynesianism in a way Gray does not: many states with high levels of welfare, most notably Germany for a large part of the postwar era, did not practise demand management policies. It is certainly true that full employment during the Long Boom of 1945–73 kept the cost of welfare states down, but high levels of growth and full employment had multiple causes across the advanced world and existed in both Keynesian and non-Keynesian states (Hall 1989).

States with low levels of trade to GDP, like Japan or the US, could get away with vestigial or imperfect welfare states, using other policies to sustain economic performance and, therefore, employment: in Japan industrial policy and in the US demand management and federal spending on defence and infrastructure. Rodrik argues cautiously that the very factors that increase the need in all the advanced countries for welfare to provide insurance against and adaptation to external shocks may now work against the implementation of such policies. He says that 'globalization presents this dilemma: it results in increased demands on the state to provide social insurance while reducing the ability of the state to perform that role effectively' (1997, p. 53). The danger of a high level of external exposure is that the mixture of extensive welfare and free trade becomes unstuck. Capital becomes mobile and will move if domestic economic policies and tax regimes threaten economic returns available elsewhere. Capital can intimidate both national governments and workers in particular firms with threats to defect. How seriously these threats are taken will depend on the conjuncture. Major manufacturing firms with large fixed investments are unlikely to move lock, stock and barrel. Financial institutions, however, can move pensions and insurance investments offshore and the markets can refuse to buy government bonds except at an interest premium. Thus, in an open economy, capital will resist high levels of corporate taxation and payroll taxes paid by employers. It will try to increase its income take from firms by demanding wage restraint without compensating bargains: a form of 'postcorporatist', one-sided bargaining typical of the US. The costs of welfare will, therefore, be forced on to workers' incomes. At the same time, the elite of high-paid and relatively mobile workers will resent high levels of tax. Thus the tax base will erode as incomes from capital and higher salaries are increasingly exempt.

Rodrik's case depends centrally not merely on the mobility of capital, but on the use of such mobility as a threat in distributional bargaining. It supposes a delocalized and postcorporatist business class. Obviously, the threat is real – very high levels of taxation on investment incomes in an open economy, cutting into pensions and personal saving, will threaten middle-class support for the welfare system, as well as lead to defections abroad by major institutional investors. Inevitably, welfare and government expenditure generally will have to be funded out of taxes on incomes, sales and targeted services like airline journeys or insurance policies. This means that the public must both want such welfare services and be willing to pay for them. It implies both solidaristic values and appropriate political institutions that force decision-makers to respond to those values. Hence both attitudes and institutions become central, in the form of distinct national legacies that favour solidarism and public consumption. Societies without such inheritances or the means to invent them will thus feel the pressure. The degree of international exposure *per se* is not the issue: rather it is the domestic political response to it. Moreover, to attitudes and institutions must be added effective macroeconomic and welfare policy responses by elites: pressure on public spending can be made much worse by poorly conceived or inappropriate policies (as we shall see in the case of Sweden).

This implies that welfare states already funded out of general taxation probably have a head start on those funded from employers' contributions, taxes on capital and high levels of public borrowing. Pay-as-you-go welfare states will be viable, ones that avoid excessive budget deficits and rely on domestic sources of revenue. It also implies that not only is welfare spending a means of insurance against external shocks, it is also a means of macroeconomic adjustment. In a severe externally induced crisis, corporatist bargaining may centre not merely on wage restraint but on the containment or retrenchment of public expenditure. As we shall see, the two are connected: the employed will contain wage demands more readily if tax bills are held down. This means bringing public expenditure and welfare programmes into the domain of bargaining, deciding which programmes must be maintained to help adjust to shocks (training, active labour market measures) and which programmes may involve temporary or long-term cutbacks in benefits or entitlements. In an advanced corporatist economy, the representatives of the recipients of welfare should be brought into the bargaining, as economic agents with a role in generating consensus and not merely as passive objects of policy.

Ireland, for example, has its corporatist National Economic and Social Council but also the National Economic and Social Forum. The former represents the traditional and social partners and bargains primarily over national wage policy; the latter represents other social interests, including the unemployed. So far, the interests represented by the Forum have not been included directly in national bargaining. However, if effective use is to be made of such extended corporatist representation to achieve consensus on a wide basis and to prevent the Forum turning into a source of special pleading by claimants for more government programmes, in an essentially negative and passive role, then the Council will have to include them too. Ireland has had a high rate of growth (5.7 per cent in the years 1991–5), but persistent high unemployment (Sabel 1996; O'Donnell and O'Reardon 1997).

This is to get ahead of ourselves. If we accept that welfare states do face some added constraints in a period of high capital mobility and international exposure to trade, then the issue is how can these be met. One way is to return to Katzenstein's theme of small states in world markets and look at how very open economies with extended welfare states have fared. The examples chosen are Sweden, because it is always cited as a classic case of retrenchment through international pressures, but also Denmark and Holland because they illustrate the possibilities of successful adaptation and survival both in economic performance and in welfare policy. In both cases the story is not one of simple expansion of welfare: rather welfare has played its part as a variable in macroeconomic adjustment, both through strategic cutbacks at difficult conjunctures and long-term shifts in welfare policy and provision. They are also very different institutionally. For some time Denmark has lacked centralized corporatist bargaining over wages, unlike the Netherlands and Sweden (Lind 1997). Denmark has been seen as having a 'Scandinavian' welfare state and the Netherlands a 'continental' one (Esping-Andersen 1990, 1996c). Thus they offer a crucial experiment: small highly internationalized states facing similar pressures but with different industrial and institutional structures. If the effect of internationalization is to undermine welfare, it should be visible here. If societies can contain these external pressures, then the ability of different complexes of institutions to adapt and respond shows that policy does have an effect and that there are options at the political level.

A Swedish crisis and a Danish surprise

The economic difficulties experienced by Sweden in the 1990s have been widely cited as evidence that globalization has removed the option for distinctive national economic policies. For example, Gray claims: 'What happened in Sweden has implications for social market economies everywhere' (1998, p. 92). In particular, Sweden has been forced to retreat from full employment policies based on the expansion of the public sector and to cut back on entitlements in its extensive and universalist welfare state. Sweden's crisis is taken to be decisive because it was perceived internationally to be the classic embodiment of a social democratic 'third way' between state socialism and laissez-faire capitalism. If Sweden could not sustain its welfare system, then what hope for other states?

One cannot dispute the severity of the crisis. Over the period 1990–5 growth was virtually stagnant at an average for the five years of 0.4 per cent

GDP; in 1991–3 GDP growth was negative (OECD 1997a, statistical summary). Unemployment rose from 1.6 per cent in 1990 to 7.7 per cent in 1993, and if one includes those in active labour market programmes, from 2.1 per cent to 12.5 per cent (Stephens 1996). Total government expenditure in relation to GDP rose from 60 per cent in 1989 to 74.1 per cent in 1993, before falling back to 66 per cent in 1995 (Goul Andersen 1997c, table 1, p. 2; OECD 1997a). Sweden suffered a particularly sharp crisis in the early 1990s as a result of three interrelated phenomena that acted together to drive down employment and output: first, the movement of Swedish capital abroad in anticipation of the completion of the European single market and before Sweden's own entry into the EU; second, the widespread depression of the early 1990s in Europe; third, the struggle to maintain a fixed parity of the krona against the Deutschmark after the abandonment of the policy of competitive devaluations of the 1980s.

There are two responses to this crisis. One is to claim that it is a typical and inevitable feature of excessive public spending and overextended welfare entitlements. Sweden is simply an extreme case of a general problem with European welfare states. The other, represented for example by Esping-Andersen (1996b), is to see the crisis as primarily conjunctural. Sweden's economy will recover, indeed is recovering, and, with appropriate retrenchment, the welfare state will survive. This view has some merits, but clearly there are structural features that need addressing too. The defect of the first view is that it neither accepts a substantial amount of conjunctural contingency nor does it allow for Swedish specificity. We should not let Sweden's status as an exemplar of welfare capitalism hide the very distinctive features of its economy and economic policy that explain why it was so exposed to international constraints in the early 1990s.[2] Thus Sweden's problems may not be intrinsic to welfare states in advanced countries, and such countries may have other more extensive options than Esping-Andersen's expectation of muddling through and retrenchment.

Sweden is distinctive in the degree of its export orientation in manufacturing and the dominance of the internationally exposed sector by a few highly concentrated corporations. As a direct consequence of its post-1945 export success Swedish manufacturing has become highly multinational, with approximately half of the output of Swedish firms being produced abroad. Increasingly, Swedish large firms have used their internationalization to oppose some of the distinctive features of the Swedish model. The major employers came to reject the corporatist bargaining and governance arrangements that had served them so well until the 1980s, the Swedish Employers Federation (SAF) abandoning centralized wage bargaining in 1990 and withdrawing from tripartite institutions of economic governance altogether in 1991 (Martin 1995, pp. 279–80; Dølvik and Martin 1997, pp. 106–9). The big firms increasingly threatened to defect abroad if governments and unions failed to adopt the employers' policy prescriptions.

Swedish society might be said to be paying the price for making firms like L. M. Ericsson and Saab into world companies. In the post-1945 period Swedish economic policy was dominated by the goals of full employment and promoting export performance. Swedish industry was sustained by 'forced draught' macroeconomic policies aimed at providing it with a stable domestic environment, internationally competitive wages in the export sector and low-cost investment. Exchange controls and credit controls served to give governments a high degree of autonomy in managing the domestic economy. From the 1950s to the end of the 1970s centralized corporatist bargaining determined wages policy. Industry, labour and the state all pursued policies emphasizing wage restraint and wage solidarity between sectors (Martin 1995, p. 265). Taxation policy restrained domestic demand and thus prevented overheating, and yet ensured full employment by steadily expanding public sector employment and welfare services. Investment was promoted by low interest rates.

By the 1980s the elements of this policy consensus became unstuck. The unions objected to the excess profits for the major firms created by the wage solidarity policy. The firms themselves objected to rising wage costs and inflexible wage structures, and chafed at exchange controls limiting their capacity to operate abroad. In the 1980s Swedish governments dismantled the apparatus of exchange and credit controls. They also adopted the policy of using devaluations to restore competitiveness. The effect of the removal of credit controls largely negated the benefits of devaluing the krona. A credit-fuelled consumer boom led to overheating and inflation, and to the collapse of wage restraint. In responding to this the currency was pegged to the German mark and the public sector was expanded to sustain employment, leading to the crises of the early 1990s (Dølvik & Martin 1997, pp. 110–13). Sweden's problems are clearly due to a mixture of economic structure, policy errors and conjunctural factors, but the heavy dependence of the economy on large multinational manufacturing exporters, on the one hand, and public employment, on the other, severely limited the options available.

However, the idea that all advanced economies would face a crisis deriving from the pressure of their extended welfare states on the international competitiveness of their export sectors is belied by other societies that have had very different experiences in the same period of the late 1980s and early 1990s. One has only to cross the Sound to Denmark. Superficially, Denmark is a typical Scandinavian welfare state with high unemployment and a high percentage of government expenditure to GDP: in 1993 unemployment stood at 10.7 per cent and public expenditure at 63.8 per cent of GDP. Denmark had experienced relatively high unemployment and sluggish growth throughout the 1980s: in the early 1980s it had an early experience of welfare state retrenchment when entitlements and compensation ratios were cut back. It also provided an early example of populist protest against excessive public expenditure when the taxpayers' Progress Party won 15.9 per cent of the vote in 1973–4.

Yet since the early 1990s Denmark has experienced a strong economic recovery with above average growth, a reduction in unemployment and a positive balance of payments. It thus seems to be bucking a trend towards welfare states in crisis, and, moreover, public support for welfare remains high. If extended welfare states were such a threat to international competitiveness and economic performance then Denmark ought not to work, but it does.

In an article on the history of small-scale production in Denmark, Kristensen and Sabel (1997) argue that the survival and success of small farmers and firms in that country appear to be an exception, but they contend that a concatenation of circumstances and outcomes, many of which were present in other countries, here produced a distinct variant (see also Kristensen 1995). In other words, Denmark was not so much an exceptional case as a possible world. It would be too much to see Denmark as a model, whether of successful small-scale production or of a modern welfare state. A model implies that the experience can be readily copied and applied. Rather it serves as an indication that such variants are possible, that extended welfare and economic performance can go together in a small and highly internationalized economy. As Esping-Andersen (1990, 1996c) argues persuasively, welfare states, even where they are equally extensive and in countries with a common level of development, exhibit distinct structural and institutional features that make them more or less able to respond to the forces of European integration, economic internationalism and social change.

What are the distinctive features of its economy and welfare state that have led Denmark to be able to survive and adapt? The first point to notice is that, unlike Sweden, Denmark has an economy in which numerous small and medium-sized firms are salient, and that these span a number of sectors. The Danish private business sector is less homogeneous than Sweden's. It speaks with more voices, and is less concentrated and less multinational. Firms thus have a long history of adapting to international markets and of being obliged to do this for themselves without lobbying as privileged insiders, in a highly centralized corporatist structure, for compensatory policies from government and organized labour. Denmark's exports are now overwhelmingly industrial goods (72 per cent in 1995). Many small firms are dynamic and innovatory, and industrial districts, like those in West Jutland, have been dynamic focuses of growth. Denmark has not had centralized national wage bargaining in the private sector.

Unemployment benefit is closely tailored to the features of this small firm economy. Employment protection measures are among the weakest in Europe, lower than in the UK (Nickell 1997, table 4, p. 61). Unemployment benefits have been easy to get, with a long period of compensation and a relatively high level of compensation of lower incomes which tapers off sharply. They are close to flat-rate benefits organized as insurance funds, but where the bulk of financing is provided by the state out of general taxation (Goul Andersen 1996, pp. 160–1). Access and availability were tightened up in 1995. The system thus allowed employers to adjust to changing conditions without imposing a severe burden on lower-paid workers. As Loftager comments, 'the unemployment benefit system has not only served the interests of the employees. Corresponding to the generous benefits, the rules for dismissal have been relaxed considerably, thereby becoming more favourable to the employers. And especially in an economy like the Danish characterised by many small firms this has contributed to flexibility and competitiveness' (Loftager 1996b, pp. 144–5).

The universalism of the benefits system thus has obvious advantages for flexibility. Both unemployment benefit and basic pensions are paid out of general taxation (taxes in 1995 were 51.6 per cent of GDP, the highest in the EU, and primarily composed of income tax and value-added tax at 25 per cent; corporation taxes were low). They can thus be varied to suit economic conditions, and indeed have been (as in the case of the retrenchment in the early 1980s). Denmark is thus not burdened with unsustainable income-related public pension entitlements, or with a system of welfare like that in France where benefits are tied closely to one's existing job. Welfare policy can be adjusted, and labour mobility is not discouraged by such inflexible job-specific methods of providing benefits as those in France and Germany where benefits are funded substantially through social insurance paid by employers.

The OECD argues that high taxes depress labour demand and, combined with readily available benefits, ensure that wages at the lower end have a high floor (OECD 1997a, p. 51). This may be so, but the system has many advantages that outweigh the flexibility provided by very low pay and poor benefits. As Goul Andersen remarks, 'the Danish welfare system is a universalist system with some resemblance to a citizen's income system' (1996, p. 160). Only a very small proportion of the population is not covered by some automatic citizen's entitlement to income support – only about 50,000 people or about 1.5 per cent of the population, mostly women at home, have no income right of their own (Loftager 1996a, p. 17). It might therefore be assumed that the disincentives to work mean that the burden of dependants to active citizens will become intolerable.

The evidence does not bear this out. First, its demographic profile means that Denmark will have a lower than average proportion of people aged sixty and over because of higher than the European average fertility rates: roughly 4:1 of the economically active age to over-60s in 2020 in contrast to Germany's 3:1 (Goul Andersen 1997c, table 7, p. 15.). The OECD calculates that the burden of future transfer commitments places Denmark in the middle range of OECD countries – net present value of social security payments as a percentage of 1994 GDP = 235 per cent in Denmark as against Germany's 348 per cent, France's 318 per cent and Italy's 401 per cent (OECD 1997a, table 15, p. 59).

Secondly, a readily accessible universal welfare system does not seem to have reduced labour market participation: the participation ratio in 1993 was 82.6 per cent, above the US at 75.9 per cent and the EU15 average of 66.9 per cent. Female participation rates have risen from 43.5 per cent in 1960 to 78.3 per cent in 1993 (Goul Andersen 1997c, table 7, p. 15). Most Danish households of working age are one-and-a-half or two income households. Thus the fact that 20 per cent of those aged 19–66 receive their income from public transfer payments does not mean a large proportion of households excluded from labour market participation and condemned to low incomes.

Denmark appears to have very high levels of both passive income support and active labour market programmes, ranking highest for both in the EU12 in 1992 (Goul Andersen 1996, fig. 3, p. 164). The effect of flexible labour markets and strong active measures means that there is a good deal of conjunctural and frictional unemployment, and a fair bit of 'resting', but very much less long-term unemployment than one would anticipate. Indeed, 'Denmark had generally had the lowest proportion of long-term unemployed in the European Union' (Goul Andersen 1996, p. 163).

Thirdly, the effect of this combination of strong passive income support and active labour market measures ensures that the unemployed are not marginalized. Denmark has among the highest levels of equality in disposable incomes in the OECD and did not experience a major shift towards inequality in the 1980s, unlike many other countries, most notably the UK and New Zealand (Goul Andersen 1997c, table 12, p. 24). Denmark had only 3 per cent of households with a principal wage earner unemployed below the poverty line in 1988, compared to close to 50 per cent in the UK (Goul Andersen 1997c, fig. 2, p. 25). Some 61 per cent of unemployed workers who are married or cohabiting are homeowners (Goul Andersen 1996, p. 170). Again, among the married, a high proportion of the unemployed are women (some two-thirds) and long-term unemployment among the married is even more heavily concentrated among women (75 per cent of those with 4–5 years unemployment are women) (Goul Andersen 1996, p. 171). The absence of social exclusion makes the unemployed much like the rest of the population, and therefore more easily employable. However, dual-income families and readily available benefits mean that poverty is not a pressure driving citizens into low-paid work. This factor has prompted the recent Danish reforms of 1993–5 which reduced entitlements to unemployment funds, restricting benefit to five years of which three will be spent in active labour market programmes. This switch in policy does seem to have contributed to a reduction in unemployment, the 'active line' being the factor pushing people to seek work rather than the crude threat of poverty.

Fourthly, private employment in Denmark has been almost flat since 1980: indeed, the level was only marginally higher in 1997 than in 1948 (1,789,000 compared with 1,782,000) (Goul Andersen 1997a, table 3). Public employment grew from 691,000 in 1980 to 800,000 in 1997. Public employment is heavily concentrated in services. The Danes have a very high level of collective and public service consumption – for example, the widely available public daycare for children that enables dual-income families to function, and good public transport. Given a high level of income equality and ready access to good public services and universalist benefits, most citizens irrespective of income or occupation are consumers of public services and benefit from them. Hence the viability of a high-tax, high-service regime. There is little evidence that public employment has 'crowded out' the private sector. Public employment has absorbed those who would otherwise have been displaced by 'jobless growth'. GDP has grown far faster than employment: GDP at factor cost was some 65 per cent greater in 1990 than in 1970, whereas employment was just over 10 per cent greater (Loftager 1996a, p. 5).

Moreover, public services (which absorb 30 per cent of the labour force) should not be seen as a pure cost but rather as collective consumption: taxes are 'buying' services and enabling them to be available to all. The Danish welfare state is service intensive rather than benefits intensive. It is a widespread perverse tendency, reinforced by national income accounting conventions, to treat public expenditure as a deduction from private welfare, as if public services were value destroying. Given a reasonable level of efficiency of service provision in both public and private sectors, then the choice between private and collective consumption is just that, a political choice in how and why services are provided. Public services have the advantage of promoting equality of access, thus reducing cost constraints for lower income groups. Thus women on lower incomes are able to work because of publicly provided daycare.

Fifthly, the Danish transfer payments system is not, despite popular perceptions, inordinately expensive in comparison with comparable neighbouring countries like Germany or the Netherlands. Danish welfare is overwhelmingly paid out of current taxes, and income taxes and VAT are both highly visible. However, when one aggregates taxes and social insurance payments, then as Goul Andersen argues, 'this composite income tax as a percentage of GDP resembles most other North European countries' (1997c, p. 5). Recalculated after deduction of interest payments and correcting for the taxation of income transfers, public expenditure as a percentage of gross factor income in 1987 was 40.9 per cent for Denmark, approximately 40 per cent for the Netherlands, and 38.1 per cent for Germany (Goul Andersen 1997c, table 2).

Lastly, such a level of welfare is not unsustainable, given the political will and political support. Jorgen Goul Andersen has presented extensive survey data on public perceptions of the welfare state, and overall some 67 per cent of those surveyed agreed that the welfare state should be maintained rather than reduced. Even among private sector employees with no experience of unemployment some 24 per cent more supported the existing level of welfare provision than thought it had gone too far (Goul Andersen 1996, p. 179). This is further evidence that Denmark is not divided into insiders and outsiders, differentiating between the stably employed, especially in the private sector, and those dependent on state benefits, seen as a burden. There is evidence that younger Danes are less solidaristic, particularly students who see the unemployed who enter university given superior terms, but given the high levels of taxation in Denmark, public resistance to welfare is much lower than one would expect. One can surmise that equality, non-marginalization of welfare recipients and a common experience of collective consumption do lead to high levels of solidarity. People contribute but they also benefit. This contrasts with exclusionary welfare states, where exclusion and pauperization lead employed taxpayers to see services and entitlements for the poor and unemployed as a pure cost.

There is a good deal of academic and elite criticism of Danish government institutions and of public expenditure in particular. Danish political science has had a strong strand of public choice theory and neoclassical economics has been influential. Denmark thus does not lack the elite voices that have been so successful in transforming countries like the UK and then New Zealand in an anti-welfare direction. What has been missing is the political capacity. Most Danish governments have been coalitions without large majorities. Confronted with strong public support for welfare, political parties have hesitated to follow arguments for radical reform. Political power is also highly diffused in Denmark. Local government is very decentralized and has a high degree of autonomy. Corporatism may be weak at national level, but is strongly entrenched within the different branches of the public sector. It is thus difficult to drive through change against the resistance of local authorities and welfare professionals. It is significant that both the UK and New Zealand are highly centralized 'Westminster' systems, characterized by winner-take-all party government. In both countries the first past the post electoral system has meant that governments could enjoy effective majorities while appealing to narrow and exclusive bases in the constituencies. Thus in the UK the public has continued to support higher public spending on health and education, yet since the 1970s successive governments have been able to ignore these mass attitudes.

According to public choice theory Denmark should have experienced institutional deadlock and ever-escalating public expenditures as entrenched interests fought budget cuts and sought to expand their own programmes. Yet Danish governments have been able to restrain budget growth and cut back on entitlements. The reason, argue Albeck et al., is that within the state and public sector organized interests have traded off short-term budgetary gains for preserving long-term institutional autonomy (n.d.,

'Introduction'). Danish citizens and organized interests seem to have been willing to adapt to crises, making sacrifices in periods of economic difficulty. Undoubtedly, equality and inclusion help to promote such solidaristic and public-minded behaviour: citizens and organized interests have a high degree of influence in the political process and a reasonable expectation of fairness in the behaviour of governments and other political actors. Unlike polarized societies in which the losers can expect to be penalized in distributional conflict, solidaristic behaviour in this situation is a rational choice.

A Dutch miracle?

Visser and Hemerijck's book on the Netherlands, *A Dutch Miracle* (1997, hereafter V&H 1997), is an extremely valuable study of the institutional conditions and policy measures which enable a small and highly internationalized advanced economy to adapt to the intensified competitive pressures of the 1990s and in doing so preserve an extensive system of social welfare. The authors show how the Netherlands is an exception to Esping-Andersen's (1990, 1996c) analysis that welfare states, once institutionalized, are very difficult to change. It is widely accepted that extensive welfare states create powerful political constituencies, vested interests and organized groups with veto powers that obstruct change in either structures or entitlements, however real and necessary may be the economic pressures for adaptation. Such rigidities are a block to effective macroeconomic adjustment to the pressures of the world economy. At the same time Esping-Andersen argues that welfare states come in distinct institutional complexes, some of which (like the continental European model) have more serious effects on the level of unemployment and the capacity to control public expenditure and welfare entitlements than others. It would be an exaggeration to say he believes that the institutional structure chosen at the beginning of welfare reform is fate, but the analysis claims a high degree of path dependency and a high tendency to adaptive sclerosis.

The Netherlands is close to being a crucial experiment for the effects of globalization on the welfare state, since it is one of the most highly internationalized economies in the world and has been so for some time. Its ratio of commodity exports and imports to GDP puts it in a league with Singapore at 83.4 per cent in 1995 (although still lower than it was in 1913); the ratio is over twice that of the UK, itself at the top end for industrial countries (see table 2.3 above).

The Dutch invest substantially abroad, some 17 per cent of the financial assets of households being held overseas in 1995, whereas the proportions for the UK, Canada, Denmark, Germany, Italy, Norway and Sweden were all under 10 per cent and for France, Japan and Spain under 5 per cent (see figure 2.5 above).

Until the late 1980s the Netherlands appeared to be a classic example of the defects of a continental welfare model. The Dutch system, like the French and German, concentrated on benefits for full-time working bread-winners, with high social insurance costs per employee. Firms adapted to competitive pressures by productivity growth and by shedding labour on to the social security system. Together the employers and unions, who controlled access to the employment and sickness insurance funds through the consociational governance system, accepted large-scale early retirements and a huge increase in disability benefits.

In 1986 some 27 per cent of those of working age were on disability benefits, unemployment benefits, early retirement, social assistance or special employment measures (V&H 1997, p. 9). The labour force participation rate for males aged 60 to 65 fell from 70 per cent in 1973 to 22 per cent in 1991 (p. 17). In 1973 women's participation in the labour force was a mere 29 per cent and in 1983 just 34.7 per cent, well below the European average (table 4, p. 25 and p. 33). In 1983 the employment/population ratio was 52 per cent, the lowest of all OECD countries (p. 24). In 1989 the number of people receiving disability benefits approached 1 million in a population of just over 15 million. In 1983 unemployment was 9.7 per cent (table 3, p. 25).

Whatever one's stance in economic theory, the Netherlands was faced with a potentially unsustainable burden of dependants to active participants in the labour force. The tendency to adapt by shedding labour on to the social welfare budget drove up both the costs of employees for firms, and the tax take on workers' incomes. The result was a cycle of maladaptive responses. Workers became unwilling to continue the wage moderation policies that had enabled the strongly externally oriented Dutch economy to compete in world markets. Employers were reluctant to hire labour and sought to drive up productivity: after 1960 productivity rose from 54 per cent of US levels to 92 per cent in 1987 and 99 per cent in 1995 (OECD 1997a, table 24, p. 94). Only this high rate of growth in productivity could sustain the welfare system, but it had the inevitable consequence of 'jobless' economic growth. Moreover, as it was approaching US levels by the mid-1990s, there were distinct limits to improving competitiveness further by this route.

Consider then the following facts. The labour force has increased by 25 per cent between 1982 and 1996 (V&H 1997, p. 23). Unemployment fell to 6.5 per cent in 1996 by standardized measures, and to 5.2 per cent in 1997 – comparable with the US (V&H 1997, p. 24; OECD 1998b, fig. 1, p. 23). Employment growth averaged 1.8 per cent per annum between 1983 and 1993, compared to a mere 0.4 per cent EU average (V&H 1997, table 2, p. 24). In 1994 employment growth was 0.8 per cent, in 1995 2.4 per cent, in 1996 1.9 per cent and projected for 1997 2 per cent (ibid.). Between 1991 and 1996 GDP growth was 2.2 per cent compared to an EU average of 1.5

per cent (table 1, p. 11). Inflation remains low at 2.5 per cent. The budget deficit was 2.2 per cent of GDP in 1996 – in 1980 it was 7.2 per cent (p. 10). Thus the Netherlands seems to have somehow achieved a remarkable turn-around, boosting employment, reducing the costs of welfare without fundamentally undermining the welfare state and achieving modest but non-inflationary growth. The Netherlands has broken out of the path apparently ordained by its institutional structure.

How was this possible? First, let us look at where most of the new jobs have come from and who has filled them. The labour force has grown by 1.4 per cent per year between 1982 and 1995, compared with an EU average of 0.5 per cent (V&H 1997, p. 24). This is a result of above average population growth and the entry of women into the labour force. The Netherlands has switched from an employment pattern centred on a single-breadwinner family to a 1.5 job per family pattern. Women's employment increased from 34.7 per cent of the labour force in 1983 to 55 per cent in 1996, above the EU average and comparable to France and Germany (table 4, p. 25). Most of the new jobs are temporary, part-time or less than 35 hours. Since 1987 60 per cent of all new jobs have been part-time, part-time jobs growing rapidly to 36.5 per cent of employment in 1996 (p. 30). Part-time jobs are mainly held by women, some 75 per cent.

Most new jobs can be attributed to the effects of the policy for wage moderation. Job growth was restored in 1983 as the Netherlands emerged from recession and the Wassenaar Accord of 1982 on wages began to take effect. Unit labour costs in manufacturing in 1994 were lower than in Western Europe or Scandinavia, and lower than in the US (V&H 1997, table 5, p. 27). The Central Planning Bureau claims that institutionalized wage restraint has been 'Holland's single most important weapon in international competition' and attributes two-thirds of employment growth in the latter half of the 1980s to the effect of wage restraint (V&H 1997, p. 26).

If wage moderation contributed to the competitiveness of the manufacturing sector, most of the new jobs created are in services. Manufacturing represents just 18.2 per cent of total employment in 1996; commercial services grew from 20 to 27 per cent of total employment between 1960 and 1996 (V&H 1997, pp. 28–9). Non-marketed services have grown much less rapidly – thus job growth in Holland has not been by expansion in public employment, unlike Scandinavia.

Job growth has not come primarily from a reduction of the working week of full-time employees: full-time hours have not been reduced as in Germany. Certainly, the new jobs have not been filled by the long-term unemployed. Since 1984 50 per cent or more of the unemployed have been out of work for one year or more (V&H 1997, p. 36), and only one-seventh of the new jobs created between 1984 and 1990 went to the unemployed. This means that new entrants took most new jobs in the labour market, that is, young people or women leaving the home for work. Older workers have certainly not returned: only 41 per cent of men aged 55–64 were in work in 1996 (p. 38).

The shift towards new entrants, part-timers and women has not led to a marked growth in earnings inequality. The effect of the new policies has not been a reduction in the real wages of unskilled workers as in the US – the Netherlands has a lower incidence of low pay and earnings inequality than the Anglo-Saxon economies or Japan, France and Germany (V&H 1997, p. 40, OECD data). Visser and Hemerijck cite a Dutch econometric study by Roorda and Vogels that shows there is no robust relationship between earnings inequality and employment growth. They also point out that wage restraint and job growth have been consensual policies supported by the unions, and that wage moderation has affected higher earnings too. Undoubtedly, without a commitment to equality and fairness these policies would have been unsustainable. The Netherlands has avoided the mixture of 'winner takes all' for the top 20 per cent and widespread working poverty that characterizes the otherwise impressive American employment growth since the early 1980s, and renders it improbable as a route for the reform of advanced European economies. Moreover, Visser and Hemerijck's analysis is broadly supported by the 1998 OECD economic survey of the Netherlands (1998b) which extensively discusses social security reform.

Visser and Hemerijck's study is especially valuable in analysing the possibilities and limitations of corporatism under modern conditions. To identify corporatism with highly centralized bargaining, with large-scale standardized mass production and with Keynesian policies conducted within the constraints of exchange and credit controls is to mistake a member of the class for the class. The Netherlands exhibits a network of dense corporatist institutions, and, in particular, strong aspects of consociational governance. It ought to generate the vested interests and veto groups that inhibit change and lead to the accumulating inefficiencies that add up to maladaptation. But it has not. Why?

This is not because there were not periods of immobilism and crisis, when the corporatist partners were deadlocked, nor because there were not strong pressures against consensus from below. The unions persisted in the policy of wage restraint in the 1980s despite continuing job losses and falling membership, and despite the policy being unpopular. Likewise, the coalition partners, the Christian Democrats and Social Democrats, lost heavily in the 1994 general election in protest at their cuts in benefit levels and tightening up on access to disability benefits.

The answer seems to be that the Netherlands adapted through a mixture of inescapable economic pressures that forced a response, decisive action by governments and a willingness to persist in dialogue while seeking to find new policy options by the social partners. In theory, hierarchies such as Westminster-style governments with exclusive control of executive and legislative powers ought to be the most effective institutional and least path dependent forms for breaking with previous arrangements. But the experience of the UK shows that this leads to adventurism in macroecomonic policy, radical and excessive deviations from the previous course of policy and a neglect in seeking the cooperation of the social interests. The Netherlands seems to have had the lucky combination of enough hierarchy on the part of government to break the deadlock between the organized interests, but not so much as to destroy negotiated social governance in all policy areas.

In the case of the policy of wage moderation the Wassenaar Accord of 1982 was negotiated in the 'shadow of hierarchy' (V&H 1997, p. 40; see also ILO 1995) and in the face of an accelerating economic crisis: during the 1981–3 recession 1 in 25 firms in manufacturing went bankrupt and 300,000 jobs were lost (V&H 1997, p. 13). The government threatened to impose a wage freeze and the employers and the unions struck an accord rather than lose all autonomy in wage determination. The deadlock of 1976–82 was broken by the unions recognizing the need to restore competitiveness through wage moderation. Equally, the employers recognized the need for a deal, because they feared that in the context of a wages freeze the government would enforce job sharing and job subsidy programmes that would undermine their autonomy too. Similarly, the New Course deal of 1993 was negotiated in the recession of the early 1990s and the social partners were faced again with the threat of a government-imposed wage freeze. The role of the government in pushing the partners towards an agreement is central, as is the commitment of the partners to a form of negotiated governance characterized by realism and accommodation.

In the case of disability benefits, the government chose to act independently of the social partners, since in claiming to represent the general interest it regarded the system of negotiated social governance of social welfare as beyond repair. That the unions remained in other spheres of bargaining despite this, and accepted the new active labour market policies and also the development of part-time work, is evidence of their political maturity and ability to judge policies by their effects. Visser and Hemerijck's emphasis on the combination of power and social learning in this process is well judged. Without a measure of objectivity in analysing outcomes and a commitment to stay in the process, neither the employers nor the unions could have continued with the system of corporatist governance. Had the state gone beyond the shadow of hierarchy and relied on its substance as the main means of achieving policy, then the delicate balances on which compliance for its policies depended – aided by judiciously timed threats – would have broken down. The lesson is that enough corporatism to win the commitment of the social partners in certain policy spheres and enough hierarchy to remove blockages and to unravel serious policy failures are both necessary. Something similar can be seen in Denmark. To dispense with governance by negotiation and to rely on hierarchy and the market alone has been the aim of most economic liberals. Yet the example of the

Netherlands shows how a form of negotiated social governance in a post-Keynesian context can work and can deliver the goods better than strong states enforcing free markets.

Welfare state reform in Italy

It might be objected that the examples we have chosen are nothing like a 'crucial experiment'. Denmark and the Netherlands may be instances of the successful adaptation and maintenance of welfare states, but these countries are exceptional and therefore misleading bases on which to generalize about the ability to absorb international competitive pressures. Although highly internationalized, both countries are small and highly solidaristic – they are of a scale that permits a certain kind of politics and public-spiritedness. The situation is surely different in the larger European states, with their more diverse interest groupings and potential sources of conflict. Even states, like Germany, with established traditions of collaborative decision-making between industry, organized labour and the state have found tackling the problems of market flexibility, welfare state reform and unemployment exceedingly difficult. Thus in Germany the unions, the government and the employers all proposed radically different versions of the Alliance for Jobs in 1995–6. The unions concentrated on reducing unemployment, the state and employers on welfare cuts. Needless to say, no agreement, let alone a social pact, was concluded (Bispink 1997).

In more conflictual polities with less cooperative unions, like France, attempts to drive welfare reform through from the top failed miserably. The welfare reforms proposed by the Juppé government were destroyed in a massive wave of strikes and protests in 1995–6. The same happened to the Berlusconi government in Italy in late 1994. Governments may perceive welfare reform to be necessary, but citizens and organized labour have refused to accept the reduction of their acquired rights. Europe thus seems stuck between the pressures of the EMU convergence criteria and international competition, and the unwillingness of its populations in the larger states to abandon the achievements of national democratic politics. Social pacts may have returned in parts of Europe – in Finland, Ireland, Portugal, Norway and Spain – but not in the larger advanced industrial states.[3]

Except that, against all expectations, Italy from the early 1990s has seen the conclusion of a series of relatively successful agreements between industry, organized labour and the state on wage determination, industrial relations and welfare state reform. It seems that the Berlusconi episode of attempting to impose solutions from above by state fiat was an exception and that both the employers' association, Confindustria, and the Italian trade union confederations have played a constructive role in the reform of Italian economic institutions. That it is Italy that shows that it is possible to have concerted action for reform is extremely surprising. It proves that history is not fate, and that given appropriate conditions, societies can break out of their previous path of development. Italy would have seemed highly unpropitious material for effective concertation between the social interests and the state, and for public-spirited action by the unions to promote reform.

Locke (1995) argues persuasively that Italy is not a coherent 'national model': government policies, economic institutions and social interest actions have radically different consequences in the different subunits of which the economy is composed. This is not just the familiar divisions of northern, southern and the 'third' Italy. As he shows, even within the north, and under the same formal ownership arrangements, outcomes can be radically different. Thus Fiat in Turin and Alfa Romeo in Milan restructured their sections of the automobile industry on quite different bases, the former defeating and excluding organized labour, and the latter successfully cooperating with it. Locke relates these differences to different patterns of association and sociopolitical networks, those in Turin polarizing the different interests and those in Milan promoting cross-connection and communication between them (1995, ch. 4). Economic governance in Italy is heavily dependent on such localized features as the different experiences of the textile industry in Prato, which found it difficult to adapt to the crisis of the 1980s, and in Biella, which successfully upgraded and renewed itself (Locke 1995, ch. 5). Interests of both employers and unions are difficult to aggregate, locally fragmented and often contradictory between different sectors and regimes. Moreover, Italy has been characterized by a 'weak state', captured and parcellized by party interests, and by weak governments of short duration. Thus the political centre in Italy was also an ineffective and inconsistent partner in tripartite negotiations.

The classic literature on corporatist concertation (Schmitter 1981; Lehmbruch 1984) specified an institutional structure quite different from the Italian one. Effective concertation required highly centralized monopoly representation of the major interests, given official recognition and semi-public status by the state, and able to act as disciplined partners in binding negotiations. The state, in turn, needed to have effective bargains to offer the interests in return for cooperation, presupposing a substantial degree of control of macroeconomic and fiscal policy.

As Mario Regini (1997) shows, none of these features was present in Italy. Italian governments had little to offer, they were trapped by the excessive concessions of the 1970s and the early 1980s. In fact the agreements of the 1990s worked by bringing the unions into the core of policy definition and legitimation (Baccaro and Locke 1996) and devolving governance of labour markets and collective bargaining to unions and employers (Negrelli 1997; Regini and Regalia 1997). Italian unions are neither centralized nor insulated from the rank and file, and therefore it is difficult to agree bargains at peak level and impose them from above. Indeed, the unions have been threatened by fragmentation between the different confederations (their alliance split up in 1985), and by a crisis of representation as they were challenged by the 'autonomous' unions and the unofficial grassroots labour organizations, the *comitati de base*. However, as part of the process of concertation, the unions were able to reconstruct real organizations in the workplaces and to use these as part of a process of democratic dialogue and consultation with the membership that provided democratic legitimacy for pensions reform (Baccaro and Locke 1996). Thus, in this case, devolution and democratic consultation in the workplace rather than the centralized authority of the union federation helped to promote effective grassroots agreement to the results of negotiated social governance. Italian corporatism has thus been built out of quite different and looser textured materials than those specified in the corporatist literature of the 1970s and 1980s, which drew on the experiences of such countries as Austria. Indeed, it is better suited to a more diverse economy and a conflictual polity, and to more volatile economic conditions.

In the early 1990s both the Italian economy and the welfare state were in crisis. Italy had fully industrialized in the 1950s and 1960s, utilizing large labour reserves from the south and benefiting from low wages. In the postwar period unions were effectively excluded from workplace bargaining, they had little legal protection, and elements of the Fascist labour code remained operative until the late 1950s. In the 'Hot Autumn' of 1968–9 labour took its revenge with a wave of strikes and demonstrations. Labour was strengthened by an alliance between the union confederations in 1972 (Sabel 1982). In 1975 the *scala mobile* system of 100 per cent indexed wage increases was established and this was generalized from manufacturing to the public sector, thus locking in inflation. Also, in an attempt to contain the labour unrest of the Hot Autumn, the government increased the compensation ratio for pensions to 74 per cent of previous pay and indexed pensions to prices (Baccaro and Locke 1996, p. 7). As a consequence of these two measures, inflationary shocks were locked into the economy. Inflation remained well above the G7 average from 1973 into the mid-1980s (peaking at 21.2 per cent in 1980 and 19.5 per cent in 1981) (Locke 1995, table 1.4, p. 9). Thus by the early 1980s all three main players – unions, employers and the state – were seeking an anti-inflationary agreement. In January 1983 the centre-left government agreed an exchange in which the *scala mobile* was revised and the government made compensatory bargains for employers and workers. This attempt at concertation was a one-off. The government could not readily offer equivalent concessions again, faced as it was with a large budgetary deficit. As an effect of this failure in the 1984 negotiating round, the union alliance split – with the largest confederation, the Confederazione Generale Italiana del Lavoro, opposing the deal. This finished any prospect of social pacts for the rest of the 1980s.

In the early 1990s the Italian economy was in recession, yet inflation at 6.5 per cent in 1990–1 was well above that of major competitors like France, Germany and Japan (Locke 1995, table 1.4, p. 9). Growth rates had fallen to 1.3 per cent in 1991 and 0.9 per cent in 1992 (Locke 1995, table 1.6, p. 11). Unemployment had grown rapidly to above the EU average. By 1987 Italy's public debt had risen to 103.9 per cent of GDP, roughly three times the G7 average (Locke 1995, table 1.5, p. 10). In 1995 it stood at 123.8 per cent of GDP, and by the 1990s servicing the public debt was consuming some 10 per cent of GDP and crippling the state budget (Ferrara 1997, p. 231). The combination of high inflation and a large budget deficit under-mined the lira, and Italy was forced to devalue in 1992, thus negating its efforts to remain in the ERM.

Yet Italy remained an effective industrial economy. As Locke points out, the economy presents a very different picture depending on the situation one chooses to highlight: 'although still macroeconomically fragile and plagued by a variety of other worrisome problems, the Italian economy has nonetheless generated impressive rates of growth, exports, labour produc-tivity, firm profitability and private fixed investment' (1995, p. 10). Italy had levels of investment in machinery and equipment through the 1980s equalled only by Japan among the G7, and a personal savings rate as a per-centage of disposable income consistently higher than Japan's and the highest in the G7 (Locke 1995, table 1.8, p. 13 and table 1.9, p. 14). Italy has an efficient and profitable manufacturing core with well-paid and produc-tive workers – in that sense both sides of industry have an interest in common, to contain the effects of macroeconomic mismanagement on real economic performance.

In the 1990s Italy faced the twin pressures of recession and the condi-tions of the ERM membership and then subsequently the convergence criteria for EMU. Even without these pressures, the public finances and the welfare state would have required serious attention. Italy did not have an overextensive welfare state by northern European standards: public expenditure on social protection stood at 24.5 per cent of GDP in 1990, below most of its EU partners. However, Italy's pension system was chaotic, underfunded and ultimately unsustainable. Governments had used the enhancement of entitlements in the pensions system as a low-cost option to buy industrial peace and appease militant interest groups. Real pension benefits grew at an average annual rate of 6.5 per cent between 1960 and 1975 and 8.2 per cent between 1975 and 1981 (Baccaro and Locke 1996, p. 6). Rather than impose realistic social security contributions, successive governments chose to subsidize the pensions system from the public trea-sury, and they chose to cover expenditure by borrowing. By the early 1990s the future of Italy's pay-as-you-go pensions system was clearly grim: the decline in fertility rates to 1.26 children per woman threatened a very low ratio of economically active age groups to pensioners in the early twenty-first century; moreover, a combination of unemployment, early retirement and late entry into the labour market reduced the ratio between active and retired workers in the principal fund to 1.1 in 1994 as against 2.62 in 1963 (Baccaro and Locke 1996, p. 7).

As in the Netherlands, the problem was less international pressures than the growth of a system of entitlements that could not be sustained. The Italian welfare state would have needed reform even if Italy were in a state of complete autarchy. The pressures of public debt meant that budgets were being squeezed, with an impact on public services, and yet taxes were relatively high, and could not easily be raised without reducing demand (Ferrara 1997). Hence pensions were crucial to reform: only a reduction in entitlements could control future costs.

The move towards concertation was aided by a collapse of the old political system in 1992. This broke the old clientelistic political parties that had colonized the state and diverted it to their own ends, thereby reducing state competence, efficiency and legitimacy. Equally the implication of many leading industrialists in corruption scandals delegitimated industry, and yet at the same time probably strengthened the position of its representatives in Confindustria vis-à-vis the major firms. The unions emerged in this evolving and reforming political system as a relatively clean and representative force.

In 1992, after several years of stalled tripartite negotiations, the partners signed an agreement that abolished the *scala mobile* and froze wage bargaining for 1992–3. A new accord signed only in 1993 confirmed the end of the old system and set out a new framework for income policy and collective bargaining (Regini and Regalia 1997; ILO 1995). It established a dual-level system of national basic agreements and local collective bargaining, and this gave greater autonomy to unions and to firms. In the case of pensions, a limited reform began under the technocratic government of Guilio Amato in 1992, and it was not militantly opposed by the unions. As we have seen, Berlusconi's attempt to force further reform through in 1994 was defeated by mass mobilization and the defection of his coalition partner, the Northern League, on this issue. Confindustria also pressed for dialogue. After the fall of the centre-right government the technocratic government of Lamberto Dini began a dialogue on reform that gave union experts a central place in shaping the outcome. This reform tried to bring order into the chaos of the funds, and equity between various classes of worker, as well as restricting entitlements.

After signing the accord on pensions in May 1995, the unions implemented a process of democratic dialogue in workplaces and then a referendum on the reform on 30 May and 1 June 1995. The result of this national referendum was a 64 per cent vote in favour, with some 4.5 million voting (Baccaro and Locke 1996, p. 23). Certain sectors opposed the reform, including the metalworkers and secondary school teachers, and among the workers in Lombardy 52.62 per cent opposed the reform against 47.38 per cent endorsing it (Baccaro and Locke 1996, table 8). In a decentralized industrial struggle these key groups would have been sufficient to undermine the whole process. Yet they had agreed to abide by the outcome of the democratic dialogue and the national vote, and the National Assembly was able to vote the reforms into law in July 1995. The unusual character-istic of this referendum and democratic dialogue is that it built legitimacy from below, but aggregated decisions on a national basis, thus marginaliz-ing powerful but self-interested minorities. The unions benefited from the reform of industrial relations, and thus were able to reach into virtually every major workplace. They delivered an accord not by centralized and disciplined monopoly representation, but by mass participation. Italian unions and workers, including the militant teachers and northern engi-neering workers, showed they could act in a public-spirited way without coercion.

If Italy, with its history of militant industrial conflict and dogged defence of acquired privileges, can reform, then it is possible that other medium-sized nation-states could do so too – given the right political conditions. Reform in Italy was not merely a matter of cutting welfare entitlements; rather it has put pensions on a more equitable and sustainable footing.

Monetary union as a threat to the welfare state?

Italy's move towards collaboration between industry, labour and the state has been driven not only by the crisis of the early 1990s but also by the need to qualify for monetary union. The European Union is popular in Italy and there is widespread commitment to further economic integration. There has been nothing like the anti-EMU backlash that occurred in France, where unpopular welfare reforms were justified as inevitable and necessary in the face of intensifying international competition and the need to achieve mon-etary union. As Rodrik (1997) points out, this strategy of politicians blaming 'globalization' for unpopular policies simply discredits international open-ness and breeds nationalist and protectionist sentiments.

The problem is that, issues of globalization apart, the EU has rapidly created the world's largest economic space. As Scharpf points out in a pen-etrating analysis (1997; see also 1996), the Single European Act created a free market in capital, labour, goods and services that has fewer barriers internally than in the United States: the US still has substantial barriers in the form of different state standards for professional accreditation, for example. The US is a federal state, whereas the EU is not a state. The EU performs certain governance and legislative functions, and has primacy over national states in respect of these, but it does not perform others. Welfare provision is still the prerogative of the national states.

Scharpf's main point is that a market has been created whose scope is out of kilter with the methods for governing its consequences. He argues that the mobility of capital and skilled labour means that high taxes on income from capital, high welfare contributions for employers and high taxes on the incomes of skilled and mobile labour in particular national states will tend to provoke defections by firms and employees.[4] They can locate elsewhere and enjoy the benefits of the same market. This will tend to produce regulatory competition between states, as in the US, but with no possibility of compensatory policies at the European level. National states will adapt to this fact, and begin to cut welfare entitlements and taxes to promote their competitiveness against other EU states. Indeed, one could argue that this process of regulatory competition has already begun in that it was the explicit strategy of the Thatcher government in the UK that signed up to the Single European Act. Britain under the Conservative government, and seemingly under Tony Blair's government too, has sought to compete by attracting firms on the basis of labour market flexibility and low taxes on capital and the upper levels of income.

Yet it should be obvious that this process of regulatory competition has limited possibilities for the advanced states in the EU. The EU is made up of states with very different levels of GDP per capita: Sweden cannot hope to compete with Portugal in a cost-cutting strategy, let alone with possible EU entrants like Poland. Until the mid-1990s trade unionists and social democratic politicians throughout the EU imagined that they could build a new 'social Europe'. Europe could thus serve as a bulwark against international competitive pressures. Europe would develop common welfare policies within and would be large enough and economically strong enough to resist pressures from without, threatening trade sanctions against 'social dumping'. Quite clearly this was an illusion, not because of global markets, but because Europe was built out of competing states at very different levels of wealth and welfare entitlements. Europe could not easily be harmonized 'upwards' in terms of welfare benefits, except at the cost of a vast amount of redistributive taxation channelling benefits from north to south, and from centre to periphery. Such policies are difficult to sustain *within* nation-states, as the example of Italy shows, let alone between them. What harmonization there is, is of a minimalist kind. Thus the European Social Chapter is a framework document on workers' rights, but carefully avoids prescribing European standards for substantive welfare benefits like pensions or unemployment compensation. Even if there can be no levelling up, equally there can be no levelling down of European social standards to create a common norm that serves as a level playing field for competition. Even if that were the aim, as Scharpf points out, the problem of harmonization is further complicated in that it is not only the levels of welfare funding that are divergent but also the packages of welfare services offered and the methods by which they are funded. To harmonize, whether up or down, would require the creation of a federal state with welfare as one of its core competencies.

Such a state is neither in the offing, nor would it be likely to have legitimacy with the publics of Europe's nation-states. Yet are national welfare states to be eroded in the absence of such harmonization? Scharpf sees this impasse in governance as a threat to democracy. Thus French voters may explicitly choose to maintain their welfare state and yet the French government may still be powerless to preserve it. Scharpf argues that national societies and the EU as a whole do have significant options to preserve extensive welfare states, even if defections of capital were to become a real threat. He makes a series of proposals for national reform and coordinated European action.

First, he argues – as we have seen in the case of Denmark – that a welfare state funded from taxation, especially taxes on consumption like VAT, has an advantage in containing defections over systems that draw a substantial portion of funding from taxes on business and payrolls and give workers employment-specific entitlements. Secondly, he argues that the state should require all those who can afford it to take out health insurance and protection against other social risks, and that it should subsidize the premiums of those who are too poor to afford insurance. Third, that the EU could avoid the unacceptable alternatives of either its current high levels of unemployment or widespread poverty wages, as in the US, if member states were to adopt some form of citizen's income based on tax credits, allowing low-wage jobs to be created without the full consequences of poverty and income inequality. Fourthly, he argues that if incomes from capital are lightly taxed then, in the interests of fairness, workers should begin to benefit from them too. He advocates promoting the distribution of equity as part of income, and therefore, as employees' funds build up, workers would derive at least part of their incomes from equity. Fifthly, he argues that while member states cannot harmonize incomes between north and south in Europe, they could at least develop a pact not to lower their spend on welfare as a percentage of GDP below the average level for countries with a similar level of national income. Lastly, he makes the point that if citizens, workers and unions want to avoid a policy of competition between states in terms of cuts in taxes and welfare benefits, then they must accept the need to raise business profitability. He advocates industrial policies and industrial relations and labour market reforms that boost productivity and profitability.

These are sensible proposals in the context of a worst case analysis based on rational choice assumptions. Many of Scharpf's proposals have been widely advocated by welfare reformers and have merit even if regulatory competition does not prove a significant threat.[5] Arguments for some form of guaranteed minimum income are widespread. For example, one of the authors (Hirst 1993, 1998b) has argued for a citizen's income in order, among other objectives, to boost low-wage employment without the consequence of poverty. This is part of a wider strategy of associative welfare reform that attempts to counter tax aversion and flight to private provision by making individual citizens stakeholders with a substantial measure of control over both policies and resources. Only reforms that give citizens the individual ability to craft the package of services they receive to suit their needs, choosing between service providers, and also collective control over the content of services, will lead them to identify closely with the welfare state and be willing to pay for it. The way to do this is to base welfare on public entitlements delivered by self-governing voluntary welfare associations. Only a system that provides a decent minimum, but gives the better off the option of topping it up with services of their choice, will maintain social solidarity and prevent the separation of welfare into private insurance-based services and a tax-funded public safety net that all pay for but only the desperate use. Welfare states are coming under intense pressure on costs and types of service for a variety of reasons – ageing population, high rates of family break-up, rising costs and complexity of health care, and increasing diversification and professionalization of services – and of these the openness of the national economy to external shocks is neither the principal reason nor a new factor. Pressures to welfare reform should not be identified with globalization, although reforms may help to reduce the impact of external competitive pressures and economic shocks.

The worst case analysis proves welfare states still have options, but it does not follow that the worst case will occur. Capital flight by major employers is by no means a widespread phenomenon. Scharpf is writing in a context of alarm in Germany. Instances of relocation to the Czech Republic, for example, have shocked a country where banking and business circles have traditionally been solidly nationally oriented. Fears of a loss of competitiveness seem to have been heightened by the recession in Germany, making such alarmist diatribes as Martin and Schumann (1997) bestsellers. Such fears may well decline as evidence of the recovery in Germany filters through. Believers in capital flight may be surprised to see that it is marginal locations like the UK that relied on low wage costs that have suffered substantially as major South Korean firms have cancelled investments and firms like Siemens have relocated from the north-east of England to core plants in Europe.

Moreover, the widespread adoption of social pacts in Europe from Finland to Portugal shows that both governments and the social partners have fully recognized the need to control inflation and wage costs as part of a strategy of maintaining price competitiveness – and boosting company profitability. These pacts are beginning to generate a new literature of commentary and analysis (Fajertag and Pochet 1997; ILO 1995; Rhodes 1996, 1997). Rhodes (1997), in the most sustained example of this new analysis, contends that such pacts are examples of a new 'competitive corporatism' aimed primarily at enhancing international competitiveness, rather than sharing the egalitarian and redistributive social goals of the 'old' corporatism. Rhodes's distinction is perhaps a little too clear-cut and one might question how far it holds good: the old corporatist strategies had national macroeconomic management as a primary aim, and were particularly concerned to maintain international competitiveness. For example, the Swedish wages solidarity policy was explicitly designed to enhance that country's international competitiveness by pushing less efficient firms in the direction of enhancing productivity and allowing efficient firms to gain export markets and to reinvest high retained profits (Martin 1995). What is different now in national corporatist bargaining is that governments under fiscal constraints and limited in their scope for borrowing can offer fewer entitlements and rights in exchange for workers' and employers' commitment to such policies. What they can offer workers is voice and the ability to shape labour market and welfare policies. Even in the context of strategic reductions in welfare benefits, as with the case of Italian pensions reform, the ability to co-determine how such changes are accomplished is a definite advantage to organized labour.

The existence of widespread social pacts across Europe might appear to offer the possibility of an alternative mechanism to contain inflation that might lessen the need for the kind of 'sound money' anti-inflationary policies in the EU, in the context of a successful launch of the euro. The danger is that such pacts, in combination with the restrictive remit of the European Central Bank, will do the opposite. Each state competing with the others in restraining wages could lead to the locking in and reinforcing of the deflationary bias of monetary policy. Each state competing in wage costs and seeking to boost the export performance and profitability of its own firms will tend to restrict demand below the level needed to contain accelerating inflationary pressures. Generalized 'competitive corporatism' will lead to winners and losers, it cannot be a win-win strategy. As Martin provocatively remarks:

> the next stage of European integration . . . is stuck with a particular institutional form which has a price stability macroeconomic regime built into it. And this is essentially why there is nothing much that social pacts can do in the present historical context except redistribute work. But let there be no illusion that that is a means for reducing unemployment. (1997, p. 41)

Macroeconomic policy still has its place, and has not been eliminated by international openness or capital mobility. Ton Notermans (1997) offers a powerful criticism of the notion that the growth of global financial markets and the removal of exchange controls have imposed fundamental constraints on growth-oriented policies and act in favour of restrictive macroeconomic policies (see also Notermans 1993). He argues that history does not bear this out. He goes on to claim that the removal of exchange controls and the adoption of monetarist policies in a number of European countries in the mid-1970s to early 1980s were not the result of external pressures but were designed to defeat domestic inflation. The full employment and tight labour markets of the 1950s and 1960s led to wage push inflation and also to the locking in of external inflationary shocks. No union federation could reliably deliver the sort of income policies that could contain such pressures for a decade or more. The error of export-oriented countries like Sweden was to persist with reflationary policies in a context of generalized movement away from macroeconomic policies prioritizing growth. The analysis by Notermans is a powerful attack on both liberal fatalism and social democratic illusions, especially the belief that the combination of restrictive monetary policy and supply-side policies to improve training and labour flexibility will ensure long-term sustainable growth. Such beliefs are now dogma among ex-social democrats across Europe. However, the analysis also shows that a crucial element in escaping from restrictive policies is autonomy in exchange rate policy, with the option of appropriate and judicious devaluations that stabilize the economy at a more competitive level.

The problem with the Notermans stance in the context of EMU is that the euro will deny member states just this option. This implies that the European Central Bank will have to be given a revised remit to pursue more growth-oriented policies once the new currency has established itself. The EU will then have to seek to contain inflation by coordinated social pacts in the member states. Competitive corporatism would be replaced by coordinated concertation as an arm of European policy. The latter is a tall order, given the radical differences in economic performance and the real advantages of free riding as a short-term strategy. Yet a growth-oriented policy will falter if a significant number of states fail to contain domestic inflation.

This shows that the EU has still failed to develop an effective division of labour in economic governance with the member states in order to manage a continental-scale economy successfully. We return to this in chapter 8. It can only contain inflationary pressures at present by placing the European Central Bank above democratic politics and giving it a restrictive remit as part of its constitution. The result will inevitably be low growth and high unemployment. In the absence of alternatives, the welfare state policies of member states will have to adapt to this regime. This will favour those states with relatively high capacities for solidarity and with appropriate welfare institutions. For those with less sustainable institutions, it will favour those with the political resources to evolve and reform in the sorts of directions Scharpf indicates. Globalization has not eliminated the scope for extensive welfare, and even within the constraints of the EU, states have clear options so long as they have the political resources.

7

Economic Governance Issues
in General

This chapter concentrates on the existing mechanisms for economic governance in the international economy. It also considers the possibilities for future enhanced economic governance, particularly with respect to international financial markets. In chapter 9 we shall consider the broader political aspects of international governance and the continuing role for the nation-state in such regulatory mechanisms. Here we begin by outlining the five levels at which governance can operate, from that of the world economy to that of regional economies within nation-states. We argue that at each of these levels there are possibilities for the enhancement of the scope of governance and the development of more effective regulatory mechanisms. These five levels are:

1 Governance through agreement between the major political entities, particularly the G3 (Europe, Japan and North America), to stabilize exchange rates, to coordinate fiscal and monetary policies, and to cooperate in limiting speculative short-term financial transactions.
2 Governance through a substantial number of states creating international regulatory agencies for some specific dimension of economic activity, such as the WTO to police the GATT settlement, or possible authorities to police foreign direct investment and common environmental standards.
3 The governance of large economic areas by trade and investment blocs such as the EU or NAFTA. Both are large enough to pursue social and environmental objectives in the way a medium-sized nation-state may not be able to do independently. Both are capable of enforcing adequate minimal standards in labour market policies or forms of social

protection. The blocs are big enough markets in themselves to stand against global pressures if they so choose.

4   National-level policies that balance cooperation and competition between firms and the major social interests, producing quasi-voluntary economic coordination and assistance in providing key inputs such as R&D, the regulation of industrial finance, international marketing, information and export guarantees, training, etc., thereby enhancing national economic performance and promoting industries located in the national territory.

5   Governance through regional level policies of providing collective services to industrial districts, augmenting their international competitiveness and providing a measure of protection against external shocks.

These five levels are interdependent to a considerable degree. Effective governance of economic activities requires that mechanisms be in place at all five levels, even though the types and methods of regulation are very different at each level. Thus the forms of coordination of world financial markets are very different from the processes of balancing cooperation and competition in specific industrial sectors at the regional level. The upshot of this interdependence of levels is that those national and regional economies that are not well regulated by appropriate means would benefit least from extended international economic governance, such as the effective stabilization of world financial markets and the management of world trade through international agreements and the practices of supranational trade blocs. However, interdependence is relative: strong mechanisms of national and regional governance can compensate for volatility at the international level and provide reinsurance for specific economies against shocks caused by weak governance of world markets. National and regional economies remain significant, as we shall see later in this chapter.

This chapter concentrates first on levels one and two, and then goes on to consider levels four and five. We consider the third level mainly in chapter 8, when we examine the EU as the most institutionally developed trade bloc. Levels one and two, and four and five, respectively, are closely interwoven into two linked couples. We begin with a discussion of the relationship between the G3 and G7/8 economies,[1] and then move on to the second level, that is the wider range of countries assembled into the institutions that have been formed to manage aspects of the international economy. In a similar way, at levels four and five, effective regional governance depends very much on the policies of national states, and the degree to which they recognize the need for effective local knowledge in promoting coordination and cooperation between firms and between economic actors more generally.

A central plank of this argument, applying to all five levels, is that market economies need to be appropriately governed if they are to perform effectively in meeting the substantive expectations of a wide range of economic actors. Markets are an effective means of economic allocation only if the conditions in which they operate are controlled. The degree of that governance and the specific mechanisms of achieving it vary with the character and scale of the markets in question. Most markets need to be embedded in a context of non-market social institutions and regulatory mechanisms if they are to produce effective outcomes. This social embeddedness of markets is complex and it changes as economic conditions change. It is thus not amenable to a simple elegant general theory, and the ideas which explain it must be revised constantly to meet changed circumstances. The dogmatic advocates of economic liberalism deny this need for market institutionalization. They use a simple elegant general theory of markets to advocate that markets be freed from the interventions of other social institutions. For economic liberals, sales and purchases can function as an effective mechanism of economic coordination in and of themselves. The problem is that the deliberate liberalization of international economic relations since the 1970s has appeared to create a *fait accompli* in favour of the economic liberals' case. This has given rise to the widespread belief that global markets are ungovernable. As we shall see below, this is far from being the case, and even in a period of economic liberal ideological dominance, structures of public regulation of markets have been built up or maintained at the international level.

However, appropriate concepts of economic governance, capable of recognizing the five interdependent levels of activity from world markets to regions, have hardly begun to develop. One reason for this is that the best established argument for governed and socially embedded markets, the theory of the 'mixed economy', was developed for national level economic management. We need a new and equivalent theory which recognizes that certain key aspects of economic activity can no longer be under direct national control and that a changed international environment needs new governance strategies and institutions. The concept of polycentric economic regulation, relying on a number of governance loci and a variety of regulatory mechanisms, is a necessary successor to doctrines of national economic management developed in the 1930s and put into practice in a number of advanced economies after 1945.

This is not to say that the post-1945 practices of national economic management did not have an international context. However, the *international* institutions appropriate to and complementary to the era in which national economic management was the dominant form of regulation, centred on managed multilateralism between the major advanced economies, now also need rethinking and adaptation. Whether such a new polycentric version of the mixed economy will emerge remains to be seen. We now move on to consider the general governance of the international economy as it currently exists.

Governing world markets

What are the current prospects for a more orderly international economic environment in the relationships between world markets, countries and trade blocs? As indicated in chapter 2, there is still a great deal of volatility and increased uncertainty in the international economy relative to the stability of the period between 1950 and 1972. However, it is not inevitable that the adverse trends giving rise to those uncertainties are set and robust. Countertrends do exist: thus the inauguration of the EMS, and particularly its ERM component, in 1979 initially decreased the volatility of the member states' exchange rates. It also led to some convergence of underlying monetary conditions. Although the EMS was substantially undermined by market pressures in late 1992 and early 1993, the EU still represents an arena of potential stabilization for the international economy as a whole, as well as for its member countries. This is likely to mature as the euro is introduced after 1999. In addition the G7/8 summit system of policy coordination has seen some successes, particularly in its early days and in 1991 (Artis and Ostry 1984; Putnam and Bayne 1987).

These instances of international policy coordination have so far been of only limited scope. They have primarily involved monetary issues. Although in recent years the monitoring – if not the active coordinated management – of real variables such as growth rates has been added to the deliberative agendas of such bodies as the G7. However, 'monitoring' is still far from an active cooperation to change policy. By and large the G7 countries have each gone their own way on domestic economic policy issues, and the divergence of their basic philosophies and approaches has been evident over the last ten to fifteen years. This is further registered by the recent divergence in the business cycles of the advanced countries indicated in chapter 2. We should not dismiss outright these attempts at limited exchange rate and monetary coordination, but neither should we overexaggerate their importance or success.

The problem inhibiting further coordination at present is the divergent interests that still characterize the international economy, where, despite the claims of the globalization enthusiasts, the major nation-states of the advanced countries and increasingly the emerging trading blocs are the dominant players. If nothing else, the very different underlying economic conditions of the Japanese economy and the American economy should testify to a divergence of interests that limits active and positive cooperation between their governments.

This is not to suggest that complete non-cooperation will develop between the major players in the international economy; only that the probability is either that cooperation will be of a minimalist nature – cooperation to manage periodic international crises – or that it will be cooperation by default as policies in the stronger economies dictate those in the weaker ones. To this must be added the very obvious continuing differences in economic policy frameworks and outlooks that typify the main international trading countries, which will inhibit coincidental agreements on more developed cooperative ventures. Some national states do not have the domestic institutional frameworks to implement ambitious policies agreed within an international negotiating structure, even if they were more actively canvassed there. Coordinated fiscal policy initiatives are an obvious example. For instance, it is unlikely that a properly functioning fiscal federalism could be rapidly constructed even within the EU, as we shall see in chapter 8.[2]

But these necessary caveats should not blind us to the ways in which the international economy has become integrated to the degree that an outright return to overt protectionism between the major trading blocs, while still a possibility, remains unlikely. The case of the financial balances between the major blocs illustrates this point, something already referred to in chapter 2. Figure 7.1 shows that the EU was in rough balance on its ratios of savings and investment to GDP over the period between 1960 and 1994. This was also the case for the US and Japan up until the early 1980s. Then the US went into a dramatic international 'deficit' as its savings collapsed while inward investment remained high (to support its balance of payments and budget deficits). This twin deficit was financed by the Japanese, and to a lesser extent by the EU in the mid-1980s. Thus despite some volatility in the overall trends, which show large swings in investment and savings to GDP ratios, the three main bloc powers appear to be locked together in a reciprocal relationship. In particular, the Japanese economy could hardly continue to exist in its present form without the US markets for its manufactured goods, while the US currently needs Japan as a source of finance for its domestic spending. Japan and the US need one another because their economic fates interlock, despite their divergent interests in manufacturing and in monetary policy.[3]

These complex and often conflictual relationships came to the fore in the wake of the severe financial crisis that hit the world economy in 1997–8, when the Japanese economy in particular was pushed further into recession. This has raised fears about the possibility of a worldwide economic collapse. Japan seems unable to revive its economic fortunes, having slipped into a classic liquidity trap and low-level equilibrium. Even with real interest rates set at virtually zero and domestic tax cuts, the economy has so far failed to revive. Expectations of falling prices mean that neither domestic consumers nor investors have been willing to spend. Great uncertainty and memories of recent speculative failures have further dampened the prospects for economic revival. The resulting 'credit crunch', with domestic savings ratios increasing and with the possibility of the liquidation of Japanese investments abroad, has sent shudders around the world.

Clearly, given the situation depicted in figure 7.1, if Japanese investors were to retreat into an autarchic policy stance and begin to liquidate their real and financial investments in the US and Europe, this could have a more dramatic effect on the other two Triad members. But with US and EU assets

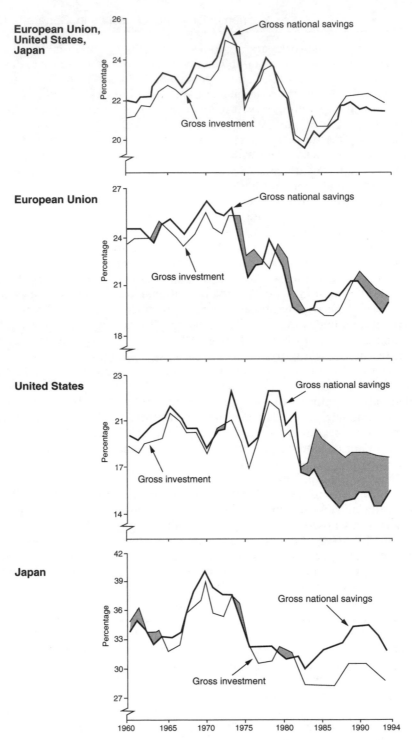

Figure 7.1 Evolution of savings and investment in the EU, US and Japan, 1960–1994 (percentage of GDP)

Source: European Commission services

Table 7.1 Selected trade shares of the Triad countries, 1996 (as percentage of exports)

	EU15		*US*		*Japan*	
Trade with:	EU15[a]	60	Canada	23	China and NIC4[b]	29
	EFTA[c]	12	Latin America	18	Rest of Asia	14
Memorandum	CEEC[c,d]	12	EU15	22	EU15	16
items:	US and Canada[c]	21	Japan	9	US and Canada	29

[a] As a percentage of total EU15 exports.
[b] NIC4-Korea, Taiwan, Hong Kong and Singapore.
[c] As a percentage of extra-EU15 exports only.
[d] CEEC-Central and Eastern European countries, including Russia.
Sources: Compiled from European Commission, Comtrade database/Eurostat; WTO, *Annual Report 1997*, vol. 2

more or less the only performing ones for Japanese institutions and companies, these are the least likely to be called in, even if the domestic credit crunch were to intensify. The first investments to be liquidated would be domestic non-performing assets (of which there are many) and those in East Asia, where the economic collapse has been most severe. Indeed, withdrawal of Japanese capital has been a significant factor in the South East Asian crisis. Thus the prospects for an outright 'global' economic collapse resulting from the Japanese domestic credit crunch, while real, still looked an avoidable eventuality at the end of 1998.

These points about relations between the blocs are reinforced if we look at the structure of trade *within* them. The percentage of total trade that each bloc leader conducted with its immediate partner countries in 1996 is shown in table 7.1. The most integrated bloc as regards trade is the EU; neither the US nor Japan trade to such an extent with their natural 'bloc associates'. Rather, the US and Japan must still look to the wider international environment for their trading partners. This should reinforce their mutual commitment to an 'open' trading environment. The US may have much to fear from Japanese import penetration in its manufacturing sector; there may be added pressure from the rest of East Asia as these countries try to seize the opportunity to export their way out of recession, their currency values having fallen heavily against the US dollar.

But the US remains a major exporter of manufactured goods and services and primary products, and it relies on a liberal regime of world trade to do so. Japan is vitally dependent on the markets of the US and its East Asian neighbours. The US is still committed to free trade and will remain so, up to and until the point where Japanese or other foreign competition threatens a catastrophic collapse of its domestic manufacturing base.

Figure 7.2 shows the shares of world exports of goods accounted for by the three Triad members from 1963 to 1996, and demonstrates that these

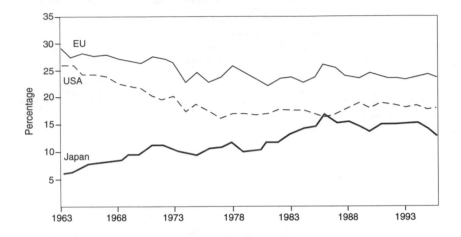

Figure 7.2   Percentage shares of world exports of goods accounted for
by the Triad countries, 1963–1996

Source: European Economy, no. 63: Annual Report for 1997, EU, 1998, graph 15, p. 47

have been converging over the period. But there were still significant differences between the three in 1996, with the EU at 24 per cent and Japan
at under 15 per cent. Figure 7.3 gives an indication of the importance of
trade in goods to these economies between 1960 and 1996 expressed as a
percentage of their GDP. There had also been a remarkable convergence
here up to the late 1980s, but some divergence since. The data in figure 7.3
is made up of imports and exports, and there have been important differences between the trends in each category. The US in particular experienced
an almost continuous growth of imports, from under 3 per cent of GDP in
1960 to over 11 per cent in 1996. For Japan and the EU, on the other hand,
although there was significant volatility in the ratio of imports to GDP
between 1973 and 1986, the overall proportion was much the same at the
end of the period as at the beginning (about 8 per cent). In the case of
exports, the trend has been more consistent, a convergence of all three
economies to a figure of around 10 per cent of GDP in 1996. This similar-
ity in shares of trade and in the levels of trade to GDP ratios for the three
main players indicates a certain symmetry in their external relations that
could enhance the prospects of broader agreements between them. The
current account balances resulting from these trends are indicated in figure
7.4, with the US moving into deficit after 1975, while the Japanese trade
surplus soared and the EU's position remained roughly in balance (in fact,

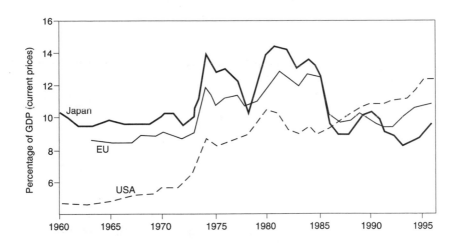

Figure 7.3 Trade in goods of the Triad countries as a percentage of their GDP, 1960–1996

Source: *The European Union as a World Trade Partner*, Directorate-General for Economic and Financial Affairs, EU, graph 4, p. 26

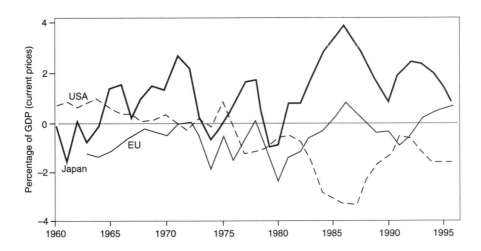

Figure 7.4 Current account balances of the Triad countries as a percentage of GDP, 1960–1996 (current prices)

Source: *The European Union as a World Trade Partner*, EU, graph 7, p. 28

these are the counterparts to the savings and investment flows indicated by the data in figure 7.1).

The most vulnerable economy remains that of Japan. It is the only one of the three that is not a continent-wide economy. Its vulnerability is signalled by its consistently low import penetration ratio, which makes it vulnerable to pressures for 'market access'. While discriminatory trading blocs have been formalized in Europe and North America, Japan has no such formal arrangements with its neighbours, and the prospects for this developing in East Asia with Japanese leadership seem slim (Kirkpatrick 1994; Panagariya 1994). Thus Japan has a more restricted 'natural hinterland' for its trade than the other two main players, even though they all share a similar combined aggregate total of trade to GDP ratio. Japanese export trade in particular is concentrated in a small number of sectors (motor vehicles and consumer electronics, in particular), which would make it highly vulnerable to selective US and EU trade policy. The comments made above about the current 1998 conjunctural weaknesses of the Japanese economy add to this structural vulnerability.

This is where the analysis of the relative importance of the Triad countries in the international economy as reported at the end of chapter 2 and in chapter 4 becomes significant. There it was suggested that the centre of gravity within the Triad could shift back towards the Atlantic and away from the Pacific as Japan and the East Asian economies fade in relative economic importance. The key relationship will be between the US dollar and the euro. Clearly, the US is likely to be suspicious of too successful a launch of the euro, particularly if it challenges the dollar as the major reserve currency. Unless the yen can increase its importance as a regional currency in East Asia, as and when these economies and Japan revive, the prospects for Japan's influence in international governance issues will remain limited. Quite how the exchange relationship between the euro and the dollar will be handled remains an open question, but it threatens to become the most important issue confronting economic governance at the beginning of the twenty-first century.

Returning to the actual relationships in the late 1990s, the point of this account is to confirm the emergence and continuing dominance of the three main players in the international economy. The US and the EU are roughly of the same economic size and standing, and the degree of diversity in their aggregate external relations is decreasing. Until recently Japan looked to be becoming the third equally strong member of this Triad. But perhaps the reality is less a Triad than a somewhat less stable 2.5-bloc governance mechanism at the heart of the international system.

This situation still offers the prospect of a minimal level of management of the international economy by cooperation between the three leading economies. It is easier to achieve agreement between three even unequal players than it would be for the whole OECD, if for no other reason than that there are fewer actors involved. This does not mean, of course, that new policy agreements will be forged. That depends on the economic issues and circumstances that arise and require management. The immediate prospects for extended cooperation are not auspicious. As we saw earlier, there remain significant policy differences on the form and style of economic management between the three main players, which could constrain even a conscious and determined attempt on their part at international policy coordination or cooperation. In addition, a more active practice of coordinated international management requires that the blocs will form into coherent managerial/regulatory entities themselves. The current state of affairs is not encouraging in this respect. This is partly an issue of political will and momentum. Nowhere is the political leadership or the prevailing economic ideas conducive to an ambitious extension of international economic governance. In the next chapter we consider the internal evolution of the EU and again draw relatively pessimistic conclusions. The gap between the potential for extended governance and the perceptions and policies of the major actors remains substantial. But this could change, particularly under the pressure of events. A deepening international crisis could force action. Unfortunately, although the idea of international economic liberalization has lost its intellectual hegemony as a result of the present crisis, it persists by default in the minds of the international technocracy and central bankers. We need an alternative policy doctrine, and quickly, to legitimate coordinated action to preserve output and employment.

This analysis suggests that a minimal modified multilateral international governance structure will prevail for the immediate future. It will be modified as against the previous regime of multilateralism under US hegemony, in the direction of a trilateral regime based on the three main blocs. To this will be added bilateral negotiations that are emerging between the three main players and other lessor actors. This latter phenomenon is termed *minilateralism* and is discussed below. Quite what the full consequences of this configuration might be for the management of international economic affairs remains an open question. Overt and widespread inward-looking protectionism on the part of the major blocs is unlikely. The present minimal level of modified-multilateral cooperation would seem to be enough to ensure the continued 'openness' of the international economic system, even as that system continues to move further away from the traditional postwar type of full liberal-multilateralism.

One thing is clear: the world economy will remain centred on its existing main players. The predictions of the World Bank that by 2020 China, India, Indonesia, South Korea, Thailand and Brazil would be among the ten largest economies, leading to a more polycentric world economic system, now seem hollow (as we saw in chapter 5). The G3 will continue to set the agenda in monetary, investment and trade policy.

Specific aspects of international financial governance

Having introduced the general background to issues of international economic governance, it is useful to develop its various features more fully. In this section we examine the first two levels outlined at the beginning of this chapter together, since, as will become apparent, they overlap significantly in terms of institutional evolution.

The international financial regime

That part of the international economy attracting most attention from commentators – and the one that seems to have internationalized to the greatest extent – is the financial system (chapters 2 and 5). This is also the most controversial area, particularly since the great regime shift of the early 1970s heralded the transition from what Padoa-Schioppa and Saccomanni have characterized as a government-led international monetary system (G-IMS) of the Bretton Woods era to the market-led international monetary system (M-IMS) of today. Padoa-Schioppa and Saccomanni list six main features that characterize the M-IMS (1994, p. 246):

1   the internationalization of financial portfolios consequent on the widespread domestic liberalization of capital movements;
2   the decline in the importance of banks relative to markets as agencies of financial intermediation (signalled by the rise in importance of securitization, bond issues, derivatives, etc.);
3   the financial market determination of exchange rates in the light of the growth in the scale of international financial transactions relative to trade transactions;
4   market volatility – the amplification of shocks across the system – which they attribute largely to the growth of information and communications technology;
5   market concentration, where a relatively small group of institutions trade simultaneously across international markets, employing similar conventions of analysis and behaviour; and finally;
6   the paradoxical emergence of an exposure of countries to exchange rate pressures at the same time as this does not effectively 'discipline' them in terms of their domestic economic policies.

As a response to these changes in the international financial system there have been developments in three distinct areas of regulation. The first concerns the general relationship coordinating and regulating the monetary, fiscal and exchange rate relations mainly between the key players of the G3. Broadly speaking, in practice this has been restricted to the determination of the global money supply and exchange rate manipulation, since the coordination of fiscal policies has not been in the forefront of economic

policy thinking since the late 1970s. As discussed in chapter 2, the attempts
to manage international liquidity multilaterally collapsed after 1979. This
led to the principal mismatch in governance characterizing the present
period, that is, an institutional gap between the increasingly international
nature of the financial system and the still predominantly 'national' remits
of the major central banks and the wider nationally located regulatory
mechanisms for financial markets and institutions.

How might this institutional gap be closed? The G3 to G7/8 summit
meetings, while providing an arena in which these broad issues have been
addressed, still lack a proper institutional base: there is no permanent
secretariat attached to these summits; they are conducted in an informal
atmosphere without tight procedural rules or functionally specified
agendas; there is no proper external accountability for decisions taken; and
few if any sanctions can be applied to national actors if the implementation
of agreements is not forthcoming. The upshot is that in terms of controlling
international liquidity, the summits have had only partial success, often as
much by chance as design. The 'exchange of views' that they embody has
led to a number of ad hoc monetary initiatives of an interventionary kind
rather than a permanent regime of institutionalized management. But while
a formalized international central bank is absent from the M-IMS, as argued
in chapter 2, the task could still fall to a particular country and its central
bank. Thus the US Federal Reserve Board has been instrumental in
developing initiatives in respect to governance and regulation, as we shall
see below.

More developed institutional arrangements are characteristic of the
second important governance aspect of the M-IMS: international payments
mechanisms. Clearing and settlement systems for international financial
transactions may not seem a particularly significant aspect of the international monetary regime but they are crucial for the continuance of all types
of financial activity, whether it be organized as banking or as securities
markets. This activity is redolent with 'public goods' features; it begs to be
organized in a collective manner but suffers from severe free-rider problems. At the national level, central banks play an important role in the
creation and supervision of payments mechanisms, the provision of 'final
money' services being a key part of the central banks' 'lender of last resort'
obligations. While this central banking function remains unfulfilled at the
international level, the risks of default increase and disturbances threaten
to become magnified across the whole system.

Among the international banking community the growth in international
financial transactions has been recognized as raising important issues for
efficient payment services and has been addressed in a number of G10
reports (Angell Report in 1989; Lamfalussey Report in 1991; Noel Report
in 1993). The result is a growing network of cooperative and coordinative
institutionalized mechanisms for monitoring, codifying and regulating
such transactions (centred on the Bank for International Settlements and

headed by the Group of Experts on Payment Systems). These G10 central bank initiatives have been paralleled by similar developments within the EU, which has now developed an effective cross-border clearing system in anticipation of the euro being fully introduced early in the next century. This could quite easily be extended to encompass Central and Eastern Europe when necessary as candidate members of the EU are admitted (Padoa-Schioppa and Saccomanni 1994, pp. 255–7).

The third area of regulation of the newly internationalized monetary system concerns supervision of those organizations conducting banking and financial market business. Here the landmark policy initiative was the G20/30 1975 Basel concordat that established the BIS's leading role in the supervision of international financial institutions. Following on from this the Basel Committee's 1988 Capital Accord was probably the most significant international agreement to date in the field of bank supervision. This established both a framework for further developments and a set of rules for measuring capital adequacy and fixing minimum standards of business conduct for banks involved with international activities. Recently this credit risk approach has been extended to include market risk and derivative assessment procedures, among a range of other matters. Again, the Basel agreement structure has been mirrored by developments within Europe, where the EU approved a comprehensive capital adequacy directive for banks in 1989.

Much like the monetary summits of the G3 to G7/8 the Basel Committee was initially designed as a forum for the exchange of ideas in an informal atmosphere with no set rules or procedures, let alone decision-making powers. But although it maintains this original informal atmosphere, its evolution has been towards much more involvement in hard-headed rule making and implementation monitoring. The Committee does not take as its brief the further liberalization of capital and banking markets; that is left to the policy of national governments. What it has done is respond to the effects of this liberalization on organizations conducting the business of international finance, and the central banks involved with them. It has been led by the demands of the banks, security houses and governments for a more codified and ordered international financial environment, rather than initiating discretionary action on its own part. The Basel Committee's activity with respect to the banking community is paralleled by the International Organization of Securities Commissions (IOSCO), a more recent and less robust body dealing with other aspects of international financial transactions, notably security market supervision. This was established in 1986, and although in a dialogue with the Basel Committee framework, it has yet to mature to the same extent.[4]

The issue raised by the emergence of these bodies (and other similar ones discussed in a moment) is why and how have they come about in an era of increased ideological emphasis on market-led solutions to international economic relationships? Why create new coordinative bodies to regulate and manage markets and transactions when such regulation and management are supposed to be increasingly frowned on by policy-makers? We outline an answer here. The Basel Committee responded to demands made elsewhere, both by governments, through their central banks, and by commercial companies involved in financial intermediation activity itself. One paradoxical consequence of the financial innovation unleashed by national liberalization and deregulation of financial markets in the 1980s, and of the technological development of information and communication systems introduced in its wake, was a sense of organizational 'loss of control' experienced by both central bankers and the managers of financial institutions. The development of fee-based 'off balance sheet' activity (options, swaps, forwards and futures, etc.) by banks and other organizations undermined well-established and well-understood practices of commercial management within both countries *and* firms. Paradoxically, a technology introduced in the expectation that it would provide up-to-date information, and so help managers, actually led to them feeling a loss of control. The players no longer quite understood what their 'capital base' was or how it functioned in terms of credit and market risk. This knowledge had been disrupted by the innovative financial engineering of the 1980s. The rapidity of the introduction of new financial instruments, the very pace of trading activity itself, and the necessity for 'on the spot' decisions to be made by floor dealers or in the OTC (over-the-counter) markets meant that even managers of commercial banks became unsure of their risk exposure and the real worth of their firms. Bank officials, along with their traditional national supervisors, the central banks, thus had an interest in re-establishing greater transparency in the light of the new circumstances they faced in international dealings. In many ways, then, managers of financial institutions are as 'dazed and confused' as the average citizen in terms of how the international financial system works and what to do about its proneness to speculative bubbles.

As a number of commentators have pointed out (Helleiner 1994; Kapstein 1994; Padoa-Schioppa and Saccomanni 1994), this concern among central bankers, governments and mainstream commercial banks was first fostered (and later reinforced) by a number of banking crises/failures of the 1970s and 1980s (Bankhaus Herstatt in Germany, Franklin National Bank in New York and British-Israel Bank in London, all in 1974; Banco Ambrosiano in 1982–3; BCCI in 1992; Barings in 1995). These banking crises were successfully 'managed' by the judicious intervention and cooperation of national governments. So the trend was set for *national governments* to cooperate more fully over a wider range of supervisory and monitoring tasks in this field.

Indeed, the central role of the policy of national governments in the creation of the M-IMS and its continued relevance for international financial governance is stressed by both Helleiner and Kapstein in their analyses. These authors dispute the view that the move from the G-IMS to the

M-IMS was the result of inexorable economic or technological forces rather than policy changes, and further that it has thereby undermined either the will or the ability of national governments to manage the present system.

The move to a nationally liberalized financial system in the 1980s was the result of deliberate political decisions taken in the face of a range of definite choices available to policy-makers (Helleiner 1994). Similarly, the subsequent development of a new regulatory regime was also driven by national governments, and according to Kapstein (1994) it is national governments that remain central to the nature of that regime. For instance, it was the US that took the lead in securing the 1988 Basel Accord. Within this framework, home country supervision of financial institutions came to dominate that of host country supervision: what Kapstein calls the principle of *international cooperation based upon home country control*. This was then gradually accepted by all the participant states and remains the dominant characteristic of the system. Although there have been tensions between home country and host country control, and also among multinational organizations with a stake in the regulation and supervision of financial institutions, the central role of the home nation-state in the process remains. This was most recently demonstrated by the Barings crisis of March 1995 when it was the Singapore authorities, the market in which the problems occurred, that took the lead in the investigations into Barings, and the eventual prosecution of Barings personnel. This procedure was accepted and endorsed by the UK government and the City of London supervisory network.[5]

What is more, according to Kapstein (1994), those countries not directly involved with the Basel Accord process have been keen to attach themselves to its regulatory framework. This was pressed on them by the banks operating within those countries. The dynamic of the system is fostered by a market-led desire to achieve a certain 'credit status' commensurate with that of the G20 sanctioned banks, a status dependent on operating within the Basel Accord guidelines.

However, a problem with these guidelines emerged during the 1998 financial crisis. They were found to be less than satisfactory in their regulation of short-term bank lending to emerging market countries (see chapter 5). The BIS capital adequacy ratios for short-term international bank lending require a lower weighting of reserves than for long-term lending, thereby actually encouraging short-term lending to developing countries as against long-term investment.

This crisis has raised a series of regulatory problems with international lending more generally. It has exposed the underlying problem in the case of capital flows: the rapid transition from full quantitative controls on capital movements to the totally free movement of capital. This is analogous to a transition from quotas on manufacturing trade to full free trade without passing through a tariff stage of international trade. The issue then is to bring 'tariffs' to bear again on capital flows, particularly short-term flows. At present the way the international system works is to subsidize short-term capital movements and to penalize long-term capital. In effect this is what the BIS criteria amounted to. Second, the IMF rescue packages initiated as a response to the crisis proved particularly pernicious since they have more or less completely guaranteed committed short-term funds, while forcing all the adjustment to be made by long-term capital and the real economy. Proposed mechanisms to bring tariffs to bear again on short-term loans include a small tax on short-term capital movements (the 'Tobin tax'), the imposition of non-remunerative reserve requirements on new short-term capital inflows (as in Chile), and George Soros's proposal for an International Credit Insurance Corporation that would guarantee international loans to countries for a modest fee (see chapter 5). Thus the 1998 financial crisis exposed the need both for better immediate 'fire-fighting' responses from the international governance system, and for reforms of the regulatory regime to enforce a more 'prudential' approach towards financial market supervision. The proposal for a Tobin tax and other policy responses are discussed at greater length in a moment.

One positive consequence of the BIS supervisory process is that the 'informality' of the system's decision-making activity actually fosters an emphasis on the active involvement of affected parties. In many ways, the success of this informal rule-making process speaks against the idea of substituting for it by the creation of a new formal multinational body to regulate and supervise *all* capital market activity under one roof, such as the Capital Markets Supervisory Authority suggested by Bergsten (1994, p. 361). The present system of national cooperation based on home country control is firmly in place in the case of banking supervision, and in embryonic development in the case of securities markets. The issue is to strengthen both these initiatives rather than to undermine them with the creation of yet another top-down multilateral body.

What we have then is not totally unregulated markets but an elaborate system for the detailed management of international financial transactions. National governments have not proved totally powerless in the face of an overwhelming 'globalization' of international finance. They have joined together in various ways to organize the supervision of the new situation. This remains, nevertheless, a limited *supervision* of a market-led international economy. Regulation does not attempt to alter price fixing by markets or the direction of financial flows. Currency markets are left to operate broadly unhindered, and exchange rates to find their own levels. Thus massive short-term speculative capital flows can still bring chaos to well-founded national economic management policies. There are no grounds for complacency about the existing system: rather, the desperate need is to strengthen the existing supervisory apparatuses and to begin the difficult task of redirecting financial flows along more sensible and sustainable lines. The 1998 financial crisis was much more than a simple and necessary 'corrective' to a system otherwise operating efficiently. It demonstrated the fundamental irrationality of speculative activity and the potentially destructive and hazardous nature of a totally free market in international finance.

Thus what are left out by the current supervisory organizations are ways of checking the unhindered operation of these market processes. Here the development of 'acceptable' exchange rate bands – commensurate with Williamson-type 'economic fundamentals' – within which currencies are allowed to fluctuate would seem highly desirable (Atkinson and Kelly 1994, p. 33; Holtham 1989). Such bands would have to be wide ones however: they would operate only as 'indicators' of the sustainable economic fundamentals in the anticipation that this would help form expectations and direct market sentiment as to the authorities' intentions, enhancing credibility and consistency in both policy-making and market reaction as a result. Narrow bands or pegged systems that are closely defended under all circumstances have proved almost unworkable and destructive in practice. But a wide band regime is clearly preferable to completely floating rates in the degree of certainty and stability it offers, it is more attainable than semi-fixed rates, and it is less likely to trigger speculative activity in periods of crisis or transition (as was the case with old EMS-type adjustable peg rates). This could be considered as a new strategy of governance of markets along with the introduction by those states with major financial centres of a tax on short-term (speculative) foreign exchange trading, thereby reducing the possible gains from simply specializing in the recycling of money.

As suggested by Tobin (1978, 1994; Eichengreen, Tobin and Wyplosz 1995; see also Grieve Smith 1997; Arestis and Sawyer 1997), a small transactions tax on the purchase and sale of foreign exchange could 'throw sand in the wheels of international finance' without necessarily preventing long-term investment or indeed all speculative activity. But it is questionable how effective this could be without further restrictions on certain key elements of the international financial system (Davidson 1997). The trouble is that 'financial churning' is so extensive, with gearing and exposure of two to three hundred times an institution's capital base, that such a tax could easily become meaningless and be overwhelmed by the speculative frenzy at just the moment it is supposed to work to dampen things down. Of course, it might operate quite effectively as a tax revenue generating device rather than to prevent speculation, but this would then raise the further difficulty of who should appropriate the revenue and how it should be used.

As has been emphasized by Holtham (1995, pp. 244–5) and Kenen (1995, p. 189), some 'managed' speculation is warranted since it can genuinely work to reduce risks, stabilizing currencies and reducing volatility. The issue is to prevent speculative activity for its own sake, and while 'target zones' might be useful in conjunction with the Tobin tax, other measures would also be necessary to isolate the purely 'superspeculative' element in foreign exchange dealing. One way to tackle this would be for national authorities to put legal limits on the number of financial institutions allowed to engage in such activity, so that a smaller number of players could be more easily monitored. Bringing the derivatives business into an ordered institutionalized framework – say, by restricting this business to regulated banking organizations only – would thus add another sensible layer to this governance strategy. Hedge funds are a case in point. While they operated as a basic intermediary, a kind of insurance policy against volatility, their activity was economically useful and sound. It was when they began to expand the range of their business, to operate on their own account for instance, that problems arose. This dramatically affected both their own stability as the parameters of volatility moved (larger than expected swings in exchange rate and interest rate movements, for instance), and the economies of the currencies in which they were speculating.

In addition, this raises the connected issue of how to prevent 'spillovers' from one market into another. An increasingly interdependent financial system can mean both a rapid 'lateral' spread of problems from one financial arena into another, as with the relationship between foreign exchange markets and securities markets, as well as an increasing momentum to panics and crises. The policy response here is to erect 'fire walls' between different arenas so as to 'ring fence' against spillovers, and to introduce or extend 'stops' or interruptions in trading activity to allow 'cooling off' periods.

These measures would go some way to 'cool the casino'. However, their introduction is not without serious technical difficulties (Akyuz and Cornford 1995; Garber and Taylor 1995), and would require agreement between at least the G20 (but perhaps just the G3 in the case of some of these measures). This is difficult to envisage in the immediate future, but is by no means impossible in the longer run. The more thoughtful international monetary experts and central bankers are beginning to talk about a limited, managed monetary multilateralism under the slogan of a 'new Bretton Woods'. The use of the rhetoric of Bretton Woods shows a desire to restore the *functions* and *objectives* of those international institutions, to promote growth in output and full employment, rather than the specific mechanisms established for those purposes in the heyday of the system. Restoring the pre-existing regime is hardly an option; there is little prospect of a new hegemon to assume the role the US played from 1954 to 1972, and no analogue of full convertibility. Fundamentally, these issues are not 'technical' but 'political' – they require a political will on the part of the leaders of the major nations. This is discussed further in the concluding chapter.

Governing trade

After the major financial markets, the second most important area of the international economy is that of trade. Here an already highly tuned regulatory regime has been firmly in place and it is not our intention to describe the development of this regime in any detail, as it is well known. But there

are a number of issues that arise in the context of the GATT treaty framework which are worth considering separately in this section.

First, the traditional liberal multilateralism of the initial phase of GATT
came under increasing pressure after 1965 from two sources. One was a
move towards *bilateralism* in the form of a set of negotiations and agreements between pairs or smaller groups of countries, conducted outside the
formal GATT multilateral framework. The second source of tension arose
with the creation of regionalized trading blocs, and particularly the 1980s
and 1990s development of supranational dispute settlement mechanisms
between the EU, NAFTA and Japan. Both these trends constitute what
Yarbrough and Yarbrough (1992) have called a move towards *minilateralism*. While minilateralism does not hold to the cherished GATT cornerstone
of non-discrimination and 'most favoured nation' status, neither does it necessarily abandon 'openness' in trade relationships. Thus it would be perfectly possible to have a widely supported, open and liberal trading regime
without having one based on the principles of multilateralism.

The tensions between multilateralism, bilateralism and minilateralism in
international trade have yet to fully work themselves out. However, the
current *modus operandi* for world trade was formalized by the second
important development considered here, the conclusion of the Uruguay
Round of GATT negotiations in 1994 and the formation of the World Trade
Organization (WTO) in 1994–5.[6] The point to emphasize about these particular negotiations is the relative revival in the fortunes of multilateralism
initiated by the conclusion of this round. But strong bilateral and minilateral forces still linger in the international system, as indicated by the way it
was concluded and the difficulties experienced in the process of ratifying
the agreement, and they could still be quite quickly revived. The key to
bringing the negotiation to a successful conclusion, for instance, was a deal
struck between the US, Japan and the EU over agricultural issues, but these
have still not been finally resolved. All three players continue to subsidize
agriculture in one way or another, which adds to the tensions between them
in discussion over these issues. It also makes smaller players suspicious
about the pressures brought to bear on them over agricultural trade
matters.

Meanwhile, in anticipation of final ratification, the WTO was formed
during 1994 to become operative sometime in 1995. The Final Act established the WTO as a fully fledged international governing institution recognized in international law (GATT Secretariat 1993; Jackson 1994). It
brings together and supersedes the previous diverse and sometimes
ambiguous agreements, articles, codes, clauses and treaties of the entire
post-1947 GATT process, binding them into a single package. At the same
time it incorporates the agreements and articles of the Uruguay Round:
these have become mandatory on all members of the WTO by imposing
binding legal obligations on them. The result is a comprehensive bureaucratic administration of the 'rules of conduct' for undertaking international

trade, the establishment of an enlarged and streamlined disputes mechanism, and a unified framework for future rounds of negotiations. Although this is an international organization its structure remains essentially 'representational': the members make the decisions as representatives of their governments, and decision-making is on the basis of various forms of majority voting (still with a number of 'escape clauses'). Thus 'national sovereignty' would seem to be little more compromised than under the old GATT procedures.

The conclusion of the Uruguay Round leaves almost as many problems for regulating world trade as it has solved. Four of the most pressing involve agriculture, environmental standards, labour standards and the protection of Third World interests. All these in turn involve the future of the protectionism versus free trade debate. In many ways the four issues are interlinked through the problems confronting some of the less developed economies in the face of the Uruguay Round. There will continue to be legitimate objections to the appropriation of genetic engineering outputs from agricultural experiments by advanced country firms. The potential for the distortion of Third World agricultural output towards providing for standardized First World market demands remains. The general viability of an environmentally sustainable agricultural system as integrative trade pressures grow needs careful thought. In addition, the question of the continued subsidization of First World agricultural output and trade has not been properly solved by the Uruguay Round, and this regime of subsidy continues to characterize all the G3 players to greater or lesser degrees.

The issue of sustainable agricultural development under the new post-GATT regime can be seen as part of the wider problem of global environmental governance. The Uruguay Round, by strengthening the liberalization of trade under the notions of non-discrimination and mutual treatment, could make it harder for different and higher environmental standards to be maintained by particular nation-states. The pressure could mount for these standards to be watered down or cut back altogether, under the rules for fair and non-discriminatory trade treatment (Lang and Hines 1993). While more rigorous standards might increase the cost of goods and services originating from a single country, they also harden the overall standards regime, preventing the discrimination of imports from those countries that undercut in standards and costs. The environmental code of the WTO has come under considerable attack on this score, from US environmental interests in particular (though much criticism is also directed at the NAFTA agreement with Mexico). It should be remembered, however, that many Third World countries argued against the imposition or maintenance of high standards, fearing they would be unable to compete if these were imposed on them (Anderson 1996; Kruger 1996). Thus the minimizing of labour and environmental standards has as much to do with the resistance of Third World governments as it has to do with MNCs. The key to unlocking this in the long term must be a genuine redistribution of global resources, so that the fears of Third World governments that these standards are but another attempt by the industrialized world to gain competitive advantage are addressed.

These dilemmas have rekindled the protectionist and anti free trade argument in new forms (Lang and Hines 1993; Nader et al. 1994; Goldsmith 1994). There are legitimate concerns raised in this debate, which spans the political spectrum and includes both left and right. These concerns should not be ignored, but the solution is not a generalized restriction of trade, even in the name of a 'new protectionism'. Rather prosperity and growth of the world economy are more likely with an open and broadly liberal trading order. Environmental concerns can better be addressed by diverting the revenue of a growing and prosperous international economy than in a stagnant one, which would be a real danger if widespread protectionism ensued. The lessons of the 1930s are that widespread protectionism not merely helped to prevent recovery from the Great Depression, but that it promoted antagonistic and self-defeating competition between states. This is hardly an encouraging scenario in which to protect the environment or to benefit poorer and weaker economies.

The agricultural issues mentioned above would not necessarily be any better dealt with by protection either. What are needed are sensible new negotiations on terms for trade, rather than their abandonment in the name of localist autarchy. Protection of specific sectors over defined time periods may be justifiable at times, and this would be less damaging for individual economies in a world where trading blocs took sole responsibility for these decisions as relationships between them evolved. But, as far as possible, an open liberal trade regime is the most desirable. And it is still possible, though the revitalization of multilateralism with the setting up of the WTO may have closed off some options.

Minilateral negotiations are also still possible, however (and if circumstances dictate, nation-states will make them possible by overriding the strict multilateralism of the WTO). Minilateralism may provide a better basis on which to tackle some of the problems identified above (for instance, in the case of agricultural subsidies, where negotiations between just the G3 countries, who are the principal subsidizers, could produce positive results). Trilateral and bilateral forms of open economy negotiations have provided powerful levers for a wider trade liberalization in the past (Oye 1994, pp. 156–61).

Finally in this section a caveat needs to be introduced on much of the above discussion. The way the issue is set up corresponds to the traditional notion that international trade takes place 'in the open', as it were, between national states. However, as was pointed out in chapter 3, up to a third of international trade is actually carried out within the boundaries of MNCs, that is, it is intra-MNC trade. This raises a whole new set of problems, associated as much with the general regulation of international businesses as with international trade itself. However, the issues explored in this subsection are not necessarily undermined by this observation. They remain vitally important even in an environment where it is companies that are conducting trade internally. It is issues like 'transfer pricing', international accounting conventions, tax and profit declaration procedures that arise in the new context. Such issues are probably better tackled in a multilateral negotiating environment like the General Agreement on International Business framework discussed in the next section.

In itself this raises yet another important issue in the context of contemporary international governance. An area of growing concern is the proliferation of international standard-setting activity. Of course, this is a feature of the well-established supranational organization of management, through bodies such as the World Bank, IMF and WTO. These already lay down many standards for the conduct of trade, investment and official loan business. But in addition to these, we see the growth of what are unofficial and informal modes of standard setting, though they are often not clearly recognized as such. Thus in the field of commercial matters, accounting standards and legal standards are increasingly being codified internationally, usually around Anglo-American practices. Companies' voluntary adherence to such standards and to practices of independent commercial arbitration is often a condition for their access to contracts or a requirement of international loans.

In addition there is the more formal development of quality standards for production activity organized by the ISO 9000 process, and by the ISO 14000 process for environmental standards (Clapp 1998). But who knows where the ISO is located, let alone who appoints its officers? Then there are the better known 'private' credit rating agencies like Standard and Poor, and Moody's. Increasingly, these determine the creditworthiness not only of companies but also of countries, a classic example of power without responsibility. While this kind of activity is by no means new – UK financial institutions set credit ratings in the late nineteenth and early twentieth centuries, Norway and the UK captured the setting of marine classification standards, the Federal Aviation Administration in the US effectively did the same for international air transport in the 1960s – so that it cannot be used to explain 'globalization' as a new process, it does give enormous power to those organizations conducting this kind of activity. Fundamentally these standard-setting practices are part of the international trading system: they exist to facilitate international trade and investment, yet they also determine the fate of economic actors in ways that confer real political power. Strange (1996) draws attention to these practices and sees them as the most significant aspect of globalization (for her they are far more important than cross-border trade) and internationalization that does not show up in official international statistics. These processes are obviously significant, but they are also compatible with an economy rooted in distinct national bases rather than one centred on supranational market forces.

The question arises, what exactly are these organizations? Are they public or are they private? Perhaps the best way to describe them is as both claiming and exercising a public power while being neither wholly private nor wholly public organizations. They represent a different breed of semi-private/semi-public institutions, part of the change in the international system referred to above. They are part of the newly emerging governance system, and they need both greater attention from scholarship and more supervision from traditional public authorities and state actors.

The regulation of FDI and of labour migration

The international management of FDI can be considered in terms of three possible approaches to governance: (a) the development of a multilateral and multinational approach, via something like a parallel organization to the GATT/WTO – a General Agreement on International Investment or as part of a General Agreement on International Business; or (b), to proceed along more functionally specific lines to negotiate over specific aspects of international direct investment in separate forums; or finally (c), to pursue the minilateralist option of bilateral or trilateral (G3) bargaining (see chapter 3).

This is an area where strengthening the international public policy regime is most pressing, given the dramatic growth of FDI and its increasing strategic importance for the future shape of the international economy. Many of the recent policy moves here have been designed to increase market access and further liberalize FDI flows, particularly in the case of service sector investment (such as the 1997 WTO Financial Services Agreement). One possibility would be to push this trend further by explicit public policy of the major states, extending the range and cover of FDI liberalization moves. This would mean the further extension of essentially ad hoc initiatives, developing the existing patchwork of bilateral and trilateral agreements while attaching any remaining genuine multilateral issues to the WTO framework (Julius 1994). On the other hand, those who see the problem of inconsistency in the regulation of FDI emerging, who are worried about partial coverage and who see the need for a deeper coordination on FDI matters and not just further liberalization, have pressed for the multilateral option and the development of a new institutional structure (Bergsten 1994). This is essentially what the OECD's proposed Multilateral Agreement on Investment would involve. At present this initiative is stalled – it has come up against fierce opposition from development oriented NGOs and also from governments (the French government, for instance, has declared that it will not sign such an agreement), because it would virtually dismantle any governmental control over the terms and conditions for inward FDI. It is hoped that this initiative is now 'dead in the water' for the foreseeable future. Its advocacy occurred within the economic liberal technocracy, pushing ahead even as their dogmas were discredited by the current economic crisis. The danger is that such ideas are virtually indestructible in bodies like the OECD; the Multilateral Agreement on Investment may have failed but that organization will prevent coherent alternatives with different objectives.

None of these approaches sees the problem as one of redirecting FDI flows on a global basis so that FDI not only moves towards those countries at present disadvantaged in terms of flows and amounts, but so that it is also directed towards investment in specific economic sectors at present starved of such funds. Such a system could involve a modest levy (say 0.5 per cent) on FDI flows between OECD countries, and between them and the ten largest developing country recipients of FDI, which would be used to create an investment fund for those countries at present almost ignored by MNC FDI activity. The fund would be administered by a new organization alternative to and competing with the World Bank, and would be used to subsidize and augment Western corporate investment in the poorest developing countries. A 50 per cent subsidy, with firms required to raise 50 per cent commercially, might persuade companies to undertake what they might otherwise dismiss as risky ventures in the poorest countries.

This discussion of FDI regulation has so far concerned only possible international cooperative moves. We have left out of account policy initiatives that might be made at the purely domestic level. There exists a generalized feeling among political radicals and extreme globalization theorists that little can be done here. The left in particular sees MNCs as predatory and beyond the control of any particular government. However, as we saw in chapter 3, this attitude is unnecessarily pessimistic; it is also politically disarming and needs to be challenged. The bulk of the business activity of international companies remains specific to their country of origin (or region of origin). One modest but realistic possibility is the institution of a system of national monitoring of the activity of home-based MNCs (Bailey, Hart and Sugden 1994). Countries like the UK have no such monitoring structure, though it is common to a greater or lesser extent in other comparable advanced countries. The suggestion of Bailey et al. is to institute, develop or strengthen these forms of enquiry across the advanced world so that they at least provide good quality information and analysis on what the exact impact of both inward and outward investment is on an economy.[7] Their proposal is to set this in an elaborate social accounting framework, which could be extended to incorporate the general business issues mentioned above in connection with intra-MNC trade. This would then form the basis for developing consensus policy measures between the major nation-states to tackle any adverse effects identified. Given our results in chapter 3, the options for regulating MNCs in this way remain a distinct possibility, particularly since they are unlikely to quit their national bases. It would provide a further example of Kapstein's (1994) 'international cooperation based upon home country control'.

Another approach to dealing with MNCs at the national level – an approach that attempts to neutralize their adverse consequences – is to try to 'bypass' them by stimulating an alternative domestic oriented sector through the use of favourable fiscal and other incentives. The 'mutual sector', broadly conceived, fits this bill. The restrictions put on 'discrimination' in trade or investment matters by international treaties of the character of the WTO/OECD liberalizations of capital movements can be circumvented by a policy aimed solely at domestically oriented activity of a cooperative nature. This type of measure would involve corporate reforms, and is best considered below in the context of stimulating local industrial initiatives, regional economic networks and the like.

Another area of economic governance that, potentially at least, straddles the international and the national in its appropriate level of regulation involves labour and migration matters. This is often neglected as a governance issue, but it is likely to become an increasingly important one, as the analysis of migration in chapter 2 showed.

Among the proposals to deal with this in an international context would be to create a new international regulatory function and to institutionalize it by using and expanding an existing body like the International Organization for Immigration (part of the United Nations High Commission for Refugees) or the International Labour Organization (ILO). Such a body would take responsibility for negotiating common standards and procedures for the migration and entry and exit of labour, dealing with questions of illegal entry and of family and refugee movements, and establishing fair and efficient disputes procedures, etc. The aim of such common criteria would be to avoid racism and promote at least some mobility into the First World, especially for those threatened by oppressive regimes. It could also extend the main work of the ILO, laying down common standards of employment conditions, industrial relations, etc. The existing structures in this area are extremely weak, so to build a new international migration/labour regime along these lines would prove very difficult. These are also particularly sensitive areas of economic policy-making. Up until now international cooperation has been aimed more at restricting migrants' movements than at liberalizing them.

An alternative is to think along rather more regional or subregional lines (Lee 1996). This would build on current trends and emerging arrangements, which are increasingly mirroring the regionalization of trade and investment. But even here one suspects that handing over further policy formation and control to intergovernmental bodies would prove politically difficult. Within the EU, the most advanced of the regional configurations, developments along these lines have progressed very unevenly, particularly in respect to immigration into the Union. Thus for the foreseeable future we suspect that national governments will continue to preserve their own prerogative in these sensitive matters. The result will be a patchwork of differing criteria and procedures, with the likelihood of more draconian measures to try to control migration of all kinds.

Managing economic development and economic transition

The final area considered in the context of the first two of our five levels of governance involves the traditional institutional arrangements for dealing with economic development, and also the way these have expanded to deal increasingly with societies in transformation from authoritarian regimes.

Here it is the World Bank and the IMF that have been centrally involved. The Bank set the pattern for multilateral development lending to govern- ments in the Bretton Woods era, involving its own activity and that of a set of regional development banks for Latin America, Africa and Asia. The IMF concentrated on shorter-term assistance, mainly associated with liquidity for balance of payments crises and stabilization policies. Although the IMF was heavily involved with managing the 'petro-dollar' shocks of the 1970s, with the spread of floating exchange rates its specific role in liquidity provision has diminished, and the rationale for the IMF has been somewhat undermined. The role of the World Bank has also changed since the related 1980s 'debt crisis' period, which saw the rise in importance of commercial banks in the financing of official Third World government debt. The emergence of regional economic configurations like the EU has also undercut many of the IMF's functions.

Both organizations have responded to these developments by looking for new policy approaches and for new areas in which to offer 'assistance'. The new approaches are signalled by a move from the centrality of the cri- teria of 'conditionality' in their dealings with client states, to that of 'good governance', by which the World Bank basically means good public admin- istration (World Bank 1994). The new areas were rather fortuitously offered in the form of the 'economies in transition' in Eastern Europe and the former Soviet Union after 1989 (or more properly, 'economies in trans- formation', see Thompson 1995b), and the Bank and the IMF eagerly embraced these areas for the deployment of their advice and activity.

Along with the emergence of 'good governance' as a criterion for assis- tance, other 'softer' targets and criteria have risen in importance. Thus human development and poverty alleviation, the production of knowledge and provision of technical assistance, and the protection of the environment have all entered the vocabulary of these organizations, alongside their tra- ditional concerns with project finance and external resource transfers. To some extent these softer criteria have made the organizations and the activ- ity they are there to monitor more difficult to manage. With strict 'condi- tionality' criteria, at least the objectives of policy were clear and precise (however perniciously they were applied at times), but 'good governance' and 'human development' are imprecise, loose criteria, which vary significantly between situations and are thus difficult to monitor consistently as constraints. Indeed, such criteria may give international organizations wider discretionary powers and may be more invasive of the sovereignty of member states than were the old examples of strict monetary and fiscal objectives.

The other important change in the case of the World Bank is the insistence on 'trade regime neutrality' in its dealings with the newly emergent economies in transformation. Thus there has been a move away from support for either import substitution or export-led growth strategies, both of which are thought to implicate discretionary interventionist policy-making on the part of governments. This is all part of a further move towards market-led solutions to the economic problems faced by these economies.

However, formally at least, it is this new 'softer' monitoring regime that will guide these organizations in the conduct of their main business with the economies in transformation. At the same time there is growing pressure for a fundamental reform in the World Bank structure, in particular to make it more 'businesslike' and complementary to private capital lending (Gilbert et al. 1996). As yet its outright privatization has been resisted, but the Bank already conducts a major section of its business effectively in the private sector (for instance, the International Finance Corporation and the Multilateral Investment Guarantee Agency). Proposals to extend this abound, particularly as its lending to middle-income countries – a major part of the IBRD business – and its development funding (International Development Agency) is now heavily complemented by private sector flows. However, the 1998 financial crisis may undermine this private sector involvement in 'development assistance' and restimulate the original public sector rationale for World Bank activity. Moves to recapitalize it through the injection of private sector funds could prove difficult and costly in the long run. Its partial privatization is not off the agenda, however. Perhaps the best way to proceed would be to encourage competition in development strategies, building a radical competitor to the World Bank (Unger 1996). This would give developing country governments an option, thus reducing the scope of the World Bank to dictate wider issues of policy as a condition for loans.

In the case of the World Bank's fellow organization, the IMF, there are perhaps even stronger and more pressing needs for reform. Do we need an international lender of last resort? Clearly, the answer is yes. But only if part of its remit and the conditionality for future assistance is the encouragement of policies at national level that act to constrain volatility, for instance, by accepting controls on the capital account for developing countries and imposing restrictions on the riskier financial markets (such as the OTC trade and derivatives) for the advanced countries. Secondly, only if the IMF's policies are directed towards concentrating on providing liquidity for trade and on maximizing domestic output. The IMF has done just the opposite in the Asian crisis (see above and appendix to chapter 5), and had its strictures not been strongly resisted in South Korea, it would have made matters worse than they are.

The major institutions need reform. Rationalizing the IMF and the World Bank into a single superorganization might appear tidy, but it concentrates power and merges quite different functions. Public development assistance can best be performed by a limited variety of competing agencies – sufficient to embody different development strategies and thus permit alternative routes to the future. Competing economic institutions are essential for promoting economic evolution. The IMF, by contrast, has one function and barely enough funds to perform its current roles; therefore, the need is to maximize the funds available.

National economic governance

There can be no doubt that the combined effects of changing economic conditions and earlier public policies of dismantling exchange controls have made ambitious and internationally divergent strategies of national economic governance far more difficult. Also reduced has been the capacity of states to act autonomously on their societies. This is because the range of economic incentives and sanctions at the state's disposal has been restricted as a consequence of this loss of capacity to deliver distinctively 'national' economic policies.

Most obvious is the case of macroeconomic management. The current impossibility of ambitious Keynesian strategies at a national level hardly needs to be demonstrated, particularly after the failure of the ambitious reflationary programme of the French Socialist government in the early 1980s. But nationally distinctive monetarist policies of an ambitious nature have proved hardly more viable. Thus the UK was saved from accelerating losses of employment and output in the early 1980s by international impacts that reduced the value of sterling against the dollar and brought down interest rates, but that had nothing to do with national policy.

If macroeconomic management is problematic, so too is that supply-side alternative, a centralized, state-directed industrial policy. Technologies are currently changing too rapidly for the state, however competent and well informed its officials are, to 'pick winners' on a national basis. Moreover, the population of firms that the state would have to bring into such a policy is less stable and easy to interact with than it was in the 1960s. Many major products are now the result of complex interfirm partnerships. Changed economic conditions favour risk sharing between firms, diversification and flexibility, and put a premium on specialist and local knowledge. These are factors that traditional state institutions and uniform systems of industrial administration find hard to cope with.

Despite the foregoing, national governmental policies to sustain economic performance remain important, even if their methods and functions have changed. This is true even when states are part of a supranational entity. In the EU some hitherto important areas of specifically national economic management will obviously be restricted by the free movement of capital, labour, goods and services from the end of 1992, monetary union as provided by the Maastricht Treaty, and greater political integration as a result of the 1996 intergovernmental conference. But these events will make others more important, giving a new significance to non-monetarist fiscal and supply-side policies for instance. Moreover, by stabilizing the external economic environment, they make other national policies more effective and less subject to disruption.

While national governments may no longer be 'sovereign' economic regulators in the sense traditionally, if somewhat fallaciously, claimed for the 'Keynesian era', they remain political communities with extensive powers to influence and to sustain economic actors within their territories. Technical top-down macroeconomic management is now less important. However, the role of government as a facilitator and orchestrator of private economic actors has become more salient as a consequence. The *political* role of government is central in the new forms of economic management. As we shall see in chapter 8, neither the financial markets nor the officials of the European Commission in Brussels, to take the case of the most developed supranational economic association, the EU, can impose or secure the forms of social cohesion and the policies that follow from them that national governments can. National governments can still *compensate* for the effects of internationalization and for the continued volatility of the financial markets, even if they cannot unilaterally control those effects or prevent that volatility.

Before going into more detail on features of political orchestration through national policy, let us look at the more overtly economic character of (non-monetarist) fiscal policy. Fiscal policy has been in the shadow of monetary policy ever since the demise of Keynesianism. During the late 1970s and the 1980s it became very difficult to argue for an 'independent' fiscal policy, one that was both nationally autonomous and independent of monetary policy. However, that may be about to change.

One thing closer economic and monetary union within Europe (and more generally, the relative 'cooling of the casino' internationally) could do is to help 'disengage' fiscal from monetary policy once again. Take the case of the EU. The closer monetary union becomes, the more individual countries may be able to engage in independent fiscal policies. This does not mean that they will be totally free to do as they wish on the fiscal front. The post-Maastricht guidelines for government fiscal balances, for instance, are very tight (around 3 per cent of GDP). But these are only meant to be guidelines and in practice they may be quite flexible. They are likely to be more flexible than monetary guidelines, for instance, which are under the direction of the 'independent' European Central Bank. The President of the ECB made it clear during the 1998 financial crisis that the Bank would pursue a very conservative line both on disclosure of its deliberations and in terms of the monetary policy it intended to follow. Thus, as decisions on monetary policy are increasingly taken elsewhere, that is centrally, individual governments will be able to decide their own fiscal policies relatively independently of monetary policy. This could enable some quite innovative fiscal responses as a result. Any new fiscal regime will also be operating in an environment of increasing financial and labour market integration, and this would need to be taken into account by policy-makers.

However, this must be considered against the changing background of attitudes towards taxation among voters in advanced countries. There has been a widespread move towards tax resistance in advanced countries, which is often put down to the effects of 'globalization'. But globalization has little to do with this. It was fostered by domestic policy initiatives to gain electoral advantage, and in the name of the supposed incentive effects of lower taxation. The consequence is, however, that raising additional government revenue for elaborate expenditure plans is proving increasingly difficult. Considered alongside the growing difficulty of levering up economic activity and employment by the simple deployment of public expenditures, the framework for conducting a macroeconomic fiscal policy may have radically changed.

The problem this will pose is how to develop tax systems that minimize both the incentives to avoid individual national taxes and the ability to do so. Broadly speaking the need is to think in terms of factor mobility in relationship to taxation. Capital and money markets will probably integrate most rapidly and thoroughly, so there may be little scope for nationally differential corporation taxes or taxes on savings (via taxes on savings institutions). Nationally differential taxes on domestic consumption may also be difficult, but this depends on how internationally mobile purchasers are in the face of tax rates. Will they be prepared to travel long distances just to exploit tax differences? There may be more scope for difference here.[8] In the case of income taxes this again depends on how integrated labour markets become. Clearly there are likely to be degrees of integration. A lot of work overseas is temporary. But in general the highest paid and the lowest paid tend to be potentially the most internationally mobile. In the case of indigenous EU workers, cultural and linguistic barriers may still be high in terms of labour mobility, and a lot will depend on how quickly and efficiently mutual recognition of professional qualifications and standards develops. In general there may still be some scope for differential income taxes before (dis)incentive effects become rife and undermine their effectiveness. The most immobile factor is likely to remain property of one kind or another. People cannot just up and away with their houses, for instance.

Thus there may be some innovative scope for new forms of property taxes as this becomes an increasingly attractive source of tax revenues for governments.

One other significant area where new tax and revenue-raising strategies may be available to national states and to subsidiary regional and local governments is energy consumption and environmental pollution (Hewitt 1990). Taxes on the consumption of non-renewable types of energy and the widespread adoption of the 'polluter pays' principle through taxes on industrial emissions, vehicle use, etc., may well be the major sources of revenue of the future. Such taxes have three advantages: they attract less stigma from international financial markets than direct taxation (mainly because they have not yet been factored into the market-makers' calculations); they appear to be more acceptable to citizens than taxes on income; and they serve the dual purpose of raising revenue and forcing both firms and final consumers to internalize the environmental costs of their actions. Thus energy taxes seem to offer one of the best ways of decoupling fiscal and monetary policy and attaining a measure of autonomy in revenue raising.

Returning to the general theme of the nation-state in regulating the economy, there are three key functions it can perform which stem from its role as orchestrator of an economic consensus within a given community. States are not like markets: they are still to some extent communities of fate which tie together actors who share certain common interests in the success or failure of their national economies. Markets may or may not be international, but wealth and economic prosperity are still essentially nationally determined phenomena. They depend on how well national economic actors can work together to secure certain key supply-side outcomes. National policy can provide certain key inputs to economic performance that cannot be bought or traded on the market. Markets need to be embedded in social relations. Political authority remains central in ensuring that markets are appropriately institutionalized and that the non-market conditions of economic success are established. National governments thus remain a crucial element in the economic success of their societies, providing cohesion, solidarity and certain crucial services that markets of themselves cannot (Hutton 1995). The three key functions of states are as follows.

(1)   The state, if it is to influence the economy, must construct a societal *distributional coalition*, that is, win the acceptance by key economic actors and the organized social interests representing them of a sustainable distribution of national income and expenditure which promotes competitive manufacturing performance (among other things). The major components of such a coalition are the balance of national income devoted respectively to consumption and investment; a broad agreement on the level of taxation necessary to sustain state investment in infrastructure, training and collective services for industry; and a framework for controlling wage settlements,

the growth of credit and the levels of dividends such that inflation is kept within internationally tolerable limits.

(2)   Such a distributional coalition is only possible if the state performs another function, that is, the *orchestration of social consensus*. Such coalitions only work when they emerge from a political culture that balances collaboration and competition, and in which the major organized interests are accustomed to bargaining over national economic goals, to making ongoing commitments to determine policy by such bargaining and to policing their members' compliance with such bargains. Industry, organized labour and the state can be related in various ways, perhaps much less rigidly than the highly structured national corporatism practised in states like West Germany and Sweden into the 1990s. The social pacts that have re-emerged in Europe in the 1990s (as discussed in chapter 6) are examples of such new forms of codetermination through negotiated governance. The point is to ensure that the key components of the economic system are in dialogue, that firms cooperate as well as compete and that different factors of production (such as labour and management and capital providers and firms) relate in other than just market terms. Such systems will not be devoid of conflict, nor will interests be wholly compatible, but there will be mechanisms for resolving such differences. An overall consensus like this can only work if it is also keyed in with the effective operation of more specific resource allocation mechanisms, such as the system of wage determination and the operation of capital markets.

(3)   The state must also achieve an adequate balance in the distribution of its fiscal resources and its regulatory activities between the national, regional and municipal levels of government. The centralization of EU policy is promoting the increasing importance of effective *regional* government. The regional provision of education and training, industrial finance, collective services for industry and social services is gaining in prominence. Regional governments are better able to assess the needs of industry because they possess more localized, and therefore more accurate information and because they are of a scale where the key actors can interact successfully. Regional government has to be seen not as something inherently opposed to national economic management, but as a crucial component of it. It is the national state which determines the constitutional position, powers and fiscal resources of lower tiers of government. Those national states that allow a considerable measure of autonomy to regional governments tend to have the best and most effective supply-side regulation at the regional level. In a European context, Germany and Italy offer obvious examples. The most prosperous *Lander*, like Baden-Württemberg and Bavaria, or the most successful Italian regions like Emilia-Romagna have achieved a high level of devolution of the tasks of economic management (Sabel 1988).

The main problem about the ways in which nation-states continue to have a salience as a locus of economic management is that such activities now depend on social attitudes and institutions that are not equally available to all states. The new mechanisms of economic coordination and regulation give primacy to the high level of social cohesion and cooperation that the state can both call on and develop. The new methods of national economic regulation in a more internationalized economy are not like, for example, the post-1945 demand management version of Keynesianism, that is, a technique of macroeconomic policy that was in principle available to every substantial and competently administered modern state if it chose to adopt such a strategy. Rather the new methods rest on specific ensembles of social institutions and these are more difficult to adopt or transfer by deliberate choice. States are thus constrained by the legacies of social cohesion they inherit. Countries like the US cannot just decide to adopt the more solidaristic and coordinative relations between industry, labour and the state that have hitherto prevailed in Germany and Japan. However, the evidence of policy innovation and institutional reform in Italy and the Netherlands, for example (discussed in chapter 6), shows that history is not fate and that given the right political conditions, societies can change and adapt.

This still means, however, that between blocs and within blocs there will be fundamental differences in the ability to respond to competitive pressures and changing international conjunctures. Those societies that have emphasized short-term market performance, like the UK and the US, are still threatened by the competitive pressures of societies that have concentrated on enhancing long-term manufacturing competitiveness and have had the social cohesion to achieve it, like Germany. Japan, despite its macroeconomic difficulties, remains a formidably competitive manufacturing exporter. Countries like Korea show how central social solidarity is in responding to the crisis. Economic nationalism is a powerful force promoting adaptation. The political process and the interest group culture in societies like the UK and the US do not favour rapid adaptation in a more cooperative direction; rather they emphasize competition and the dumping of social costs on those who are at once the least organized or influential and the least able to bear them. This tends to push such societies away from effective international or bloc cooperation. The US, by contrast with its role between 1945 and 1972, will refuse to bear any substantial level of cost to secure a more stable international economic environment: it will pursue narrow and short-term considerations of national advantage.

It might appear in one sense as if the less solidaristic and more market-oriented societies like the UK or US may actually have an *advantage* in a more internationalized economy where national-based economic governance is less effective. This seems particularly true in the wave of triumphalism engendered by the economic boom in the US and the *schadenfreude* occasioned by the Asian crisis, with its denunciation of 'crony capitalism'. British and American firms are used to putting competition before cooperation and to fending for themselves in the face of narrowly self-interested financial institutions. It is not only that activist macroeconomic management and a centralized, state-directed industrial policy are increasingly obsolete, but also that a range of social and economic changes – and not just the internationalization of major markets – are making national uniform systems of corporatist intermediation more difficult to sustain. Industrial structures and divisions of labour are becoming more complex and differentiated throughout the advanced industrial world. Large, highly concentrated national firms with stable and highly unionized manual workforces are becoming less salient (Kern and Sabel 1994). Thus countries like Japan and Germany will find that their (very different) national systems of corporatist coordination are less and less representative of industry and, therefore, less effective.

The danger with Anglo-Saxon triumphalism is that it attempts to limit capital markets, corporate structures, company governance and market regulation to the forms common in the US. Not only are these forms virtually impossible for many societies to adopt constructively, but this advocacy rests on the assumption that there is only one appropriate institutional form for capitalism. Not only is this not the case, but economic liberal advocacy would restrict the options available, favouring one model of capitalism over other potentially effective competitors. This limits competition to that between forms within one model, rather than also between social systems or models of capitalist institutions. It damages the prospects of long-run economic evolution, imposing an institutional monoculture. The current enthusiasm for US institutions as an international norm is thus no better founded than the naive assumption of inherent Japanese superiority and American failure found in authors like Herman Kahn and Ezra Vogel in the 1980s. The aim of any sensible international economic policy must be to permit and preserve different ensembles of national institutions and different styles of national policy. Without such pluralism, and, therefore, national strategies adapted to local conditions and institutional legacies, effective economic management at the international level will fail. Societies can only contribute to such management if they are secure at the national level, have space for their own practices, and do not feel they have to sacrifice chosen objectives to alien international goals derived from foreign models. Pluralism, with a continued place for different national models, is thus vital for international cooperation in governance.

Thus, whatever the difficulties of some solidaristic models, the conclusion is not sustained that less solidaristic countries will actually *benefit* from the changed conditions. It is difficult to see how the future of complex social systems, investment in manufacturing, training, public infrastructure, etc., can be left in the hands of firms that compete but cannot cooperate and to the workings of weakly regulated markets alone. In fact, societies like Japan and Germany will continue to enjoy major competitive advantages even if their national systems of corporatist representation decline, precisely because their forms of non-market economic governance are diverse and multilayered. In both countries strong patterns of cooperation and solidarity *within* firms and effective forms of governance through regional institutions or patterns of interfirm cooperation continue to give them advantages in supplementing and sustaining market performance. The general functions performed by political authority in promoting competition and coordination remain important, even if some of the means by which they have been delivered heretofore are changing.

Regional economic governance

The growing importance of regional economies and industrial districts, and the contribution of public and private forms of local economic governance to their continued success, are now well recognized (Sabel 1988; Zeitlin 1992). It is not our purpose here to discuss such regional economies and their diverse forms of governance in and of themselves; rather we consider why such forms of local regulation have become important in a more internationalized economic environment, and how they can help societies to cope with the competitive pressures and market shocks of a more open economic system.

The major reason for the re-emergence of regional economies at the very point when many markets in manufacturing goods internationalized is the changing structure of industry, especially the increasing importance of more diversified and flexible production, and, as a consequence, the continued survival and growth of small and medium-sized enterprises. Flexible forms of production can cope with shifting and volatile patterns of international demand. Populations of smaller firms sharing work and collective services, or in partnership with larger ones, are more able to resist market shocks and adapt to rapid changes than are large hierarchically organized firms. Large firms themselves are changing, entering into partnerships with other firms, diversifying internally, reducing hierarchy and layers of management (Moss Kanter 1991; Sabel 1991). In the period of national economic management, large firms could expect to supply growing national markets with standard industrial goods. Such management was supposed to smooth out the economic cycle and promote full employment and industrial growth. Firms could therefore, at least in theory, plan for long runs and adopt relatively inflexible mass production methods (Piore and Sabel 1984). The new production strategies and increasing importance of regional economies are thus in part a direct response to the internationalization of markets in manufacturing goods and the complex and changing patterns of demand brought about by servicing diverse markets in a period of volatile trading conditions and uncertain growth. The point to emphasize is that both small and large firms are less exposed and more secure in cooperative relationships: these include partnerships that share expertise and risk in the case of large firms, and industrial districts that provide the cost advantages of collective services and the benefits of cooperation with other firms, for example in work sharing, for smaller firms (Lorenz 1988, 1992).

Public governance of an appropriate kind clearly reinforces the advantages of a closely integrated population of firms in a region or district. An industrial 'public sphere' (Hirst and Zeitlin 1989) provides an industrial district or region with the means to anticipate and respond to change, to reconcile cooperation and competition and to restructure both production and common services in a way difficult for a less organized and articulated population of firms. Public governance, especially in partnership with private governance institutions like trade associations, is thus important in protecting regions against external shocks and in responding to major changes in trading conditions. It is clearly the case that some national states are better able to sustain such regional governance institutions and some regions are more capable of responding to the needs of their local economy than others. In this respect societies like the UK are singularly disadvantaged (Zeitlin 1994).

Another significant aspect of regional economies in the context of an internationalized economy is their role in the face of the perceived threat of capital mobility. One way of responding to remote financial institutions that invest across the globe as economic advantage dictates is to build up a financial sector dedicated to industrial finance and governed by public policy. Such low-cost finance is unlikely to be well founded unless its disbursement is based on local knowledge, and nor is the public likely to invest in such institutions unless they can enjoy both low-risk investments and ones that bring a distinct advantage in work and output to their own locality. For these reasons such an alternative financial sector is likely to be closely linked to regional economic governance and to local economies. Such alternative institutions, combined with other forms of public governance at the regional level, and a population of firms strongly rooted in and oriented to the locality, could result in very robust decentralized economic systems relatively independent of wider capital markets but capable of trading effectively. This model has much to recommend it both as a means of reversing industrial decline and as a way of protecting successful industrial districts from the full ravages of international competition (Hirst 1993). The regional level of governance is capable of a good deal of development, and for the wider national society such experimentation at local level is less risky than ambitious centralized state-sponsored investments in a few key main technologies or major initiatives of national institutional reform. Provided the national state is not actively hostile to such local governance, the regional is probably the one of the five levels outlined above that is capable of the most rapid enhancement. Such extensions of effective regional economic governance would, in consequence, secure advanced industrial societies at the local level against at least some of the effects of increased international openness.

8

The European Union as a
Trade Bloc

This chapter is a bridge between the general discussion of the possibilities of economic governance in the preceding chapter and the consideration of the wider political issues in the one that follows. The role of the European Union is central because it is at one and the same time the most developed and the most complexly structured of the major trade blocs. The evolution of the EU's capacities for coordinated common action by its member states will determine to a considerable degree whether the governance of the world economy is strong or minimalist.

As we have seen, trade blocs represent a vital intermediate level between general institutionalized governance mechanisms for the world economy as a whole, such as the WTO, and the economic policies of the nation-states. The Triad of the EU, Japan and NAFTA currently dominates the world economy, and it is likely to account for a majority share of the world manufacturing output, world trade and FDI for a long time to come. The Triad could, therefore, effectively control the direction of the world economy if it chose to act in concert. Loosely organized trade blocs with mutually incompatible interests will inevitably lead to minimal (if still vitally necessary) governance, patching up the existing world institutions and engaging in periodic crisis-avoidance measures. The strong governance of the world economy towards ambitious goals (such as promoting employment in the advanced countries and raising output and incomes in the developing world) requires a highly coordinated policy on the part of the members of the Triad. If they did embrace such ambitious goals and devise the governance mechanisms to fulfil them, they could impose a new tripartite 'hegemony' on world financial markets, international regulatory bodies and other nation-states comparable to that exercised by the US between 1945 and 1973. It is just not the case that any attempt to further regulate the international financial system by the means discussed in the previous chapter, for instance, would immediately be undermined by the 'flight' of financial business to new 'offshore' locations, because those locations could be quickly put out of business if there were the political will to do so. Why should small island states be allowed to hold the rest of the world to ransom? The preconditions for such coordination are that the three component parts of the Triad remain roughly equal with one another in terms of economic power, that they find a common doctrine of governance, and that each bloc develops the internal consistency needed for external action.

It should be clear to those interested in the sustainable future of the international economy that an active public governance of the world trading system is vital. A pure free market is fragile and volatile, and the implications of such markets on the global scale are terrifying, as the tumult in the international financial system in late 1998 testifies. The question that arises therefore is the precise nature of such governance mechanisms and the forces that will organize and drive them. John Ruggie (1993) has argued that 'embedded liberalism' represented the parameters in which that governance was organized over much of the post-1945 period. In its classic form this lasted at least into the late 1970s. Embedded liberalism tied together national and supranational governance. At the domestic level it involved a consensual social compromise between industry, labour and the state to set both a floor and a ceiling on the redistribution of income. At the international level such stabilized states supported an open and multilateral trading system, which was organized in the interests of international capitalism by the intergovernmental and supranational institutions that became familiar after 1945, like the GATT, the IMF, etc.

This picture has been changing for some time, both at the domestic and the international levels, affecting the EU countries in particular. At the domestic level the welfare state compromise seems to be needlessly eroding in many countries in the headlong dash of policy elites towards economic competitiveness and inequality (chapters 4 and 6). At the international level new forms of regulatory mechanisms are arising which, at least on the surface, might seem to undermine the continuation of managed multilateralism. Nationalistic unilateralism in trade and commercial matters, bilateral agreements and deals, and regional configurations of economic interest all indicate an acute uncertainty by the players about the future of traditional multilateralism. At the least we are unlikely to see a return to a period of empire building or hegemonic project by a single country: both these have in the past served as at least partial frameworks for the governance of the international system. But these are expensive regulatory orders both to organize and sustain.

We would argue that a minimal multilateralism, based on the strengthened trilateral relationships between North America, the EU and Japan, now represents the most likely prospect for effective governance mechanisms of the world economy.[1] Multilateralism in one form or another has proved to be the most economical and least costly form of governance for international economic stability. It has also provided the most effective framework for the consolidation of national sovereignty within the international state system. Multilateralism has provided an international basis for the legitimation of domestic authority: the state is recognized as having certain attributes and its external relations are codified. Such recognition and the stabilization of economic activity achieved by multilateral institutions has enhanced rather than diminished the domestic governance powers of the nation-state (Hirst 1997). The fact that such multilateralism has never existed in a pure form (it was underwritten by British hegemony between 1870 and 1914 and American hegemony between 1945 and 1973), and that it now depends on the control of a Triad of the major economies at its heart should not divert us from the fact that the basic 'efficiency' of this system remains, and that it continues to represent the contours within which liberal 'national sovereignty' could be most effectively remoulded.

This evolving structure of modified multilateralism is itself a complex combination: classic liberal embedded multilateralism with the new trilateralism at its centre. There is a significant degree of asymmetry between the three components of the Triad. A key element in it is the EU. The EU is the most ambitious project of multinational economic governance in the modern world, but it is still far from being completed. It has major problems of internal articulation and different perceptions of its future evolution that currently restrict its capacity for concerted external action. NAFTA is dominated by the US, and Japan is a bloc-sized economy based on a nation-state; both are thus less ambitious in their governance strategies and more like traditional political entities. Given that Japan and the US could agree on a common agenda and each obtain internal support for it, they could coordinate policy in much the same way as nation-states have done in the past. The EU's problem is to reconcile divergent interests within it and to settle the course of development of its own institutions. Thus what happens to the EU will be crucial to the whole structure of the governance mechanism that eventually matures for the international economy as a whole.

The EU is at a crossroads in regards to both its internal development and its external relationships. While for convenience we treat the EU as a single entity in much of the following analysis, this should not blind us to the difficulties the EU faces in securing its common identity or capacity to act. In extreme circumstances it would still be possible for the EU to fragment. Perhaps we should continue to think of the EU as an often fractious combination of fifteen national entities many of which as yet remain ambiguous in their commitment to the full EU ideal. In fact, this provides a first point of departure, since we must clarify exactly what the EU amounts to in the present period.

The European Union as a political entity

The European Union's capacities for effective economic governance are closely tied to the further development of its political institutions. Such development is confronted with two serious difficulties. One of these is that the EU is a new venture for which pre-existing political models are of little use in guiding its evolution. The other and most important is that there are substantial differences in economic performance, social standards and, therefore, political interests between the component countries.

The Union is not and will not become a nation-state writ large. Its development cannot be modelled on a continental-sized centralized federal state like the US. Rather the Union is a new kind of political entity to which the conventional constitutional categories do not readily apply. Such categories have been derived from the institutions of the nation-state: at the most basic level, the sovereignty of the principal legislature and the accountability of the central executive to that legislature. In contrast to this, the Union has no single and sovereign source of law and nor does it possess a central multifunctional executive that is democratically accountable through a single channel to representatives of the people (Harden 1995).

The Union is far from resembling the constitutional forms of a nation-state. Most of the Union's powers derive from treaties between the member states. Much of its legislation depends on incorporating common framework initiatives at the level of the member states, and it also depends on the executive branches of those states to carry out common policies. The system of common decision-making still depends to a great degree on agreements between national governments and the relatively secret and nationally unaccountable deliberations of the Council of Ministers. Europe's nation-states retain many distinct and important governmental functions, and the nations have distinct languages, cultural traditions and legal systems that will continue to make complete European integration impossible. Even if a common foreign and security policy is developed after 2000, it would depend on the majority decision of the representatives of the member states and would require the donation of nationally controlled and funded military units to support common policies. The Union will never become a political entity that remotely resembles the old national unitary states.

Federalism and confederalism revisited

In this political context it is useful to return to the debate about the differences between *federal* (*Bundestaat*) and *confederal* (*Staatsbund*) political formations. It is often argued that the 'old' European Economic Community was a confederal formation while the 'new' EU is the beginning of a federal one (CEPR, 1993). Confederal formations are accused of lacking the structural clarity of federal state-like bodies. Much of the debate about clarifying and operationalizing the concept(s) of subsidiarity has to do with the movement from confederal to federal organizational forms.

There are two basic conditions that distinguish confederalism from federalism. The first of these we can call the 'principle of secession'. The powers of confederations are always limited by treaties, which have to be renegotiated as new issues of coordination or common activity arise. Thus there is the continuing possibility, and indeed legal right, for any of the confederees to secede from the union. This is not the case for federalism, where the 'federal state' takes legal precedence (for federal purposes) over the federated state governments, and where as a result there is no legal right to secede. The second main feature distinguishing confederations from federations involves the 'principle of direction of authority'. For confederations, this moves from the confederees to the confederal centre, so that powers are only granted upwards on an issue-by-issue basis and the lower levels preserve their rights to determine this. Within federations, on the other hand, the direction of authority is from the federal centre to the federees, so that powers are essentially granted downwards from the centre to the state governments.

Clearly there are many variations and hybrid forms of these confederal/federal arrangements. But in as much as one can distinguish between them, the two principles just outlined capture the essential differences. The first implication is that federal states are more like unitary states than are confederal ones, though this is not to deny the enormous differences existing between unitary and federal forms.[2]

A second implication of this analysis is that the notion of subsidiarity – in as much as a consistent meaning for this term can be found – does not quite correspond to the idea of confederal authority presented here. The term would seem to presuppose that decentralized powers are to be preferred unless there are good reasons for centralization. But it also clearly implies that there is a federal competence that decides on the issue of the precise degree of centralization or decentralization for those specific powers. The federal or leading power has *Kompetenz Kompetenz*, as the Germans say. In addition, the original meaning for subsidiarity did not just imply a decentralization of decision-making and the return of powers to *national governments*, but a thoroughgoing potential decentralization to national, regional or local levels of public *or* private governance. It is successive layers of public and private confederational arrangements that better meet this primary meaning of subsidiarity.[3]

The present European configuration

The argument in this section is twofold. First, that broadly speaking existing EU governance mechanisms remain predominantly confederal in form. And secondly, that they will remain so for the foreseeable future despite the flurry of activity associated with the recent enlargement debate and the intergovernmental conference that took place in 1997. The second of these arguments is clearly the most controversial, but we begin with the first.

The 1957 Treaty of Rome continues to be the foundation of the EU and its powers. Most recognize this as a confederal type treaty in its role of establishing governance mechanisms. The Treaty of Rome has limits on its scope, and the states are unified for certain specific purposes only. A *confederal state* is different from a *confederation of states* designed to achieve certain common objectives, which the EU probably still is. Since 1957 there have been additional amendments and treaties, some of which have established quasi-federalist principles and capacities for Community regulations and initiatives, often in particular and limited areas, though there seems little consistency between these.[4] The competences of the Union remain delegated by the member states (they are 'derived' competences), and the Union has no general mechanism for the allocation of competences within it. What is more, the 'Luxembourg compromise' (1966) ensured a *de facto* ministerial veto power on important decisions, which was not entirely eroded by the Single European Act (which introduced qualified majority voting and the 23-vote 'blocking majority' issue), or even by the 1994 'Greek compromise' (now a 27-vote blocking majority) associated with the entry of Austria, Finland, Norway and Sweden into the Union. Formally, the Council of Ministers remains the key decision-making arena, though it has delegated powers to the Commission, and the Commission has effective power to determine much commercial policy (by dint of the Treaty of Rome). Legislative *implementation* remains the prerogative of the national governments which incorporate Community-agreed directives into domestic law (though subject to the final judgments of the European Court).

All this makes for a complicated array of decision-making dimensions, but one still largely confederal in form, we would suggest. These powers in no way constitute a confederal *state*. Of course, the EU displays certain state-like features, but it is best described as constituting a configurative 'confederal public power' (with some affinity to the concept of 'confederal consociationality' current in the discussion of EU governance mechanisms, see Chryssochoou 1995, 1997; Taylor 1990). This term is meant to signify the operation of a complex of public bodies at the European level, subject to various forms of accountability and quasi-democratic control, but lacking full constitutionalized establishment and rights, or full citizenship legitimation. It forms a system of 'governance without government', exercising 'statesmanship without a state'.[5]

The question is whether a political hybrid such as this can survive and even develop. Our argument is that it will and indeed that it must mature in this form if it is to survive.

The alternative to this idea of a confederal public power governing the Europe of the future is the idea of a fully federal state. The argument against this latter option actually developing (independently of its desirability) is that at present most mainstream European politicians are too risk-averse and too concerned with emergent ultranationalistic and regionalist forces to contemplate this policy. In addition, it would inevitably fundamentally empower Brussels at the expense of the national governments and will be resisted by the majority of the national leaders and parliaments for that reason.

The underlying reason for believing that the mainstream European political leadership would be wary of allowing for the full-blooded emergence of a federal state in Europe is because of strong contemporary centrifugal forces within the continent. The first of these involves the collapse of political homogeneity. From its inception in 1957 the Union was dominated by a political spectrum from centre-right to centre-left. More recently there was a shift, not towards the far left, but towards the ultra-right, and more importantly, towards populist, nationalist and regionalist parties. There are clear signs of political revolt against the established parties in several European countries and dissatisfaction with the nation-state itself. This was most obvious in the 1992 and 1994 Italian elections with an across-the-board loss of support for the established parties and a strong showing by ultra-right, populist and federalist regional parties. As the established national parties were challenged by right-wing nationalism or by regional secessionism they tended to retrench politically, to defend the state, and therefore to resist the ceding of further power to the EU.[6]

Another centrifugal force encouraging caution is the prospect that European economic growth will further falter, with the possibility of a widespread and prolonged economic depression throughout continental Europe. That has not occurred since the Treaty of Rome was signed. The integration of Europe has hitherto been achieved without serious costs. All continental states have experienced rises in output and real incomes (though with significant fluctuations). Were growth to falter, however, the pressures towards national protective measures could grow. These would not be for new tariff barriers within Europe, but towards reversing EU competition policy, which is designed to reduce state aids to industry, and towards greater independence in fiscal and monetary policy than the current EMU process would allow. The EU could begin to disintegrate as national states sought to protect their own economic bases and as established politicians attempted to avert the threat of political competition from the far right and regional political forces.

Yet it would be wrong to overemphasize the political weakness of the European Union. The Union *has* displaced the national states in a number of areas of governance. The states are no longer 'sovereign' entities, as they once claimed to be. The European Parliament, especially after the Maastricht Treaty, does exercise certain important legislative and accountability functions. The Commission plays an important role in creating legislative initiatives, consulting on major policies across Europe, and directly exercising certain regulatory powers and supervising others in their exercise at national level. Those aspects of European legislation giving implementation to the single market take precedence over national legislation and thus radically abridge national legislature sovereignty with respect to certain functions. Europe's peoples are, after the Maastricht Treaty, common citizens of the Union and enjoy certain supranational rights guaranteed and overseen by a superior judiciary.

The Union thus fits into no established constitutional schema. It is not like a unitary, a federal or a confederal state; rather it could best be called an ongoing association of states with certain functionally specific governance functions exercised by a common public power. It should be seen as a complex polity made up of common institutions, member states, and peoples. There is both strength and weakness in this newly evolved, very distinctive and slightly cumbersome structure. Strength because it minimizes the conflicts that occur when one set of institutions is to have primacy, as when an attempt is made to build a unitary state from diverse political institutions. In the short term, it has a serious weakness, because such a complex association limits the rapid development of certain very necessary common governance functions.

The point is that Europe's political evolution will have to build on and make a virtue of this complexity. One cannot, as some enthusiastic 'federalists' imagined in the late 1980s, scale up to the European level national forms of government and accountability. The European Parliament cannot be expanded into a superior legislature and national assemblies reduced to the role of subordinate authorities in a national state: it is just not an omnicompetent sovereign body and lacks the common legitimacy to exercise such functions. Likewise the Commission cannot evolve into a European executive, primarily answerable to the Strasbourg Parliament and taking precedence over national governments. Political development is most likely to be successful if it concentrates on enhancing the common decision-making procedures of the association of states, rather than by seeking to supplant national-level political institutions. Both the Union and national levels can gain in authority and governance capacity if they can cooperate and coordinate; as we shall see in chapter 9, it is by no means the case that 'sovereignty' is a fixed quantum and that what one agency gains in governance capacity must be at the expense of another. It is time the old Bodinian view of sovereignty was buried, along with the conceptions of exclusive governmental powers on which it is based (Bodin 1992).

The European Union's national states continue to have a vital role. They remain a crucial locus of political legitimacy and democratic accountability without which the Union would find it impossible to function. Politics and citizen identification at the national level remain compelling in a way that, for the foreseeable future, European politics and a common European identity will not be. But this strength of the Union's member nations can be turned to positive advantage in the governance of the Union. Too rapid a development of Europe's central institutions might in fact threaten their legitimacy, leading to justified fears of remote, technocratic and unaccountable government.

National politicians too readily see their role, if they are democrats, as protesting at the institutional defects of the EU and, if they are pragmatists, of bargaining for the best narrowly self-interested deal for their nation within its councils. Democratic radicals, especially Members of the European Parliament (MEPs) and their advisers, raise the spectre of a 'democratic deficit' at the centre of the Union. This criticism has some force to the degree that bureaucratic and technocratic conceptions of policy-making have predominated among Europe's elites. But this view is mistaken when such critics see the problem as being *like* that of a lack of accountability within the nation-state but on a bigger scale, and as being capable of remedy by political mechanisms derived from the national level and scaled up to the European one. On the contrary, democracy and accountability can best be bolstered by seeing the EU as a polity in which the nation-states are the most significant sources for the representation of the people *at the European level*. Some of this enhanced accountability can be quickly achieved, without large structural changes, providing there are significant changes in attitude on the part of Europe's politicians. Thus greater majority decision-making by representatives of the member states in the common councils of the Union will require both MEPs and national ministers to perceive and to exercise their roles as 'continental electors' in a wider polity (a notion we will develop further towards the end of chapter 9).

To facilitate this the role of the Council of Ministers and the scope of majority decision-making within it needs to be enhanced and made constitutionally explicit as the principal thrust of political union. The decisions of the Council and the deliberations of the Parliament need to be made transparent to Europe's citizens. The actions and votes of national ministers in the Council need to be more fully debated and made known to the parliaments of the member states so that they are directly accountable to national elected representatives. Ministers have to recognize that their actions when they speak and vote in Brussels are no longer intergovernmental, but *governmental*. They have to think and act as national representatives in a supranational forum, shaping policy in a constitutionally ordered association of states.

This is not a Eurosceptical argument. The EU could not long remain a weakly structured association of nation-states and not suffer the consequences of weak and partial governance of a continental-scale economy. Strong government is not, however, necessarily centralized and exclusive government. Strength can be had by consultation, coordination and division of labour in governance functions. The great danger in Europe is of competition between nation-states and conflict between them over common policy. This will lead both to overlapping and conflicting competencies and to 'gaps' in the scope of governance. Capacities for governance vanish into these gaps and diminish the competing powers, weakening exclusively self-interested governments at the *national* level because of failures of effective control at the European level. The creation of a single market and the continuing concentration and integration of production at the European level have created phenomena that can neither be governed by national-based policies nor left to the workings of unregulated markets. Weak common and cooperative governance by the national states at the European level will lead to bitter and divisive struggles between unevenly performing and competing national economies over those dimensions of policy that states acting alone can no longer control. Eurosceptics who want to reduce the Union to a loosely structured free trade area, and localist dissenters who seek to reduce the governance powers of the Union by turning the doctrine of 'subsidiarity' against Brussels, thus threaten not only the project of the Union but the powers of their own national states over large areas of economic life. European economic governance needs to be extended, but it cannot be done by creating a superstate. Instead such extension will involve a division of labour involving national and regional governments, cooperating with Union institutions with considerable power but limited functions.

One of the main problems of responding coherently to these issues is the paucity of political thinking to span the gap between the global and the national. The extreme theorists of globalization are particularly pernicious in this respect because they argue that there is no need to try: they deny both the need for strong supranational governance and the possibility of national-level action. They are pessimists of the intellect and of the will. The need to develop a balance of powers between the regional, national and Union levels of governance in Europe highlights the fact that there is no commonly accepted theory of the art of government required to practise such distribution, and therefore no compelling model of an institutional architecture to replace those derived from nation-states. This is one reason why the debates on the political future of Europe are so difficult, the terms so confused, and why so many people are arguing at cross-purposes.

In fact such a theory is not that difficult to develop, once the issues are clearly recognized, and nor do Europe's states lack some common grounds for action despite conflicting national interests. But cooperation between states in the Union, necessary to make it an effective polity of states, can only be refocused if there is some strong common basis for action. It now looks very likely that EMU will begin on time and involve enough of the members to make it a success. But it must be said that the EU has done best when it has looked outside of itself to its external environment and negotiations. There has been less dispute between its members in these instances than when the Union has focused inwards on internal developments. External considerations also give Europe a basis for cohesion, balancing cooperation and competition between its component national interests in the course of pursuing a strategy that attempts to promote cooperation between the major players in the world economy towards common goals.

But in some ways there are *too few* disputes in the international system, between the members of the Triad for instance. The US tends to get its way too easily and too often. Over the completion of the Uruguay Round of trade negotiations, for instance, the EU gave in too easily to the US's persuasion on a number of key matters, not least of which involved intellectual property rights and agricultural trade. A more resolute EU could have fought for the interests of Third World countries in the area of agricultural trade, particularly as it has more sympathy and closer ties with these countries than either Japan or the US. There can be, then, too much 'common ground' within the international community on economic matters. Some added disagreement would serve to define the system more clearly, push the specific interests of the EU and its allies more forcefully and enable the EU to consolidate its internal position further (since 'external' conflict adds to integrative pressures). With more intra-Triad conflict the Union could exercise its powers more clearly, and this would tend to provide the political conditions for a more coherent internal decision-making process to develop.

Here the fact that the Treaty of Rome ceded competency in most external trade-related matters to the EU has served to provide a strong presence for Europe in international trade, investment and coordinative management discussions. This is not to suggest that the EU could not speak louder and with more force in these negotiations. Nor is any of this an argument for outraged conflict, protectionism or stand-offs, but rather a plea for the EU to define its particular external interests more clearly while operating within the contours of a continued commitment to multilateralism. These are not incompatible positions.

The key to the internal deepening of the Union clearly remains the relationships that unfold in respect to its external profile. As a common voice shaping an emerging agenda of international governance, its role in the GATT/WTO negotiations, for instance, shows that, while by no means well developed, this international orientation can be a source of internal unity. Clearly, the easiest way for Europe to be united externally would be as a competing and protectionist trade bloc, opposed to NAFTA and Japan, but such a focus of unity would be negative. It would favour conservative forces in Europe, and would be highly destructive of any project for extended international governance. A more open and extended agenda towards the external world, promoting stability in an open international economy, will be more difficult to pursue but is essential. Europe would ultimately gain from such reregulation of the international economy and could also gain internal coherence by such external concerted action.

Centripetal and centrifugal forces in Europe

We must now turn to the substantive sources of conflict and the potentials for extended governance in the Union. It was clear even before the prolonged ratification crisis of the Maastricht Treaty and the beginning of a period of intense turbulence in the ERM in 1992 that European integration was at a point of balance between powerful centripetal and centrifugal forces. The centrifugal forces are recent and significant. They are to be found in the collapse of the Eastern bloc and the need for a unified front against an external adversary, in the decline of political homogeneity and in the faltering of prosperity. The European Community was created in the shadow of the Soviet threat. This set limits to the political divergence of European states. The Community was not coterminous with NATO, since it had its neutralist members such as Ireland, and France had withdrawn from military force commitments to NATO, but the Soviet threat both unified Western Europe and linked it to the US. Until 1989 the EU had clear political limits, it was a *western* European entity. Now the future of 'Europe' is an open question, and the European Union's development is threatened by a potentially fatal conflict of interests between those who wish to deepen its institutions and those who wish to widen its boundaries.

The second of the centrifugal forces is the most ominous from a liberal internationalist perspective. Since the late 1940s Europe has been dominated by a political spectrum from centre-right to centre-left. The exclusion of and containment of the far left are likely to continue. The threat to polit ical homogeneity comes from the right and from new non-ideological regionalist parties. The latter are often no great challenge except to their national states, since they are centrist in policy – like Britain's separatist Scottish National Party. Far right parties are another matter. Their nationalism has two faces. It is anti-immigrant, and currently predominantly directed against non-EU migrants. But it also defines the benefits of membership of the European Union in 'national' terms and therefore limits the scope of possible European cooperation by such parties to a free trade area. Europe is for them an economic convenience, not the source of a new kind of political identity or a new level of political legitimacy. Legitimacy for the Front National, for example, as its then leader Le Pen made clear in the 1992 French referendum on Maastricht, is a matter of adherence to 'national' interests. Such ultranationalist forces must in practice be hostile to the goal of ever closer union. Whereas some of the regionalist parties or smaller nationalist parties like the SNP are, by contrast, strongly in favour of European integration.

Despite the widespread success of centre-left national governments in the late 1990s in Europe, the fundamental factor sustaining the rise of the far right, and therefore the decline in political homogeneity, is unlikely to diminish in importance in the next decade. That factor is immigration. These pressures against immigrants are likely to intensify if economic failure in eastern Europe and continuing poverty in Africa lead to strong tendencies towards attempted economic migration to Europe. A new 'wall' to keep the poor out would be a wretched irony after the collapse of the old fortified frontiers in the east. Such a tight immigration policy may be the price the political centre will be faced with and be willing to pay to contain the far right and exclude them from office.

Given that the prospects for a widening of the Union require a deepening of its internal structure for that widening to be a success, there are two sets of issues that arise here, both of them concerning what happens around the Union's borders in the near future. Europe faces serious political and economic dilemmas here.

The first of these is what happens towards the east. Many countries in eastern Europe are poor and chronically unstable, with little evidence that either market reforms or democracy will prove viable in the medium term. Belarus and the Ukraine, Albania, Romania and Bulgaria are all in such turmoil that membership of the EU is inconceivable. However, incorporating Poland or the Baltic States or Slovenia would bring these weak states directly to the borders of the EU and bring the EU directly into contact with Russia's sphere of influence.

The successful integration of any new members to the east will require a radical restructuring of their economies and polities if this process is not to undermine the development and achievements of the Union so far. But if the Union is to provide some serious 'ladder' by which potential members can climb to be ready for union, then this will itself require a comparable deepening of the Union among the existing members at the same time. This is why the present monetary union process has come at just the wrong time, despite its likely successful launch. The steps to monetary union as constructed by policy-makers are themselves deflationary, and they have coincided with a general recession in some of the Union countries, and a time when the existing economies, particularly those of France and Germany, need internal restructuring to re-establish or maintain their own competitiveness. This is a less than ideal situation, and one that could easily lead to a longer-term destabilization of the unifying European economy.

On the other hand, we have the issues that arise to the south. The *economic* relationships between the EU and the countries around its southern perimeter are more complex than those between the EU and its eastern candidate members because of a basic asymmetry in the revealed comparative advantages displayed by the two areas (Padoan 1997, table 5.1, p. 112). The countries to the east display a sectoral comparative advantage structure *complementary* to the existing EU countries, whereas those to the south show no such complementarities, and indeed have little comparative advantage in any sector of production. Thus, while there seems to be the basis for a mutually advantageous sectoral trade between the EU and the countries to the east, there seems little such basis for mutual sectoral trade advantages for those countries to the south and the EU.

But what happens around the Mediterranean, and particularly among the Muslim countries, will be crucial to the *political* development of Europe. This is because there are large Muslim populations within the Union which have the capacity to destabilize – or more likely, to be used to destabilize – its internal political development. Of particular significance here are events in the most important of the Mediterranean Muslim countries, notably in Turkey, Egypt and Algeria. Algeria is obviously unstable, Egypt may fall to the religious right and the situation in Turkey could become even more volatile. If these become radicalized then the present uneasy political equilibrium within many of the key Union states could be quite easily and severely shaken, and this could itself dramatically affect the moves towards a deepening of the Union. The Cyprus question is a serious problem, since it could be part of a broader conflict with Turkey over the Aegean. Turkey has the option to enter the EU if certain conditions are met, and Cyprus would like to. As usual, these potential political developments cannot be easily read off from the economic ones, and they are likely to involve highly contingent and very unpredictable events.

The EU has been an economic organization first and foremost, but these are matters of power politics: it is currently institutionally ill-equipped to deal with such matters, and they divide its major nation-states. The example of Bosnia is not an encouraging one. The easy option would be to build a new *Festung Europa*, hardening external borders against economic migrants and trying to ignore the poverty and strife without. Yet the short-sighted nature of this move should be self-evident. These are vast markets which could stimulate European output if they could be launched on the path to prosperity. The modern equivalent of Marshall Aid, large-scale funds for reconstruction if countries agree to meet certain political and social conditions, could serve as a carrot for political stability within and boost the prosperity of donor and recipient alike. Defensive monetarism, the present policy of EMU, and more frontier police will still leave the EU vulnerable and fail to boost growth within the wider Europe. Without policies to lift these countries on to a ladder for their full entry, the EU will simply continue as a rich nations' club. But for how long will this be secure?

Given this, there remain formidable problems. The Czech Republic (1996 GDP per capita $4,740), Hungary ($4,340) or Slovenia ($9,240) could probably be absorbed into the EU with less difficulty than either Poland (GDP per capita $3,230) or Turkey ($2,830). With populations of 39 and 62 millions respectively, and with GDP per capita a fraction of that of Germany ($28,870) or France ($26,270), how could Poland and Turkey successfully accede to the Maastricht Treaty? This makes citizens of member states common economic citizens of the Union. Moreover, how could either of them become full members of the Common Agricultural Policy (CAP)? If the EU wants both further integration within the core and extension of its territory to the periphery, it will have to create variable geometry options that allow different degrees of integration on different dimensions (see CEPR 1995). If the EU frustrates Turkish hopes completely, for instance, it will further undermine the present political settlement in that country. Yet it would be dishonest to string Turkey along with the prospect of full membership in the medium term.

These issues require serious thought and urgent action. Yet currently, the EU is too absorbed in its next phase of reform to see how a positive external policy towards its neighbours could boost its own growth and create the basis for future markets. This is a key aspect of EU external policy that cannot be safely ignored.

The most serious of the centrifugal forces has been the prospect that Europe has lost its greatest unifier and pacifier, economic growth and prosperity. Until the recession which began in earnest in 1991 the European Community as a whole had not suffered a serious and prolonged interruption of growth since the Treaty of Rome creating it was signed in 1957. Integration of member states into the Community has been achieved without serious national costs. All states have experienced rising output and rising real incomes, and some, like Italy and Spain, have made spectacular leaps towards the first rank of the advanced industrial countries. Europe is currently entering a phase of economic recovery. But the prospects for growth could be severely shaken by the turbulence in the world's financial markets that accelerated in August 1998. However, it may be that growth will stagnate across Europe for structural rather than conjunctural reasons. If that were so, and if the divergences in economic performance within the Union became even more marked, then the pressures towards national protective measures within the EU would grow. These pressures are unlikely to be for tariff barriers *within* Europe. Within the Union there may be competitive devaluations of those states outside the euro zone, and pressures towards reversing the common competition policy (which is to reduce state aids to industry) and for greater independence in fiscal policy than the current policies of the European Central Bank would allow for. If Europe were to suffer from relative economic failure this might lead to pressure for the creation of protective tariff walls against major and threatening competitors outside the Union, particularly the US and Japan. In fact, if Japan, or other East Asian countries, were to regain their competitiveness but retain their resistance to European imports, Europe might actually *gain* in the short run from exclusionary measures and the strengthening of its role as a trade bloc. The far right might have a certain economic logic to bolster their chauvinism. The nationalist far right is not wedded to economic liberalism, and should another major crisis occur, its advocacy of national protective measures will press centrist politicians towards divergence from the common European objectives outlined at Maastricht and from the new WTO regime.

The right should not be overrated, given the current centre-left dominance in Europe, but it is not a spent force, as its success in countries like Belgium and Austria shows.

Europe is still at the point where a great deal of institutional work needs to be done to complete effective economic integration. Yet at a primitive economic level, as a single market, integration *is* virtually irreversible. It will also be almost impossible to unscramble the effects of common citizenship of the Union and extremely difficult to reimpose national limits on work and residence. The creation of common economic citizenship as part of market openness has thus eroded a central component of national sovereignty. Those British Conservative politicians who support the notion of Europe as a 'free market' but oppose the erosion of 'national sovereignty' are caught in a fundamental contradiction: the measures needed to ensure the free movement of goods, capital and labour will inevitably remove certain powers from Europe's nation-states.

As well as sources of strain and divergence, there are also centripetal forces in Europe. Crudely put, the Union's national states have lost the effective capacity to serve as regulators over certain vital dimensions of economic activity, for which regional governments are even less effective. But the central institutions of the Union have not acquired the political capacity to exercise these economic functions. This functional imbalance will put continuing pressure on both national policies and the institutions of the EU. How such an imbalance can be resolved is another matter.

Hitherto it was assumed by most pro-Europeans that economic integration would inevitably draw political union in its wake. Now, on the contrary, it is becoming clear that effective economic governance of the EU depends on major political institutional reforms. It is now clear that there is no inevitable and automatic economic logic that will unite Europe. The creation of the single market has not given the boost to growth across Europe that some enthusiasts hoped, nor will market openness in itself reduce inter-regional inequality. It is also the case that the reverse is not true. The construction of new forms of political legitimacy for European institutions would not of itself ensure effective economic governance. Rather, that legitimacy, even if it could be achieved, will be wasted unless political union *does* transform the European economies. Effective political union cannot ultimately be built out of a series of states and regions with radically divergent economic performances. Only with great difficulty would a Europe of 'tiers' be either economically integrated or politically united. The differences over substantive policy issues in that case would threaten to tear the political union apart. Political union will be blighted from the start for the economic losers if it promises to do nothing for them and if the existing forms of economic integration simply expose them to the competitive pressures of the winners. Such economic divergence, if it continues, will threaten to fragment the Union into a united prosperous core and a poor and marginalized periphery.

The issue is not just the integration of markets or the transfer of national regulatory functions upwards to EU institutions, but the creation of new mechanisms, objectives and policies of economic governance appropriate to the level of the Union as a whole. The EU is an agency of economic governance of continental dimensions. It has the potential to do things medium-sized nation-states like France and Italy cannot, but at the same time it cannot effectively and efficiently perform certain governance functions that nation-states traditionally have done. The question remains one of a balance between regional, national and EU economic regulation.

The problem of divergent regional economic performance and the role of regional economic governance in Europe

The wider policy dimensions of the regulation of the new European single economic space and of European-level economic and social issues also raise serious questions about both the need for such common programmes and the difficulty of attaining them within existing institutions. How, for example, can Europe have a 'single market' unless it also has not only rules to ensure market openness but also effective mechanisms to compensate for some of the regional effects of that market's workings? Such a market carries the danger that it puts firms and capital markets beyond effective national control, so that they are able to impose social costs and to avoid paying for them. Most European politicians are not happy with hard-core economic liberalism and still subscribe to Christian democratic or social democratic principles. They aim for the highest measure of market liberalization consistent with long-run social efficiency. That means common European standards and regulation where they are necessary – in environmental protection, in company law and the regulation of capital markets, in social, health and safety legislation. Existing European Union institutions can and do perform many of these regulatory functions and enjoy legitimacy in doing so. The EU creates common 'framework' legislation, a common structure of rights and regulations that enables all economic actors to operate with a measure of certainty throughout Europe. The problems begin to occur at the point where programmes of regional harmonization involve major spending, for example on common standards of environmental protection or compatible social benefits. Not all nations and regions can afford to comply with the emerging 'first tier' conceptions of a healthy environment, nor can there really be a single labour market until there are common basic social entitlements. As we have seen in chapter 6, there are possibilities for common procedural rules about entitlements and for conventions that prevent regulatory competition on welfare between states at comparable levels of development. But even the extensive refinement of such rules would leave Europe divided into different welfare regimes.

The same difficulties will occur in other areas of policy: in particular there will be great resistance to a European regional policy that seeks to improve the efficiency of weaker regions by further substantial investment in infrastructure and in crucial supply-side factors like education and training. Policies to promote economic revitalization are essential on narrow economic grounds and are ultimately of benefit to the richer regions too. Widespread success and growth are needed to maintain a base of effective demand to sustain an extensive, growing and productive advanced industrial sector. Baden-Württemberg or Rhône-Alpes cannot ignore their poorer fellow-regions in Europe like Cornwall or Reggio-Calabria. The idea of a Europe of 'tiers' where capital can profit by exploiting low wage zones is ultimately self-defeating. Such zones will also be low demand peripheral areas and thus limit the scope and competitiveness of the 'first tier' core of regions by restricting the growth of their markets. Moreover, no European Union region can compete in this respect with the vast low wage 'third tier' of countries that has opened up in Eastern Europe.

The drive to regional harmonization and social homogeneity makes sense in the long run and from the perspective of the whole Union. The problem is that richer regions and states, like wealthier social groups within a nation-state, will not be prepared to spend on fiscal redistribution and social harmonization if they can avoid it. Europe needs to challenge its own version of the 'culture of contentment' (Galbraith 1991) if it is ever to develop into a fully integrated economic zone. If it does not, then the differences in real economic performance between centre and periphery could well begin to lead to disintegration.

Nation-states will remain crucial in a uniting Europe in that, among other things, it is they that provide the domestic constitutional framework and policy support for effective regional governments. States differ massively in size and the categories 'nation-state' and 'region' have no ultimate coherence: Bavaria is a 'region' but could easily be a 'state'; Ireland and Luxembourg are states with smaller populations than many regions. As we saw in chapter 7, regional governments are now key agencies of economic governance, in that they are more able to assess the needs of industry because they possess more localized and therefore more accurate information, and because they are of a size that enables the key public and private actors to interact and cooperate successfully. Regions are small enough to possess 'intimate knowledge' and yet sufficiently large to aid and regulate local economies through a significant revenue base. The regional provision of education and training, industrial finance and collective services for industry is gaining in importance in Europe. It is also a vital component of the new 'supply-side' policies that promote industrial efficiency and reverse the trend of European economies towards declining competitiveness.

The most successful national economies are those that have allowed the measure of local autonomy necessary to regional regulation and have developed strong industrial districts. The UK has failed most conspicuously in this regard. Its governments have relentlessly promoted centralization since the 1960s. The Conservatives reduced local government to client status (and UK local authorities are too small to be regional governments). Recent Conservative governments have denied the need for local industrial policies or public–private partnerships to provide collective services. Business has also concentrated massively: through mergers and acquisitions local firms have been turned into subsidiaries of remote headquarters and regional cross-linkages between firms have been severed. It remains to be seen how far the Labour government will address these issues. Greater autonomy for Scotland and Wales may help them to develop effective regional economic governance. The Greater London Authority too may become a focus for such initiatives in London. But the rest of England could lose out in any further European-wide move towards the regional governance of economic activity. It could suffer both from the competitive pressures of the single market and from those competitive pressures stemming from the enhanced efficiency available to foreign firms through their use of regional economic cooperation and collective services.

In other states regional governments have compensated for ineffective national policies. As we showed in chapter 7, Italy is the obvious example, with the more successful industrial districts and regions in the north and the 'third Italy' providing effective economic assistance to firms. One should note that the very weakness and paralysis of the Italian state aided this process in the 1980s. Italy did not fall prey to fashionable monetarist doctrines and its lax government allowed a strongly expansionary (and inflationary) policy. For a time this benefited the more 'post-Fordist' enterprises and industrial districts, at the expense of Italy's large firms, big cities and the south. But even such regions have an interest in containing excessive public indebtedness and excessive inflation. Italy seems to have moved from the threat of fragmentation towards national reform. This process has been spurred on by the demands of monetary union and the Italian perception that membership of the euro is crucial for national competitiveness.

However, a 'Europe of the regions' remains rhetorical and at present has no precise form. Most of continental Europe's nation-states may accept the need to facilitate regional government – France has at least partially decentralized, for example. But the national states are not about to sponsor their own dissolution, even if they are strongly regional-federal like Germany. The European Union could not conceivably create central institutions fast enough and with enough legitimacy to achieve an effective federal-regional division of labour, marginalizing national governments in most economic regulatory functions. The danger is that a 'Europe of the regions' will emerge not as a result of an equitable balance of power between federal, national and regional levels, but from the reverse. Much of Europe will be divided into successful and failing regions, in conflict within their nation-states and with the Union over the direction of policy and the distribution of resources. National states will continue to differ considerably in their capacities for economic management and for effective cooperation with their own regional governments. Strife between rich and poor regions, and violent divergences over the direction of the EU's economic governance could then help to ensure the unsettled character of European institutions and prevent a generous policy towards the countries in the east. The future of Europe as a whole may be decided by differences within the European Union that prevent it from acting to unite the European continent.

The worst and quite possible prospect for the beginning of the next century would then be a divided and weakened European Union, with aspects of its economic affairs beyond the control of either the member states or of Brussels, faced with the eastern half predominantly plunged in poverty and strife, and confronted with a tide of refugees and economic migrants that will promote ever more repressive measures against immigrants. Only if European politicians see the need for policies that link the rich and poor regions in the EU and that link the rich states of the EU with the poor ones of Eastern Europe in a common search for prosperity can there be any hope of evading such a future. The problem is that politicians in the national states and in the richer regions of the Union can currently see only the costs and dangers and not the hopes and benefits in such programmes. 'Self-protective' policies at national level will most probably prevent progress to the economic and political integration of Europe. Europe will only develop if its national leaderships and its central institutions are able to exploit the advantages that the pooling of sovereignty and the resources of the largest trade bloc in the world make possible.

The issue of monetary union

Monetary policy provides a striking example of the contradiction between the need for integration and the impossibility of merely scaling up national policies and institutions. The Maastricht Treaty establishes a politically independent central bank that will determine monetary policy and operate without direct accountability to national economic policy-makers. It will pursue the same economic priorities as the Bundesbank, economic stability and an anti-inflationary policy. The problem is that such a central bank and a single currency can only exist after a period of real economic 'convergence'. But it is now widely acknowledged that many of the Union's national economies that have qualified for EMU may not have actually experienced real and sustained convergence. The last thing Europe will need as it approaches the new century, and if it continues to come out of recession, is a widespread deflationary dose of Euromonetarism, though this will most likely be in prospect in order to consolidate the single currency if the underlying economic cycles in the EMU states reappear and 'divergence' emerges once again.

Germany's economy survived the policy objectives of the Bundesbank, once it acquired full autonomy in monetary policy after 1972, because its export-oriented manufacturing sector was strongly competitive by international standards and because its unions tended to practise wage restraint and thus put less pressure on the central bank's anti-inflationary policy. Even so, and especially in the late 1980s, Germany traded lower growth and higher unemployment as the tariff for price stability. These conditions do not apply in Europe as a whole. Manufacturing output grew substantially in the 1980s in most European states except Britain, but it is doubtful if much of Spanish and Portuguese industry, or even much of Italian industry, for example, could be competitive under a combined regime of Euromonetarism and relatively open trade with the world outside.

The implications of this are twofold. First, the process of a forced march to 'convergence' may damage longer-term European integration. The alternative of a slower process of monetary union with looser targets and wider objectives has now been ruled out. Rather, we have a process with at least two stages, with a fast and slow lane. The danger with this latter option is the creation of a partial monetary union and the virtual exclusion of some of the weaker currencies from the possibility of convergence. Already EMU has created what looks like a permanent first tier of European countries, followed by a second tier comprising the UK, Sweden, Denmark and Greece. In addition, there is the prospect of a possible third tier composed of the next round of entrants early next century.

Secondly, the idea of an 'independent' central bank at the EU level is highly problematical. Unlike the Bundesbank, which has a broadly representative council that both protects its substantial degree of independence and ensures its accountability (Kennedy 1991), such a bank will lack legitimacy. That lack will be reinforced by its divorce from wider economic policy-making and by its tendency to set constraining conditions for the latter. The effect of the 'independence' of a European Central Bank would be to allow virtually unaccountable officials to dictate economic policy, at a time when the central organs of the EU will still lack legitimacy and citizen identification. The result could all too easily be a disaster for the process of building support for EU economic and political integration (Grahl and Thompson 1995). The issue of Britain's ambiguous relationship towards the development of the EU is nowhere more starkly demonstrated than in regard to this debate about the impending launch of EMU. In many ways the prevailing British attitude has been either to wish it would go away or to try to remain blissfully unaware of its impending onset. But it did not go away. Until mid-1998 there was a genuine possibility that it might not happen at all, but that no longer looks likely.

However, this does not mean that everything is settled. The 1998 turmoil in the international financial markets testifies to the instability and unpredictability of events. One of the reasons for the appreciation of the pound during 1997 and 1998 had to do with it being well outside the EMU process.

While market sentiment was uncertain about EMU starting on time and without problems, a move into the pound acted as a safety measure. There could still be significant turmoil in the markets in the run up to EMU if things do not run smoothly. The difficulty is to predict exactly what might happen to the main currencies. The pound, while still outside the fray, could continue to strengthen. On the other hand, if things were to go terribly awry, market sentiment could easily turn towards the German mark as the key currency within the EU.

But the most likely course now is for the pound to slowly weaken as the markets get used to the idea of a stable euro being introduced after 1999. One of the problems for the EU then will be the existence of a strong euro just when the two main integrationist economies, France and Germany, in their own very different ways require a weak exchange rate to help restore their individual international competitiveness. To a large extent the whole EMU enterprise has come just at the wrong time for Europe since it has diverted the attention of Germany and France away from the deep and necessary restructuring of their own domestic economies, away from the real problems associated with a successful expansion of the EU to the east, and away from the EU taking a lead in serious initiatives to manage the international economy more widely.

A particular problem in this respect involves the management of the euro exchange rate. The new ECB does not have formal responsibility for the exchange rate, though it may well become partly responsible for it by default. Clearly, the ECB is likely to develop a key role, but this will be shared with a number of other parties: the Ecofin (European Finance ministers' meetings), the full Council of Ministers and the Commission could all claim some authority over setting the exchange rate. This looks as though it will result in a muddle, which could be particularly dangerous in times of economic crisis when decisions about the exchange rate have to be made quickly and under pressure.

So where does this leave Britain? More or less out in the cold, one suspects. The idea that any EU country can conduct an independent monetary policy while outside EMU is quite unrealistic. Abstainers will either be dictated to by the international markets, effectively fall under the sway of the euro anyway, or be pushed towards following the lead of the US Federal Reserve Board and US dollar. There is no guarantee that conditions for entry will be any better a few years after the establishment of EMU than at the time of its inception. The effect of a long-term hostility will be to marginalize the UK pound and other currencies as small rump currencies on the periphery of Europe, of little consequence and with no voice. It is impossible to continue to prosper in Europe by adopting an abstentionist policy stance. The euro will go ahead whether the British or other governments like it or not. The old debate as to the pros and cons of EMU is over. British industry in particular, and even the City as a key financial centre, could become marginalized and left on the edge of Europe. But while British industry does not have the option of informally entering EMU, the City – which acts very much as an offshore part of the UK economy anyway – may be able to exercise that option by in effect going over to euro business and largely ignoring that conducted in sterling. This will not ease the problems of the UK authorities, however, who will still have to wrestle with conducting a defensive exchange rate and domestic monetary policy in an increasingly uncertain world. The pound could, at worst, become a form of 'coupon' for domestic use, exporters and the UK financial markets opting out and into the euro. Monetary policy would then depend on the wishes of an externally oriented sector trading in another currency. The UK's only remaining advantage would be periodic devaluations.

What this debate also leaves out of account is the key task of properly integrating the candidate economies to the east. Here, the EU, despite failing to take prompt action in the early 1990s, still has before it a situation in which it has the chance to reconstruct the whole continent if it takes a decisive lead. It would be possible to stave off depression in Western Europe in the course of aiding Eastern Europe: a form of 'continental Keynesianism'. Such a programme would most productively take the form of large-scale infrastructure investment aid and long-run trade credits for Eastern Europe. Such infrastructure investment would enable those states to support their citizens' living standards in the course of their transition to a market economy, offering the unemployed jobs on public works, and trade credits would allow them to obtain essential capital goods in order to reconstruct. The effect of such trade credits on the order books of firms in Western Europe would be immediate, stimulating in particular the depressed capital goods sector. Rising employment in Western Europe would increase both domestic effective demand and the tax base for European social harmonization measures. If Eastern Europe could be started on the path to rapid economic recovery, then its markets would offer to the EU the best prospect available of recreating the long economic boom after 1945.

The scale of the European economy makes possible policy options of this kind that no medium-sized national government can contemplate. The problem is that such options cannot be realized within the existing structures of governance of the EU. The national governments of the member states rejected Jacques Delors's proposals greatly to expand the central EU budget and to spend a sizeable chunk of that revenue on an aid programme for Eastern Europe.

The EU can best ensure its security by promoting prosperity in the east and increasing living standards in its poorer southern states. Internal harmonization and external action to promote growth in its neighbours are related rather than contradictory objectives. Seeking *military* security in the east and countering threats from its southern Mediterranean littoral are expensive and economically inefficient options, involving high levels of unproductive defence expenditure: promoting prosperity in its neighbours and its weaker members is a more effective security strategy. The problem is that the EU currently finds it difficult to act externally and internally in this way and is foregoing, through caution and because it cannot overcome institutional obstacles, policies that stem from its position as the world's largest trading bloc (Hirst 1995).

Our point in drawing attention to this issue is not that we expect such a continental Keynesian option to be followed, given existing attitudes and structures. It is simply to point out that this option is in principle possible and that the EU is potentially capable of far more effective action as a trade bloc than it is currently delivering. In terms of its future development, only success in substantive areas can secure the long-term legitimacy of the European Union as a political entity. It is in essence an association founded on *economic* objectives, not cultural homogeneity or collective security (it can rely on all the military force it requires through its member states, NATO and the Western European Union to ensure its survival). Promoting growth within and raising prosperity among its neighbours, and developing its own policies accordingly, are preconditions for its successful evolution and internal institutional development.

This is where the existing debate about the future of European monetary union again becomes crucial. While the UK economy was experiencing something of a cyclical upswing between 1993 and 1997, the other continental economies remained caught in a coincidental recession. This was prolonged, one suspects, because of the determination of these other economies to meet the Maastricht convergence criteria, which are basically growth inhibiting and deflationary. The struggle to adhere to the Maastricht criteria represented an added burden on economies like those of France and Germany which needed to undertake their own restructuring, with pressures that these economies could have well done without.

Thus when monetary union begins on time in 1999, if the two main economies are still in recession, a further and much more serious deflationary spiral could unfold. One possible move under these circumstances would be to argue for a 'weak euro' policy by the European Central Bank. Although this might appear as anathema to conventional European political and economic opinion, it would potentially open a space for a devaluation-led recovery of the newly integrated economies. Recent past experiences with devaluations by national economies like that of the UK have demonstrated that this can be achieved without the prospect of renewed inflationary pressures (but perhaps not repeatedly, as the case of Sweden demonstrates).

Problems of political cooperation and the limits to integration

Unfortunately, the Union needs to make *rapid* progress towards concerted common policies towards Eastern and Southern Europe if it is to seize the opportunities of the moment and ensure the prosperity of all parts of the continent. The odds against moving quickly towards such very necessary common objectives are high. But even if such progress were to be made, the European Union as a political entity would still for the foreseeable future be a complex amalgam of overlapping powers and responsibilities. For the most ambitious policy goals to be realized there would have to be a substantial measure of political coordination between the European Union and national and regional levels. Even if the central institutions of the EU were to gain considerably in citizen support and political legitimacy, they could not substitute central social coordination for the more complicated processes of the orchestration of consensus and consent at national and regional levels. Nations and regions are the sites of social solidarity, and some of these entities have a far stronger capacity to coordinate the social interests than do others.

If one considers the sorts of policies that could become possible, given the continental scale of the EU, the necessity and the difficulty of achieving this complex division of labour becomes obvious. Thus the Commission – even with an expanded budget – is not in itself a large enough fiscal actor in relation to total EU GDP to provide the stimulus for 'Euro-Keynesian' policies without coincident fiscal and monetary policies in at least the majority of the member states. Assuming that the EU could orchestrate such a policy on the demand side, it is even more the case that its central institutions could not create the complementary non-monetary policies to contain money wage growth and prevent inflation. Such income restraint would fall to national governments. Some like Germany might still be able to deliver because of the continued, if weakened, presence of corporatist structures and a relatively disciplined union movement. Others like France would probably be able to comply because its unions are weak in conventional wage bargaining. In a category of its own is Britain, manifestly incapable of constraining wage growth during periods of rapid expansion without highly restrictive macroeconomic policies. A European-level policy of boosting demand and output would, therefore, lead to patchy results: those states most able to restrain wages growth would benefit, those unable to do so would lose out through accelerating unemployment or nationally imposed deflations.

It is difficult to see how the discrepancy between the different national experiences and institutional legacies can be eliminated. There is no prospect, for example, of a strong 'Euro-corporatism' that might bring the social partners from different countries together to make binding agreements at Union level (see chapter 6). Business will not present itself at this level as a single 'social partner'. It is too divided by national and sectoral interests, and it would prefer to lobby for those interests with national governments and the directorates of the Commission on an issue-by-issue basis. Its national collective bodies are divergent in their degree of organization, in their objectives and in their willingness to enter into partnership with labour. German industry remains highly organized on the employers' side, with strong sectoral and peak employers' associations, whose member firms follow collective policy in a disciplined manner. German employers, despite a growing internationalization of outlook, still retain strong commitments both to industry-wide bargaining on wages and working hours and to the codetermination system of consultation with labour at enterprise level.

British employers' associations are, by contrast, almost exclusively concerned with representing the most general perceived interests of their members to government, and have few powers to discipline their members or get them to take part in coordinated consultation with labour. Wage bargaining has undergone massive decentralization in Britain since the 1970s, with very few industry-wide agreements left (Hirst and Zeitlin 1993). British employers are actively hostile to the idea of an extended dialogue with organized labour to build consent for national policies: this is 'corporatism' and has no place in the modern British manager's lexicon. This stark contrast shows that the European Union will find it difficult to create institutionalized means of orchestrating consensus for macroeconomic policy at suprastate level. European labour, through its supranational federations, may well wish to try to enter into a dialogue with the Commission about policy coordination and the orchestration of consent across the Union. It will have problems if it alone is interested and the employers refuse to cooperate, but even greater problems on its own side too – for European-level consultations will not be able to deliver disciplined continental commitments by member unions in the nation-states in such key areas as labour market policy and wage restraint.

This tells us that *some* nation-states will remain the crucial actors in constructing a *political* basis of consent for the macroeconomic policies of the Community and for their own fiscal, regulatory and industrial policies. Only at the national level can effective *distributional coalitions* be built, that is, as we saw in chapter 6, broad brush agreements between the major parties and social actors about the conditions for and the sharing of the necessary costs of economic success. For example, Social Democrats and Christian Democrats in Germany both continue to agree on a wide range of policies and institutions sustaining the economy, but also enter into intense and open political competition. Such coalitions may be tacit or more orchestrated: what matters is that cooperation and competition between the major interests are in a rough balance. In either case it involves the commitment by social actors and organized social interests to a sustainable distribution of national income between consumption and investment, and to a pattern of expenditure that promotes manufacturing performance. For example, despite substantial recent internationalization, a critical mass of the German financial community still accepts the priority of investing in German firms at terms and conditions that protect their competitiveness. The mainstream political parties, organized labour and employers' organizations all accept the need for public and private investments in education and training. In other countries such commitments and their orchestration would require explicit government action: the UK is the prime example, and Conservative and Labour governments alike have seen this as no part of their task. It will be more difficult to extend such national distributional coalitions to cover the costs of ensuring competitiveness at Union level. Labour seems as hostile to such cohabitation-building as the Tories, marginalizing organized labour and paying little attention to the need to rebuild *organized* business interests at industry level as effective sectoral actors.

Britain's government is no longer congenitally Eurosceptical, but it holds a relatively limited vision of the EU, far below its potential for economic governance. Britain is unwilling to learn from other centre-left governments and seeks to promote its own limited vision. Until this changes the UK will remain an obstacle to the development of alternative governance strategies for Europe's continental economy.

Conclusions

Thus Europe is still at the point where a great deal of institutional work needs to be done to ensure that its effective economic integration is irreversible. At a primitive level, as a single market, integration is probably irreversible. The same does not hold for the development of the extended economic governance of this single economic space. For those committed to European union the hope must be that there is no serious and sustained depression in the early twenty-first century, that centrist politicians can contain the worst of the rightist pressures, that the issue of immigration does not become explosive and a gift to the right, and, therefore, that space is left for centripetal forces to exert countervailing pressures towards integration.

For a long time European elites talked as if a federal solution were possible. They got way ahead of Europe's populations. They thought that the economic logic of integration would produce a *de facto* union, without the need for legitimacy. Europe would pay for itself, and technocratic measures would suffice as the people enjoyed rising prosperity. The hubris of that view is now clear; it coloured much of the Maastricht Treaty and led to fierce opposition to it in Britain, Denmark and France. A 'federal' solution has too little political credibility now, because few see the need to boost Europe alongside its nation-states as an object of citizen identification. Europe will have to go forward in its governance mechanisms and its further integration more clearly concerned with the political conditions of their implementation.

As we have seen, the Maastricht process has resolved none of the issues of the balance of power between Union, national and regional levels of governance in Europe. To be realistic, the EU is very unlikely to evolve into a continent-wide single unified state, even of a federal form. There are things that unified states can do that looser configurations cannot. For certain purposes a federal state like the US has considerable advantages over the present EU arrangements. But it is unlikely that Europe can advance to a federal status. Existing political forces are not in the mood to cede the necessary powers to Brussels. Any attempt to force this through would rapidly lead to the break-up of the EU. Rather, what is most likely is that some form of *confederal* arrangement will emerge, as suggested above. The EU will at best be a European 'public power', its capacities continuing to be derived from treaties between the member states and from processes of decision-making in which those states will have the major part to play. If the EU becomes inescapably confederal in matters of both revenue and military power, the nation-states will retain the power of decision, but they will make community-level policy by majority vote. This also means that the legal possibility of seceding from the Union remains for all nation-states.

It must develop, however, some mechanisms for securing citizen identification with and political legitimacy for Union institutions if it is not to forgo some of the main benefits of a continental scale of organization. In part, the construction of such an identity can only come with processes of integration, as indeed legitimacy is linked with the strengthening of central political institutions. This will in most likelihood involve the further development, maturing and deepening of the public powers of institutions of economic governance. Most members of European elites accept that a single market requires a unit of regulation to match it. The main limits of possible policy in Europe are *political* and concern the capacity of Brussels to mobilize citizen support for continental-scale policies involving major fiscal commitments and political risks.

9

Globalization, Governance and the Nation-State

So far we have been mainly concerned with the economic aspects of globalization, and have considered governance primarily in terms of its economic necessities and possibilities. In this chapter we consider the wider political issues raised by globalization theorists, and consider in particular whether the nation-state has a future as a major locus of governance.

We begin with a reminder that the modern state is a relatively recent phenomenon, and that 'sovereignty' in its modern form is a highly distinctive political claim – to exclusive control of a definite territory. We emphasize the *international* aspects of the development of sovereignty, that agreements between states not to interfere in each other's internal affairs were important in establishing the power of state over society. We go on to consider the development of the nation-state's capacity for governance and how these capacities are changing in the modern world, especially after the end of the Cold War.

While the state's capacities for governance have changed and in many respects (especially as national macroeconomic managers) have weakened considerably, it remains a pivotal institution, especially in terms of creating the conditions for effective international governance. We shall make the following main points in our discussion of the possibilities of governance and the role of the state:

1   If, as we have argued in earlier chapters, the international economy does not correspond to the model of a globalized economic system, then nation-states have a significant role to play in economic governance at the level of both national and international processes.
2   The emerging forms of governance of international markets and other economic processes involve the major national governments but in a

new role: states will come to function less as 'sovereign' entities and more as the components of an international 'quasi-polity'; the central functions of the nation-state will become those of providing legitimacy for and ensuring the accountability of supranational and subnational governance mechanisms.

3   While the state's claim to exclusive control of its territory has been reduced by international markets and new communication media, it still retains one central role that ensures a large measure of territorial control: the regulation of populations. People are less mobile than money, goods or ideas, and in a sense they remain 'nationalized', dependent on passports, visas, residence and labour qualifications. The democratic state's role as the possessor of a territory is that it regulates its population, and this gives it a definite and unique legitimacy internationally in that it can speak for that population.

The rise of 'national sovereignty'

Political theorists and sociologists commonly assert, following Max Weber, that the distinctive feature of the modern state is the possession of the monopoly of the means of violence within a given territory (Weber 1968, p. 56). In the seventeenth century the modern state system was created and mutually recognized by its members. Central to that recognition was that each state was the sole political authority with exclusive possession of a defined territory. The 'state' became the dominant form of government, accepting no other agency as rival. The Middle Ages had known no such singular relationship between authority and territory. Political authorities and other forms of functionally specific governance (religious communities and guilds, for example) had existed in overlapping forms that made parallel and often competing claims to the same area (Gierke 1988). Some would claim that the period of the domination of the nation-state as an agency of governance is now over and that we are entering into a period when governance and territory will pull apart, when different agencies will control aspects of governance and some important activities will be ungoverned (Cerny 1998). This is questionable, but the claim of nation-states to exclusivity in governance is historically specific and by no means preordained.

The modern state did not acquire its monopoly of governance by its own internal efforts alone. After the Treaty of Westphalia in 1648 governments gradually ceased to support co-religionists in conflict with their own states. The mutual recognition by states of each other's sovereignty in the most important contemporary matter, religious belief, meant that states were willing to forgo certain political objectives in return for internal control and stability (Hirst 1997). By exploiting the autonomy from external interference sanctioned by this mutual and international agreement, states were able to impose 'sovereignty' on their societies. The agreement of states changed the terms of conflict between territorial authority and confessional groups in favour of the former. Thus to a significant degree the capacity for sovereignty came from *without*, through agreements between states in the newly emerging society of states.

The rise of the modern state as a territorially specific and politically dominant power thus depended in part on *international* agreements. The doctrine of the 'sovereignty' of states in the new international law, and the mutual recognition of their internal powers and rights by European states, thus played a central part in the creation of a new relationship between power and territory, one of exclusive possession (Hinsley 1986). These international understandings made possible an 'internalization' of power and politics within the state. States were perceived as the primary political communities, with the capacity to determine the status of and to make rules for any activity that fell within contemporary understandings of the scope of legitimate authority. States were sovereign and hence each state determined within itself the nature of its internal and external policies. States monopolized not only internal but also external violence. Only the state could make war and use force externally, pirates and private armies being gradually suppressed by interstate agreements and enforcement (Thomson 1994).

The society of states thus became a world of self-sufficient entities, each acting on its own will (Bull 1977). International relations could be conceived as 'billiard ball' interactions, limited by mutual recognition and the obligation to refrain from interfering in the internal affairs of other states (Morse 1971). The anarchical society of external interactions between states, their autonomy one from another, was thus a precondition for an effective monopoly of power within. In the nineteenth and twentieth centuries liberal and democratic governments inherited from the earlier absolutist regimes these claims to sovereignty within a coherent and exclusively governed territory, and brought to them new and powerful legitimations.

So to this fundamental sovereignty postulated by seventeenth-century states could be added, without excessive contradiction, most of the other features of modern politics. States were autonomous and exclusive possessors of their territory, and this fact did not alter whether they were dynastic or national, autocratic or democratic, authoritarian or liberal. The notion of a 'nation' state actually reinforces the conception of a sovereign power having primacy within a given territory. Nationalism is in essence a claim that political power should reflect *cultural* homogeneity, according to some common set of historically specific political understandings of the content of the nation.

Nationalism thus extends and depends on the scope of 'sovereignty', requiring certain kinds of cultural conformity for citizenship.[1] In this respect the advent of nationalism did not alter our understanding of states as 'sovereign' bodies, but rather it required it. The concept of a culturally homogeneous and therefore legitimately sovereign territory could justify both the formation and the break-up of states. The result of the various waves of nationalism from the early nineteenth century onwards has been to increase the population of the anarchical society of sovereign states, rather than change its nature. Indeed, if anything, nationalism rendered international cooperation more difficult, reinforcing the notion of the national community as the master of its fate.

Democracy had no greater effect on the fundamental characteristics of the sovereign state, a political entity created in a pre-democratic era. Democracy, in the sense of representative government based on universal suffrage, has become a virtually universal ideology and aspiration in the late twentieth century. Non-democratic regimes are now signs of political failure and chronic economic backwardness. The notion of a sovereign people could easily replace the 'sovereign', annexing the latter's claims to primacy in the making of political decisions within a given territory. Similarly, democracy and nationalism can, at a price, be made compatible. Democracy requires a substantial measure of cultural homogeneity (or publicly recognized cultural difference within some overarching political identity) if it is to be tolerable (Hindess 1992). Bitterly divided communities cannot accept the logic of majority rule or tolerate the rights of minorities. National self-determination is a political claim that derives its legitimacy from the notions of democracy and cultural homogeneity in equal measure, its essence being a plebiscite on independence in a territory claimed to have a degree of distinctive cultural coherence (Nairn 1993).

Modern political theory – that is, the theory of government and political obligation in a sovereign state – evolved before mass democracy but adapted relatively easily to it. This is not just because it was possible to substitute the people for the monarch. It is also because the nation-state is simply the most developed form of the idea of a self-governing political community, and the very possibility of a distinctive 'political' theory has been bound up with that idea (Hindess 1991, 1996). Democracy is a source of legitimacy for government and a decision procedure within an entity seen to be self-determining. From the Greek polis, through the civic republicanism of the Italian city-states, to seventeenth-century ideas of government by consent, the notion of the community that controls its social world through collective choice has been central to our understanding of politics. Modern democratic theory blended together what had hitherto tended to be two contradictory ideas: that the community was sovereign, power being ultimately derived from the people, so that government must be by consent; and that the ruler was sovereign, state and society being separate entities, with the sovereign as an uncommanded commander, not bound by prior agreements (Hinsley 1986). Democratic elections legitimated the sovereign powers of state institutions, and thus provided a better foundation for a state viewed as the organ of a self-governing territorial community than did the will of a prince. Democratic sovereignty *includes* citizens and binds them through a common membership that is denied to others.

The notion of the self-governing community has ancient sources, but in the form of the modern nation-state it acquired a distinctive credibility. First, in its pre-democratic guise, the state (as a distinct entity separate from society) monopolized violence, imposed uniform administration and provided a form of the rule of law. States claimed to guarantee a substantial measure of security to citizens from external enemies and internal tumults. This claim, advanced as the justification for enlightened autocracy, only became fully credible when states became representative democracies and matters of war and peace ceased to be determined by princely ambitions and dynastic considerations. Since Kant's *On Perpetual Peace*, the proposition that liberal states will not attack one another has been the foundation for the hope that a world of nation-states could be a peaceful one, that democracy within would temper the anarchical relations between states (Kant 1991; Doyle 1983). Second, the modern state based on representation could govern its territory with a degree of completeness and comprehensiveness unavailable to previous regimes. Representative government reinforced and legitimated the state's capacities for taxation and, given this fiscal power and the removal of competing and subordinate authorities, it could create a uniform national system of administration. On this basis it could extend social governance, for example, creating universal systems of national education or bringing in public health measures. Third, but only in the twentieth century, states acquired the means to manage or direct national economies, either through autarchy and state planning, as with the state-directed economies in Britain and Germany in the two world wars, or through Keynesian measures, using monetary and fiscal policy to influence the decisions of economic actors and thus alter economic outcomes.

Thus by the 1960s the state appeared to be the dominant social entity: state and society were virtually coterminous. The state governed and directed society in both the Communist and Western spheres, albeit in rather different ways. Communist states used one variety of national economic management, through permanent central planning. In the 1960s the excesses of forced socialist construction seemed to be over and reformers like Khrushchev were promising greater prosperity and peaceful coexistence rather than open conflict with the West. In the advanced Western industrial states it was widely believed that national economic management could continue to ensure both full employment and relatively steady growth. Industrial states, in the East and in the West, were ramified public service agencies, omnicompetent to supervise and to provide for every aspect of the life of their communities. In Western societies still shaped by the industrial revolution, in which the majority of the employed population remained manual workers even into the 1960s, uniform and universal national services in health, education and welfare remained popular. Populations that had only recently escaped the crises of unregulated capitalism continued to welcome collective state social protection, even as they began to enjoy the new mass affluence created by full employment and the long boom after 1945.

This perception of the state has changed out of all recognition and with surprising rapidity. The revolutions of 1989 in Eastern Europe and their aftermath have led to a widespread perception of the modern world as one in which nation-states are losing their capacities for governance and national-level processes are ceding their primacy to global ones. What 1989 ended was a specific structure of conflict between allied groups of nation-states, the Cold War. The driving force of this conflict was mutual fear between two armed camps, a fear exploited on both sides for ideological purposes, but it was not primarily a clash of ideologies. The Cold War reinforced the need for the nation-state, for its military capacities and for the national-level forms of economic and social regulation necessary to sustain them. The states system was frozen into a pattern of rigid passive confrontation at the centre, with conflict by proxy at the margins. The state remained necessary, even though its powers remained in reserve in a suspended conflict. Until 1989 it remained possible, although unlikely and mutually suicidal, that the two superpowers and their allied states might go to war. This eventuality, the fear of a mobilized and immediate enemy, made nation-states necessary. If they weakened or lost their capacity to control their societies, then the enemy might overrun them, and, depending on one's viewpoint, destroy the gains of socialism or impose communist tyranny. This blocked conflict preserved the saliency of the national level of government in a way that delayed or masked the changes that would subsequently weaken it.

The political rhetoric of 'globalization'

We have seen that it has now become fashionable to assert that the era of the nation-state is over, and that national-level governance is ineffective in the face of globalized economic and social processes (Horsman and Marshall 1994). National politics and political choices have been sidelined by world market forces which are stronger than even the most powerful states. Capital is mobile and has no national attachments, locating wherever economic advantage dictates, but labour is both nationally located and relatively static, and it must adjust its political expectations to meet the new pressures of international competitiveness. Distinct national regimes of extensive labour rights and social protection are thus obsolete. So too are monetary and fiscal policies contrary to the expectations of global markets and transnational companies. The nation-state has ceased to be an effective economic manager. It can only provide those social and public services deemed essential by international capital and at the lowest possible overhead cost.

Nation-states are perceived by authors like Ohmae (1990, 1993) and Reich (1992) to have become the local authorities of the global system. They can no longer independently affect the level of economic activity or employment within their territories: rather that is dictated by the choices of internationally mobile capital. The job of nation-states is like that of municipalities within states heretofore, to provide the infrastructure and public goods that business needs at the lowest possible cost.

This new political rhetoric is based on an anti-political liberalism. Set free from politics, the new globalized economy allows companies and markets to allocate the factors of production to their greatest advantage, and without the distortions of state intervention. Free trade, transnational companies and world capital markets have liberated business from the constraints of politics, enabling it to provide the world's consumers with the cheapest and most efficient products. Globalization realizes the ideals of mid nineteenth-century free trade liberals like Cobden and Bright; that is, a demilitarized world in which business activity is primary and political power has no other task than the protection of the world free trading system.

For the political right in the advanced industrial countries the rhetoric of globalization is a godsend. It provides a new lease of life after the disastrous failure of their monetarist and radical individualist policy experiments in the 1980s. It has argued that labour rights and social welfare of the kind practised in the era of national economic management will render Western societies uncompetitive in relation to the newly industrializing economies of Asia and must be drastically reduced.

For the radical left the concept of globalization also provides release from a different kind of political impasse. Confronted with the collapse of state socialism and of Third World anti-imperialist struggles, the left can see in globalization evidence of the continued reality of the world capitalist system. It can also see the futility of national social democratic reformist strategies. The revolutionary left may be weakened but the reformists can no longer claim to possess a pragmatic and effective politics.

Left and right can thus mutually celebrate the end of the Keynesian era. National economic management, full employment and sustained growth, standardized mass production with large semi-skilled manual labour forces, corporatist collaboration between industry, organized labour and the state – these factors, central to the period of the post-1945 long boom, created conditions that favoured the political influence of organized labour, and that confined credible political policies to a centrist and reformist path. The dominance of volatile international markets, the change to flexible methods of production and the radical reshaping of the labour force, fitful and uncertain growth in the advanced countries, the decline of organized labour and corporatist intermediation, all these, it is claimed, have rendered reformist strategies obsolete and reduced the centrality of national political processes, whether competitive or cooperative.

There is some truth in the proposition that national politics in the advanced countries is increasingly a 'cool' politics (Mulgan 1994). It is no longer a matter of war and peace, or of class conflict. It is no longer a matter of mass mobilization for common life-or-death national efforts. For the globalists national-level politics is even less salient because it cannot greatly alter economic and social outcomes, unless foolish interventionalist strategies are adopted that undermine national competitiveness.

Once national politics is held to become more like municipal politics, a matter of providing mundane services, energy drains out of conventional politics, away from established parties, and first-rate people cease to be attracted by a political career. Energy flows into the politics of morality, into issues like abortion, gay rights, animal rights, the environment, etc. Activist or 'hot' politics can be played as primary politics without fear that this will distract or divert attention from vital 'national' issues – for these are now mundane.

The decline in the centrality of national-level politics, of war, of class conflict and revolution, of effective economic management and social reform, frees political forces from the need to cooperate against enemies without or to collaborate within to maintain national prosperity. Subnationalities and regions can assert their autonomy with less fear: being, for example, an active advocate of Breton culture and interests will no longer have the effect of weakening France in its life or death conflicts with Germany. Equally, cultural homogeneity at the 'national' level is less central in advanced states linked to world markets, since the nation-state as a political entity can offer less. Hence religious, ethnic and lifestyle pluralism can expand within such states, and groups within national states grow in significance as alternative focuses of allegiance for their members.

These arguments have some force. There is no doubt that the salience and role of nation-states have changed markedly since the Keynesian era. States are less autonomous, they have less exclusive control over the economic and social processes within their territories, and they are less able to maintain national distinctiveness and cultural homogeneity.

The changing capacities of the nation-state

There are certain areas in which the role of the state has changed radically and its capacities to control its people and domestic social processes have declined as a consequence. The first of these is war. The state acquired a monopoly of the means of violence within, the better to be able to mobilize the resources of a territory for external conflict. From the sixteenth century to the present the primary defining capacity of the modern state has been the power to make war, and to draw on the lives and property of its citizens in order to do so. As we saw, the Cold War kept this power alive. Mutual enmity between East and West reinforced the need for permanent mobilization against an ever present threat of war. The development of nuclear weapons, however, has had the effect of making war impossible, in the traditional sense of the use of force to attain some objective. Classically war was seen as a means of decision, victory settling an issue between states that could be resolved in no other way. Clauswitzian war was purposive, and to that degree rational, the continuation of policy by other means. Nuclear war between roughly equal combatants could only end in mutual destruction and the negation of any rational policy pursued by the officials of the participating states. As Bernard Brodie (1946, 1965) perceptively observed (immediately after Hiroshima), the sole function of nuclear weapons was deterrence: the greatest military force could no longer be employed to reach a political decision but could now only be effective if it prevented its own use and thus gave politicians time to devise means to bring it under political control by the mutual agreement of the nuclear states.

Brodie was right, even if it took half a century of extreme risk and the danger of extinction before such political measures finally became possible. The Cold War was insupportable, deterrence unstable and nuclear stalemate bought at ever higher cost. Periods of intense competition between the superpowers, seeking technological advantage through arms races, were followed by periods of détente. The major nuclear states have forgone 'sovereignty'; they have created a world civil order by their treaties, not merely limiting wars, but granting to other states powers of inspection and supervision, of notification of military manoeuvres etc., of a kind that render effective war mobilization extremely unlikely.[2] States have had to accept a hitherto intolerable level of interference in their internal affairs to make peace credible. The ultimate force that nuclear arsenals represent is useless: it cannot make war, and political agreements, if they can be institutionalized, will make deterrence unnecessary.

War between nuclear states became impossible, whether they were liberal or illiberal, provided their leaders were possessed of minimal rationality. Non-nuclear conflicts could only occur in peripheral regions, conflicts by proxy where the defeat of one side would not lead to the threat of nuclear war. The possession of nuclear weapons thus also ended the possibility of conventional war between nuclear states.[3] Nuclear weapons drove war out of international relations between advanced states, being no longer an alternative means of decision but the threat of a terrible mutual disaster that needed to be negotiated away.

Armed forces are thus virtually an irrelevance for the major advanced states in their dealings with one another. Weapons have evolved to the point where they have rendered war obsolete and with it much of the rationale and capacities for control of the state. Armed forces will not cease to exist, but they will matter less and less as a means of political decision (Van Creveld 1991). They cannot decide matters between advanced states. And the disparity of forces between the great powers and major states in the Third World is so great that when the great powers perceive their vital interests to be at stake, the latter cannot rearrange matters to their advantage by conventional armed force, as the Gulf War of 1991 proved.

This does not mean we shall live in a peaceful world. Lesser states will fight one another. Advanced states will be threatened by terrorism. Revolutionary movements will continue to arise on the impoverished periphery, new but local 'beggars' armies' like the Zapatistas in Chiapas, Mexico. Revolutionary movements will articulate specific local antagonisms, but they will no longer seem to be detachments in a single struggle united by a common anti-capitalist and anti-imperialist ideology. But it does mean, in the advanced states at least, that governments are unlikely to have the occasion to call on the lives and property of their citizens for war. They will no longer be able to mobilize their societies and demand and create the solidarity and common identification with authority necessary to the effective pursuit of total war. War, the presence of a genuine enemy, reinforced national solidarity and made credible the claim to national cultural homogeneity.

Without war, without enemies, the state becomes less significant to the citizen. When peoples really faced enemies, invaders and conquerors, they needed their state and their fellow citizens. The liberal state, claiming to live peacefully with its neighbours and to make limited demands on its own people, could claim great legitimacy if attacked, thereby rousing its people to a degree of commitment and common effort that authoritarian states could seldom match. These legitimations are gone, and with them whole classes of provision for 'national' needs justified by the possible contingency of war: 'national' industries, health and welfare to promote 'national efficiency', and social solidarity to unite rich and poor in a common struggle. Social democracy profited from industrialized conventional war: it could deliver organized labour to the all-out war effort at the price of economic and social reforms.

States in the advanced world no longer have war as a central support for their claims to 'sovereignty'. They are no longer conceivable as autonomous actors, free to pursue any external policy in an anarchical society of states. The society of states has passed from an anarchical condition to a quasi-civil one. The vast majority of states are bound together in numerous ways in what amounts to an international political society, and, in the case of the major advanced states of the G7 and OECD, a virtual standing association of states with its own rules and decision procedures. This does not mean that national states are irrelevant, but it does mean that their claim to a monopoly of the means of legitimate violence within a given territory is no longer so defining of their existence.

Just as nuclear weapons have transformed the conditions of war, weakening the central rationale for the state in the process, so too the new communications and information technologies have loosened the state's exclusiveness of control of its territory, reducing its capacities for cultural control and homogenization. It is a commonplace that digitalized communications, satellites, fax machines and computer networks have rendered the licensing and control of information media by the state all but impossible, not merely undermining ideological dictatorships but also subverting all attempts to preserve cultural homogeneity by state force.

Modern communications form the basis for an international civil society, people who share interests and associations across borders. The international media also make possible a set of cosmopolitan cultures, elite and popular, scientific and artistic, linked through the medium of English as a universal rather than a national language. Such cultures, from children watching Tom and Jerry cartoons on TV to physicists gossiping on e-mail, are inevitably international. Cultural homogeneity becomes increasingly problematic, since 'national' cultures are merely one of several cultures in which people participate for different purposes. Cosmopolitan and national cultures interact. Complete cultural homogeneity and exclusiveness are less and less possible. 'National' cultures that aim to be dominant over the individuals who belong to them are increasingly projects of resistance to and retreat from the world. Inward-looking nationalism and cultural fundamentalism are, to put it bluntly, the politics of losers. It is virtually impossible to continue to operate in the various world markets and still ignore the internationalized cultures that go along with them. Such inward-looking nationalisms do exist and will continue to develop, but to the degree that their political projects are successful, they have the effect of marginalizing their societies. Although they are responses to economic backwardness, such nationalisms act to reinforce it. The same is true of social groups within advanced states that claim an all-pervasive identity, be that ethnic, religious or whatever: they condemn their members to social marginality.

The existence of different languages and religions, as Kant argued, virtually guarantees cultural diversity (Kant 1991). Distinct local cultural traditions will continue to coexist with cosmopolitan cultural practices. What is threatened, however, is the idea of an exclusive and virtually self-sufficient 'national' culture, of which individuals are simply exemplars, sharing a common language, beliefs and activities. States strenuously attempted to create such cultures through common systems of national education, military service, etc. (Anderson 1991). That such projects are no longer possible for advanced states means that they have to seek bases of citizen loyalty outside of primitive cultural homogeneity. In the major cities of most advanced states dozens of languages and almost every conceivable religion are commonly used and observed. As we shall see, the state will probably find a new rationale in managing this very diversity, acting as the public power that enables such parallel communities to coexist and to resolve conflicts. Space and culture have no definite relation. In the great cities of the advanced countries at least, the cultures of the world are more or less randomly mixed. The state in the era of 'nation building' tried to turn its people into artefacts of itself, representative specimens of the 'national' culture. In the interest of individual liberty and the values of cosmopolitanism and cultural diversity, we should be grateful that states can make fewer and less credible claims on our imaginations and beliefs.

The state may have less control over ideas, but it remains a controller of its borders and the movement of people across them. As we have seen, apart from a 'club class' of internationally mobile, highly skilled professionals, and the desperate, poor migrants and refugees who will suffer almost any hardship to leave intolerable conditions, the bulk of the world's populations now cannot easily move. Workers in advanced countries have no 'frontier' societies to migrate to as they did in huge numbers to countries like Australia or Argentina in the nineteenth century and in lesser numbers into the 1970s. Increasingly the poor of Eastern Europe and the Third World are unwelcome in advanced countries except as 'guest workers' or illegal migrants working for poverty wages. Western societies are shedding labour and local unskilled labour finds it harder and harder to get jobs, hence the pressure to exclude poor migrants. In the absence of labour mobility, states will retain powers over their peoples. They define who is and who is not a citizen, who may and who may not receive welfare. In this respect, despite the rhetoric of globalization, the bulk of the world's population lives in closed worlds, trapped by the lottery of birth. For the average worker or farmer with a family, one's nation-state is a community of fate. Wealth and income are not global, they are nationally and regionally distributed between poorer and richer states and localities. For the vast majority of people nation-states cannot be regarded as just municipalities or local authorities, providing services that one chooses according to their relative quality and cost.

Nationally rooted labour has to seek local strategies and local benefits if it is to improve its lot. The question is whether business is similarly constrained, or whether it can simply choose new and more optimal locations. Internationally open cultures and rooted populations present an explosive contradiction. The impoverished can watch *Dallas*. They know another world is possible, whether they are watching it in a slum apartment in an advanced country or a shanty town in a Third World country. The ideology of socialist revolution may have few takers, but one should not imagine that the world's poor will remain cowed or passively accept their poverty. Their responses, whether through street crime or guerrilla struggles as in Chiapas, will be far harder to cope with than old-style revolts in the name of communism. Such responses will be local, and less aggregated in ideological terms with other conflicts. Hence these struggles will be left in the main to local states and local elites to contain. The advanced world currently does not think its frontier begins in the jungle of Yucatan in the way it once thought it did in the jungles of Vietnam or Bolivia.

As the advanced countries seek to police the movement of the world's poor and exclude them, the capriciousness of the notions of citizenship and of political community will become ever more evident. Advanced states will not be able to make effective use of the claim to cultural homogeneity as a principle of exclusion – for they are already ethnically and culturally pluralistic. Exclusion will be a mere fact, with no other logic or legitimacy than that states are fearful of the consequences of large-scale migration. A world of wealth and poverty, with appalling and widening differences in living standards between the richest and the poorest nations, is unlikely to be secure or stable. Industrial workers in the advanced countries fear the cheap labour of well-educated and skilled workers in the upper tier of developing countries like Taiwan or Malaysia. The poor of the Third World see themselves as abandoned by a rich world that trades more and more with itself and with a few favoured NICs. Both groups are stuck within the borders of states, forced to regard their countries as communities of fate and to seek solutions within the limits of their enforced residence.

However, as we have argued above, mere nationalism as such will provide no solution to these problems. The assertion of ethnic, cultural or religious homogeneity may serve as a cultural compensation for poverty, as an opium of the economically backward, but it will not cure it. It is to the poor and excluded that fundamentalist Islam or other forms of cultural nationalism appeal. Such localizing ideologies will continue to be politically successful in areas where significant numbers of people see they have not benefited at all from the world free trade order. But such ideologies will not alter the fact of poverty.[4]

Third World national revolutions as projects of economic and social modernization have proved failures. They required autarchic withdrawal from world markets, the socialization of agriculture and forced-march industrialization. Where such revolutions were most complete, as in Albania or North Korea, they led to societies that reproduced the worst features of the Soviet system. Unfortunately for the world's poor they could not exit the free trade system and transform their societies by their own efforts within their own borders. The problem is that without a transformation in the international economic order, without new strategies and priorities in the advanced countries towards the Third World, and without large-scale foreign capital investment, poor countries are unlikely to benefit much from turning away from autarchy either. The point is that in the 1960s the national state solution still seemed viable for the Third World, using the state power available after independence and the legacy of solidarity from the anti-colonial struggle to build a new society. Such Third World revolutionary strategies are no more viable now than are conventional social-democratic national Keynesian strategies in the advanced countries.

Governance and the world economy

There can be no doubt that the era when politics could be conceived almost exclusively in terms of processes within nation-states and their external billiard-ball interactions is passing. Politics is becoming more polycentric, with states as merely one level in a complex system of overlapping and often competing agencies of governance. It is probable that the complexity of these superimposed authorities, both territorial and functional, will soon come to rival that of the Middle Ages. But this complexity and multiplicity of levels and types of governance implies a world quite different from that of the rhetoric of 'globalization', and one in which there is a distinct, significant and continuing place for the nation-state.

We should make it clear again at this point that the issue of control of economic activity in a more integrated internationalized economy is one of govern*ance* and not just of the continuing roles of govern*ments*. Sovereign nation-states claimed as their distinctive feature the right to determine how any activity within their territory was governed, either performing that function themselves or setting the limits for other agencies. That is, they claimed a monopoly of the function of governance. Hence the tendency in common usage to identify the term 'government' with those institutions of state that control and regulate the life of a territorial community. Gover*nance* – that is, the control of an activity by some means such that a range of desired outcomes is attained – is, however, not just the province of the state. Rather it is a function that can be performed by a wide variety of public and private, state and non-state, national and international institutions and practices.[5] The analogy with the Middle Ages simply helps us to grasp this by thinking back to a period before the attempt at the monopolization of governance functions by sovereign nation-states. That is its only and limited purpose.

Some authors like Cerny (1998) and Minc (1993) press the analogy with the Middle Ages. The reference back to the Middle Ages is, however, at best metaphoric and in some ways is far from apt. We are *not* returning to a world *like* the Middle Ages and before the development of national 'sovereignty'. This is not just because national states and the 'sovereign' control of peoples persists. The scope and role of forms of governance is radically different today, and this has distinct implications for the architecture of government. In the Middle Ages the coexistence of parallel, competing and overlapping authorities was possible, if conflictual, because economies and societies were less integrated. The degree of division of labour and economic interdependence was relatively low, whereas today communities depend for their very existence on the meshing and coordination of distinct and often remote activities. Markets alone cannot provide such interconnection and coordination – or rather they can only do so if they are appropriately governed and if the rights and expectations of distant participants are secured and sustained (Durkheim 1964).

Hence governing powers cannot simply proliferate and compete. The different levels and functions of governance need to be tied together in a division of control that sustains the division of labour. If this does not happen then the unscrupulous can exploit and the unlucky can fall into the 'gaps' between different agencies and dimensions of governance. The governing powers (international, national and regional) need to be 'sutured' together into a relatively integrated system. If this does not happen then these gaps will lead to the corrosion of governance at every level. The issue at stake is *whether* such a coherent system will develop, and it takes priority over the question of whether international governance can be democratic (as force-fully argued by Held 1991, 1995, for example). The answer to this former question remains moot. But simplistic versions of the globalization thesis do not help to resolve it because they induce fatalism about the capacity of the key agencies in promoting coherent national strategies.

The nation-state is central to this process of 'suturing': the policies and practices of states in distributing power upwards to the international level and downwards to subnational agencies are the ties that will hold the system of governance together. Without such explicit policies to close gaps in governance and elaborate a division of labour in regulation, then vital capacities for control will be lost. Authority may now be plural within and between states rather than nationally centralized, but to be effective it must be structured by an element of design into a relatively coherent architec-ture of institutions. This the more simplistic 'globalization' theorists deny, either because they believe the world economy is ungovernable, given volatile markets and divergent interests, and therefore that no element of design is possible, or because they see the market as a mechanism of coordination in and of itself that makes any attempt at an institutional architecture to govern it unnecessary. They see the market as a substitute for govern*ment* because it is held to be a satisfactory mode of govern*ance*, producing optimal outcomes when its workings are least impeded by extra-neous institutional regulation.

Extreme globalization theorists like Ohmae (1990) contend that only two forces matter in the world economy, global market forces and transna-tional companies, and that neither of these is or can be subject to effective public governance. The global system is governed by the logic of market competition, and public policy will be at best secondary, since no govern-mental agencies (national or otherwise) can match the scale of world market forces. To repeat, this view considers that national governments are the municipalities of the global system, that their economies are no longer 'national' in any significant sense and that they can only be effective as gov-ernments if they accept their reduced role of providing locally the public services the global economy requires of them. The question, however, is whether such a global economy exists or is coming into being. As we have seen, there is a vast difference between a strictly *globalized* economy and a highly *inter-nationalized* economy in which most companies trade from their bases in distinct national economies. In the former, national policies are futile, since economic outcomes are determined wholly by world market forces and by the internal decisions of transnational companies. In the latter, national policies remain viable, indeed essential in order to preserve the distinct styles and strengths of the national economic base and the com-panies trading from it. A world economy with a high and growing degree of international trade and investment is not necessarily a globalized economy in the former sense. In it nation-states, and forms of international regulation created and sustained by nation-states, still have a fundamental role in providing governance of the economy.

The issue, therefore, turns on what type of international economy exists at present or is coming into being: one that is essentially supranational, or one in which, despite high levels of international trade and investment, nationally located processes and economic actions still remain central. The evidence we have considered so far on the key aspects of this question – the character of the world financial markets, the pattern of world trade and FDI, the number and role of MNCs, and the prospects for growth in the developing world – all confirms that there is no strong tendency towards a globalized economy and that the major advanced nations continue to be dominant.

This can be illustrated by the continued importance of the national border between the US and Canada. If true globalization had emerged, then surely this border would have been one of the first to have lost its pertinence as far as trade, investment and their governance were concerned. But, in fact, this border continues to play a central role in the distribution of trade and investment, even after the NAFTA treaty came into force after 1994. Both McCallum (1995) and Engel and Rogers (1996) demonstrate that this border continues to have a decisive impact on continental trade patterns and in terms of the differentiation of price dispersion across locations. The significance of national markets in determining the organization of trade and the formation of prices remains even in the case of the relatively close proximity and integration of the US and Canadian economies.

Given this is so, we should ditch the overfashionable concept of 'globalization' and look for less politically debilitating models. The issue here is not merely one of assessing evidence, but of providing political concepts that restate the possibilities for economic governance and the role of the modern state in such governance.

Earlier in the book we saw that the ongoing battles between the public policy of the advanced nations and the major financial markets are by no means settled, but that there is no reason to believe that market forces will invariably and inevitably prevail over regulatory systems, despite setbacks like the unravelling of the EMS. The financial crisis of 1997–8 has produced extensive calls for reregulation and the reform of major international institutions like the IMF. There is a clear recognition of the need for preventive action to forestall crises in emerging markets and to constrain the activities of hedge funds like Long Term Capital Management. Thus the public culture of discussion has swung away from gung-ho economic liberalism, and policy and practice are likely to follow. This will lead to some measure of coordination in policy, although not to a new world exchange rate regime. However, the advent of the euro will create a large zone of monetary stability on the ruins of the EMS.

The reason for such pressures towards reregulation is that most players in the international economy have an interest in financial stability, including the major companies, for whom a reduction in uncertainty is of obvious advantage in their planning of investment and in their production and marketing strategies. It has become obvious that derivatives, once turned into speculative investment, no longer offer adequate means of containing risk: they show the advantages of stabilization of the international financial system by public regulation. The idea common among extreme globalization theorists that major companies will benefit from an unregulated international environment remains a strange one. Calculable trade rules, settled and internationally consistent property rights, the containment of excessive volatility in security markets, and exchange rate stability add up to a level of elementary security that companies need to plan ahead, and therefore a condition of continued investment and growth. Companies cannot create such conditions for themselves, even if they are 'transnational'. Stability in the international economy can only be had if states combine to regulate it and to agree on common objectives and standards of governance. Companies may want free trade and common regimes of trade standards, but they can only have them if states work together to achieve common international regulation.[6]

Equally, the notion that companies should wish to be 'transnational' in the sense of extraterritorial is also a strange one. The national economic bases from which most companies operate actually contribute to their economic efficiency and not just in the sense of providing low-cost infrastructure. Most firms are embedded in a distinct national culture of business that provides them with intangible but very real advantages. Managers and core staff have common understandings that go beyond formal training or company policies. Genuinely transnational companies, with no primary location and a multinational workforce, would have to try to create *within* the firm the cultural advantages and forms of identification that other firms get almost free from national institutions. They would have to get core workers to put the company first as a source of identification and build a cohesive non-national managerial elite that can communicate implicitly one with another. This transnationality has traditionally only been achieved by non-economic organizations with a strong ideological mission providing a focus of loyalty alternative to countries and states, such as the Society of Jesus. This would be difficult for companies to match. After all, the Jesuits are culturally distinct even if multinational, products of a distinctive Latin Catholic environment and education. It is difficult to make the firm the exclusive *cultural* focus of an individual's life, and for individuals to make an ongoing commitment to one company, entirely removed from national connections. The Japanese managers and core workers who see the firm as a primary and ongoing social community do this in a *national* context where this makes sense.

Companies benefit not just from national business cultures, but from nation-states and national communities as social organizations. This is emphasized by the literature on national systems of innovation (Lundvall 1992; Nelson 1993; Porter 1990) and on national business systems (Whitley 1992a, 1992b). These national business systems are quite distinct from the forms of homogeneity preached by cultural nationalists, but they remain tenaciously distinctive in a way that many other forms of national culture do not. Companies benefit from being enmeshed in networks of relations with central and local governments, with trade associations, with organized labour, with specifically national financial institutions oriented towards local companies and with national systems of skill formation and labour motivation (chapter 7). These networks provide information, they are a means to cooperation and coordination between firms to secure common objectives and they help to make the business environment less uncertain and more stable. A national economic system provides forms of reassurance to firms against the shocks and risks of the international economy. As we have argued, such national business-oriented systems have been most evident in the developed world in Germany and Japan, both of which have had strongly solidaristic relationships between industry, labour and the state, and in the developing world in such countries as South Korea and Taiwan.

But national advantages are not confined to those societies whose institutions promote solidarity in order to balance cooperation and competition between firms and between the major social interests. The US has a national business culture that emphasizes competition and the autonomy of the individual corporation. But, contra fashionable arguments like those of Reich (1992), US firms find that there are very real benefits in remaining distinctly American that stem from the power and functions of the national state (Kapstein 1991; Tyson 1991; Doremus et al. 1998): for example, that the US dollar still largely remains a key medium of international trade, that regulatory and standard-setting bodies like the Federal Aviation Administration and the Food and Drug Administration are world leaders and work closely with US industry, that the US courts are a major means of defence of commercial and property rights throughout the world, that the federal government is a massive subsidizer of R&D and also a strong protector of the interests of US firms abroad (chapter 7).

The extreme globalization theorists paint a picture of a world set free for business to serve consumers. States and military power cease to matter in the face of global markets. In this view, economics and politics are pulling apart, and the latter is declining at the expense of the former. As markets dominate and the results of markets are legitimated by free competition and seen to be beyond national control, so states come to have less capacity to control economic outcomes or to alter them by force. Attempts to use military force for economic objectives against the interests of world markets would be subject to devastating, if unplanned, economic sanction: plunging exchange rates, turbulent stock exchanges, declining trade, etc. War would cease to have any connection with economic rationality – most societies would have become inescapably 'industrial' rather than 'militant'. War would become the recourse of failed and economically backward societies and political forces, driven by economically irrational goals like ethnic homogeneity or religion. This world free for trade is the dream of classical economic liberalism since its inception.

Markets and companies cannot exist without a public power to protect them, whether it is at the world level where the major states confront authoritarian regional powers that seek to annex wealth by force, as with Saddam Hussein's seizure of Kuwait, or at the local level of policing against pirates or gangsters. The advanced states do at present trade predominantly one with another and, indeed, are unlikely to fight one another. But the world's free trading order does require military force to back it and this only the advanced countries, and in particular the US, can provide (Hirst 1994a).

The advantages provided by public power to companies and markets are not confined to the national level. Indeed, for many vital services to business and forms of cooperation between firms, national-level institutions are too remote for adequate local knowledge and effective governance. We argued earlier that regional governments are providers of vital collective services to industry throughout the advanced industrial world. In particular, regional governments are the public articulation of industrial districts composed of small and medium-sized firms, and are a major reason why such firms can be internationally competitive and enjoy advantages comparable to the economies of scale of larger firms. The existence of regional economic governance, of thriving industrial districts and of an effective partnership and division of labour between national states and regional governments is a central component of the success of national economies in world markets.[7]

If the foregoing arguments have any merit then the majority of companies, large and small, that are active in international markets have a strong interest in continued public governance, national and international, of the world economy. Internationally they seek a measure of security and stability in financial markets, a secure framework of free trade, and the protection of commercial rights. Nationally they seek to profit from the distinct advantages conferred by the cultural and institutional frameworks of the successful industrial states. If companies have such interests then it is highly unlikely that an ungoverned global economy composed of unregulated markets will come into existence. Globalization theorists tend to rely either on the providentialist assumptions derived from a simplistic reading of neo-classical economics, that as markets approach perfection and freedom from external intervention they become more efficient as allocative mechanisms, or on the gloomy suppositions of the Marxist left, that international capital is an unequivocally malevolent force and one indifferent to national or local concerns. In the former case, the public power is a virtual irrelevance and its actions (beyond essential tasks like the protection of property) can do little but harm. In the latter case, political authority submits to the will of capital and can do nothing to counter it within the existing world system.

In this and previous chapters we have argued that there are good economic grounds for arguing that the international economy is by no means ungovernable. To recap from chapter 7, therefore, governance is possible at five levels from the international economy to the industrial district by means of:

1   agreement between the major advanced states, and particularly the G3;
2   a substantial number of states creating international regulatory agencies for some specific dimension of economic activity, like the WTO;
3   the governance of large economic areas by trade blocs such as the EU or NAFTA;
4   national-level policies that balance cooperation and competition between firms and the major social interests;
5   regional-level policies of providing collective services to industrial districts.

Such institutional arrangements and strategies can assure some minimal level of international economic governance, at least to the benefit of the major advanced industrial nations. Such governance cannot alter the extreme inequalities between those nations and the rest in terms of trade and investment, income and wealth. Unfortunately, that is not really the problem raised by the concept of globalization. The issue is not whether the world's economy is governable towards ambitious goals like promoting social justice, equality between countries and greater democratic control for the bulk of the world's people, but whether it is governable *at all*.

The 'new' sovereignty

If such mechanisms of international governance and reregulation are to be initiated then the role of nation-states is pivotal. Nation-states should no longer be seen as 'governing' powers, able to impose outcomes on all dimensions of policy within a given territory by their own authority, but as loci from which forms of governance can be proposed, legitimated and monitored. Nation-states are now simply one class of powers and political agencies in a complex system of power from world to local levels, but they have a centrality because of their relationship to territory and population.

Populations remain territorial and subject to the citizenship of a national state. States remain 'sovereign', not in the sense that they are all-powerful or omnicompetent within their territories, but because they police the borders of a territory and, to the degree that they are credibly democratic, they are representative of the citizens within those borders. Regulatory regimes, international agencies, common policies sanctioned by treaty, all come into existence because major nation-states have agreed to create them and to confer legitimacy on them by pooling sovereignty. Sovereignty is alienable, states cede power to suprastate agencies, but it is not a fixed quantum. Sovereignty is alienable and divisible, but states acquire new roles even as they cede power, and in particular they come to have the function of legitimating and supporting the authorities they have created by such grants of sovereignty. If 'sovereignty' is of decisive significance now as a distinguishing feature of the nation-state, it is because the state has the role of a source of legitimacy in transferring power or sanctioning new powers both 'above' it and 'below' it. Above – through agreements between states to establish and abide by forms of international governance. Below – through the state's constitutional ordering within its own territory of the relationship of power and authority between central, regional and local governments and also the publicly recognized private governments in civil society. Nation-states are still of central significance because they are the key practitioners of the art of government as the process of distributing power, ordering other governments by giving them shape and legitimacy. Nation-states can do this in a way no other agency can; they are pivots between international agencies and subnational activities because they provide legitimacy as the exclusive voice of a territorially bounded population. They can practise the art of government as a process of distributing power only if they can credibly present their decisions as having the legitimacy of popular support.

In a system of governance in which international agencies and regulatory bodies are already significant and are growing in scope, nation-states are crucial agencies of representation. Such a system of governance amounts to a global polity and in it the major nation-states are the global 'electors'.[8] States ensure that, in a very mediated degree, international bodies are answerable to the world's key publics, and that decisions backed by the major states can be enforced by international agencies because they will be reinforced by domestic laws and local state power.

Such representation is very indirect, but it is the closest to democracy and accountability that international governance is likely to get. The key publics in advanced democracies have some influence on their states and these states can affect international policies. Such influence is likely to be increased if the populations of major states are informed and roused on an issue by the world 'civil society' of transnational non-governmental organizations. Such NGOs, like Greenpeace or the Red Cross, are more credible candidates to be genuine transnational actors than are companies. It is easier to create a cosmopolitan agency for common world causes like the environment or human rights than it is to build a rootless business whose staff are asked to identify with its mundane activities above all else in the world.

Moreover, the category of non-governmental organizations is a misnomer. They are not governments, but many of them play crucial roles of governance, especially in the interstices between states and international regulatory regimes. Thus Greenpeace effectively helps to police international agreements on whaling. Equally, where nation-states are indeed as weak and ineffective as the globalization theorists suppose *all* states to be, as in parts of Africa, NGOs like Oxfam provide some of the elementary functions of government such as education, as well as famine relief.

An internationally governed economic system in which certain key policy dimensions are controlled by world agencies, trade blocs and major treaties between nation-states ensuring common policies will thus continue to give the nation-state a role. This role stresses the specific feature of nation-states that other agencies lack, their ability to make bargains stick: upwards because they are representative of territories, and downwards because they are constitutionally legitimate powers. Paradoxically then, the degree to which the world economy has internationalized (but not globalized) reinstates the need for the nation-state, not in its traditional guise as the sole sovereign power, but as a crucial relay between the international levels of governance and the articulate publics of the developed world.

Nation-states and the rule of law

So far we have discussed the persistence of the nation-state primarily in terms of its role within a system of international governance. There is, however, another reason to argue that the 'nation' state will persist as an important form of political organization, a reason closely connected with one of the central traditional claims to 'sovereignty', that is, to be the primary source of binding rules – law – within a given territory. This role of the state as monopoly lawmaker was closely connected with the development of a monopoly of the means of violence and with the development of a coherent system of administration providing the principal means of governance within a territory. Today, however, this role of upholding the rule of law is relatively independent of those other elements in the historical process of the formation of the modern state.

To sum up the argument in advance: nation-states as sources of the rule of law are essential prerequisites for regulation through international law, and as overarching public powers they are essential to the survival of pluralistic 'national' societies with diversified forms of administration and community standards. States may be the key source of the rule of law without being 'sovereign' in the traditional sense, that is, standing against all external entities as the sole means of government in a territory, or standing above subnational governments and associations as the body from which they derive their powers by recognition and concession. Omnicompetence, exclusivity and omnipotence of the state are not necessary to the rule of law: indeed, historically they have been the attributes of states, deriving from the portmanteau theory of sovereignty, that have served to undermine it.

States have been janus-faced: substantive decision-making and administrative powers, on one hand, and sources of rules limiting their own actions and those of their citizens, on the other. These two aspects may be pulling apart, and in large measure for the good. The power of nation-states as administrative and policy-making agencies has declined. We have seen that the decline in the salience of war and the restriction of the scope of national economic management have lessened the claims that states as governing agencies can make on their societies. This does not mean that the lawmaking and constitutional ordering functions of states will decline in the same measure. One aspect of the state is substantive and outcome oriented, a matter of political decision and the implementation of such decisions through administration; the other aspect is procedural and concerns the state's role as regulator of social action in the widest sense, of rules as guides to action and of constitutional ordering as adjudicating between the competing claims of corporate entities and citizens.

The state as a source of constitutional ordering, limiting its own and others' powers and guiding action through rights and rules, is central to the rule of law (Hirst 1994b). Commercial societies require that minimum of certainty and constancy in the action of administrators and economic actors that the rule of law implies. Western societies have been economically successful and reactively civilized in their treatment of their members when they have provided the security and the certainty of the rule of law, limiting the harms that citizens, companies and governments could do. Politics, ideology and state policy have frequently undermined the rule of law, governments abandoning the civilized limits of state action in the pursuit of overarching political goals.

If we are moving into a more complex and pluralistic social and political system then the rule of law will become more important rather than less. Even more so than in the sphere of administrative regulation, 'gaps' between jurisdictions are fatal to the certainty and security necessary for actors in a commercial society, for they allow the unscrupulous to evade their own obligations and to violate others' rights. For example, tax havens, flags of convenience, dumping grounds for pollution, etc., all allow advanced world economic actors to avoid First World obligations. A world composed of diverse political forces, governing agencies, and organizations at both international and national levels will need an interlocking network of public powers that regulate and guide action in a relatively consistent way, providing minimum standards of conduct and reliefs from harms. In this sense we are considering constitutional ordering and the rule of law in their aspect as a *pouvoir neutre*, not as part of issue-oriented politics or administrative regulation. Our model for such a power remains the *Rechtsstaat*, and national states are its primary embodiment in so far as they correspond to that conception of authority as a source of law that is itself lawful and limited in its action by rules.

Within states the role of such an independent public power that arbitrates between other powers, that is neutral between plural and competing social communities with different standards and that provides highly individuated citizens with a common procedural basis on which to regulate their interactions will become more important rather than less. A pluralistic system of authority and pluralistic communities require a public power as the medium through which they may contain their conflicts. As Figgis (1913) argued at the beginning of the century, the decline of the excessive claims of state 'sovereignty' does *not* mean the end of a lawmaking public power. The state may no longer be 'sovereign' in this old sense, it may share authority with subnational governments whose specific autonomous powers are guaranteed, it may no longer view associations and corporate bodies as legal fictions that have been granted what powers they have by its own revokable *fiat*, but it will define the scope of legitimate authority and legitimate action in its roles as constitutional arbitrator and lawmaker.

In an individualistic and pluralistic society, where there are few common standards, where strong binding collectivities have declined and been replaced by communities of choice, and where informal social sanctions have weakened, then the rule of law is more rather than less necessary. This does not mean that states will be able to cope fully with the multiple problems and conflicts that arise from the growing pluralism of modern societies; rather we are claiming that without a public power that mediates between these plural groups through the rule of law, such conflicts will become intolerable (Hirst 1993, ch. 3). In a sense the decline of war as a source of national cohesion and the lessening role of the state as an economic manager reduce the powers and claims that states can exert over society as administrative agencies and focuses of political identification. They have less capacity to impose external cohesion on groups. The other consequence of this is that they are becoming less janus-faced, less encumbered with the need to balance their roles as primary administrator and neutral public power in a way that makes it easier for them credibly to give primacy to the latter role. A cooling of national politics gives states the space to expand their role as an arbiter between conflicting interests, something that the excessive and overcharged claims to 'sovereignty' as omnicompetence made problematic.

Externally, the role of states as sources of the rule of law will also become more central. If international economic, environmental and social governance expands, so the role of international law will increase. International agencies, international regimes based on treaties and interstate agreements, international 'civil' agencies performing world public functions in the defence of human rights and environmental standards, all imply an extension of the scope of international law. However, international law cannot function without national states, not merely as its material supports and the agents to whom it is addressed, but as *Rechtsstaats*, agencies that create and abide by law. International law without a significant population of states that are sources of the rule of law is a contradictory enterprise. It is like states imposing laws on citizens who do not internalize rules or govern their actions by such rules. An international society as an association of states cannot rely on supranational bodies to make and enforce laws but requires states that accept constitutional limitations above and below them. In this sense the move from an anarchical society of states to a world in which states are part of a common association requires that the member states of that association accept international legal obligations and also govern internally according to the requirements of the rule of law. In this sense the state as the source and the respecter of binding rules remains central to an internationalized economy and society.

Notes

1 Introduction: Globalization – a Necessary Myth?

1   This distinction between MNCs and TNCs is not usual. There is a tendency to use the terms interchangeably, with TNC increasingly adopted as a generally accepted term for both types. Where we use the term TNC it should be clear that we are referring to *true* TNCs in the context of discussing the strong globalizer's view.

2   Obviously, conjunctural changes *could* result in a change of the international economic system: the question is whether they have? Our point here is to caution against citing phenomena generated by such changes as if they were part of and evidence of a process of structural transformation driven by deep-seated causes, called 'globalization'.

2 Globalization and the History of the International Economy

1   By the term 'autonomy' we mean the ability of the authorities in a national economy to determine their own economic policy and implement that policy. This is obviously a matter of degree. Autonomy is closely linked to 'openness', 'interdependence' and 'integration', three other categories used in this and subsequent chapters. Openness implies the degree to which national economies are subject to the actions of economic agents located outside their borders and the extent to which their own economic agents are orientated towards external economic activity. This is in turn linked to the degree of interdependence of the economic system in which these agents operate. Thus interdependence expresses the systemic links between all economic activity within a system or regime. Integration is the process by which interdependence is established.

2   France devalued twice, in 1957 and 1958, Germany in 1961, Britain in 1967 and Germany and France again in 1969; all against the US dollar, hence the designation of this period as a dollar standard.

3   This refers to the exchange rate element of the BWS only. The total BWS
    package comprised not just its exchange rate part but also the activity of
    the International Monetary Fund and the World Bank. In so far as these two
    institutions still exist and function much as planned at the Bretton Woods
    conference, these elements of the BWS still operate.

4   Take possibly the simplest case of short-term interest rate differentials. These
    rates will be affected by local regulations, by the riskiness and precise duration
    of the loans, by local structural conditions, by the possibilities of generating
    monopoly rents, and so on. Thus differences between rates in financial centres
    could be due to these conditions rather than to the integration or separation
    of markets as such.

5   This scepticism is registered in the careful analyses contained in Banuri and
    Schor 1992.

6   An analysis using the Feldstein–Horioka framework for the EU countries'
    savings and investment ratios over two subperiods 1971–89 and 1990–5 found
    an ambiguous change in the value of the β coefficient, but concluded that this
    indicated 'weak, but positive evidence that the EU as a whole has been more
    open to the rest of the world as regards capital movements' (European Union
    1997a, box 1, p. 5).

7   Of course this emphasis on the relationship between domestic savings and
    domestic investment might seem to reinforce the neoclassical view of invest-
    ment determination. The critique of this from an essentially post-Keynesian
    perspective is that the constraint on investment is not savings but the ability to
    raise finance for investment. In an advanced industrial economy with a devel-
    oped financial system, credit creation is the key to investment; it is the access
    to 'liquidity' that determines economic activity, and this is endogenously
    created.
        Formally we would agree with this analysis for mature advanced economies
    with a developed banking system operating efficiently in an essentially stable
    financial environment. However, we would emphasize that there are two excep-
    tions to this image. The first is for those societies that remain less developed,
    that have an *underdeveloped* banking system in particular. The second is for
    those economies that have an *overdeveloped* financial system typified by spec-
    ulation and instability. In both these cases, the 'normal' financing system for
    investment either simply does not exist, or breaks down in the face of specu-
    lative pressures. In addition, we would argue that it is this second case that
    increasingly typifies the position faced in the advanced industrial countries.
    In both of these cases, however, we are thrown back on to a more 'primitive'
    conception of what determines investment, namely the brute fact of national
    savings.

8   Of itself convergence is not an adequate indicator of integration. In systems
    theory and evolutionary biology, for instance, there is a tendency for elements
    and species to converge despite there being no necessary *relationship* between
    them. Thus the key to integration is to specify a relationship, which convergence
    does not of itself provide.

9   Before 1870 the British suspended convertibility in 1847, 1857 and 1866, but
    each time restored it quickly again at the previous parity. It should be noted,
    however, that there were a large number of suspensions of, withdrawals from
    and readmissions to the system among the peripheral economies.

10   This is a somewhat controversial position: the general sentiment is that the US Federal Reserve Board was unique among central banks in being able to unilaterally stabilize its own price level – inclusive of tradable goods.

3   Multinational Companies and the Internationalization of Business Activity

1   However, this was down from 75 per cent for a similar group of countries during the 1980s (see Hirst and Thompson 1996, table 3.2, p. 68).
2   In 1993 the six most important country investors abroad were the US ($50,244 million), the UK ($25,332 million), Japan ($13,600 million), France ($12,166 million), Germany ($11,673 million), and the Netherlands ($10,404 million) (*Financial Market Trends* (OECD), no. 58 (June 1993), table 1, p. 16). Thus this analysis covers the main externally investing countries in the late 1980s and early 1990s.
3   Thus the 'home region' for German companies in all years comprises Germany itself, the rest of Europe, the Middle East and Africa (although these latter two areas account for a very low proportion of overall sales); 'home region' for Japanese companies comprises Japan and South East Asia; for the UK it comprises the UK itself, the rest of Europe, the Middle East and Africa (here, too, the latter two areas were not very important for sales); and for US companies it includes the US and Canada. These aggregations are dictated by the way it was possible to code the 1987 data.
4   Assets are measured as total assets for these calculations (total assets include financial assets and inventories as well as fixed assets). A better indicator would be either net fixed assets or operating assets, which relate more closely to the real capital stock. These were not extractable from the company accounts. Thus these data probably overestimate the value of real capital assets involved. These problems become more acute for some of the financial institutions included in the 'service' category of companies.
5   The analysis conducted here mainly refers to manufacturing, banking and new IT technologies. But the traditional service sectors are also internationalizing, as indicated by the quantitative analysis reported above. In fact, the case of accounting and law firms largely confirms the points already made. The strategic management of these firms and the way they 'fit' into the business systems where they are newly locating is evolving in a similar way to that analysed in the case of manufacturing firms (see Barrett, Cooper and Jamal 1997; and Spar 1997).

4   North–South Trade and International Competitiveness

1   NICs included here are Hong Kong, Taiwan, Republic of Korea, Singapore, Thailand, Indonesia, Malaysia, Philippines, India, China, Argentina, Brazil, Mexico, Czechoslovakia, Hungary and Poland.
2   In fact, as explained in chapter 2, the ratio of trade to GDP is likely to exaggerate the extent of 'openness' of economies, because trade is a consumption measure while GDP is a value-added measure.

3   The European Union increased its imports of manufactures from the NICs from 0.22 per cent of its GDP in 1970 to 1.30 per cent in 1990 (Krugman 1995, table 4, p. 337).
4   The level of merchandise trade between the Triad and the non-NIC LDCs was always less than 1 per cent of Triad country GDP in 1996.
5   Politically this protectionist sentiment at the time was strongly registered by Ross Perot and Pat Buchanan in the US and by Sir James Goldsmith in Europe (see Goldsmith 1994).
6   We leave land out of this for the moment, though see Wood and Berge 1997.
7   And also, clearly, in the South, though this aspect is less well researched in the literature.
8   The Minford, Riley and Nowell estimate is a rogue one from the point of view of the mainstream, and may be the result of the extreme nature of the general equilibrium model employed. For instance, it assumes a perfectly competitive international market in the long run (1997, p. 5). In fact, the whole H-O approach is couched in a constant returns, entry barrier-free world, though there have been attempts to recast this in a more oligopolistic framework (see Helpman 1981).
9   In fact, this differential experience in respect to labour market operations as between continental Europe and the US has led to the addition of another explanation for the collapse of US unskilled wages and employment prospects. Thurow suggests that the reason lies not in the relationship between the US and the 'South', but in the relation between the US and Europe and Japan. His explanation is an intra-OECD one. Given the greater importance of trade between the US and Europe and Japan than that between the US and the 'South' (see figs 4.2 and 4.4), the more likely adjustment concerns intra-OECD factor price equalization as trade has developed between the US and Europe and Japan (1997, ch. 8).
10 The analysis on which table 4.5 is based straddles the period of the rapid loss of competitiveness of the UK economy over the period 1979 to 1981 as well as the following period of the growth in competitiveness. This accounts for the *average* loss of competitiveness shown in the table over the entire period 1978–94 (measured by RULC).

5   The Developing Economies and Globalization

1   The example of India stands as the exception to the rule when attempts are made to link democracy and prosperity, even though, given the tribulations of democracy in India, it shows how difficult it is to combine democracy with gross and widening inequality (see Khilnani 1997).

6   Can the Welfare State Survive Globalization?

1   For more balanced surveys of the literature on the issue of globalization and the welfare state see Martin 1996 and Rhodes 1996.
2   On Sweden's specific institutional features see Ivesen 1996 and Pontusson and Swenson 1996.

3   Fajertag and Pochet 1997 and ILO 1995 give details of the major pacts and their content.

4   As Nickell (1997) points out, there is little econometric evidence for the proposition that high social costs on employment do tend directly to high levels of unemployment (see chapter 4 above): Scharpf is hypothesizing a rational actor here. He may be wrong, but, whatever the statistical evidence, employers do tend to perceive things in this way.

5   Many of Scharpf's proposals have been widely scouted. Thus the former UK social security minister Frank Field has proposed a very similar system of 'top-up' pensions in the context of reforming the British pensions system, which is low in cost and sustainable but with the consequence of very poor benefits and widespread poverty among the elderly (Field 1996). There have been many advocates of employee share ownership, the most articulate of whom is Weitzman (1984), who sees advantages not just in greater worker involvement or control, but in the strong incentives that an equity income provides and the redistributive benefits of workers' access to the income stream from profits in the company. Of course, the problem when such income becomes a normal part of workers' pay is that it is far more volatile than wages. Large numbers of employees are already indirect holders of equity and dependent on occupational pension funds for their retirement incomes. Typically, however, they have neither individual nor collective control of these funds. Perhaps pension fund trustees should be encouraged to take a more active role and ensure that fund managers behave in such a way that their members' employment is preserved as well as their retirement income. As a large amount of capital is generated from the incomes of labour, it could be used more responsibly and with regard to the national economy. In the US tax credits for low-income workers are envisaged as an alternative to welfare benefits and entitlements, but there is no reason why they should be used in this way in Europe, where they could supplement wages but not replace benefit rights. On citizen's income see Atkinson 1996; McKay 1998; Van Parijs 1992.

7   Economic Governance Issues in General

1   The G7 are the US, Germany, Japan, the UK, France, Canada and Italy. The addition of Russia comprises the G8.

2   As another example, the domestic structure and organization of Japanese retailing can preclude the implementation of internationally agreed norms for 'market access', and there is little that Japanese governments can do about this.

3   Clearly, this relationship between the US and Japan would seem to break the high correlation between national saving and investment ratios discussed in chapter 2. However, while it does this for these two countries, there is no indication that things have dramatically changed in other countries, and Europe as a whole has not followed the trend (European Union 1997a, p. 5, and the discussion in chapter 2 above, pp. 38–42). This also pertains to overall financial flows, not necessarily just to private real resource flows. Finally, of course, there is no necessary reason why this situation should continue indefinitely. The old relationships could be re-established.

4   The IOSCO promotes harmonization and cooperation between different national regulatory environments. Among the major issues discussed at its

recent meetings have been capital adequacy standards, supervision of financial conglomerates, international auditing standards, coordination between cash and derivatives markets, money laundering, means of combating insider dealing, transparency in secondary market transactions, and emerging securities markets. It has set up a number of technical committees to investigate these areas, with an aim of agreeing regulatory principles for them.

5   The collapse of the US hedge fund, Long Term Capital Management, in October 1998 offered another example of this process at work: the US Federal Reserve Board led and secured its rescue.

6   The Final Act was signed in Marrakesh, Morocco, on 15 April 1994.

7   At the international level UNCTAD conducts this kind of an analysis from the Geneva headquarters of its Division on Transnational Corporations and Investment. UNCTAD and the DTCI also have extensive expertise on issues such as transfer pricing.

8   Clearly, the case of the UK alcohol market has shown that some people will travel to continental Europe to obtain their purchases at a lower tax rate. While an important example, this should not be exaggerated: there is extensive compliance with the existing situation by most consumers.

8   The European Union as a Trade Bloc

1   We say this despite all the contemporary hype about the future role of China in the world economy. As chapter 3 has shown, the Triad of North America, Japan and the EU accounted for 60 per cent of world trade, 70 per cent of world GDP and 75 per cent of FDI flows over the early 1990s. Thus what happens with respect to these three players will for all practical intents and purposes determine the course of the world economy for the foreseeable future.

2   Clearly one might expect some things to be better done in the context of unitary state forms than federal ones, like securing redistributive objectives for instance: see CEPR 1993 for an interesting discussion of the range of economic functions that are best secured under different governmental formations.

3   Of course, subsidiarity should not be taken as the sole criterion for the present debate about the limits of centralization and decentralization in Europe. There are at least three others: harmonization, common treatment and the idea of a 'level playing field'. Each of these would need to be examined in the light of the confederal/federal distinction developed here.

4   The most important, of course, are the 1986 Single European Act and the 1992 Maastricht Treaty.

5   The positive argument for a confederal public power solution can itself be bolstered by a further set of political categories having their origin in the notion of 'associationalism'. This constitutes a further grounding principle for the confederal form. (On associationalism and a defence of genuine political plurality in constitutional matters, see Hirst 1989, 1993). For some detail on the emergent forms of this associationalism in respect to the regional and local economic mechanisms in Europe, and the political impact of these for extended forms of economic governance and the role of the central supportive mechanisms, see Thompson 1993.

6 Britain has a particularly rabid and silly form of resistance to the EU –
   'Euroscepticism'. This attacks all extensions of the scope of European policy,
   all future integration and any increase in common decision procedures as
   'federalism'. This is constitutionally foolish, since no major European leaders
   or parties support ceding power to a European state.

9 Globalization, Governance and the Nation-State

1 This discussion of nationalism draws on two quite contrary approaches, that of
   Benedict Anderson (1991) which stresses the character of cultural homogeneity as a political project, and that of Eric Hobsbawm (1992) whose scepticism
   about nationalist politics and whose practice of confronting the rhetoric of
   nationalists with the political and cultural complexities they seek to homoge-
   nize is a healthy corrective.
2 This is in many ways the entry of states into a 'civil order' and no longer an
   anarchy: it moves international relations on beyond the 'deterred state' and
   closer to the solution to the nuclear stand-off advocated by Schell 1984.
3 Proliferation is unlikely to undermine this proposition. The mutual possession
   of nuclear weapons by antagonistic regional powers (like India and Pakistan)
   will result in a state of deterrence and also a curb on conventional military
   adventures. Indeed, the BJP-led coalition government's foolish decision to go
   nuclear has had the effect of negating India's vast conventional military superiority over Pakistan. Major nuclear powers will strive to disarm pariah states
   like Iraq or North Korea, in the case of Iraq with some modest degree of
   success. The real dangers stem from the break-up of unstable regimes with
   nuclear weapons and nuclear terrorism. The former will probably be subject to
   political and military sanction by the great powers, and the latter, while a real
   threat, cannot be contained either by deterrence or by conventional war – it is
   an intelligence and police matter.
4 It has become fashionable to erect political Islam, and other anti-Western
   movements, into a major threat (see for example Huntington 1993, 1997). Huntington argues that after the ending of the conflict of ideologies we are moving
   into a new era of the 'clash of civilizations'. Four points can be made against
   this claim: (1) it is not evident that there are homogeneous 'civilizations' intrin-
   sically opposed one to another – rather there are relatively brittle politico-
   religious ideologies that are highly particular constructions of Islam or, among
   fundamentalist conservatives in the West, Christianity; (2) radical political
   Islam lacks a coherent and practical strategy for economic and social life; (3)
   in the case of Islam such politics are those of protest rather than general and
   allegedly hegemonic alternatives to capitalism, as socialism claimed to be in the
   East and West; (4) Islamic fundamentalist regimes are radically different in
   character and often extremely hostile one to another. On political Islam, see
   Zubaida 1993.
5 For an interesting series of discussions of the difference between governance
   and government and of the possible forms of non-state regulation in international arenas, see Rosenau and Czempiel 1992; see also the World Bank's
   attempt to define the roles of states in respect to good governance in its 1994
   report *Governance*.

6   It is probably the case that Keynes's main legacy to the modern world is not his account of the management of national economies in *The General Theory* but his long-term emphasis on the corrosive effects of uncertainty on investment, output and trade and the value of a calculable international monetary framework in stabilizing expectations. Skidelsky's biography (1992) is exceptionally valuable and suggestive in demonstrating the value of Keynes's ideas today, for it shows him (especially in the 1920s) wrestling with the problem of national policy in a highly internationalized and volatile world economy.

7   See Ohmae (1993) for the argument that region states can become salient in an era when nation-states are declining. Region states or networks of city-states are another thing entirely from organized industrial districts or subsidiary regional governments, and although they are a fashionable idea (building on the success of Singapore or Hong Kong), they are unlikely to become a widespread *alternative* to nation-states. They rely both on strong international economic governance and on the collective security provided by major states. They are too small to survive alone in the face of less economically successful but militarily strong political powers. They cannot bear the full costs of security or economic regulation alone without losing competitive advantage, and larger political entities will not allow them to free ride if they become differentially successful and put competitive pressure on their own economies.

8   The reference here is to those princes of the Holy Roman Empire who enjoyed the right to elect the Emperor. The Empire was not a 'sovereign' state but a political entity made up of associated institutions with varying powers of governance: its policies were determined by the Emperor, the Electors and the Imperial Diet. It could hardly be a model for the modern world, but given our need to understand emerging political relationships it has some limited value as an analogy. For debates on the constitutional status of the Empire in the period of the formation of the modern state, see Franklin 1991.

References

Akyuz, Y. and Cornford, A. (1995) Controlling capital movements: some proposals for reform. In J. Michie and J. Grieve-Smith (eds), *Managing the Global Economy*, Oxford: Oxford University Press.

Albeck, E. et al. (n.d.) Managing the Danish welfare state under pressure: toward a dynamic theory of the dilemmas of the welfare state. MS.

Allen, J. and Thompson, G. F. (1997) Think global, and then think again: economic globalization in context. *Area*, 29(3), pp. 213–27.

Anderson, B. (1991) *Imagined Communities*. London: Verso.

Anderson, K. (1996) Environmental standards and international trade. In M. Burno and B. Pleskovic (eds), *Annual World Bank Conference on Development Economics 1996*, Washington DC: IBRD, pp. 317–38.

Archibugi, D. and Michie, J. (1997) The globalization of technology: a new taxonomy. In D. Archibugi and J. Michie (eds), *Technology, Globalization and Economic Performance*, Cambridge: Cambridge University Press.

Arestis, P. and Sawyer, M. (1997) How many cheers for the Tobin transactions tax? *Cambridge Journal of Economics*, 21, pp. 753–68.

Arthur, W. B. (1996) Increasing returns and the new world of business. *Harvard Business Review*, July–Aug., pp. 100–9.

Artis, M. and Ostry, M. (1984) International policy coordination. *Chatham House Papers*, no. 30. London: Royal Institute for International Affairs.

Asheim, B. T. and Isaksen, A. (1997) Location, agglomeration and innovation: towards regional innovation systems in Norway? *European Planning Studies*, 5(3), pp. 299–330.

Atkinson, A. B. (1996) The case for a participation income. *Political Quarterly*, 67(1), pp. 67–70.

Atkinson, D. and Kelly, R. (1994) *The Wrecker's Lamp: Do Currency Markets Leave Us on the Rocks?* London: IPPR.

Atkinson, M. (1998) Which next hot spot is anyone's guess. *The Guardian*, 12 Jan., p. 17.

Auerbach, P. (1996) Firms, competitiveness and the global economy. In M. Mackintosh, V. Brown, N. Costello, G. Dawson, G. Thompson and A. Trigg (eds), *Economics and Changing Economies*, London: International Thompson Business Press.

Baccaro, L. and Locke, R. (1996) Public sector reform and union participation: the case of Italian pension reform. Paper presented at APSA conference, San Francisco.

Bailey, D., Hart, G. and Sugden, R. (1994) *Making Transnationals Accountable*. London: Routledge.

Banuri, T. and Schor, J. B. (eds) (1992) *Financial Openness and National Autonomy*. Oxford: Clarendon Press.

Barrell, R. and Pain, N. (1997) The growth of foreign direct investment in Europe. *National Institute Economic Review*, no. 160 (Apr.), pp. 63–75.

Barrett, M., Cooper, D. J. and Jamal, K. (1997) 'That's pretty close' and the 'friction of space': managing a global audit. In *Accounting Time and Space, Proceedings*, vol. 1, ed. Helle K. Rasmussen, Copenhagen: Copenhagen Business School.

Barrington Moore, J. M. (1967) *The Social Origins of Dictatorship and Democracy*. London: Allen Lane.

Bartlett, C. A. and Goshal, S. (1989) *Managing across Borders: The Transnational Solution*. Boston: Harvard Business School Press.

Bayoumi, T. (1990) Saving-investment correlations: immobile capital, government policy or endogenous behaviour? *IMF Staff Papers*, 37(2), pp. 360–87.

Bayoumi, T. and MacDonald, R. (1995) Consumption, income and international capital integration. *IMF Staff Papers*, 43(3), pp. 552–76.

Bayoumi, T. A. and Rose, A. K. (1993) Domestic savings and intra-national capital flows. *European Economic Review*, 37, pp. 1197–202.

Bergsten, C. F. (1994) Managing the world economy of the future. In P. B. Kenen (ed.), *Managing the World Economy: Fifty Years after Bretton Woods*, Washington DC: Institute for International Economics.

Bhagwati, J. (1998) The capital myth. *Foreign Affairs*, May–June, pp. 7–12.

BIS (1996–7) *Annual Report*. Geneva: Bank for International Settlements.

BIS (1998) *68th Annual Report*. Geneva: Bank for International Settlements.

Bispink, R. (1997) The chequered history of the Alliance for Jobs. In Fajertag and Pochet 1997, pp. 63–78.

Bodin, J. (1992) *On Sovereignty* (1576), ed. J. H. Franklin. Cambridge: Cambridge University Press.

Borjas, G. J., Freeman, R. B. and Katz, L. F. (1997) How much do immigration and trade affect labor market outcomes? *Brookings Papers on Economic Activity*, no. 1, pp. 1–90.

Borrus, M. and Zysman, J. (1997) Globalization with borders: the rise of Wintelism as the future of global competition. *Industry and Innovation*, 4(2), pp. 141–66.

Bosworth, B. P. (1993) *Saving and Investment in a Global Economy*. Washington DC: Brookings Institution.

Brodie, B. (1946) *The Absolute Weapon*. New York: Harcourt Brace.

Brodie, B. (1965) *Strategy in the Missile Age*. Princeton: Princeton University Press.

Bull, H. (1977) *The Anarchical Society: A Study of Order in World Politics*. London: Macmillan.

Cantwell, J. (1992) The internationalisation of technological activity and its implications for competitiveness. In O. Granstrand, L. Hakanson and S. Sjolander (eds), *Technology Management and International Business*, Chichester: Wiley.

Casson, M., Pearce, R. D. and Singh, S. (1992) Global integration through the decentralisation of R & D. In M. Casson (ed.), *International Business and Global Integration*, Basingstoke: Macmillan.

Castles, S. and Miller, M. J. (1993) *The Age of Mass Migration*. Basingstoke: Macmillan.

CEPR (Centre for Economic Policy Rescarch) (1993) *Making Sense of Subsidiarity: How Much Centralization for Europe?* Monitoring European Integration Report 4. London: CEPR.

CEPR (Centre for Economic Policy Research) (1995) *Flexible Integration: Towards a More Effective and Democratic Europe*. Monitoring European Integration Report 6. London: CEPR.

Cerny, P. (1998) Neomedievalism, civil war and the new security dilemma: globalization as a durable disorder. *Civil Wars*, 1(1), pp. 36–64.

Chang, H. J. (1998) Korea: the misunderstood crisis. *World Development*, 26(8).

Chesnais, F. (1992) National systems of innovation, foreign direct investment and the operations of multinational enterprises. In Lundvall 1992.

Chryssochoou, D. N. (1995) European Union and the dynamics of confederal consociation: problems and prospects for a democratic future. *Journal of European Integration*, 23(2–3), pp. 279–305.

Chryssochoou, D. N. (1997) New challenges to the study of European integration: implications for theory building. *Journal of Common Market Studies*, 35(4), pp. 521–42.

Clapp, J. (1998) The privatization of global environmental governance: ISO 14000 and the developing world. *Global Governance*, 4, pp. 295–316.

Cline, W. R. (1997) *Trade and Income Distribution*. Washington DC: Institute for International Economics.

Coe, D. T. and Helpman, E. (1995) International R & D spillovers. *European Economic Review*, 39 (May), pp. 859–87.

Coe, D. T., Helpman, E. and Hoffmaister, A. (1997) North–South R & D spillovers. *Economic Journal*, 109, pp. 134–49.

Corley, T. A. B. (1994) Britain's overseas investments in 1914 revisited. *Business History*, 36(1), pp. 71–88.

Cosh, A. D., Hughes, A. and Singh, A. (1992) Openness, financial innovation, changing patterns of ownership, and the structure of financial markets. In Banuri and Schor 1992.

Coyle, D. (1998) Guiding global markets. *Prospect*, Jan., pp. 16–19.

Davidson, P. (1997) Are grains of sand in the wheels of international finance sufficient to do the job when boulders are often required? *Economic Journal*, 107 (May), pp. 671–86.

Dicken, P. (1992) *Global Shift: The Internationalization of Economic Activity*, 2nd edn. London: Paul Chapman.

Dicken, P., Forsgren, M. and Malmberg, A. (1994) The local embeddedness of transnational corporations. In A. Amin and N. Thrift (eds), *Globalization, Institutions, and Regional Development in Europe*, Oxford: Oxford University Press.

Dølvik, J. E. and Martin, A. (1997) A spanner in the works and oil in troubled waters: the divergent fates of social pacts in Sweden and Norway. In Fajertag and Pochet 1997, pp. 103–34.

Doremus, P., Keller, W., Pauly, L. and Reich, S. (1998) *The Myth of the Global Corporation*. Princeton: Princeton University Press.

Doyle, M. W. (1983) Kant, liberal legacies and foreign affairs. *Philosophy and Public Affairs*, 12, part.1 pp. 205–35, part.2 pp. 325–53.

Dunning, J. H. (1993) *Multinational Enterprises and the Global Economy*. Wokingham: Addison-Wesley.

Durkheim, E. (1964) *The Division of Labour in Society* (1893). New York: Free Press.

Dutton, M. (1992) *Policing and Punishment in China*. Cambridge: Cambridge University Press.

Economist (1994) The global economy. *Economist* 1 Oct., pp. 3–46.

Economist (1997) The Asian miracle: is it over? *Economist*, 1 Mar., pp. 23–5.

Edey, M. and Hviding, K. (1995) An assessment of financial reform in OECD countries. OECD Economics Department, Working Paper 154, OECD, Paris.

Edgerton, D. (1996) *Science, Technology and the British Industrial 'Decline', 1870–1970*. Cambridge: Cambridge University Press.

Eichengreen, B. (1990) *Elusive Stability*. Cambridge: Cambridge University Press.

Eichengreen, B. (1994) *International Monetary Arrangements for the Twenty-First Century*. Washington DC: Brookings Institution.

Eichengreen, B. and Irwin, D. A. (1995) Trade blocs, currency blocs and the reorientation of world trade in the 1930's. *Journal of International Economics*, 38, pp. 1–24.

Eichengreen, B. and Irwin, D. A. (1997) The role of history in bilateral trade flows. In J. A. Frankel (ed.), *The Regionalization of the World Economy*, Chicago: University of Chicago Press.

Eichengreen, B., Tobin, J. and Wyplosz, C. (1995) Two cases for sand in the wheels of international finance. *Economic Journal*, 105 (Jan.), pp. 162–72.

Engel, C. and Rogers, J. H. (1996) How wide is the border? *American Economic Review*, 86(5), pp. 1112–25.

Esping-Andersen, G. (1990) *The Three Worlds of Welfare Capitalism*. Cambridge: Polity Press.

Esping-Andersen, G. (1996a) After the golden age? Welfare state dilemmas in a global economy. In Esping-Andersen 1996c, pp. 1–31.

Esping-Andersen, G. (1996b) Positive-sum solutions in a world of trade-offs? In Esping-Andersen 1996c, pp. 256–67.

Esping-Andersen, G. (ed.) (1996c) *Welfare States in Transition: National Adaptations in Global Economies*. London: Sage.

European Union (1997a) Advancing financial integration. *European Economy, Supplement A: Economic Trends* 12 (Dec.), EU, Brussels.

European Union (1997b) External aspects of economic and monetary union. Euro-Paper 1, Commission Services, July.

European Union (1997c) *European Union Direct Investment Yearbook 1996*, Luxembourg: EU.

Fagerberg, J. (1996) Technology and competitiveness. *Oxford Review of Economic Policy*, 12(3), pp. 39–51.

Fajertag, G. and Pochet, P. (eds) (1997) *Social Pacts in Europe*. Brussels: European Trade Union Institute/Observatoire Social Européen.

Featherstone, M. (ed.) (1990) *Global Culture: Nationalism, Globalization and Modernity*. London: Sage.

Feenstra, R. C. (1998) Integration of trade and disintegration of production in the global economy. *Brookings Papers on Economic Activity*, 12(4), pp. 31–50.

Feenstra, R. C. and Hanson, G. H. (1996) Globalization, outsourcing, and wage inequality. *American Economic Review, Papers and Proceedings*, 86(2), pp. 240–5.

Feldstein, M. and Bacchetta, P. (1991) National savings and national investment. In B. D. Bernstein and J. B. Shoven (eds), *National Savings and Economic Performance*, Chicago: University of Chicago Press.

Feldstein, M. and Horioka, C. (1980) Domestic savings and international capital flows. *Economic Journal*, 90 (June) pp. 314–29.

Ferrara, M. (1997) The uncertain future of the Italian welfare state. *West European Politics*, 20(1), pp. 231–49.

Field, F. (1996) *How to Pay for the Future: Building a Stakeholders' Welfare*. London: Institute of Community Studies.

Figgis, J. N. (1913) *Churches in the Modern State*. London: Longmans Green.

Flanders, S. (1997) Putting a spotlight on Africa. *Financial Times*, 7 Apr.

Frankel, J. A. (1992) Measuring international capital mobility: a review. *American Economic Review*, 82(2), pp. 197–202.

Frankel, J. A. (1997) *Regional Trading Blocs in the World Economic System*. Washington DC: Institute for International Economics.

Franklin, J. H. (1991) Sovereignty and the mixed constitution. In J. H. Burns (ed.), *The Cambridge History of Political Thought, 1450–1700*, Cambridge: Cambridge University Press, pp. 309–28.

Fransman, M. (1997) Is technology policy obsolete in a globalised world? The Japanese response. In D. Archibugi and J. Michie (eds), *Technology, Globalization and Economic Performance*, Cambridge: Cambridge University Press.

Freeman, R. B. and Katz, L. F. (1994) Rising wage inequality: the United States vs other advanced countries. In R. B. Freeman (ed.), *Working under Different Rules*, New York: Russell Sage Foundation.

Gaddy, C. G. S. and Ickes, B. W. (1998) Beyond a bailout: time to face reality about Russia's 'virtual economy'. *Foreign Affairs*, Sept.–Oct. pp. 53–67.

Galbraith, J. K. (1991) *The Culture of Contentment*. London: Penguin.

Gales, B. P. A. and Sluyterman, K. E. (1993) Outward bound: the rise of Dutch multinationals. In G. Jones and H. G. Schröter (eds), *The Rise of Multinationals in Continental Europe*, Aldershot: Edward Elgar.

Gallie, D., White, M., Chang, Y. and Tomlinson, M. (1998) *Restructuring the Employment Relationship*. Oxford: Oxford University Press.

Garber, P. and Taylor, M. P. (1995) Sand in the wheels of foreign exchange markets: a sceptical note. *Economic Journal*, 105 (Jan.), pp. 173–80.

GATT Secretariat (1993) The Draft Act of the Uruguay Round, press summary. *World Economy*, 16(2), pp. 237–59.

Gershenkron, A. (1966) *Economic Backwardness in Historical Perspective*. Cambridge, Mass.: Belknap Press.

Ghosh, A. R. (1995) International capital mobility amongst the major industrialised countries: too little or too much? *Economic Journal*, 105 (Jan.), pp. 107–28.

Gierke, O. von (1988) *Political Theories of the Middle Ages* (1900), ed. F. W. Maitland. Cambridge: Cambridge University Press.

Gilbert, C. L., Hopkins, R., Powell, A. and Roy, A. (1996) The World Bank: its functions and its future. Global Economic Institutions Working Paper 15, July, Centre for Economic Policy Research, London.

Gill, R. (1998) *Asia under Siege*. Singapore: Epic.

Glyn, A. (1998) Egalitarianism in a global economy. *Boston Review*, 25 (May), pp. 4–8.

Goldsmith, J. (1994) *The Trap*. London: Macmillan.

Goldstein, M. and Mussa, M. (1993) The integration of world capital markets. IMF Research Department Working Paper (WP/93/95), Dec. IMF, Washington DC.

Gordon, D. M. (1996) *Fat and Mean: The Corporate Squeeze of Working Americans and the Myth of Managerial 'Downsizing'*. New York: Free Press.

Goul Andersen, J. (1996) Marginalisation, citizenship and the economy: the capacities of the universalist welfare state in Denmark. In Oddvar Eriksen and Loftager (1996) pp. 155–202.

Goul Andersen, J. (1997a) Beyond retrenchment: welfare politics in Denmark in the 1990s. Dept of Economics, Politics and Public Administration, Aalborg University, Denmark.

Goul Andersen, J. (1997b) Changing labour markets, new social divisions and welfare state support: Denmark in the 1990s. Dept of Economic, Politics and Public Administration, Aalborg University, Denmark.

Goul Andersen, J. (1997c) The Scandinavian welfare model in crisis? Achievements and problems of the Danish welfare state in an age of unemployment and low growth. *Scandinavian Political Studies*, 20(1), pp. 1–31.

Grabel, I. (1998) Rejecting exceptionalism: reinterpreting the Asian financial crisis. Paper presented at conference on Global Stability and World Economic Governance, Robinson College, Cambridge, 13 May.

Graham, E. M. (1996) *Global Corporations and National Governments*. Washington DC: Institute for International Economics.

Grahl, J. and Thompson, G. F. (1995) The prospects for European economic integration: macroeconomics, development models and growth. In P. Arestis and V. Chick (eds), *Finance, Development and Structural Change: Post-Keynesian Perspectives*, Cheltenham: Edward Elgar.

Grassman, S. (1980) Long term trends in openness of national economies. *Oxford Economic Papers*, 32(1), pp. 123–33.

Gray, J. (1996) *After Social Democracy*. Demos: London.

Gray, J. (1998) *False Dawn: The Delusions of Global Capitalism*. London: Granta Books.

Greider, W. (1997) *One World Ready or Not: The Manic Logic of Global Capitalism*. New York: Simon and Schuster.

Grieve Smith, J. (1997) Exchange rate instability and the Tobin tax. *Cambridge Journal of Economics*, 21, pp. 745–52.

Hall, P. A. (ed.) (1989) *The Political Power of Economic Ideas: Keynesianism across Nations*. Princeton: Princeton University Press.

Harden, I. (1995) The constitution of the European Union. *Public Law*, Winter, pp. 609–24.

Harris, L. (1995) International financial markets and national transmission mechanisms. In J. Michie and J. Grieve Smith (eds), *Managing the Global Economy*, Oxford: Oxford University Press.

Hart, J. (1992) *Rival Capitalists: International Competitiveness in the United States, Japan, and Western Europe*. Ithaca: Cornell University Press.

Held, D. (1991) Democracy, the nation-state and the global system. *Economy and Society*, 20(2), pp. 138–72.

Held, D. (1995) *Democracy and the Global Order: From the Modern State to Cosmopolitan Governance*. Cambridge: Polity Press.

Helleiner, E. (1994) *States and the Reemergence of Global Finance: From Bretton Woods to the 1990s*. Ithaca: Cornell University Press.

Helpman, E. (1981) International trade in the presence of product differentiation, economies of scale and monopolistic competition: a Chamberlin-Hechscher-Ohlin approach. *Journal of International Economics*, 11, pp. 305–40.

Henderson, J. (1998) Danger and opportunity in the Asia-Pacific. In G. Thompson 1998b, pp. 356–84.

Herring, R. J. and Litan, R. E. (1995) *Financial Regulation in the Global Economy*. Washington DC: Brookings Institution.

Hewitt, P. (1990) *Green Taxes*. London: IPPR.

Hindess, B. (1991) Imaginary presuppositions of democracy. *Economy and Society*, 20(2), pp. 173–95.

Hindess, B. (1992) Power and rationality: the Western concept of political community. *Alternatives*, 17(2), pp. 149–63.

Hindess, B. (1996) *Discourses of Power: From Hobbes to Foucault*. Oxford: Blackwell.

Hinsley, H. (1986) *Sovereignty*, 2nd edn. Cambridge: Cambridge University Press.

Hirst, P. Q. (ed.) (1989) *The Pluralist Theory of the State: Selected Writings of G. D. H. Cole, J. N. Figgis and H. J. Laski*. London: Routledge.

Hirst, P. Q. (1993) *Associative Democracy*. Cambridge: Polity Press.

Hirst, P. Q. (1994a) Security challenges in post-communist Europe. In L. Freedman (ed.), *Military Intervention in European Conflicts*, Oxford: Political Quarterly/ Blackwell.

Hirst, P. Q. (1994b) Why the national still matters. *Renewal*, 2(4), pp. 12–20.

Hirst, P. Q. (1995) The European Union at the crossroads: integration or decline? In R. Bellamy, V. Bufacchi and D. Castiglione (eds), *Democracy and Constitutional Culture in Europe*, London: Lothian Foundation.

Hirst, P. Q. (1997) The international origins of national sovereigny. In Hirst, *From Statism to Pluralism*, London: UCL Press.

Hirst, P. Q. (1998a) Guiding global markets. *Prospect*, Jan., pp. 16–19.

Hirst, P. Q. (1998b) Social welfare and associative democracy. In N. Ellison and C. Pierson (eds), *Developments in British Social Policy,* Basingstoke: Macmillan, pp. 78–91.

Hirst, P. Q. and Thompson, G. F. (1992) The problem of 'globalization': international economic relations, national economic management and the formation of trading blocs. *Economy and Society*, 21(4), pp. 357–96.

Hirst, P. Q. and Thompson, G. F. (1996) *Globalization in Question*, 1st edn. Cambridge: Polity Press.

Hirst, P. Q. and Zeitlin, J. (eds) (1988) *Reversing Industrial Decline? Industrial Structure and Policy in Britain and her Competitors*. Oxford: Berg.

Hirst, P. Q. and Zeitlin, J. (1989) Flexible specialisation and the failure of UK manufacturing. *Political Quarterly*, 60(2), pp. 164–78.

Hirst, P. Q. and Zeitlin, J. (1993) An incomes policy for sustained recovery. *Political Quarterly*, 64(1), pp. 60–83.

HMSO (1994) *Competitiveness of UK Manufacturing Industry.* Trade and Industry Committee, 2nd Report, 20 Apr., HCP 41-I, HMSO, London.

HMSO (1996) *Competitiveness: Creating the Enterprise Centre of Europe*, Cm 3300. London: HMSO.

HM Treasury (1996) Overseas investment and the UK. HM Treasury Occasional Paper 8, June, HM Treasury, London.

Hobsbawm, E. (1992) *Nations and Nationalism since 1780*. Cambridge: Cambridge University Press.

Hollingsworth, J. Rogers and R. Boyer (eds) (1996) *Contemporary Capitalism: The Embeddedness of Institutions*. Cambridge: Cambridge University Press.

Holtham, G. (1989) Foreign exchange markets and target zones. *Oxford Review of Economic Policy*, 5(3).

Holtham, G. (1995) Managing the exchange rate system. In J. Michie and J. Grieve-Smith (eds), *Managing the Global Economy*, Oxford: Oxford University Press.

Horsman, M. and Marshall, A. (1994) *After the Nation State*. London: HarperCollins.

Howell, D. R. and Wolff, E. N. (1991) Skills, bargaining power and rising interindustry wage inequality since 1970. *Review of Radical Political Economics*, 23(1–2), pp. 30–7.

Howell, M. (1998) Asia's Victorian financial crisis. Paper presented at the Conference on the East Asian Economic Crisis, Institute for Development Studies, University of Sussex, 13–14 July.

Hu, Yao-Su (1992) Global or stateless firms are national corporations with international operations. *California Management Review*, 34(2), pp. 107–26.

Hu, Yao-Su (1995) The international transferability of the firm's advantage. *California Management Review*, 37(4), pp. 73–88.

Huntington, S. (1993) The clash of civilizations. *Foreign Affairs*, 72(3), pp. 22–49.

Huntington, S. (1997) *The Clash of Civilizations and the Rethinking of World Order*. New York: Simon and Schuster.

Hutton, W. (1995) *The State We're In*. London: Faber and Faber.

IFC (International Finance Corporation) (1997) *Foreign Direct Investment*. Washington: IFC.

ILO (International Labour Organization) (1995) Perspectives: experience of social pacts in Western Europe. *International Labour Review*, 134(3), pp. 407–8.

IMF (1994) *World Economic Outlook* (Oct.). Washington DC: International Monetary Fund.

Irwin, D. A. (1996) The United States in a new global economy? A century's perspective. *American Economic Review, Papers and Proceedings*, 86(2), pp. 41–6.

Ivesen, T. (1996) Power, flexibility and the breakdown of centralized wage bargaining: the cases of Denmark and Sweden in comparative perspective. *Comparative Politics*, 28, pp. 399–436.

Jackson, J. H. (1994) Managing the trading system: the World Trade Organization and the post-Uruguay GATT agenda. In P. B. Kenen (ed.), *Managing the World Economy*, Washington DC: IIE.

Jones, G. (1994) The making of global enterprise. *Business History*, 36(1), pp. 1–17.

Julius, D. (1990) *Global Companies and Public Policy*. London: RIIA/Pinter.

Julius, D. (1994) International direct investment: strengthening the policy regime. In P. B. Kenen (ed.), *Managing the World Economy*, Washington DC: IIE.

Kaldor, N. (1978) The effect of devaluations on trade in manufactures. In N. Kaldor, *Further Essays in Applied Economics*, London: Duckworth.

Kaldor, N. (1981) The role of increasing returns, technical progress and cumulative causation in the theory of international trade and economic growth. *Economie Appliquée*, 34(4), pp. 593–617.

Kant, I. (1991) Perpetual peace. In I. Kant, *Political Writings*, ed. H. Reiss, 2nd edn, Cambridge: Cambridge University Press.

Kapstein, E. B. (1991) We are us: the myth of the multi-national. *The National Interest*, Winter. pp. 55–62.

Kapstein, E. B. (1994) *Governing the Global Economy: International Finance and the State*. Cambridge, Mass.: Harvard University Press.

Katzenstein, P. (1985) *Small States in World Markets: Industrial Policy in Europe*. Ithaca: Cornell University Press.

Kay, J. (1994) *The Foundations of National Competitive Advantage*. Swindon: Economic and Social Research Council.

Kenen, P. B. (1995) Capital controls, the EMS and EMU. *Economic Journal*, 105 (Jan.), pp. 181–92.

Kennedy, E. (1991) *The Bundesbank*. London: RIIA/Pinter.

Kennedy, P. (1993) *Preparing for the Twenty-First Century*. New York: Random House.

Kern, H. and Sabel, C. (1994) Verblate Tügenden. Zur Krises des deutschen Produktionsmodells. Umbruche gessellschaftlicher Arbeiter. *Soziale Welt*, special issue 9, Göttingen: Otto Schwarz, pp. 605–24.

Khilnani, S. (1997) *The Idea of India*. London: Penguin.

Kim, L. and Yi, G. (1997) The dynamics of R & D in industrial development: lessons from the Korean experience. *Industry and Innovation*, 4(2), pp. 167–82.

Kirkpatrick, C. (1994) Regionalisation, regionalism and East Asian economic cooperation. *World Economy*, 17(2), pp. 191–202.

Kitson, M. and Michie, J. (1995) Trade and growth: a historical perspective. In J. Michie and J. Grieve Smith (eds), *Managing the Global Economy*, Oxford: Oxford University Press.

Korten, D. C. (1995) *When Corporations Rule the World*. West Hartford, Conn.: Kumarian Press.

Kristensen, P. H. (1995) *Denmark: An Experimental Laboratory of Industrial Organization*. 2 vols, Handelshøjskolen I København.

Kristensen, P. H. and Sabel, C. (1997) The smallholder economy in Denmark: the exception as variation. In C. Sabel and J. Zeitlin (eds), *World of Possibilities*, Cambridge: Cambridge University Press.

Kruger, A. B. (1996) International labor standards and trade. In M. Burno and B. Plesuovic (eds), *Annual World Bank Conference on Development Economics 1996*, Washington DC: IBRD, pp. 281–311.

Krugman, P. (1994a) Competitiveness: a dangerous obsession. *Foreign Affairs*, 73(2), pp. 28–44.

Krugman, P. (1994b) The myth of Asia's miracle. *Foreign Affairs*, 73(6), pp. 63–75.

Krugman, P. (1995) Growing world trade: causes and consequences. *Brookings Papers on Economic Activity*, no. 1, pp. 327–77.

Krugman, P. (1998) What happened to Asia? http://web.mit.edu/krugman/www/disinter.html

Krugman, P. and Lawrence, R. Z. (1994) Trade, jobs and wages. *Scientific American*, Apr., pp. 22–6.

Lang, T. and Hines, C. (1993) *The New Protectionism*. London: Earthscan.

Lash, S. and Urry, J. (1987) *The End of Organized Capitalism*. Cambridge: Polity Press.

Lawrence, R. Z. (1996) *Single World, Divided Nations? The Impact of Trade on OECD Labor Markets*. Washington DC: Brookings Institution.

Lawrence, R. Z. and Slaughter, M. J. (1993) International trade and American wages in the 1980s: giant sucking sound or small hiccup? *Brookings Papers on Economic Activity*, 2, pp. 161–226.

Lazonick, W. (1993) Industry clusters versus global webs: organizational capabilities in the American economy. *Industrial and Corporate Change*, 2(2), pp. 1–21.

Lazonick, W. and O'Sullivan, M. (1996) Organization, finance and international competition. *Industrial and Corporate Change*, 5(1), pp. 1–49.

Lee, E. (1996) Globalization and employment: is anxiety justified? *International Labour Review*, 135(5), pp. 485–97.

Lehmbruch, G. (1984) Concertation and the structure of corporatist networks. In J. Goldthorpe (ed.), *Order and Conflict in Contemporary Capitalism*, Oxford: Clarendon Press, pp. 60–80.

Leong, Siew Meng and Tan, Chin Tiong (1993) Managing across borders: an empirical test of the Bartlett and Ghoshal [1989] organizational typology. *Journal of International Business Studies*, 24(3), pp. 449–64.

Lewis, A. (1981) The rate of growth of world trade, 1830–1973. In S. Grassman and E. Lundberg (eds), *The World Economic Order: Past and Prospects*, Basingstoke: Macmillan.

Lind, J. (1997) EMU and collective bargaining in Denmark. In Fajertag and Pochet 1997, pp. 145–55.

Lipsey, R. E. (1997) Global production systems and local labour conditions. Paper for Conference on International Solidarity and Globalization, Stockholm, Oct. 27–8.

Lipsey, R. E., Blomström, M. and Ramstetter, E. (1995) Internationalized production in world output. NBER Working Paper 5385, Dec., National Bureau of Economic Research, Cambridge, Mass.

Livi-Bacci, M. (1993) South–North migration: a comparative approach to North American and European experiences. In *The Changing Course of Migration*, Paris: OECD.

Locke, R. M. (1995) *Remaking the Italian Economy*. Ithaca: Cornell University Press.

Loftager, J. (1996a) Universality vs. selectivity in public transfers and the prospect of citizen's income. Paper given to the 6th BIEN International Congress, Vienna.

Loftager, J. (1996b) Citizen's income: a new welfare state strategy? In Oddvar Eriksen and Loftager 1996, pp. 134–54.

Lorenz, N. (1988) The search for flexibility. In Hirst and Zeitlin 1988.

Lorenz, N. (1992) Trust, community and cooperation: towards a theory of industrial districts. In M. Storper and A. J. Scott (eds), *Pathways to Industrialisation and Regional Development*, London: Routledge.

Lundvall, B.-A. (ed.) (1992) *National Systems of Innovation: Towards a Theory of Innovations and Interactive Learning*. London: Pinter.

McCallum, J. (1995) National borders matter: Canada–US regional trade patterns. *American Economic Review*, 85(3), pp. 615–23.

McGiven, A. (1996) Trade with newly industrialized economies. *Bank of England Quarterly Bulletin*, Feb., pp. 69–78.

McGrew, A. G. and Lewis, P. G. (1992) *Global Politics.* Cambridge: Polity Press.

McKay, A. (1998) Social policy in Britain. In N. Ellison and C. Pierson (eds), *Developments in British Social Policy*, Basingstoke: Macmillan, pp. 112–29.

McKelvey, M. (1991) How do national systems of innovation differ? A critical analysis of Porter, Freeman, Ludvall and Nelson. In G. Hodgson and E. Screpanti (eds), *Rethinking Economics*, Cheltenham: Edward Elgar.

McKinnon, R. (1993) The rules of the game: international money in historical perspective. *Journal of Economic Literature*, 31 (Mar.), pp. 1–44.

Maddison, A. (1962) Growth and fluctuation in the world economy, 1870–1960. *Banca Nazionale del Lavaro Quarterly Review*, no. 61 (June), pp. 127–95.

Maddison, A. (1987) Growth and slowdown in advanced capitalist economies: techniques of quantitative assessments. *Journal of Economic Literature*, 25(2), pp. 649–98.

Maddison, A. (1995) *Monitoring the World Economy 1860–1990.* Paris: OECD.

Mansell, R. (1994) *The New Telecommunications: A Political Economy of Network Organizations.* London: Sage.

Martin, A. (1995) The Swedish model: demise or reconfiguration. In R. Locke, T. Kochan and M. Piore (eds), *Employment Relations in a Changing World Economy*, Cambridge, Mass.: MIT Press, pp. 263–96.

Martin, A. (1996) What does globalization have to do with the erosion of welfare states? Sorting out the issues? Arena Working Paper 17, Oslo.

Martin, A. (1997) Social pacts: a means for distributing unemployment or achieving full employment. In Fajertag and Pochet 1997, pp. 37–44.

Martin, H. P. and Schumann, H. (1997) *The Global Trap: Globalization and the Assault on Democracy and Prosperity.* London: Zed Books.

Milner, M. (1998) 'Forces of light' bring global rout to a halt. *The Guardian*, 12 Jan., p. 17.

Minc, A. (1993) *Le Nouveau Moyen Age.* Paris: Gallimard.

Minford, P., Riley, J. and Nowell, E. (1997) Trade, technology and labour markets in the world economy, 1970–90: a computable general equilibrium analysis. *Journal of Development Studies*, 34(2), pp. 1–34.

Ministry of Economic Affairs (1997) *The Danish Economy 1997.* Copenhagen: Ministry of Economic Affairs.

MITI (1996a) Summary of 'The survey of trends in overseas business activities of Japanese companies', International Business Affairs Division, Jan. (N-96-2), Ministry of International Trade and Industry, Tokyo.

MITI (1996b) The 28th survey of trends in business activities of foreign affiliates. International Business Affairs Division, Jan. (N-96-3), Ministry of International Trade and Industry, Tokyo.

MITI (1997) *The sixth Basic Survey of Overseas Business Activities.* Tokyo: Ministry of International Trade and Industry, (http://www.jef/news/970508.html).

Montes, M. F. (1998a) *The Currency Crisis in Southeast Asia*, updated edn. Singapore: Institute of Southeast Asian Studies.

Montes, M. F. (1998b) Globalization and capital market development in Southeast Asia. Paper presented at Conference on Southeast Asia in the Twenty-first Century: Challenges of Globalization, Institute of South East Asian Studies, Singapore, 30 July–1 Aug.

Morse, E. L. (1971) *Modernization and the Transformation of International Relations*. New York: Free Press.

Moss Kanter, R. (1991) *When Giants Learn to Dance*. London: Simon and Schuster.

Mueller, F. (1994) Societal effect, organizational effect and globalization. *Organization Studies*, 15(3), pp. 407–28.

Mulgan, G. (1994) *Politics in an Anti-Political Age*. Cambridge: Polity Press.

Nader, R. et al. (1994) *The Case against Free Trade: GATT, NAFTA, and the Globalization of Corporate Power*. San Francisco: Earth Island Press.

Nairn, T. (1993) All Bosnians now? *Dissent*, Fall, pp. 403–10.

Neal, L. (1985) Integration of international capital markets: quantitative evidence from the eighteenth to twentieth centuries. *Journal of Economic History*, 45(2), pp. 219–26.

Negrelli, S. (1997) Social pacts and flexibility: towards a new balance between macro and micro industrial relations: the Italian experience. In Fajertag and Pochet 1997, pp. 45–62.

Nelson, R. (ed.) (1993) *National Innovation Systems*. Oxford: Blackwell.

Nickell, S. (1997) Unemployment and labour market rigidities: Europe versus North America. *Journal of Economic Perspectives*, 11(3), pp. 55–74.

Nickell, S. and Bell, B. (1996) Changes in the distribution of wages and unemployment in OECD countries. *American Economic Review, Papers and Proceedings*, 86(2), pp. 302–8.

Notermans, T. (1993) The abdication of national policy autonomy: why the macroeconomic policy regime has become so unfavourable to labour. *Politics and Society*, 21, pp. 133–67.

Notermans, T. (1997) Social democracy and external constraints. In K. R. Cox (ed.), *Spaces of Globalization*, New York: Guilford Press, pp. 201–39.

Obstfeld, M. (1993) International capital mobility in the 1990's. NBER Working Paper 4534, National Bureau of Economic Research, Cambridge, Mass.

O'Donnell, R. and O'Reardon, C. (1997) Ireland's experiment in social partnership 1987–1996. In Fajertag and Pochet 1997, pp. 79–95.

Oddvar Eriksen, E. and Loftager, J. (1996) *The Rationality of the Welfare State*. Oslo: Scandinavian University Press.

OECD (1992) *International Direct Investment: Policies and Trends in the 1980s*. Paris: OECD.

OECD (1993) World securities markets: looking ahead. *Financial Market Trends*, no. 55 (June), OECD, Paris.

OECD (1994a) Desynchronization of OECD business cycles. *Economic Outlook*, no. 55 (June), OECD, Paris.

OECD (1994b) *Financial Market Trends*, no 58 (June). Paris: OECD.

OECD (1997a) *Denmark 1997*. OECD Economic Survey, Paris: OECD.

OECD (1997b) *Economic Outlook*, no. 62 (Dec.). Paris: OECD.

OECD (1998a) *Financial Market Trends*, no. 69 (Feb.). Paris: OECD.

OECD (1998b) *The Netherlands 1998*. OECD Economic Survey, Paris: OECD.

Ohmae, K. (1990) *The Borderless World*. London and New York: Collins.

Ohmae, K. (1993) The rise of the region state. *Foreign Affairs*, Spring, pp. 78–87.

Ohmae, K. (1995) Putting global logic first. *Harvard Business Review*, Jan.–Feb., pp. 119–25.

Oye, K. A. (1994) Comment. In P. B. Kenen (ed.), *Managing the World Economy*, Washington DC: Institute for International Economics.

Padoan, P. C. (1997) Regional arrangements as clubs: the European case. In E. D. Mansfield and H. V. Milner (eds), *The Political Economy of Regionalism*, New York: Columbia University Press.

Padoa-Schioppa, T. and Saccomanni, F. (1994) Managing a market-led global financial system. In P. B. Kenen (ed.), *Managing the World Economy*, Washington DC: Institute for International Economics.

Panagariya, A. (1994) East Asia and the new regionalism in world trade. *World Economy*, 17, pp. 817–39.

Papademetriou, D. G. (1997–8) Migration. *Foreign Policy*, no. 109 (Winter), pp. 15–31.

Patel, P. (1995) Localised production of technology for global markets. *Cambridge Journal of Economics*, 19, pp. 141–53.

Patel, P. and Pavitt, K. (1992) Large firms in the production of the world's technology: an important case of 'non-globalization'. In O. Granstrand, L. Hakanson and S. Sjolander (eds), *Technology Management and International Business*, Chichester: Wiley. (Also in *Journal of International Business Studies*, 22(1), 1991, pp. 1–21.)

Pauly, L. W. and Reich, S. (1997) National structures and multinational behaviour: enduring differences in the age of globalization. *International Organization*, 51(1), pp. 1–30.

Pertri, P. A. (1994) The East Asian trading bloc: an analytical history. In R. Garnaut and P. Drysdale (eds), *Asia Pacific Regionalism*, Sydney: Harper Education.

Piore, M. and Sabel, C. (1984) *The Second Industrial Divide*. New York: Basic Books.

Pontusson, J. (1992) *The Limits of Social Democracy: Investment Politics in Sweden*. Ithaca: Cornell University Press.

Pontusson, J. and Swenson, P. (1996) Labour markets, production strategies and wage bargaining institutions: the Swedish employer offensive in comparative perspective. *Comparative Political Studies*, 29, pp. 223–50.

Porter, M. (1990) *Competitive Advantage of Nations*. London: Macmillan.

Putnam, R. D. and Bayne, N. (1987) *Hanging Together: Cooperation and Conflict in the Seven-Power Summits*. Cambridge: Harvard University Press.

Radelet, S. and Sachs, J. D. (1998) The East Asian financial crisis: diagnosis, remedies, prospects. *Brookings Papers on Economic Activity*, 1, pp. 1–74.

Ramesh, M. (1993) Social security in Singapore: the state and the changing social and political circumstances. *Journal of Commonwealth and Comparative Politics*, 31(3), pp. 111–21.

Ramstetter, E. (1998) Measuring the size of foreign multinationals in the Asia-Pacific. In Thompson 1998b, pp. 185–212.

Regini, M. (1997) Still engaging in corporatism? Recent Italian experience in comparative perspective. *European Journal of Industrial Relations*, 3(3), pp. 259–78.

Regini, M. and Regalia, I. (1997) Employers, unions and the state: the resurgence of concertation in Italy? *West European Politics*, 20(1), pp. 210–30.

Reich, R. B. (1990) Who is us? *Harvard Business Review*, Jan.–Feb., pp. 53–64.

Reich, R. B. (1992) *The Work of Nations*. New York: Vintage.

Reisen, H. (1997) Sustainable and excessive current deficits. UNU/WIDER Working Paper 151, Helsinki.

Rhodes, M. (1996) Globalization and West European states: a critical review of recent debates. *Journal of European Social Policy*, 4, pp. 305–27.

Rhodes, M. (1997) Globalization, labour markets and welfare states: a future of competitive corporatism? European University Institute Working Paper RSC 97/36, Florence.

Rodrik, D. (1996) Why do more open economies have bigger governments? NBER Working Paper 5537, National Bureau of Economic Research, Cambridge, Mass.

Rodrik, D. (1997) *Has Globalization Gone Too Far?* Washington DC: Institute for International Economics.

Roe, M. J. (1994) *Strong Managers, Weak Owners: The Political Roots of American Corporate Finance*. Princeton: Princeton University Press.

Rosenau, J. N. (1990) *Turbulence in World Politics*. Hemel Hempstead: Harvester/Wheatsheaf.

Rosenau, J. N. and Czempiel, E.-O. (1992) *Governance without Government: Order and Change in World Politics*. Cambridge: Cambridge University Press.

Rubery, J. (1994) The British production regime: a societal-specific system? *Economy and Society*, 23(3), pp. 355–73.

Ruggie, J. G. (1993) Multilateralism: the anatomy of an institution. In J. G. Ruggie (ed.), *Multilateralism Matters: The Theory and Praxis of an Institutional Form*, New York: Columbia University Press.

Sabel, C. (1982) *Work and Politics*. Cambridge: Cambridge University Press.

Sabel, C. (1988) Flexible specialisation and the re-emergence of regional economies. In Hirst and Zeitlin 1988.

Sabel, C. (1991) Moebius-strip organisation and open labour markets. In P. Bourdieu and J. S. Coleman (eds), *Social Theory for a Changing Society*, Boulder, Colo.: Westview Press.

Sabel, C. (1996) *Ireland: Local Partnerships and Social Innovation*. Paris: OECD.

Sachs, J. (1997) The wrong medicine for Asia. *New York Times*, 3 Nov.

Sachs, J. (1998) Out of the frying pan into the IMF fire. *Observer*, 8 Feb., p. 85.

Sachs, J. D. and Shatz, H. J. (1994) Trade and jobs in US manufacturing. *Brookings Papers on Economic Activity*, 1, pp 1–84.

Sachs, J. D. and Shatz, H. J. (1996) US trade with developing countries and wage inequality. *American Economic Review, Papers and Proceedings*, 86(2), pp. 234–45.

Sandholtz, W. et al. (1992) *The Highest Stakes: The Economic Foundations of the Next Security System*. Oxford: Oxford University Press.

Scharpf, F. (1991) *Crisis and Choice in European Social Democracy*. Ithaca: Cornell University Press.

Scharpf, F. W. (1996) Negative and positive integration in the political economy of European welfare states. In G. Marks (ed.), *Governance in the European Union*, London: Sage.

Scharpf, F. W. (1997) Economic integration, democracy and the welfare state. *European Journal of Public Policy*, 4(1), pp. 16–36.

Schell, J. (1984) *The Abolition*. London: Picador.

Schmitter, P. (1981) Interest intermediation and regime governability in contemporary Western Europe and North America. In S. Berger (ed.), *Organizing Interests in Western Europe*, Cambridge: Cambridge University Press, pp. 285–327.

Schröter, V. (1984) *Die deutsche Industrie auf dem Weltmarkt 1929 bis 1933*. Frankfurt.

Segal, A. (1993) *Atlas of International Migration*. London: Hans Zell.

Serow, W. J. et al. (eds) (1990) *Handbook on International Migration*. New York: Greenwood Press.

Siebert, H. (1997) Labour market rigidities: at the root of unemployment in Europe. *Journal of Economic Perspectives*, 11(3), pp. 37–54.

Singh, A. (1993) Asian economic success and Latin American failure in the 1980s. *International Review of Applied Economics*, 7(3), pp. 267–89.

Singh, A. (1998) Growth: its sources and consequences. In Thompson 1998b, pp. 55–82.

Skidelsky, R. (1992) *John Maynard Keynes*, vol. 2: *The Economist as Saviour 1920–1939*. London: Macmillan.

Soros, G. (1997) Avoiding a breakdown. *Financial Times*, 31 Dec., p. 8.

Soskice, D. (1991) The institutional infrastructure for international competitiveness: a comparative analysis of the UK and Germany. In A. B. Atkinson and R. Brunetta (eds), *Economics for the New Europe*, New York: Macmillan.

Soskice, D. (1997) German technology policy, innovation, and national institutional frameworks. *Industry and Innovation*, 4(1), pp. 75–96.

Spar, D. L. (1997) Lawyers abroad: the internationalization of legal practice. *California Management Review*, 37(3), pp. 8–28.

Standage, T. (1998) *The Victorian Internet: The Remarkable Story of the Telegraph and the Nineteenth Century Online Pioneers*. London: Weidenfeld and Nicolson.

Stephens, J. D. (1996) The Scandinavian welfare states: achievements, crisis and prospects. In Esping-Andersen 1996c, pp. 32–65.

Stiglitz, J. (1997) How to fix the Asian economies. *New York Times*, 31 Oct.

Stopford, J. and Strange, S. (with John S. Henley) (1991) *Rival States, Rival Firms: Competition for World Market Shares*. Cambridge: Cambridge University Press.

Storper, M. (1995) The resurgence of regional economies, ten years later: the region as a nexus of untraded interdependencies. *European Urban and Regional Studies*, 2(3), pp. 191–221.

Strange, S. (1996) *The Retreat of the State*. Cambridge: Cambridge University Press.

Streeck, W. and Schmitter, P. (1991) From national corporatism to transnational pluralism: organised interests in the single European market. *Politics and Society*, 19(2), pp. 133–64.

Taylor, P. (1990) Consociationalism and federalism as approaches to international integration. In A. J. R. Groom and P. Taylor (eds), *Frameworks for International Co-operation*, London: Pinter.

Thompson, G. F. (1987) The supply side and industrial policy. In G. Thompson, V. Brown and R. Levacic (eds), *Managing the UK Economy*, Cambridge: Polity Press.

Thompson, G. F. (1993) *The Economic Emergence of a New Europe? The Political Economy of Cooperation and Competition in the 1990s*. Cheltenham: Edward Elgar.

Thompson, G. F. (1995a) Comment on 'The crisis of cost recovery and the waste of the industrialised nations'. *Competition and Change*, 1(1), pp. 101–11.

Thompson, G. F. (1995b) The market system. In M. Macintosh et al. (eds), *Economics and Changing Economies*, London: Chapman Hall.

Thompson, G. F. (1997) What kinds of national policies? 'Globalization' and the possibilities for domestic economic policy. *Internationale Politik und Gesellschaft*, no. 2, pp. 161–72.

Thompson, G. F. (1998a) Financial systems and monetary integration. In Thompson 1998b pp. 83–111.

Thompson, G. F. (ed.) (1998b) *Economic Dynamism in the Asia-Pacific*. London: Routledge.

Thompson, G. F. (1998c) International competitiveness and globalization: frameworks for analysis, connections and critiques. In T. Barker and J. Köhler (eds), *International Competitiveness and Environmental Policies*, Cheltenham: Edward Elgar.

Thomson, J. E. (1994) *Mercenaries, Pirates and Sovereigns: State-Building and Extraterritorial Violence in Early Modern Europe*. Princeton: Princeton University Press.

Thurow, L. (1997) *The Future of Capitalism*. London: Nicholas Brearley.

Thurow, L. (1998) Asia, the collapse and the cure. *New York Review of Books*, 5 Feb., pp. 22–6.

Tiberi-Vipraio, P. (1996) From local to global networking: the restructuring of Italian industrial districts. *Journal of Industry Studies*, 3(2), pp. 135–51.

Tobin, J. (1978) A proposal for international monetary reform. *Eastern Economic Journal*, 4, pp. 153–9.

Tobin, J. (1994) Speculators' tax. *New Economy*, 1(2), pp. 104–9.

Tomlinson, J. (1988) *Can Governments Run the Economy?* Fabian Tract 542, London: Fabian Society.

Tompson, W. (1998) The price of everything and the value of nothing? Unravelling the workings of Russia's 'virtual economy'. *Economy and Society*, 28(2), pp. 256–80.

Turner, P. (1991) Capital flows in the 1980s: a survey of major trends. *BIS Economic Papers*, no. 30, Bank for International Settlements, Geneva.

Tyson, L. (1991) They are not us: why American ownership still matters. *American Prospect*, Winter, pp. 37–49.

UNCTAD (1993) *Trade and Development Report, 1993*. New York: United Nations.

Unger, R. M. (1996) The really new Bretton Woods. In M. Uzan (ed.), *The Financial System under Stress: An Architecture for a New World Economy*, London: Routledge.

United Nations (1993a) *World Investment Directory 1992*, vol. 3: *Developed Countries*. New York: Transnational Corporations and Management Division, Department of Economic and Social Development, United Nations.

United Nations (1993b) *World Investment Report 1993: Transnational Corporations and Integrated International Production*. New York: United Nations.

United Nations (1996) *World Investment Report 1995: Transnational Corporations and Competitiveness*. New York: United Nations.

United Nations (1997) *World Investment Report 1997: Transnational Corporations, Market Structure and Competition Policy*. New York: United Nations.

Van Creveld, M. (1991) *On Future War*. London: Brassey's.

Van der Toren, J. P. (1997) A 'tripartite consensus economy': the Dutch variant of a social pact. In Fajertag and Pochet 1997, pp. 181–93.

Van Parijs, P. (1992) *Arguing for Basic Income*. London: Verso.

Visser, J. and Hemerijck, A. (V&H) (1997) *A Dutch Miracle: Job Growth, Welfare Reform and Corporatism in the Netherlands*. Amsterdam: University of Amsterdam Press.

Wade, R. and Veneroso, F. (1998) The Asian crisis: the high debt model versus the Wall Street–Treasury–IMF complex. *New Left Review*, no. 228, Mar.–Apr., pp. 3–23.

Wallace, I. (1990) *The Global Economic System*. London: Unwin Hyman.

Weber, M. (1968) *Economy and Society*, vol. 1. New York: Bedminster Press.

Weiss, L. and Hobson, J. M. (1995) *States and Economic Development*. Cambridge: Polity Press.

Weitzman, M. L. (1984) *The Share Economy*. Cambridge: Harvard University Press.

Whitley, R. (1992a) *Business Systems in East Asia: Firms, Markets and Societies*. London: Sage.

Whitley, R. (ed.) (1992b) *European Business Systems: Firms and Markets in their National Contexts*. London: Sage.

Whitley, R. and Kristensen, P. H. (eds) (1996) *The Changing European Firm: Limits to Convergence*. London: Routledge.

Whitley, R. and Kristensen, P. H. (eds) (1997) *Governance at Work: The Social Regulation of Economic Relations*. Oxford: Oxford University Press.

Wilkinson, F. (1983) Productive systems. *Cambridge Journal of Economics*, 7(3–4), pp. 413–30.

Williams, F. (1997) Asian tigers lose their bite as exports slump. *Financial Times*, 11 Mar., p. 8.

Williams, K., Haslam, C., Williams, J. and Adcroft, A. (1992) Factories as warehouses: Japanese manufacturing foreign direct investment in Britain and the United States. University of East London Occasional Paper on Business, Economy and Society, no. 6.

Williams, K., Haslam, C., Williams, J., Sukhdev, J., Johal, A., Adcroft, A. and Willis, R. (1995) The crisis of cost recovery and the waste of the industrialised nations. *Competition and Change*, 1(1).

Williamson, J. G. (1995) The evolution of the global labour market since 1830: background evidence and hypotheses. *Explorations in Economic History*, 32, pp. 141–96.

Williamson, J. G. (1996) Globalization, convergence, and history. *Journal of Economic History*, 56(2), pp. 277–306.

Wolf, M. (1995) A liberal world restored. *Financial Times*, 18 Sept., p. 24.

Wolf, M. (1998a) Caging the bankers. *Financial Times*, 20 Jan., p. 18.

Wolf, M. (1998b) Flows and blows. *Financial Times*, 3 Mar., p. 22.

Wolf, M. (1998c) Ins and outs of capital flows. *Financial Times*, 16 June, p. 25.

Wong, P.-K. (1997) Creation of a regional hub for flexible production: the case of the hard disk drive industry in Singapore. *Industry and Innovation*, 4(2), pp. 183–205.

Wood, A. (1994) *North–South Trade, Employment and Inequality: Changing Fortunes in a Skill-Driven World*. Oxford: Oxford University Press.

Wood, A. (1995) How trade hurt unskilled workers. *Journal of Economic Perspectives*, 9(3), pp. 57–80.

Wood, A. and Berge, K. (1997) Exporting manufactures: human resources, natural resources, and trade policy. *Journal of Development Economics*, 34(1), pp. 35–59.

World Bank (1993) *The East Asian Miracle: Economic Growth and Public Policy*. Oxford: World Bank/Oxford University Press.

World Bank (1994) *Governance: The World Bank's Experience*. Washington DC: World Bank.

World Bank (1997) Globalization and international adjustment. *World Economic Outlook* (May).

WTO (1995) *International Trade: Trends and Statistics*. Geneva: World Trade Organization.

WTO (1997) *WTO Annual Report 1996*. Geneva: World Trade Organization.

Yamazawa, I. (1998) Regional integration in the Asia-Pacific. In Thompson 1988b.

Yarbrough, B. V. and Yarbrough, R. M. (1992) *Cooperation and Governance in International Trade*. Princeton: Princeton University Press.

Yoshitomi, M. (1996) On the changing international competitiveness of Japanese manufacturing since 1985. *Oxford Review of Economic Policy*, 12(3), pp. 61–73.

Young, A. (1994a) Lessons from the East Asian NIC's: a contrarian view. *European Economic Review*, 38(3–4), pp. 964–73.

Young, A. (1994b) The tyranny of numbers: confronting the statistical realities of the East Asian growth experience. NEBR Working Paper 4680, Mar., National Bureau of Economic Research, Cambridge, Mass.

Zeitlin, J. (1992) Industrial districts and local economic regeneration. In F. Pyke and W. Sengenberger (eds), *Industrial Districts and Local Economic Regeneration*, Geneva: International Institute of Labour Studies, ILO.

Zeitlin, J. (1994) Why are there no industrial districts in the United Kingdom? In A. Baguasco and C. Sabel (eds), *Ce que petit peut faire. Les petites et les moyennes enterprises en Europe*, Poitiers: OCSEO.

Zevin, R. (1992) Are world financial markets more open? If so, why and with what effects? In Banuri and Schor 1992.

Zubaida, S. D. (1993) *Islam, the People and the State*, 2nd edn. London: I. B. Tauris.

Index

Bold page numbers refer to tables, and italic page numbers refer to figures.